Clinical Case Vignettes for Psychological Disorders

This book provides clinical case vignettes to aid in the development of diagnostic and treatment planning skills for professionals, trainees, and students across all mental health disciplines.

Clinical Case Vignettes for Psychological Disorders provides easy-to-read case examples, highlighting relevant historical information, assessment data, and current psychopathology symptoms. Answer keys that follow each case include case conceptualizations utilizing psychodynamic, cognitive behavioral, and biopsychosocial orientations, incorporating diversity and ethical considerations as well as sample treatment plans and interventions.

These cases are a vital resource for faculty and students as they can be used for in-class assignments, course exams, program-related clinical competency assessments, or during individual or group supervision meetings. This resource will also aid current practitioners in their diagnosis and treatment planning.

Veronica Regueiro, Psy.D., is a bilingual health psychologist specializing in pediatrics, behavioral health consultation, and comprehensive psychodiagnostic evaluation. She holds a doctorate in clinical psychology from the Rosemead School of Psychology at Biola University, and is licensed in California. Dr. Regueiro serves on the faculty of California Baptist University (CBU) and as the clinical director for CBEM, LLC, a crisis intervention service vendorized with California's regional center system.

Noel Cooper, Psy.D., is a clinical psychologist with specialties in clinical supervision, foster care and adoption, and clergy family issues. She holds a doctorate in clinical psychology from Fuller Theological Seminary's School of Psychology, Dr. Cooper is licensed in the state of California. She serves on the faculty at CBU and is the director of Psychological Services of Riverside, the internal training clinic for the APA-accredited Psy.D. program at CBU.

Clinical Case Vignettes for Psychological Disorders

A Resource for Professionals, Trainees, and Students

Edited by Veronica Regueiro and Noel Cooper

Routledge
Taylor & Francis Group
NEW YORK AND LONDON

Designed cover image: Getty Images

First published 2026
by Routledge
605 Third Avenue, New York, NY 10158

and by Routledge
4 Park Square, Milton Park, Abingdon, Oxon, OX14 4RN

Routledge is an imprint of the Taylor & Francis Group, an informa business

ISBN: 978-1-032-95779-1 (hbk)
ISBN: 978-1-032-95777-7 (pbk)
ISBN: 978-1-003-58653-1 (ebk)

DOI: 10.4324/9781003586531

Typeset in Times New Roman
by Newgen Publishing UK

To our patients, our greatest teachers
And to our students, whose eager participation in this project inspired us, encouraged us, and, more than anything, made us proud to serve the future of psychology

Contents

Contributing Authors

Bethany Faulds, M.A. Ms. Faulds is a doctoral student in the APA-accredited clinical psychology program at Regent University, VA. She holds a master's degree in clinical psychology from Regent University. Ms. Fauld's APA-accredited internship is in Oregon, at the Portland VAMC. She served as a teaching and research assistant for Dr. Cassandra Page in the areas of advocacy and social justice for three years. Ms. Faulds also provided culturally informed conceptualization, assessment, and treatment training to her peers for 3 years.

Elise Fisher, M.A. Ms. Fisher is a doctoral student in the APA-accredited clinical psychology program at Regent University, VA. She holds a master's degree in clinical psychology from Regent University. For 2 years, Ms. Fisher trained Psy.D. students to diagnose, conceptualize, and treat students from a culturally humble lens through her program's multicultural clinic, facilitated by Dr. Cassandra Page.

Lindsay Gonzalez, M.A. Ms. Gonzalez is a doctoral student in the APA-accredited clinical psychology program at California Baptist University (CBU). She holds a master's degree in clinical psychology from CBU. Working under the direction of licensed clinical psychologists, she has provided psychotherapy services to patients at an outpatient generalist clinic and at an outpatient clinic specializing in anxiety and depressive disorders. She has also provided psychological assessment services in an outpatient setting. Ms. Gonzalez's APA-accredited internship is in Colorado, at Diversus Health. Additionally, she has served as an adjunct professor of psychology at CBU.

Matthew Heidl, M.A. Mr. Heidl is a is a doctoral student in the APA-accredited clinical psychology program at CBU. He holds a master's degree in clinical psychology from CBU. Working under the direction of licensed clinical psychologists, he has provided psychotherapy services to patients at Psychological Services of Riverside (PSR) and at a local college counseling center. He has participated in several research projects at CBU and has guest lectured for the undergraduate psychology courses.

Jourdan Johnson, M.A. Ms. Johnson is a doctoral student in the APA-accredited clinical psychology program at Regent University, VA. Ms. Johnson was a teaching assistant for Dr. Cassandra Page in the areas of advocacy and social justice, with a particular emphasis on the intersecting impacts of sexual and gender identity within the African American community.

Emily Longfellow, M.A., M.A. Ms. Longfellow is a doctoral student in the APA-accredited clinical psychology program at CBU. She holds M.A. degrees in forensic psychology and clinical psychology. Working under the direction of licensed clinical psychologists, she has provided psychotherapy services to patients at Psychological Services of Riverside, an outpatient clinic, and Helping Hearts, a residential treatment facility for patients with severe persistent mental illness. She has also served as an adjunct professor of criminal justice and psychology at CBU.

Jessie Lowell is a licensed clinical psychologist and associate professor in the APA-accredited doctoral psychology program at California Baptist University. She earned her doctorate from Loma Linda University and completed an APA-accredited internship at Children's Hospital, Los Angeles. Dr. Lowell also completed a formal post-doctoral fellowship at Nationwide Children's Hospital in Columbus, Ohio. Dr. Lowell has specialized training in early childhood mental health, pediatric psychology, and assessment and, prior to her faculty appointment, she provided clinical assessment and intervention services at a variety of children's hospitals and community programs. Her passion is in seeing children and families thrive and providing optimal environments that allow them to foster their development in a strengths-based and faith-integrated way. As a service to her community, Dr. Lowell is an Associate Pastor at Foothill Vineyard Church and serves as the treasurer on the board of directors for Branches Homeschool Academy. She lives in California with her husband and their young children.

David J. Machado, M.A. Mr. Machado is a doctoral student in the APA-accredited clinical psychology program at CBU. He holds an M.A. degree in clinical psychology from CBU. Working under the direction of licensed clinical psychologists, he has provided psychotherapy services to patients at an outpatient clinic, at a local locked psychiatric facility for adults with severe persistent mental illness, and in a private practice setting focused on psychodynamic approaches to patient care.

Cassandra D. Page, Psy.D. Dr. Page is a licensed multiculturally informed clinical psychologist who holds a doctorate in clinical psychology from Biola University, CA. She completed her doctoral internship at Salina Regional Healthcare Center in Kansas. Dr. Page is the assistant dean of the College of Health and Behavioral Sciences and associate professor in the doctoral program in clinical psychology at Regent University, VA.

Lauren Elizabeth Ponce. Miss Ponce is a doctoral student in the APA-accredited clinical psychology program at CBU. Working under the direction of licensed clinical psychologists, she has provided psychotherapy services to patients at Psychological Services of Riverside. Prior to beginning her doctoral training at CBU, Miss Ponce was involved in conducting research at California State University, Fullerton.

Susan N. Purrington, Psy.D. Dr. Purrington earned her doctorate in clinical psychology from Biola University, CA, and is a tenured professor at CBU, teaching undergraduate, graduate, and doctoral courses. She also maintains a private practice providing counseling services for adolescents, adults, and couples.

Sabrina Zuniga, M.S. Miss Zuniga is a doctoral student in the APA-accredited counseling psychology program at the University of North Texas. Her research interests include multicultural aspects of positive psychology and spirituality. Working under the direction of licensed clinical psychologists, she offers psychotherapy services to patients diagnosed with eating disorders. Ms. Zuniga's APA-accredited internship is in Pennsylvania, at WellSpan Philhaven Hospital. She has extensive experience presenting research at both local and national conferences.

Acknowledgments

This book would not have been possible without the sacrifice of the many who have contributed to my life. To my parents and grandparents, for their courage in coming to this country with nothing and giving my brother and me everything. To the faculty at Whittier College, CA, for encouraging me, at just 19 years old, to circumnavigate the world and encounter the beauty and dignity of those we too often see as "other." To the faculty of the Rosemead School of Psychology, CA, and Loma Linda University School of Medicine, CA, your impact on my formation as a clinical psychologist is beyond the capacity of language to express. To my patients, who have shown me the depths of human suffering, resilience, and compassion. To my husband, whose unwavering support, quiet sacrifices, endless cups of coffee, and willingness to shoulder the burdens of daily life allowed me the space to write this book – it is as much yours as it is mine. To God, without whom I would not have had the fortitude to write this book. I am who I am because they all are who they are.

V.R.

I would like to thank my husband, Addison Cooper, who is my biggest cheerleader and my best friend. He supports me in all my endeavors and always has a listening ear for me. I also want to thank all those who have contributed to my journey of lifelong learning – professors, colleagues, and clients. They have piqued my curiosity to explore ever further in the field of psychology and have shared their knowledge, wisdom, and experiences, which have enriched my view of the world. I look forward to learning even more as my journey continues.

N.C.

Introduction

Veronica Regueiro

In the spring of 2024, while meeting with the Clinical Competency Exam (CCE) Committee at California Baptist University (CBU), I came to a startling revelation – I strongly dislike writing clinical case vignettes, especially when pressed for time. We had convened to discuss some changes we wanted to propose to the broader faculty – namely, how we could include a larger variety of clinical case vignettes into the rotation used for CCEs. It was then that we realized including more clinical case vignettes meant someone had to *write* more clinical case vignettes and, like most faculty at most busy universities, we collectively groaned at the thought of having to take on any additional work, especially so close to the end of the academic term. Final grades would be due soon, mandatory commencement activities would begin, preparations for the next term would then begin … the list went on, and we had not yet even begun to consider how our leadership roles in various clinical settings (not to mention personal and family responsibilities) might limit our ability to accomplish our goal. A cursory Google search did not yield any resources that might support our efforts and so we resigned ourselves to drafting a handful of new clinical case vignettes, along with answer keys, that could be used during the CCEs in the fall, with the intention of creating more another time. Later, when final grades had been submitted and commencement had been successfully navigated, I began to think more about the issue of sourcing clinical case vignettes and wondered if it might be most effective and efficient in the long run to simply create a manuscript that could be used as a general resource for faculty, clinical supervisors, and training directors who also needed a rotating collection of clinical case vignettes. Thus, the idea for this book was born.

While the idea for this project was initiated by a professional practical need, it eventually evolved into a far more meaningful endeavor – the opportunity to create a resource designed to reduce at least a small part of the burden shared by mental health professionals serving in academic and clinical settings. By compiling a variety of clinical case vignettes designed to reflect the professional experiences of contributing authors, this volume seeks to support faculty,

DOI: 10.4324/9781003586531-1

clinical supervisors, and training directors in enriching education and training experiences and developing critical thinking skills in their students. It is our hope that this collection of clinical case vignettes will not only save some time for those professionals tasked with generating clinical case vignettes for courses, exams, and other teaching opportunities, but will also contribute in some small way to the professional growth of graduate and doctoral students who are, after all, future clinicians and future colleagues.

The Importance of Clinical Case Vignettes

The field of mental health, comprised of various professionals from a variety of educational and clinical backgrounds, is shaped by research, understanding of best practice, federal and state laws and ordinances, and clinical experience. Clinicians themselves, whether trained at the master's or doctoral level, are shaped by the courses they complete, the research projects they undertake, and the supervised clinical experiences they acquire. The many, many books and articles read during the course of graduate and doctoral training, as well as during post-doctoral training for specialists, are foundational for forming a clinician's understanding of psychopathology, including etiology, course, and prognosis. Materials offered during graduate and doctoral training also inform clinical decision making, which often includes setting goals and determining interventions as well as monitoring the efficacy of such interventions. Clinical case vignettes especially offer a crucial bridge between theory and practice, supporting students at all levels and training in all fields as they seek to apply the content learned in classes to real-world patients and situations. Case vignettes have been used as a training tool for many years in medical mental health training as a way to broaden trainees' exposure to a breadth of clinical situations beyond the limitations of in vivo training (Stone & Klein, 1989; Dempsey, 2023). Vignettes offer a "safe space" for clinicians to consider a variety of different responses to a client situation without the time pressure or potential for harm of a real-world scenario. Consideration of clinical case vignettes in a group setting, moreover, allows clinicians and trainees to hear the variety of perspectives that their colleagues have to offer, and thus broaden and expand their own viewpoints.

Patients seeking mental health services, whether in outpatient or inpatient settings, bring with them unique histories, including strengths and challenges, and multiple intersecting identities set within the context of historical and personal circumstances. When conducting a clinical interview, clinicians must sort through all the information shared by the patient, some of which may be relevant to the case conceptualization and the diagnostic and treatment planning processes, and some of which may be irrelevant. Clinicians need to learn how to listen for the salient pieces of information needed to fulfill their clinical responsibilities but they also need to learn how to interpret what a patient is saying through a clinical lens, turning the story the patient in sharing into data pertaining to symptomology, symptom onset and duration, mitigating and exacerbating factors, etc. In addition, clinicians need to learn how to think through the lens of their chosen theoretical orientations and consider which interventions may be most appropriate based on the treatment modalities they have chosen. While most clinicians now practice in an integrated fashion, students often need support in clarifying the nuances between various theoretical orientations and treatment modalities, which includes learning the relevant specific vocabulary and language. Being able to distinguish between and accurately articulate these differences can become critically important when completing coursework, sitting for clinical competency or professional qualifying exams, or being asked by an interviewer to articulate a preferred theoretical orientation.

This collection of clinical case vignettes was created to serve as a resource for faculty members, clinical supervisors, and training directors wanting to provide their students and supervisees with opportunities to practice case conceptualization as well as treatment planning. Given the complexity of the case conceptualization process, including the importance of integrating factors related to diversity and law and ethics, it is essential that graduate and doctoral students have opportunities to practice applying theoretical knowledge to clinical case vignettes. Clinical case vignettes support the development of case conceptualization skills as well as treatment planning skills in a low-risk situation. By engaging thoughtfully with the clinical case vignettes provided in this collection, graduate and doctoral students will have the opportunity to learn how to think critically though the various aspects of a patient's presentation so that they can formulate an accurate case conceptualization, including diagnostic impressions. They will also have the opportunity to practice their treatment planning skills and exercise their knowledge of diversity, law, and ethics. Ultimately, it is our hope that this resource will support graduate and doctoral students in developing the skills needed to serve a diverse patient population competently and with compassion.

Using This Book

The first two chapters of this book discuss the importance of diversity, equity, and inclusion in clinical practice, with an additional note pertaining to the practice of cultural humility. After those initial chapters, the book is organized so that it roughly follows the structure of the *Diagnostic and Statistical Manual* (Fifth Edition, Text Revision) (DSM-5-TR) (APA, 2022). Each chapter offers a brief overview of the shared diagnostic features of the disorders included in the chapter but is primarily composed of clinical vignettes intended to illustrate particular diagnoses. Each vignette, in turn, includes demographic information as well as information pertaining to diversity considerations and ethical and legal considerations. Each vignette also includes examples of how to conceptualize the case from psychodynamic, cognitive behavioral, and biopsychosocial perspectives.

Faculty members, clinical supervisors, and training directors are encouraged to provide their students and supervisees with clinical case vignettes taken directly from the book. Clinical case vignettes can be read aloud during classes or provided in photocopied form, to facilitate either class discussion or small group work. Students can be assigned clinical case vignettes and asked to either write papers or create PowerPoint presentations for in-class projects. Clinical case vignettes can also be given to students as part of an exam, to assess developing competencies. In clinical settings, the case vignettes included in this book can be utilized in either individual or group supervision to facilitate discussion and improve both case conceptualization and treatment planning skills. In offering these clinical case vignettes for use in both classroom and clinical settings, we hope to foster critical thinking skills in students and supervisees while also instilling an appreciation for three very distinct ways of conceptualizing patients and planning care.

Most of the clinical case vignettes included in this volume represent actual patients encountered in the various settings in which our contributing authors serve. Of course, creative liberties have been taken to ensure no patient can be identified based on the demographic information provided, and each case was de-identified before those creative liberties were taken. Each clinical case vignette was also simplified for inclusion in this volume, primarily because this book is meant to serve as a teaching resource for graduate and doctoral students still learning how to conceptualize psychopathology properly while also thinking through diversity, ethical, and legal components. As such, each clinical case vignette represents one primary diagnosis. While in real clinical settings patients often present with co-morbid or co-occurring diagnoses, the decision to simplify the clinical case vignettes was made in the spirit of wanting to support first- and second-year students particularly, who are the students generally enrolled in psychopathology courses and who are also the students just beginning to practice clinically. Faculty, clinical supervisors, and training directors are encouraged to add complexity to the clinical case vignettes as needed.

Additionally, not every disorder included in the DSM-5-TR was included in this volume – in some cases, entire chapters were left out. For example, disorders included in the first chapter of the DSM-5-TR, which pertains to neurodevelopmental disorders, were not included. Similarly, neurocognitive disorders were not included, and so on. The decision to exclude certain diagnoses was two-fold. First and foremost, certain disorders in the DSM-5-TR have etiologies so intricately grounded in medical and/or genetic conditions that offering psychodynamic or cognitive behavioral conceptualizations could trivialize the nuances of the disorder or the treatment planning process, or both. As a pediatric psychologist, the disorder that comes to mind when thinking about a diagnosis that would have been inappropriate to include in this volume is intellectual disability. As a neurodevelopmental disorder, intellectual disability is, by definition, present across the lifespan and also impairing across the lifespan. There is no psychodynamic intervention or cognitive behavioral intervention that can suddenly make an individual no longer meet the diagnostic criteria for intellectual disability – these criteria, after all, include the individual's performance on an objective measure of intelligence. As such, intellectual disability and other disorders were not included in this volume. Second, there are some disorders included in the DSM-5-TR that serve as a method of categorizing/labeling a patient when full criteria for another disorder have not been met. These diagnoses, of course, are the "other specified" or "unspecified" disorders. Only clinical case vignettes representing patients meeting full diagnostic criteria for the disorder they are meant to exemplify were included, for ease of teaching. Just as the decision was made to exclude certain diagnoses because to include them may have been clinically inappropriate, so too was additional attention paid to some diagnoses and/or diagnostic categories with which faculty members, clinical supervisors, training directors, and/or their students might be less familiar. For example, most mental health professionals and their students and supervisees are likely familiar with mood disorders, anxiety disorders, etc., but substantially less familiar with somatic symptom and related disorders, largely because patients with such disorders are most commonly seen in medical settings, not mental health settings. As such, to best familiarize faculty members, clinical supervisors, training directors, and their students with these diagnoses prior to reviewing the included clinical case vignettes, much more attention was given to the explanation of these disorders.

In summary, in creating this volume of clinical case vignettes, our purpose was to provide an accessible resource that could support training across a wide range of professions – clinical psychology, counseling, social work, etc. This collection of clinical case vignettes was designed specifically to meet graduate and doctoral students wherever they might find themselves in their developmental journeys and to highlight key features of the most common disorders both found in the DSM-5-TR and encountered in classrooms and at practicum and internship sites. By beginning with chapters that highlight the critical importance of diversity, equity, and inclusion, as well as cultural humility, we hope to emphasize how foundational these precepts are in both conceptualizing patients accurately and providing high-quality patient care that values human diversity and dignity. Our purpose in organizing the chapters in a manner that generally corresponds to the structure of the DSM-5-TR was to facilitate easy integration into existing curricula and supervision models across a variety of institutions and professional training programs. Although certain disorders and categories of disorders were intentionally excluded and although individual clinical case vignettes were simplified, it is our hope that the clinical case vignettes included will serve as supports for the development of clinical competencies in a manner that reduces the mental and practical workload of faculty members, clinical supervisors, and training directors.

The Importance of Theoretical Orientation in Clinical Practice

The utilization of a clearly defined theoretical orientation is foundational to ethical and effective clinical practice, specifically because a clinician's theoretical orientation serves as a structured framework through which the clinician can conceptualize psychopathology, including etiology. Use of a clearly defined theoretical orientation can also guide treatment planning, precisely because it allows a clinician to evaluate and understand what exactly is causing patient distress and, therefore, what might be helpful (Norcross & Lambert, 2019). Ultimately, use of a clearly defined theoretical orientation supports this process specifically because it allows a clinician to organize information shared by a patient into meaningful patterns (Kuyken et al., 2015). Use of a clearly defined theoretical orientation supports clinical consistency as well as the use of evidence-based practice (Sperry & Sperry, 2020). Additionally, well-established theoretical orientations provide disparate clinicians with the common language necessary for clinical training, ongoing professional development and continuing education, and interdisciplinary collaboration (Prochaska & Norcross, 2018). Clinical practice without the use of a well-applied theoretical orientation through which a patient can be conceptualized has the potential to compromise patient outcomes specifically because it can allow for more reactivity and subjectivity on the part of the clinician.

Psychodynamic Psychotherapy

Each of the clinical case vignettes included in this volume is conceptualized from the perspective of three distinct theoretical orientations, the first of these being the psychodynamic approach. Psychodynamic psychotherapy is related to and stems from psychoanalysis, as practiced by Sigmund Freud and modified by later theorists such as Carl Jung and Melanie Klein. In 1900, Freud published his landmark work, *The Interpretation of Dreams*, where he introduced concepts related to the unconscious mind. In his work, he emphasized the influence of unconscious processes on behavior as well as the therapeutic value of bringing this unconscious material into conscious awareness. Freud practiced classical psychoanalysis, with required frequent sessions with his patients, the use of free association, and the analysis of transference and countertransference (Freud, 1912). As time progressed, both Freud's contemporaries and later theorists either elaborated on his ideas or challenged them. Melanie Klein, for example, worked primarily with children and therefore focused on her patients' internalized relationships with their early caregivers, which ultimately led to the development of object relations theory. Psychodynamic psychotherapy has continued to progress but has consistently remained true to its historical roots, namely, its focus on the internal world of the patient and how the structure of that internal world influences their overall functioning. Although not always included in lists of evidence-based practices, empirical studies and meta-analyses have demonstrated that psychodynamic psychotherapy is indeed effective in addressing symptomology related to a variety of mental health disorders (Shedler, 2010; Leichsenring & Rabung, 2008).

Modern psychodynamic psychotherapy now requires fewer sessions each week than deemed necessary by classical psychoanalysis and also allows for the clinician to assume a much more relational posture towards the patient (Gabbard, 2017). Whereas Freud famously maintained a "blank screen" approach to treatment, whereby patients could freely project onto the ultimately unknowable person of the clinician, modern psychodynamic psychotherapists recognize the bidirectional intersubjective nature of the therapeutic relationship (Mitchell, 1988). Additionally, treatment modalities grounded in psychodynamic psychotherapy, such as mentalization-based treatment (Bateman & Fonagy, 2004) and transference-focused psychotherapy (Kernberg, 2006) continue to emerge, evidence that over a century after its precepts were introduced, psychodynamic psychotherapy remains a relevant theoretical orientation for clinicians wanting to address the suffering associated with psychological distress.

Psychodynamic psychotherapy's longevity is based, in part, on continuously emerging research demonstrating that long-term psychodynamic psychotherapy is not only as effective as short-term treatments but, for some complex forms of psychopathology, leads to more significant improvement (Shedler, 2010; Leichsenring & Rabung, 2011; Driessen et al., 2015). Based on the results of his landmark meta-analysis, Shedler (2010) argued that psychodynamic psychotherapy not only reduces symptoms associated with mental health disorders but also fosters long-term personality change that endures even after termination.

Psychodynamic psychotherapy's longevity can also be credited to how easily it can be integrated with other approaches. As a theoretical orientation and treatment modality grounded in developmental theory, attachment, and unconscious processes, psychodynamic therapy offers a flexible framework that can complement a variety of other theoretical orientations and treatment approaches (Shedler, 2010), setting the foundation for a truly integrated approach to patient care. Integrating psychodynamic psychotherapy with other treatment modalities allows clinicians to conceptualize patients while taking defense mechanisms, relational patterns, and early childhood experiences into account while also providing patients with the practical and/or solution-based approaches commonly utilized in community mental health settings, college counseling centers, medical settings, etc.

Unfortunately, issues pertaining to accessibility have historically negatively impacted both student clinicians' ability to receive adequate training in psychodynamic psychotherapy and patients' ability to access psychodynamic psychotherapy as a form of treatment. Psychodynamic psychotherapy is not a manualized approach to care and so training in this form of treatment can take much more time than it takes to train student clinicians in how to provide manualized forms of treatment, such as cognitive-behavioral therapy (CBT). Additionally, there is an argument to be made for the fact that training in psychodynamic psychotherapy requires much more nuance, largely because of how interpretations, transference, and countertransference are used as interventions. Short-term interventions are often perceived as being more cost-effective (Leichsenring et al., 2018) both by patients needing to pay for mental health services themselves and by the insurance companies helping other patients to access care. Additionally, in mental healthcare settings where the number of patients on waitlists far exceeds the number of clinicians providing services, short-term care is deemed most desirable, as it allows clinicians to move through waitlists more quickly. Lastly, bias against psychodynamic psychotherapy remains an obstacle, in both academic and clinical training centers and among the general public, as psychodynamic clinicians are often perceived as aloof and impersonal, obsessed with their patients' childhood memories and disconnected from the need to help patients obtain tangible results in the present moment. That said, emerging research from the field of neurobiology continues not only to support the work being done by psychodynamic psychotherapists but also, possibly, to provide evidence that such care may be worth both the time and money required to access clinical training and treatment in this form of care (Schore, 2012).

Because the emphasis in psychodynamic psychotherapy is on the exploration of unconscious processes and relational dynamics, its interventions focus on facilitating insight and emotional awareness as well as the resolution of internal conflicts. Historically, psychodynamic psychotherapy has utilized the same interventions championed by Freud, namely, free association and interpretation, but modern psychodynamic clinicians use a much broader range of interventions.

Interpretation, psychodynamic psychotherapy's flagship intervention, allows patients to bring unconscious internal conflicts, defense mechanisms, and relational patterns into conscious awareness, largely through the exploration of transference dynamics. Generally speaking, interpretations must be delivered when the clinician intuits that the patient is ready to hear the interpretation (Blagys & Hilsenroth, 2000) and target repressed affective experiences, problematic relational patterns, and defenses that maintain psychopathology. Working-through, another longstanding intervention utilized by psychodynamic psychotherapists, allows patients to re-examine unconscious conflicts and patterns over time, which supports long-term personality change (Shedler, 2010). Modern iterations of psychodynamic psychotherapy also emphasize empathic validation and emotional attunement (Maroda, 2010). Empathic validation and emotional attunement are understood not only to enhance the therapeutic alliance but also to support the patient's ability to regulate affect. Modern psychodynamic psychotherapists increasingly also use countertransference as a form of clinical information (Gelso & Hayes, 2007) to improve case conceptualization and inform clinical interventions. Additional interventions include, but are not limited to, those interventions utilized specifically by more recent treatment modalities rooted in psychodynamic psychotherapy, such as mentalization-based treatment and transference-focused psychotherapy.

Despite the accessibility issues associated with clinical training and patient care, psychodynamic psychotherapy remains a valuable and relevant theoretical orientation in which are grounded well-established treatment modalities supported by empirical evidence. Reasons for its enduring success can be found in its nuanced attention to the therapeutic relationship as well as its ability to foster deep, abiding change in patients' lives, even in the face of significant psychopathology. Psychodynamic psychotherapy continues to evolve, integrating evidence from emerging fields such as those grounded in neuroscience, without losing its connection to its historical underpinnings. The interventions commonly utilized by psychodynamic psychotherapists exemplify both the breadth and the flexibility offered by psychodynamic approaches to treatment as its clinicians work to alleviate psychological suffering.

Cognitive Behavioral Therapy

CBT is rooted in the work of B. F. Skinner, Joseph Wolpe, and Aaron Beck, theorists working in the 1950s and 1960s, half a century after the consolidation of psychology as a field. B. F. Skinner and Joseph Wolpe are known for their work in the field of behaviorism (i.e., classical and operant conditioning) and how classical and operant conditioning can contribute to the development of maladaptive behaviors as well as maintain those behaviors. Aaron Beck is best known for developing cognitive therapy, established on the principle that distorted thinking patterns contribute to and maintain both emotional and behavioral dysregulation. Beck postulated that internal schemas held by patients about both themselves and their world contribute to automatic thoughts that, in turn, contribute to emotional distress (Beck, 1967). CBT brings together the work of all three theorists to explain the interrelated nature of cognitions, emotions, and behavior in the development and maintenance of psychopathology. CBT is one of the most, if not *the* most, widely researched and practiced forms of psychotherapy, largely due to its structured, goal-oriented approach to patient care. CBT is considered to be an evidence-based treatment suitable for addressing a variety of mental health disorders, and meta-analyses have demonstrated that patients enrolled in CBT show more improvement than patients solely prescribed medication (Cuijpers et al., 2013).

Because CBT emphasizes manualized treatment protocols and measurable outcomes, it is widely endorsed by professional practice organizations and lauded as the gold standard in evidence-based practice. Similar to psychodynamic psychotherapy, it has evolved over time to better meet the needs of patients. Indeed, CBT's ability to be modified as needed to meet the needs of diverse patient populations and also address very specific mental health concerns contributes to its enduring success as an evidence-based practice. CBT interventions have been modified to address racial and ethnic differences (Hinton & Jalal, 2014). CBT has also been expanded to include several new manualized evidence-based approaches. While these approaches still incorporate historical CBT precepts regarding the role maladaptive cognitions and behaviors play in developing and maintaining psychopathology, they also take into account both the context and the function of maladaptive thoughts (Hayes et al., 2004). These new treatment modalities, grounded in CBT, include acceptance and commitment therapy (ACT), dialectical behavior therapy (DBT), and mindfulness-based cognitive therapy (MBCT). Whereas traditional CBT has clinicians challenge and restructure maladaptive thoughts while encouraging behavioral changes that incorporate exposure to feared stimuli, behavioral experiments, etc., these newer treatment modalities promote the acceptance of difficult experiences and affective states as well as the incorporation of mindfulness-based practices.

Just as psychodynamic psychotherapy often faces criticism, so, too, does CBT. Specifically, there has been some argument that, because CBT is a manualized approach to care, it promotes a one-size-fits-all approach that neglects individual patient needs and differences (Persons, 2008). Additionally, there has been some criticism regarding the superficial nature of CBT, arguing that it fails to capture the nuance of the difficult experiences often shared by patients in clinical settings (Westen et al., 2004). Finally, as with psychodynamic psychotherapy, CBT requires high-quality training and supervision. Unfortunately, many student clinicians appear to believe that they are implementing CBT whenever they present patients with worksheets, but CBT is a far more intricate treatment approach that requires clinician attention to treatment protocols (Barrett et al., 2008) as well as adherence to the manualized approach.

Because CBT is based, in part, on the theory that maladaptive cognitions are at the root of psychopathology, many CBT interventions are designed to restructure maladaptive thoughts. Cognitive restructuring, a hallmark of CBT, supports patients in identifying and challenging automatic thoughts, which research shows can mitigate symptoms of many mental health disorders (Clark & Beck, 2010). While cognitive restructuring often occurs within the context of a CBT session, other CBT interventions targeting maladaptive cognitions can be completed independently by the patient, as is the case with thought records. CBT is also based in part on the theory that maladaptive behaviors contribute to psychological distress and so many CBT interventions also target these maladaptive behaviors. Behavioral activation, just one of many CBT interventions designed to target behavior, was developed to support patients in increasing engagement in pleasurable activities specifically to counteract the social withdrawal that can reinforce symptoms of depression (Martell et al., 2010). Behavioral experiments, developed to encourage patients to test the validity of their beliefs through experiential learning (Bennett-Levy et al., 2004), involve actively testing cognitive distortions within the context of the patient's real life. Exposure therapy, an intervention developed to gradually expose patients to feared stimuli, extinguishes fear responses through habituation (Foa & Kozak, 1986). As CBT has developed, the new treatment modalities grounded in CBT have also incorporated mindfulness-based practices to develop cognitive flexibility (Segal et al., 2018) as well as cognitive defusion to help patients create distance between themselves and their thoughts (Hayes et al., 1999). Prior to any interventions being implemented, as well as throughout the course of therapy, CBT clinicians utilize Socratic questioning to encourage patients to examine their assumptions and beliefs critically. Additionally, CBT clinicians consistently request that patients complete homework assignments, specifically to support them in continuing to develop new, more adaptive skills outside of the therapy room.

Ultimately, CBT is an empirically supported approach that, just like psychodynamic psychotherapy, continues to evolve as time progresses. CBT clinicians continue to conceptualize patients in a manner consistent with historical CBT, while incorporating interventions responsive to modern sensibilities, such as the desire for mindfulness-based practices. CBT remains the gold standard of evidence-based treatment but also continues to grow, so as to serve diverse patients with varying needs better. While critics remain concerned about CBT's rigidity and potential superficiality, manualization of a treatment modality does not necessarily mean that the treatment approach itself is rigid; rather, that a specific structure has been found to be helpful in mitigating symptoms of psychological distress associated with certain mental health disorders. Even within a manualized approach, the best clinicians are still personable and emotionally responsive. Despite critiques, CBT provides its clinicians with a wide range of interventions from which to choose when supporting patients struggling with mental health concerns. As with psychodynamic psychotherapy, skillful clinicians can leverage CBT interventions to promote healing and growth.

Biopsychosocial Model

The biopsychosocial model does not focus on unconscious processes, maladaptive cognitions, or maladaptive behaviors to understand the etiology of psychopathology, but rather proposes that psychological disorders result from the ways in which biological, psychological, and social factors interact with one another (Engel, 1977). In his 1977 paper, Engel argued that both the biological and the psychological models of psychopathology were too reductionistic to account for the total experience of the human person suffering from psychological distress, largely because those models did not take into account social or environmental factors. From Engel's (1977) perspective, only the biopsychosocial model fully integrated simultaneous and systematic interaction of biological, psychological, and social factors influencing patients. Engel's work built upon previous models proposed by Adolf Meyer and Harry Stack Sullivan, indicating a general move in psychology to understand psychopathology within the context of environment and circumstance instead of accounting all mental health symptoms to individual biological and/or psychological factors. Within the field of clinical psychology, the biopsychosocial model is specifically associated with health psychology, a specialty recognized in the 1970s and 1980s (Taylor, 2017). The biopsychosocial model supports a whole-person approach to care and emphasizes not just environmental and social stressors but also environmental and social supports.

The biopsychosocial model enjoys some popularity as a theoretical orientation, especially among health psychologists and social workers. Many professional organizations, including the American Psychological Association, the American Psychiatric Association, and the World Health Organization, encourage clinicians to utilize a biopsychosocial approach when conceptualizing patients (World Health Organization, 2013). The biopsychosocial model is well utilized, especially in medical and psychiatric settings, as it encourages a multidisciplinary approach to patient care, comprehensive diagnostic assessments that account for diversity variables, and integrated treatment plans that allow for the inclusion of community resources. The biopsychosocial model acknowledges the inherent interconnectedness of the mind and body as well as the fact that treating patients as though their greater environmental and social contexts are irrelevant can lead to suboptimal outcomes.

Of course, the biopsychosocial model has critics, one of the most significant criticisms being that while the biopsychosocial is helpful when conceptualizing cases, clinicians using the biopsychosocial model to conceptualize often revert to biomedical reductionism in practice (Ghaemi, 2009). Some critics argue that the biopsychosocial model is not fully operationalized as a treatment approach and so does not provide clear guidance regarding how to select interventions (McLaren, 1998). For example, psychodynamic psychotherapy, as a theoretical orientation, operates based on the premise that psychopathology stems from unconscious conflicts and problematic relational patterns. Psychodynamic psychotherapy, as a treatment modality, implements interventions designed to bring unconscious material into conscious awareness and resolve problematic relational patterns, such as through the use of transference-based interpretations. CBT, as a theoretical orientation, proposes that maladaptive cognitions and behaviors contribute to the development of psychopathology. CBT, as a treatment modality, therefore, implements interventions designed to restructure cognitive distortions and encourage engagement in adaptive instead of maladaptive behaviors. The biopsychosocial model, as a theoretical orientation, allows for a comprehensive, whole-person understanding of variables contributing to psychopathology, whether they be biological, psychological, environmental, or social in nature. The biopsychosocial model is not, however, a treatment modality and, therefore, clinicians conceptualizing using the biopsychosocial model may deliver very different interventions when faced with the same presenting problem. Mental health professionals who prefer utilizing the biopsychosocial model are actively working to address these criticisms by refining and expanding the model but, currently, clinicians utilizing the biopsychosocial model to conceptualize are providing treatment in an integrated fashion, by utilizing other evidence-based practices as appropriate to address patient needs.

Although the biopsychosocial model may not be able to claim a particular treatment modality grounded in its precepts as a theoretical orientation, by virtue of the way in which it conceptualizes patients, treatment goals target patients' physiological health, psychological functioning, and social environment. Interventions targeting patients' physiological status often include recommendations regarding sleep and exercise as well as referrals to medical providers to address underlying genetic and/or medical concerns. Such interventions have been shown to improve mental health symptoms and so are considered a pivotal area of concern when working with patients using the biopsychosocial model (Schuch et al., 2016). Clinicians utilizing the biopsychosocial model may implement traditional psychotherapy treatment modalities such as CBT or may utilize a fully integrated approach, administering interventions curated from a variety of treatment modalities based on a particular patient's specific needs. Because the biopsychosocial approach is necessarily flexible, as it does not have an associated treatment modality, clinicians conceptualizing through the biopsychosocial lens tend to be less rigid about strict adherence to any particular treatment approach (Norcross & Goldfried, 2005). Social interventions associated with the biopsychosocial model often attempt to mitigate system barriers to care while improving social support (McDaniel, Doherty, & Hepworth, 2014) whether that support be formal or informal in nature. Importantly, the social aspect of the biopsychosocial model includes clinicians working collaboratively with other professionals to provide truly comprehensive care.

Ultimately, although flawed in terms of its utility as a treatment modality, the biopsychosocial model as a theoretical orientation offers a comprehensive framework in which the nuances of a patient's presentation can be fully understood, not just with regard to individual factors but also within the context of the patient's environment. The biopsychosocial model allows clinicians the flexibility to approach patient care from a truly person-centered perspective, when addressing medical, psychological, and social concerns. While the biopsychosocial model requires refinement as a theoretical orientation as well as further development as a treatment modality, its promise is that it can capture the complexity of the human experience and provide whole-person care to promote lasting well-being, in body and mind.

Law and Ethics

Just as adherence to a well-established theoretical orientation is foundational for providing clinical care effectively to patients in mental health settings, so too is adherence to legal and ethical standards. Laws help clinicians understand the minimum standards for the practice of their professions, whereas ethical standards are generally aspirational in nature and meant to promote patient well-being (APA, 2017). It is imperative that clinicians follow both the legal and ethical principles associated with their professions particularly because of the powers and privileges associated with being mental health professionals. Because law and ethics are not static but constantly evolving as both society and science advance, clinicians have a duty to engage in ongoing continuing education to ensure that they remain familiar with both legislative changes and updates to ethical codes (Behnke, 2008). While this volume is in no way meant to serve as a comprehensive overview of the laws guiding the practice of mental health clinicians, ethical and legal considerations for each clinical case vignette are included and, therefore, a brief overview of the laws and ethics relevant to the mental health clinicians seems relevant.

Legal Obligations

Mental health professionals, including licensed clinical psychologists, licensed marriage and family therapists (LMFTs), licensed clinical social workers (LCSWs), and licensed professional counselors (LPCCs), are all required to adhere to the wide range of legal statutes that govern their professions. Legislature governing the practice of mental health clinicians exists at both the state and federal levels and, very often, state licensing boards manage the implementation of these laws as well as the discipline required should a mental health clinician be in violation of a law. In the state of California, for example, the Board of Behavioral Sciences (BBS) governs the practice of master's level clinicians (LMFTs, LCSWs, and LPCCs) while the Board of Psychology (BOP) governs the practice of licensed clinical psychologists. These boards exist to manage the professional practice of mental health clinicians specifically because the legislative changes in question are meant to protect patients, uphold professional accountability, and maintain public trust in the field of mental health.

One of the most fundamental legal responsibilities in which a clinician must engage is the practice of obtaining informed consent prior to the initiation of treatment; for the purposes of this book, readers should assume that all patients being represented in the clinical vignettes utilized have already undergone basic informed consent procedures. In clinical settings, however, the purpose of engaging in conversations surrounding consent is to ensure patients understand the benefits and risks associated with the care they are about to receive, what to expect in terms of treatment, the limits of confidentiality, and that it is their right to withdraw from service at any time. Minors and others deemed incompetent to participate in the informed consent process, such as conserved adults, must have a legal representative provide informed consent on their behalf. They themselves should then be provided with the opportunity to assent to care. The informed consent process is grounded in the principle of patient autonomy – that an individual has the right to determine whether or not to proceed with psychotherapy services and that they have the right to fully understand the psychotherapy process before initiation of care. Part of the informed consent process necessarily includes conversations regarding privacy and confidentiality as well as their limits.

Another crucial aspect of the informed consent process, especially as it relates to the limits of privacy and confidentiality, involves clinicians' statuses as mandated reports. Being a mandated reporter in most states requires mental health clinicians to alert local and/or state authorities if they are informed of any abuse or neglect involving children, elders, or dependent adults. States define the nuances of abuse and neglect differently, but, generally speaking, abuse and neglect refer to instances of physical abuse, sexual abuse, and improper supervision that could result in injury or loss of life. For elders and dependent adults, additional categories of abuse and neglect include financial abuse, improper use of physical or chemical restraint, isolation, etc. Additionally, in some states, mental health clinicians carry a duty to either warn or protect individuals where their patients pose serious and/or imminent risk of harm. Ultimately, in situations that require clinicians to break privacy and confidentiality laws in the service of mandated reporting requirements as well as in situations where duties to warn and/or protect must be carried out, clinicians are best served by being aware of the local and state laws where they practice and, at times, consulting with other professionals, including their malpractice insurance provider, to clarify their roles and responsibilities in nuanced situations.

Additional legal obligations include keeping accurate records, which must be retained for a specified period of time, depending on the state in which the clinician is practicing as well as the age of the specified patient. As telehealth has become more frequently utilized, legislation has emerged to govern the use of telehealth. Specifically, recent laws specify where clinicians and patients must be located for telehealth services to be provided, with additional requirements for where the clinician must be licensed in order to provide care. Federal laws prohibit discriminatory practices and also require clinicians to provide reasonable accommodations as needed for patients with recognized disabilities. Many states also have laws governing professional boundaries, advertising practices, and clinician fitness. Specifically, many states require clinicians to ensure that they themselves are not impaired by medical or mental health issues. Compliance with both federal and state laws reduces risk to both clinicians and patients and maintains public trust in the professions associated with the field of mental health.

Ethical Practice

All professional organizations that support clinicians working in the field of mental health have published ethical codes to provide their constituents with guidance as to what constitutes ethical practice in that particular field. The American Psychological Association, for example, has the *Ethical Principles of Psychologists and Code of Conduct* (hereafter referred to as the "*Code of Conduct*"), the most recent edition of which was adopted in 2017. For the purpose of this discussion, the *Ethical Principles of Psychologists and Code of Conduct* will be utilized.

The *Code of Conduct* begins with general principles that are not legally enforceable but instead aspirational in nature. The five general principles include beneficence and non-maleficence, fidelity and responsibility, integrity, justice, and respect for the rights and dignity of others (APA, 2017). The first principle, beneficence and non-maleficence, is related to the notion of "doing no harm" but also incorporates active promotion of the welfare of others. Adherence to this principle requires clinicians to actively avoid actions that might cause harm while also advocating for the rights of others. The purpose of the second principle, fidelity and responsibility, is to encourage psychologists to remain trustworthy, avoid the exploitation of others, and accept responsibility for their own behaviors (APA, 2017). The third principle, integrity, specifically refers to the importance of honesty when engaging in professional activities and specifies that in situations where deceit must be utilized (such as during the course of conducting an experiment) participants are not only not harmed but also are appropriately debriefed (APA, 2017). The fourth principle, justice, is related to the notion that all individuals have the right to benefit from psychological science and practice and that it is the responsibility of psychologists to protect such access while actively managing their own potential biases (APA, 2017). The fifth and final principle, respect for people's rights and dignity, affirms the inherent worth and autonomy of all individuals and encourages psychologists to protect the rights of others, including the right to self-determination (APA, 2017). Taken together, these principles summarize the best of what psychology, indeed, what mental health practice can be at its best.

Actual ethical standards included in the ethics code address everything from how to resolve ethical issues to record keeping. While it is outside the scope of this volume to review every standard included in the ethics code comprehensively, these standards often overlap with federal and local laws related to the practice of psychology and are enforceable (APA, 2017). For the purpose of this volume, relevant ethical standards are those related to competence, human relations, privacy and confidentiality, assessment, and therapy.

The ethical standard pertaining to competence ensures that psychologists practice only within the areas in which they have received education and training (APA, 2017). Education can include coursework as part of an accredited program or continuing education course whereas training refers to supervised clinical experience, knowledge gained through consultation with other professionals, and clinical experience gathered over the course of one's practice. When confronted with patient demographics or presenting issues with which they are not familiar, the competence standard directs psychologists to acquire the education and training needed before proceeding with services (APA, 2017). A psychologist, for example, who has never been educated or trained to work with children would not ethically be able to accept a referral for a child patient without first seeking relevant education, consultation, training, or supervision. As another example, a psychologist not educated or trained to implement eye movement desensitization and reprocessing (EMDR) might be familiar with the research indicating it is effective in reducing symptoms associated with post-traumatic stress disorder, but, ethically, would be unable themselves to implement the intervention. The competence standard does allow for some flexibility in emergency situations but only until a competent clinician arrives (APA, 2017). Of note, this standard also espouses the notion that psychologists are responsible for lifelong learning; that is, that for the duration of their careers, they will participate in continuing education and remain abreast of advances in the field of psychology (APA, 2017).

The human relations standard provides general guidance regarding the ethical obligations clinicians have when interacting with others in the course of their professional duties, including patients, colleagues, and others. Specifically, this standard prohibits psychologists from unfairly discriminating against others and also prohibits psychologists from engaging in any form of harassment, including sexual harassment (APA, 2017). As is likely evident, the human relations standard is just one of the standards supporting the general principle of beneficence and non-maleficence. The human relations standard also sets forth guidance regarding the involvement of third parties in the provision of psychological services (APA, 2017). Specifically, this standard indicates that whenever a third party is involved in the provision of psychological services, whether that third party be a physician, an employer, or a court, it is the responsibility of the psychologist to clarify the nature of the professional relationship with all involved parties, including aspects relating to privacy, confidentiality, and identification of the client (APA, 2017). Of note, while some clinicians, psychologists included, might feel uncomfortable providing services to a patient when a third party is involved, the human relations standard does explicate that psychologists are expected to cooperate with other professionals if such cooperation can provide a patient with the highest level of service possible (APA, 2017).

The purpose of the privacy and confidentiality standard is to guarantee that control over a patient's personal information, including medical records, remains in the control of the patient. In service of this standard, psychologists are expected to protect the confidential information in their possession, whether digital or analogue (APA, 2017). Psychologists are also expected to discuss the limits of confidentiality with patients as soon as possible during the course of treatment (APA, 2017), ideally, in an intake session. Because it is incumbent upon psychologists to protect confidential patient information in their possession, engagement with third parties involved in the referral and/or treatment process must be thoughtful and nuanced. The privacy and confidentiality standard specifies that even when engaging with third parties, psychologists are to limit the disclosure of confidential information to only that which is necessary, relevant, and legally required. It also makes clear that these disclosures can only occur with the informed consent of the patient or when mandated or permitted by law (APA, 2017).

The assessment standard governs the appropriate and ethical use of psychological assessments, including the selection, administration, and interpretation processes. This standard specifies that when conducting psychological assessments, psychologists should strive to ensure they have gathered data from more than one source and that conclusions drawn from assessment results be evidence-based (APA, 2017). The assessment standard also specifies that interpretation of assessment data must be done within the context of the patient's history and situation, incorporating factors such as dominant language, cultural considerations, and test-taking conditions, etc.

Finally, the therapy standard provides an overview of the ethical responsibilities of psychologists when providing psychotherapy services. The nature of informed consent and when to gather informed consent is outlined in this standard, as are directions for obtaining consent from the legal representatives of patients unable to consent for themselves. The therapy standard outlines the responsibilities of psychologists when treatment is interrupted, namely, that it is the responsibility of the psychologist to make reasonable efforts to ensure continuity of care, be that referral to another provider or communicating a clear contingency plan (APA, 2017). Finally, the therapy standard specifies that psychologists are ethically required to terminate psychotherapy services if a patient is being harmed by the interventions provided, if the patient fails to participate in the psychotherapy process, or if the psychologist is being threatened by either the patient or another individual involved in the therapeutic process (APA, 2017).

Ultimately, the *Code of Conduct* offers both aspirational principles and ethical standards crucial to the appropriate, effective, and ethical practice of psychology. Although several standards have been reviewed briefly in this section, it is important to note that they represent only a small sample of the ethical standards incorporated into the actual *Code of Conduct.* Not only do they represent just a small sample of the standards included in the *Code of Conduct,* they also only apply to psychologists. LMFTs, LCSWs, and other professionals working in the field of mental health have their own professional organizations, many with their own fully articulated ethics codes. While there may be overlap between the *Code of Conduct* and the ethics codes articulated by other professions, these codes are not interchangeable, nor should they be considered so due to the unique perspective offered by distinct professions. It is also important to note that ethical standards often require interpretation within the context of whatever particular event happens to be unfolding in a clinical space. Ultimately, appropriate, effective, and ethical practice in the field of mental health is dependent upon clinician knowledge of relevant ethical codes and, more importantly, commitment to lifelong learning.

Contributing Authors

The authors who have contributed to this volume represent a variety of institutions and organizations as well as a variety of worldviews. As such, there are stylistic differences incorporated throughout the volume. For example, some clinicians refer to the subjects of their vignettes as patients; other clinicians refer to them as clients. Some clinicians completed portions of their clinical case vignettes using brief phrases as opposed to complete sentences; other clinicians wrote strictly using complete sentences. While some consideration was given to editing for uniformity across the volume, value was found in allowing each clinician to express themself in the manner consistent with his or her training and background. For example, as a pediatric psychologist who has trained and worked primarily in medical and inpatient psychiatric settings, I consistently refer to the individuals with whom I work as patients. Other licensed clinical psychologists prefer the term client. Neither of these words are right or wrong but are generally chosen by clinicians based on preferences, general approach to their particular profession within the field of mental health, socialization into the field, etc. Students utilizing the clinical case vignettes included in this volume are encouraged to notice the various ways in which the contributing authors drafted their clinical case vignettes and to consider for themselves how they wish to approach their particular professions within the field of mental health and the connotations of the language they tend to utilize.

A deliberate attempt was made, however, to maintain a somewhat casual voice, so to speak, when explaining case conceptualizations and treatment plans in the answer keys. Although some contributing authors included citations as needed in their chapters, the majority of the answers were drafted based on clinical experience as well as expertise and written in much the way the author may have chosen to deliver that same information verbally to a student or a supervisee. There are many, many books and articles available regarding the disorders, theoretical orientations, and recommendations made in this book and it is our hope that by keeping the answer keys somewhat informal in tone, anyone making use of this information will find it more accessible.

This project would absolutely not have been possible without the support and cooperation of the authors who participated. It was a particular pleasure for many of the licensed clinical psychologists involved to have the opportunity to work with doctoral students on this project. Many of the doctoral students who participated in this project had received advanced standing in their programs prior to agreeing to participate in this work. Their enthusiasm was a privilege to witness and their level of commitment and organization impressive. It was a joy to work alongside future colleagues in such a worthwhile endeavor.

Conclusion

In gathering this collection of clinical case vignettes, it was our purpose to create an accessible and user-friendly resource for faculty members, clinical supervisors, and training directors working in both academic and clinical settings. Graduate and doctoral students are, of course, also encouraged to work actively with the material contained in this volume. This volume was designed to provide graduate and doctoral students training in a variety of professions the opportunity to engage meaningfully with case material that illuminates the various ways of conceptualizing patients within the context of the theoretical orientations utilized, grounded within a framework that prioritizes diversity, equity, inclusion, and cultural humility.

This collection of clinical case vignettes was intentionally organized to parallel the structure of the DSM-5-TR, even given the deliberate omission of certain diagnostic categories that would have been inappropriate to include. Our purpose in focusing on the disorders most commonly encountered in academic and clinical training settings was to ensure that this volume would be deemed relevant, helpful, and practical, as well as easily integrated into the work already being done by faculty members, clinical supervisors, and training directors. Our intention in opening the book with chapters dedicated to diversity, equity, inclusion, and cultural humility was to reaffirm those values as foundational to the development of all other clinical competencies and to emphasize the importance of such values to the practice of competent, compassionate, ethical mental health care.

While editorial efforts were made in the curation of the clinical case vignettes ultimately included in this volume, care was made to honor and preserve stylistic differences specifically in order to reflect the diversity of thought and practice within the field of mental health. Students are encouraged to notice such differences and to consider how they themselves may wish to navigate clinical language as they develop into clinical professionals. Additionally, it was a conscious choice to maintain a somewhat conversational tone in the answer keys utilized throughout this volume, specifically to recreate the experience a student or trainee might have if they were speaking with the individual who drafted the chapter in question. It is our hope that such a decision increased the accessibility of this material for those utilizing this volume.

Again, we are deeply grateful to the authors who contributed to this work, all of whom are excellent clinicians and whose gift of time and effort reflects the spirit of collaboration with which we hope mental health, as a profession, moves into the future. It is our sincere hope that this collection of clinical case vignettes will serve not just as an academic and clinical resource but also as a reminder that the work we all do has the power to shape the lives and experiences of those we are privileged to serve – let us wield that power responsibly and well.

V. R.

References

APA (American Psychological Association). (2017). *Ethical principles of psychologists and code of conduct*. https://www.apa.org/ethics/code/.

APA (American Psychiatric Association). (2022). *Diagnostic and statistical manual of mental disorders* (5th ed., text rev.). American Psychiatric Association.

Barrett, M. S., Chua, W. J., Crits-Christoph, P., Gibbons, M. B., & Thompson, D. (2008). Early withdrawal from mental health treatment: Implications for psychotherapy practice. *Psychotherapy: Theory, Research, Practice, Training*, *45*(2), 247–267. https://doi.org/10.1037/0033-3204.45.2.247.

Bateman, A. W., & Fonagy, P. (2004). *Psychotherapy for borderline personality disorder: Mentalization-based treatment*. Oxford University Press.

Beck, A.T. (1967). *Depression: Clinical, experimental, and theoretical aspects*. University of Pennsylvania Press.

Behnke, S. H. (2008). *Ethics and law for the practicing psychologist: Contemporary issues and standards* (3rd ed.). APA Books.

Bennett-Levy, J., Butler, G., Fennell, M., Hackmann, A., Mueller, M., & Westbrook, D. (2004). *Oxford guide to behavioural experiments in cognitive therapy*. Oxford University Press.

Blagys, M. D., & Hilsenroth, M. J. (2002). Distinctive activities of cognitive-behavioral therapy: A review of the comparative psychotherapy process literature. *Clinical Psychology: Science and Practice*, *7*(2), 167–188. https://doi.org/10.1016/S0272-7358(01)00117-9.

Clark, D. A., & Beck, A. T. (2010). *Cognitive therapy of anxiety disorders: Science and practice*. Guilford Press.

Cuijpers, P., Karyotaki, E., Weitz, E., Andersson, G., Hollon, S. D., van Straten, A., & Ebert, D. D. (2014). The effects of psychotherapies for major depression in adults on remission, recovery, and improvement: A meta-analysis. *Journal of Affective Disorders*, *159*(20), 118–126. https://doi.org/10.1016/j.jad.2014.02.026.

Dempsey, K. (2023). How storytelling impacts students in their psychotherapy training. *European Journal for Qualitative Research in Psychotherapy*, *13*, 136–152.

Driessen, E., Hegelmaier, L., Abbass, A. A., Barber, J. P., Dekker, J. J., Van, H. L., & Cuijpers, P. (2015). The efficacy of short-term psychodynamic psychotherapy for depression: A meta-analysis update. *Clinical Psychology Review*, 42, 1–15. https://doi.org/10.1016/j.cpr.2015.07.004.

Engel, G. L. (1977). The need for a new medical model: A challenge for biomedicine. *Science*, *196*(4286), 129–136. https://doi.org/10.1126/science.847460.

Foa, E. B., & Kozak, M. J. (1986). Emotional processing of fear: Exposure to corrective information. *Psychological Bulletin*, *99*(1), 20–35. https://doi.org/10.1037/0033-2909.99.1.20.

Freud, S. (1912). *The dynamics of transference*. In *The Standard Edition of the Complete Psychological Works of Sigmund Freud* (Vol. 12, pp. 97–108). Hogarth Press.

Gabbard, G. O. (2017). *Psychodynamic psychiatry in clinical practice* (5th ed.). American Psychiatric Publishing.

Gelso, C. J., & Hayes, J. A. (2007). *Countertransference and the therapist's inner experience: Perils and possibilities*. Lawrence Erlbaum Associates.

Ghaemi, S. N. (2009). *The rise and fall of the biopsychosocial model: Reconciling art and science in psychiatry.* Johns Hopkins University Press.

Hayes, S. C., Strosahl, K. D., & Wilson, K. G. (1999). *Acceptance and commitment therapy: An experiential approach to behavior change*. Guilford Press.

Hayes S. C. (2004; republished 2016). Acceptance and commitment therapy, relational frame theory, and the third wave of behavioral and cognitive therapies (republished article). *Behavior Therapy*, *47*(6), 869–885. https://doi.org/10.1016/j.beth.2016.11.006.

Hinton, D. & Jalal, B. (2014). Guidelines for the implementation of culturally sensitive cognitive behavioural therapy among refugees and in global contexts. *Intervention*, *12*, 78–93. https://doi.org/10.1097/WTF.0000000000000069.

Kernberg, O. F. (2006). *Object relations theory and clinical psychoanalysis*. Jason Aronson.

Kuyken, W., Padesky, C. A., & Dudley, R. (2015). *Collaborative case conceptualization: Working effectively with clients in cognitive-behavioral therapy.* Guilford Press.

Leichsenring, F., Abbass, A., Luyten, P., Hilsenroth, M., Rabung, S., & Barber, J. P. (2015). Psychodynamic therapy meets evidence-based medicine: A systematic review using updated criteria. *The Lancet Psychiatry*, *2*(7), 648–660. https://doi.org/10.1016/S2215-0366(15)00155-8.

Leichsenring, F., & Rabung, S. (2008). Effectiveness of long-term psychodynamic psychotherapy: A meta-analysis. *JAMA*, *300*(13), 1551–1565. https://doi.org/10.1001/jama.300.13.1551.

Leichsenring, F., & Rabung, S. (2011). Long-term psychodynamic psychotherapy in complex mental disorders: Update of a meta-analysis. *British Journal of Psychiatry*, *199*(1), 15–22. https://doi.org/10.1192/bjp.bp.110.082776.

Maroda, K. J. (2010). *Psychodynamic techniques: Working with emotion in the therapeutic relationship*. Guilford Press.

Martell, C. R., Dimidjian, S., & Herman-Dunn, R. (2010). *Behavioral activation for depression: A clinician's guide*. Guilford Press.

McDaniel, S. H., Doherty, W. J., & Hepworth, J. (2014). *Medical family therapy and integrated care* (2nd ed.). American Psychological Association.

McLaren, N. (1998). A critical review of the biopsychosocial model. *Australian and New Zealand Journal of Psychiatry*, *32*(1), 86–92. https://doi.org/10.3109/00048679809062712.

Mitchell, S. A. (1988). *Relational concepts in psychoanalysis: An integration*. Harvard University Press.

Norcross, J. C., & Goldfried, M. R. (Eds.). (2005). *Handbook of psychotherapy integration* (2nd ed.). Oxford University Press.

Norcross, J. C., & Lambert, M. J. (2019). Psychotherapy relationships that work. III. *Psychotherapy*, *55*(4), 303–315. https://doi.org/10.1037/pst0000193.

Persons, J. B. (2008). *The case formulation approach to cognitive-behavior therapy.* Guilford Press.

Prochaska, J. O., & Norcross, J. C. (2018). *Systems of psychotherapy: A transtheoretical analysis* (9th ed.). Oxford University Press.

Schore, A. N. (2012). *The science of the art of psychotherapy.* W. W. Norton.

Schuch, F. B., Vancampfort, D., Richards, J., Firth, J., & Stubbs, B. (2016). Exercise as a treatment for depression: A meta-analysis adjusting for publication bias. *Journal of Psychiatric Research*, *77*, 42–51. https://doi.org/10.1016/j.jpsychires.2016.02.023.

Segal, Z. V., Williams, J. M. G., & Teasdale, J. D. (2018). *Mindfulness-based cognitive therapy for depression* (2nd ed.). Guilford Press.

Shedler, J. (2010). The efficacy of psychodynamic psychotherapy. *American Psychologist*, *65*(2), 98–109. https://doi.org/10.1037/a0018378.

Sperry, L., & Sperry, J. (2020). *Case conceptualization: Mastering this competency with ease and confidence* (2nd ed.). Routledge.

Stone, W. N., & Klein, L. D. (1989). The clinical vignette: Use in teaching and evaluation of group therapists. *Group*, *13*(1), 3–9. https://doi.org/10.1007/BF01456547.

Taylor, S. E. (2017). *Health psychology* (10th ed.). McGraw-Hill Education.

Westen, D., Novotny, C. M., & Thompson-Brenner, H. (2004). The empirical status of empirically supported psychotherapies: Assumptions, findings, and reporting in controlled clinical trials. *Psychological Bulletin*, *130*(4), 631–663. https://doi.org/10.1037/0033-2909.130.4.631.

World Health Organization. (2013). *Mental health action plan 2013–2020.* https://www.who.int/publications/i/item/9789241506021.

Chapter 1

The Importance of Diversity, Equity, and Inclusion in the Diagnostic Process

Cassandra D. Page, Bethany Faulds, Jourdan Johnson and Elise Fisher

Diagnosing, the process of providing a classification that is widely used and understood to describe the presentation of a cluster of symptoms, is a skill most mental health practitioners learn during their first years of graduate training. Understanding a patient's symptoms, etiology, duration and onset, and severity within the context of that individual's story is crucial not only to ascertaining an accurate diagnosis, but also to providing clarity for the patient and access to resources such as evidence-based treatment, psychiatric medicine, and accommodations. Furthermore, an accurate diagnosis can provide the treating clinical team a roadmap toward inclusive treatment and care, which includes an understanding of a patient's diverse needs in terms of treatment provision (e.g., financial assistance, language interpreter, parental support, elderly advocate, pronoun usage, etc.).

The current diagnostic manual utilized among mental health treatment providers is the *Diagnostic and Statistical Manual* (Fifth Edition, Text Revision) (APA, 2022), which expanded diagnostic criteria to include appropriate attention to cultural risk factors that may impact clinical presentation – for example, a patient's experience of racism and discrimination or the use of non-stigmatizing language (APA, 2022). This iteration also approached classification developmentally. Disorders often diagnosed in childhood are positioned at the beginning of the manual and those more applicable to older adulthood are toward the end (APA, 2022). Expanding upon this lifespan lens, age-related factors were added to criteria where appropriate. Specifically, criteria regarding how symptoms might manifest in children were added, and gender and cultural factors were integrated where necessary (APA, 2022). These additional details guide clinicians toward context-specific clues when utilizing a culturally competent lens as part of the diagnostic process.

Cultural factors are sometimes naturally considered by clinicians when discerning which diagnosis may best account for a patient's clinical presentation. For example, a clinician is probably more likely to diagnose a major cognitive disorder in a patient over the age of 60 rather than in a 5-year-old or

DOI: 10.4324/9781003586531-2

attention-deficit/hyperactivity disorder in a 7-year-old rather than in a 93-year-old. That is because with each diagnosis, the impact of age (and other etiological factors) is used to inform the context of the symptoms presented. Capturing the impact of a patient's individual, group, and universal traits is paramount to an accurate diagnosis, recommendation, and treatment plan (Sue, 2001). For example, if a patient has a specific learning disorder, a clinician might recommend additional testing time, one-on-one tutoring, or extra time on homework assignments, given the known impact of the diagnosis on academic achievement. The interventions chosen must align with the diagnosis provided; the recommendations must be adapted to the individual patient and be inclusive of the patient's unique needs to maximize the patient's chance of academic success.

In this chapter, the purpose is to illustrate the history of cultural considerations in the diagnostic statistical manual, including the entrance of cultural considerations in the most recent 2022 iteration. Special attention is given to some areas related to gender and sexuality to elicit historical examples of categorization and diagnostic trends informed by an increased understanding of human functioning. It is also important to understand the field's history of overdiagnosing (i.e., overpathologizing) certain populations due to misattributions of culture and its lasting impacts resulting in mental health stigma and system mistrust. At the end of this chapter is a working definition, as well as a sample application of a diversity lens, to conceptualize a patient at all identity levels and produce a holistic and best-fitting diagnosis. Two vignettes are provided to set the stage – please keep the patients' stories in mind while reading through this chapter.

Clinical Case Vignette #1: Mr. James Smith

Mr. James Smith is a 27-year-old disabled, Black, transgender male veteran. He presented to therapy stating that he had been feeling disconnected and numb since leaving his military service. Mr. Smith was reluctant to confide in his clinician, a White, neurotypical, cisgender female civilian. He expressed concern that information shared during the course of therapy and recorded in his chart would be used to threaten him. Mr. Smith additionally exhibited significant distrust and suspicion of the majority of people around him, including his clinician. He worried that others were taking advantage of him and felt certain that they would harm him in some way.

Mr. Smith reported that he had repeatedly been exposed to harassment and discrimination while in the military, including both racism and transphobia. He shared that he once overheard the other members of his unit discussing the prospect of sexually assaulting him in order to "cure [him] of [his] trans." He was reportedly unable to leave his unit or escape from these individuals. Additionally, he reported significant mistrust of his superiors and chose not to report the incident. Mr. Smith explained that he had initially joined the military to try to escape the racism that he was experiencing in his hometown. He expressed anger and hopelessness that he continued to experience racism while in the military and continued to face it as a veteran. Mr. Smith described feeling trapped by these circumstances. He also reported fatigue in the military and in his new occupation as a veteran due to trying to mask his symptoms of attention deficit/hyperactivity disorder (ADHD) as well as the impact of his disabling chronic pain, a result of his military service.

As rapport began to be established between Mr. Smith and his clinician, he described being frequently bothered by distressing violent thoughts. He shared that when he would encounter explicit racism (such as being called a racial slur at work), he would become enraged and have a strong desire to punch the offending individual. He explained that he was frightened that he would act on these urges one day. He elaborated that this felt scary because it went against his values of peace and kindness, and because he feared what would happen to him as a Black individual if he hit another individual. Between these moments of anger, Mr. Smith reported feeling numb, detached, and at times wholly separate from his body or like the world around him was a movie he observed but in which he was not participating. He expressed feeling fearful of these periods as he worried that they would lead him to one day attempt suicide. He shared that he very rarely ever experienced positive emotions such as joy or love, even when he felt he "should."

Mr. Smith additionally described that he felt guilty and ashamed after episodes of anger in which he was not physically violent towards others because he felt like a failure in that he clearly could not stand up for himself or his community. At times he expressed feelings of guilt and shame for the transphobia and racism that he experienced in the military, including "being a problem," not standing up for himself, and in some way deserving these incidents. Mr. Smith appeared to have very low self-esteem and frequently expressed that he "didn't know who [he was]." He felt conflicting guilt and pride in both his American and veteran identities. Mr. Smith reported that he used cannabis frequently to stop thinking about "bad things" that had happened, especially in the military, and to assist him with sleep, as he reportedly experienced vivid nightmares without using cannabis at night.

Mr. Smith reported that he was making efforts to connect with others now that he had left the military but that he did not trust his new acquaintances and did not feel connected to them. He elaborated that he had also been feeling disconnected from his closest friends, who he stayed in contact with via long distance communication. Mr. Smith stated that he had struggled to make and keep friends since early childhood. He also reported strained relationships with his family members; he reported a general lack of affection from his mother in childhood and experiences of gender identity-based discrimination within his family throughout his life. With regard to treatment goals, Mr. Smith reported that he would like to "feel better," increase his social support, and "move on" from stressful experiences in the military.

Consider for a moment – based on the information presented in the clinical case vignette, which working diagnosis or diagnoses might best account for Mr. Smith's presentation?

Clinical Vignette #2: Ms. Sally Jones

Ms. Sally Jones is a 38-year-old Black cisgender female who presented to individual therapy citing feelings of increasing overwhelm and approximately daily panic symptoms. She endorsed considering individual therapy as her "last resort" for decreasing her symptoms, as her experiences in medical treatment and pastoral counseling did not result in symptom reduction. Ms. Jones presented to her intake session with elevated rate of speech, extreme tearfulness, and hyperventilation, explaining that it had become increasingly difficult for her to carry out her daily activities. These responsibilities included taking care of her child with a developmental disability while working full-time in a helping profession as a single parent. As the working member of a single-income, low socioeconomic status family, Ms. Jones emphasized the importance of being able to consistently work. Of note, she reported a history of significant trauma but was not willing to divulge details.

Ms. Jones reported experiencing nausea and/or vomiting, chest pain, dizziness, paresthesia, rapid heart rate, hot flashes, and gastrointestinal distress approximately daily. She stated that these episodes of unpleasant somatic symptoms peaked within 15 minutes, with residual symptoms such as fatigue lasting about 2 hours. She additionally reported significant feelings of anxiety and racing thoughts.

She explained that she had previously self-admitted to her local emergency room due to the acuity of her physical symptoms. However, each time Ms. Jones presented to the hospital, she was met with dismissal from medical professionals who told her she simply needed to "calm down" and administered sedatives without addressing any mental health factors.

In order to cope with her intense symptoms, Ms. Jones stated that she consumed alcohol daily, often before sleeping in an attempt to fall asleep more quickly. She reported consuming larger amounts of alcohol than intended, as well as a dramatic increase in her tolerance level as well. She expressed significant concerns about this given s family history positive for substance abuse. Though Ms. Jones acknowledged that her alcohol consumption had the potential to interfere with any prescribed medications and likely exacerbated her existing gastrointestinal symptoms, she was unable to successfully achieve sobriety after multiple attempts.

Consider for a moment – based on the information presented in the clinical case vignette, which working diagnosis or diagnoses might best account for Ms. Jones's presentation?

Keep both of the above clinical vignettes in mind while continuing to read.

Diagnostic Category Shifts Across Time

Gender and Sexuality

There have been several diagnostic shifts pertaining to gender and sexuality since the first edition of the *Diagnostic and Statistical Manual* (DSM) was published in 1952. The DSM classified homosexuality as a sexual deviation along with "transvestism, pedophilia, fetishism, and sexual sadism" and was housed under the category "sociopathic personality disturbance" (APA, 1952, p. 39). This category was reserved for individuals who were deemed ill based on societal norms. It was also formally understood that "sociopathic reactions are very often symptomatic of severe underlying personality disorder, neurosis, or psychosis, or occur as the result of organic brain injury or disease" (APA, 1952, p. 39).

In the second edition of the DSM (DSM-II), homosexuality and transvestism both remained listed as sexual deviations, but now within a section titled "personality disorders and certain other nonpsychotic mental disorders" (APA, 1968, p. 41). Disorders listed in this category were considered "deeply ingrained maladaptive patterns of behavior" (APA, 1968, p. 41). More specifically, sexual deviations were defined as follows:

> This category is for individuals whose sexual interests are directed primarily toward objects other than people of the opposite sex, toward sexual acts not usually associated with coitus, or toward coitus performed under bizarre circumstances as in necrophilia, pedophilia, sexual sadism, and fetishism. Even

> though many find their practices distasteful, they remain unable to substitute normal sexual behavior for them. This diagnosis is not appropriate for individuals who perform deviant sexual acts because normal sexual objects are not available to them.
>
> (APA, 1968, p. 44)

Cultural and societal context has influenced psychology's views regarding psychopathology and informed diagnostic decisions. The portrayal of gender and sexuality in the first two editions of the DSM were largely rooted in what society deemed normal or abnormal rather than objectivity. Controversy regarding the classification of homosexuality as pathological is what led to public awareness of the DSM (Horwitz, 2021). As gay activists persisted in challenging pathological classifications pertaining to homosexuality, the American Psychiatric Association engaged in internal conversations between psychoanalysts who supported the current definitions and psychiatrists who opposed this classification and advocated to eliminate homosexuality from the DSM (Horwitz, 2021). The result of this conflict was that homosexuality as a disorder would be removed and replaced with "sexual orientation disturbance," a diagnosis meant to capture individuals experiencing distress related to their same-sex attraction and desire to change their sexual orientation (APA, 1974). This change was reflected in the 1974 edition of the DSM-II.

While the overarching categories in the DSM and DSM-II included definitions, the specific disorders within each category were not well defined. It was not until the publication of the third edition of the DSM (DSM-III) in 1980 that greater detail pertaining to symptomology regarding various disorders began to emerge. This is also when the DSM began to gain greater popularity among psychiatrists along with an increased emphasis on evidence-based understandings of mental disorders (Horwitz, 2021).

In the DSM-III, the diagnosis ego-dystonic homosexuality could be applied to an individual who "complains that heterosexual arousal is persistently absent or weak and significantly interferes with initiating or maintaining wanted heterosexual relationships; [and] there is a sustained pattern of homosexual arousal that the individual explicitly states has been unwanted and a persistent source of distress" (APA, 1980, p. 282). The DSM-III also included diagnoses related to gender identity: transsexualism, gender identity disorder of childhood, and atypical gender identity disorder (APA, 1980). Transsexualism was defined as a "sense of discomfort and inappropriateness about one's anatomic sex; a wish to be rid of one's own genitals and to live as a member of the other sex; the disturbance has been continuous (not limited to periods of stress) for at least two years; an absence of physical intersex or genetic abnormality; [and] not due to another illness such as schizophrenia" (APA, 1980, p. 264). Gender identity disorder of childhood was characterized as "a persistent feeling of discomfort and inappropriateness in a child about his or her anatomic sex and the desire to be, or insistence that he or she is, of the other sex" (APA, 1980, p. 265). Finally, atypical gender identity disorder was applicable if any individual did not meet criteria for transsexualism or gender identity disorder of childhood but still experienced discomfort and inappropriateness about their anatomic sex.

In much the same way that previous controversy led to revisions regarding how homosexuality was classified, further debate ensued with adversaries noting that if distress related to heterosexuality is not pathological, then distress related to homosexuality also cannot be classified as pathological (Bayer, 1987). This resulted in yet another revision where the DSM-III-R removed ego-dystonic homosexuality and replaced it with sexual disorder not otherwise specified. This diagnosis was considered applicable to individuals with "persistent and marked distress about one's sexual orientation" (APA, 1987, p. 296). This diagnosis was maintained in both the fourth edition of the DSM (DSM-IV) and revised text version of the DSM-IV (DSM-IV-TR) (APA, 1994, 2000).

In the fifth edition of the DSM (DSM-5), mention of sexual orientation was completely removed (APA, 2013). Additionally, classifications related to gender identity remained consistent until the publication of the DSM-5 when gender identity disorders were replaced with the single diagnosis of gender dysphoria disorder. This disorder "refers to the distress that may accompany the incongruence between one's experienced or expressed gender and one's assigned gender" and recognizes that not all individuals who experience this incongruence will experience distress (APA, 2013, p. 452). The most recent version of the DSM-5, which includes revised text (DSM-5-TR) maintains gender dysphoria disorder but utilizes more inclusive language such as "experienced gender" rather than "desired gender" (APA, 2022).

Considering Culture

Beyond the diagnostic shifts that have occurred across time, there has also been a growing awareness of how sociocultural context can influence the diagnosis an individual may receive. For example, research shows that Black adults tend to receive schizophrenia diagnoses at higher rates than White adults, whereas White adults tend to receive diagnoses with less stigma such as bipolar disorder or depression (Perlman et al., 2016; Schwartz & Blankenship, 2014). Similarly, attention deficit/hyperactivity disorder (ADHD) is often underdiagnosed in Black and Latinx children, while Black children are diagnosed with conduct disorder at higher rates (Baglivio et al., 2017; Coker et al., 2016; Tapia et al., 2024). These disparities have implications for accessing proper and equitable treatment. Yang et al. (2022) found that Black, Hispanic, and Asian children who were diagnosed with ADHD had significantly lower treatment utilization rates (i.e., lower utilization of both therapeutic services and accessing medication) when compared to their White counterparts.

Gender-related disparities have also been noted in research. One example is that women have higher prevalence rates of diagnosis with anxiety disorders (Jalnapurkar et al., 2018; Vanderminden & Esala, 2019) and depressive disorders (Salk et al., 2017) than men. Additionally, girls and women tend to be diagnosed with both autism spectrum disorder (ASD) and ADHD later in life (if they get diagnosed at all) than boys and men (Chikezie-Darron et al., 2025; Lai et al., 2022; Tapia et al., 2024). Furthermore, much of the existing literature is not inclusive and focuses on gender binaries (women and men), leaving gender minorities underrepresented in psychological research (Pedersen et al., 2022). While these are examples of racial, ethnic, and gender disparities, there are several others that exist within these domains with regard to age, disability status, sexual orientation, religious affiliation, national origin, dominant language, socioeconomic status, and more. It is necessary to become and remain aware of up-to-date research regarding sociocultural considerations for diverse clients. Likewise, individuals exist at the intersection of varying identities, some privileged and others marginalized.

Clinicians must aim to conceptualize their patients with an understanding of the intersectional impacts that may affect individuals. Yet another consideration lies within the diagnoses themselves. As revealed earlier, the DSM is an ever-changing resource that fluctuates as new research emerges and the social environment evolves. With this in mind, the DSM serves as a guide for the diagnostic process, but clinicians must have the ability to use both clinical judgment and relevant research when making diagnostic decisions. Consider the DSM-5-TR criteria for post-traumatic stress disorder (PTSD). To meet diagnostic criteria for PTSD, an individual must be exposed to "actual or threatened death, serious injury, or sexual violence" (APA, 2022, p. 304). This diagnosis, however, does not capture chronic stressors and experiences that also have the potential to result in trauma symptoms. Such experiences include, but are not limited to, adverse childhood experiences (ACES), identity-related discrimination or mistreatment, chronic illness or disability, psychological or emotional abuse, bullying, religious trauma, poverty, housing instability, food insecurity, and more. While a diagnosis to capture the traumatic effects of at least some of these experiences was proposed during the formulation of the DSM-5, the American Psychiatric Association ultimately chose to reject its inclusion in the final version of the manual (van der Kolk, 2015). Global classification systems such as the *International Classification of Diseases, 11th Edition* (ICD-11) identify the resulting distress as complex PTSD (cPTSD), but this is not formally recognized by the DSM-5-TR (Hyland et al., 2021). This gap in the conceptualization and diagnosing of trauma means that clinicians must utilize a trauma-informed lens when assessing patient experiences and symptomology. Failure to do so could result in misdiagnosing a patient, whether that means diagnosing the patient with a disorder that does not fully capture the patient's presentation (e.g., persistent depressive disorder) or overpathologizing the patient's current presentation (e.g., co-morbid borderline personality disorder, generalized anxiety disorder, and depersonalization/derealization disorder). Misdiagnosing subsequently limits patient access to effective, inclusive, and equitable treatment.

History of Task Forces

The release of the DSM-5-TR in 2022 reflected a greater and more intentional concentration on cultural elements of psychiatric diagnosis than in previous editions. The American Psychiatric Association attempted to respond to concerns in the field (Alarcón, 2014) that cultural topics be appropriately addressed through numerous strategies. Specifically, the Ethnoracial Equity and Inclusion Work Group and the Cross-Cutting Culture Review Group were formed and subsequently involved in both the updating and reviewing of the most recent text. The former was a diverse group of ten mental health practitioners who reviewed the DSM-5-TR's references to race, ethnicity, nationality, and culture; their aim was to avoid perpetuation of stereotypes. Similarly, the latter group was composed of 19 international experts on cultural psychology who reviewed the text's discussion of cultural influences on diagnostic characteristics (APA, 2022). Both the Ethnoracial Equity and Inclusion Work Group and the Cross-Cutting Culture Review Group concentrated their efforts on "the impact of culture, race, and racism on diagnosis," thus emphasizing the relevance of both an individual's cultural background and the structural systems in which an individual exists (Moran, 2022). In the DSM-5-TR, the inclusion of updated sections under each psychological disorder titled "Culture-Related Diagnostic Issues" and the revised edition of the stand-alone chapter titled "Culture and Psychiatric Diagnosis" further demonstrate this emphasis. In intentionally incorporating more diverse perspectives in its process of nosological revision, the DSM-5-TR denotes the beginning of progress toward a more emic perspective on psychopathology and diagnosis.

Case Conceptualization Through the Lens of Diversity

Case conceptualization is at the heart of both diagnosing and treatment planning. This method of information organization allows the clinician to describe the patient's symptomology, theorize the etiology and maintaining factors of that symptomology, and create a guiding plan for growth and recovery that accounts for both strengths and potential barriers (Sperry & Sperry, 2020). Typically, conceptualization utilizes precepts established by a particular theoretical orientation such as cognitive theory (Beck & Haigh, 2014), relational frame theory (Blackledge, 2003), or biosocial theory (Linehan, 1993). Clinicians who operate from an etic (culturally universal) perspective may view these theories as universally applicable to all clients. However, clinicians who operate from an emic (culturally specific) practice may use various cultural conceptualization models in combination with such theories to understand each patient within that patient's unique personal and sociocultural context (Sue & Sue, 2016). This approach allows clinicians to consider etiology, maintaining factors, and potential strengths and barriers to treatment that incorporate cultural context and various perspectives on abnormality as well as normality. Such an approach fits within a multicultural orientation (Fischer et al., 2024).

Examples of models that may assist in conceptualizing from an emic perspective include broader models such as Hays's (2024) ADDRESSING framework or Sue's (2001) Tripartite Framework of Personal Identity. Additionally, more specific models may assist a clinician in gaining an in-depth understanding of a particular identity variable's impact on a patient (i.e., Weinberg and colleagues' (1995) model of bisexual identity development). Any number of such models, as relevant, can be combined with the clinician's general theoretical orientation (i.e., relational frame theory) to create a robust case conceptualization. These models should be applied within the theory rather than added tangentially to them. Tangential application implies that the patient's cultural variables are in some way separate from the presenting psychopathology (an etic perspective) instead of understanding psychopathology within the context of applicable cultural variables (an emic perspective).

Mr. James Smith Revisited

According to Hays's ADDRESSING framework and relational frame theory, Mr. Smith's experiences of minority stress within his non-dominant intersecting identity variables likely led to the development of a verbal network that associated himself with "badness" and interactions with others with fear and anxiety. Each time that Mr. Smith experienced non-dominant identity variable discrimination, the concept was reinforced within his verbal network that other people are dangerous and should be paired with the physiological sensations of fear. Intentional conceptualization of patient pathology that includes the relevant cultural context allows for equitable application of diagnostic and treatment planning processes.

A diagnosis that did not take cultural and systemic factors into account perhaps would have mislabeled Mr. Smith as meeting diagnostic criteria for paranoid personality disorder. Though Mr. Smith did display pervasive distrust and suspiciousness of others, this suspicion typically represented healthy cultural paranoia (Newhill, 1990) and therefore did not meet Criterion A in the list of diagnostic criteria associated with paranoid personality disorder. Past repeated experiences of racism and transphobia, particularly from individuals sharing cultural variables with Mr. Smith's clinician, represents sufficient basis for an appropriate, non-clinical display of paranoia. Only with non-judgmental acceptance, openness, and application of intersectional cultural humility (Buchanan et al., 2020) was trust established between Mr. Smith and his clinician, leading to accurate diagnosis of his trauma and therefore accurate treatment planning. A misdiagnosis of paranoid personality disorder and subsequent treatment planning could have led Mr. Smith into treatment that reinforced his unhelpful trauma-informed beliefs and worsened his symptoms. Addressing his concerns as unhealthy paranoia likely would have increased Mr. Smith's self-doubt and lack of stable self-concept. At the same time, the root of his emotion regulation difficulties and marked challenges with attachment would have gone unaddressed and presumably persisted. Affirmation of all Mr. Smith's intersecting identity variables was essential in this case; indeed, due to elevated suicide risk, improper diagnosis of Mr. Smith could have led to this patient's death.

Conceptualized and diagnosed through a culturally informed lens, Mr. James Smith was diagnosed by the DSM-5-TR with PTSD with dissociative symptoms. The Criterion A trauma for this diagnosis was the threatened sexual violence that Mr. Smith experienced while in the military. A more accurate summary of his symptoms is encapsulated by the ICD-11 diagnosis of cPTSD, which is not included in the DSM-5-TR. This diagnosis focuses on prolonged, repetitive events that are extremely stressful and from which escape is very difficult or impossible. Mr. Smith in the past and currently met all core symptoms for PTSD including intrusion, avoidance, negative alterations in cognitions and mood, and marked alterations in arousal and reactivity. In addition, he displayed affective regulation difficulties (both numbing and extreme, sudden anger that he found difficult to control), disrupted self-concept, and inappropriate guilt and shame, and interpersonal challenges, especially in feeling close to others. Some of these aspects, including affective regulation difficulties and challenges in maintaining friendships, were influenced by Mr. Smith's neurodevelopmental disorder, ADHD. However, the severity of both symptom groups was significantly more than what would be expected for a patient with ADHD and both were substantially worsened by his exposure to traumatic events. Incorporation of all these factors was key to treatment planning for Mr. Smith. He engaged in stage one (stabilization) trauma treatment that focused on developing coping skills not only for core PTSD symptoms but also for affect regulation, self-concept, and attachment. Furthermore, treatment planning included appropriate accommodations for Mr. Smith's neurodivergent and disabled identities. Treatment was applied through an explicitly affirmative lens. Once stabilization was achieved, Mr. Smith was referred to a specialty clinic for identity-based trauma processing for patients with co-occurring health conditions.

Ms. Sally Jones Revisited

Integration of Sue's Tripartite Framework of Personal Identity (2001) with Beck's cognitive theory (2011) provides an emic perspective from which to conceptualize the case of Ms. Jones. Her significant trauma history as well as her family history of substance use disorders represented individual factors that contributed to greater risk for panic symptoms (Berenz et al., 2019) and a unique genetic disposition for substance abuse, respectively. Various group-level characteristics of Ms. Jones's intersectional identity can be used to understand her personal configuration of Beck's cognitive triad. For example, Ms. Jones's socialization as a Black woman in the United States, combined with her role as a caregiver in various areas of her life, led to a strong internalization of the "strong Black woman" schema (Beauboeuf-Lafontant, 2007); these factors ultimately correlated with an intermediate belief of "asking for help is a sign of weakness." Her need and desire for psychological safety, which is universal to human experience, were complicated by the intensity of her daily responsibilities and personal circumstances, leading to negative automatic thoughts (e.g., "Today is not going to go well") that reinforced and maintained Ms. Jones's avoidance behaviors and fear of further panic attacks. Continued experience of panic symptoms and her internalized belief that she could not ask for help reflected a core belief of "I am trapped." This highly negative cycle of thoughts, behaviors, and emotions was compounded by various minoritized identities that Ms. Jones held, making it essential to consider these factors as a part of the complete conceptualization.

Ms. Jones's panic symptoms and dysfunctional alcohol consumption could not be separated from her intersectional identity. Her history as a Black woman experiencing systemic racism within the healthcare system furthered her mistrust of healthcare providers. As such, treatment with her White female clinician focused heavily on building rapport and creating a strong foundation for the therapeutic relationship. The main priority for her treatment was to deliberately create a truly safe setting where Ms. Jones felt validated and that her debilitating symptoms were taken seriously. Once rapport was established, treatment aimed to foster skills of mindfulness and present-moment awareness, with the goal of increasing adaptive coping mechanisms for panic symptoms. Another important aspect of her treatment that related to the therapeutic alliance was intentionality regarding autonomy. In determining treatment goals, Ms. Jones shared that she felt open to eventually pursuing substance use treatment but first wanted to "try to be strong by [herself]." This reflection of her internalization of the strong Black woman schema was also an opportunity to affirm Ms. Jones's autonomy in the treatment process, which provided her with a corrective emotional experience for her.

Ms. Jones's symptom presentation met DSM-5-TR criteria for panic disorder and alcohol use disorder, moderate. She experienced recurrent panic attacks in settings and situations in which she was not able to identify a specific stressor, and these symptoms led to both a fear of future attacks and avoidance of unfamiliar situations. Ms. Jones's maladaptive use of alcohol to cope with her incessant anxiety symptoms warranted a co-occurring diagnosis of alcohol use disorder, illustrated in her excessive consumption despite her gastrointestinal distress, increased tolerance, and unsuccessful attempts to cease the behavior. Had the clinician not adequately considered Ms. Jones's cultural background and intersecting identity variables, it is likely that a very different diagnostic label may have been assigned. Specifically, Ms. Jones's presentation of racing thoughts and rapid speech may have been incorrectly interpreted as pressured speech, a hallmark of mania or hypomania. If Ms. Jones had been diagnosed with bipolar disorder, or even brief psychotic disorder, her treatment would have been vastly different and would not have targeted her debilitating anxiety and panic symptoms.

Conclusion

Understanding the historical evolution of professional psychology's (and psychiatry's) understanding of gender, sexuality, and cultural considerations within diagnostic systems like the DSM demonstrates how fundamentally important it is for mental health clinicians to approach their work through the lens of diversity, equity, and inclusion. As science advances, diagnostic criteria for disorders included in the DSM will continue to evolve. By embracing an emic perspective and integrating culturally responsive frameworks into their practice, clinicians can ensure that the process of case conceptualization not only leads to an accurate understanding of symptom etiology but also affirms the lived experiences of patients entering treatment and their multifaceted and intersecting identities. Prioritizing diversity, equity, and inclusion by viewing patients through an affirming multicultural lens is not only best practice, it is an ethical imperative essential for promoting justice and healing as well as honoring the dignity of all patients seeking care.

References

Alarcón, R. (2014). Cultural inroads in DSM-5. *World Psychiatry: Official Journal of the World Psychiatric Association*, *13*(3), 310–313. https://doi.org/10.1002/wps.20132.

APA (American Psychiatric Association). (1952). *Diagnostic and statistical manual of mental disorders* (1st ed.). American Psychiatric Association.

APA (American Psychiatric Association). (1968). *Diagnostic and statistical manual of mental disorders* (2nd ed.). American Psychiatric Association.

APA (American Psychiatric Association). (1974). *Diagnostic and statistical manual of mental disorders* (2nd ed.). American Psychiatric Association.

APA (American Psychiatric Association). (1980). *Diagnostic and statistical manual of mental disorders* (3rd ed.). American Psychiatric Association. https://doi.org/10.1176/aapi.books.9780521315289.dsm-iii.

APA (American Psychiatric Association). (1987). *Diagnostic and statistical manual of mental disorders* (3rd ed., rev.). American Psychiatric Association. https://doi.org/10.1176/appi.books.9780890420188.

APA (American Psychiatric Association). (1994). *Diagnostic and statistical manual of mental disorders* (4th ed.). American Psychiatric Association. https://doi.org/10.1176/appi.books.9780890423349.

APA (American Psychiatric Association). (2000). *Diagnostic and statistical manual of mental disorders* (4th ed., text rev.). American Psychiatric Association. https://doi.org/10.1176/appi.books.9780890420249.

APA (American Psychiatric Association). (2013). *Diagnostic and statistical manual of mental disorders* (5th ed.). American Psychiatric Association. https://doi.org/10.1176/appi.books.9780890425596.

APA (American Psychiatric Association). (2022). *Diagnostic and statistical manual of mental disorders* (5th ed., text rev.). American Psychiatric Association. https://doi.org/10.1176/appi.books.9780890425787.

Baglivio, M. T., Wolff, K. T., Piquero, A. R., Greenwald, M. A., & Epps, N. (2017). Racial/ethnic disproportionality in psychiatric diagnoses and treatment in a sample of serious juvenile offenders. *Journal of Youth and Adolescence*, *46*(7), 1424–1451. https://doi.org/10.1007/s10964-016-0573-4.

Bayer, R. (1987). *Homosexuality and American psychiatry: The politics of diagnosis*. Princeton University Press.

Beauboeuf-Lafontant, T. (2007). You have to show strength: An exploration of gender, race, and depression. *Gender & Society*, *21*(1), 28–51. https://doi.org/10.1177/0891243206294108.

Beck, J. S. (2011). *Cognitive therapy: Basics and beyond* (2nd ed.). Guilford Press.

Beck, A. T., & Haigh, E. A. P. (2014). Advances in cognitive theory and therapy: The generic cognitive model. *Annual Review of Clinical Psychology*, *10*, 1–24. https://doi.org/10.1146/annurev-clinpsy-032813-153734.

Berenz, E. C., York, T. P., Bing-Canar, H., Amstadter, A. B., Mezuk, B., Gardner, C. O., & Roberson-Nay, R. (2019). Time course of panic disorder and posttraumatic stress disorder onsets. *Social Psychiatry and Psychiatric Epidemiology*, *54*(5), 639–647. https://doi.org/10.1007/s00127-018-1559-1.

Blackledge, J. T. (2003). An introduction to relational frame theory: Basics and applications. *The Behavior Analyst Today*, *3*(4), 421–433. https://doi.org/10.1037/h0099997.

Buchanan, N. T., Desdamona, R., & Case, K. A. (2020). Intersectional cultural humility: Aligning critical inquiry with critical praxis in psychology. *Women & Therapy*, *43*(3), 235–243. https://doi.org/10.1080/02703149.2020.1729469.

Chikezie-Darron, O., Sakai, J., & Tolson, D. (2025). Analysis of disparities in diagnosis of autism spectrum disorder in the military health system pediatrics population. *Journal of Autism and Developmental Disorders*. https://doi.org/10.1007/s10803-024-06703-w.

Coker, T. R., Elliott, M. N., Toomey, S. L., Schwebel, D. C., Cuccaro, P., Tortolero Emery, S., Davies, S. L., Visser, S. N., & Schuster, M. A. (2016). Racial and ethnic disparities in ADHD diagnosis and treatment. *Pediatrics*, *138*(3), Article e20160407. https://doi.org/10.1542/peds.2016-0407.

Fischer, O., Cox, D. W., Mickelson, J. M., & Lyons, K. (2024). Bridging the multicultural orientation framework with sexual and gender minority psychotherapy: A mixed studies systematic review. *Psychotherapy*, *61*(1), 1–30. https://doi.org/10.1037/pst0000518.

Hays, P. A. (2024). Four steps toward intersectionality in psychotherapy using the ADDRESSING framework. *Professional Psychology: Research and Practice*, *55*(5), 454–462. https://doi.org/10.1037/pro0000577.

Horwitz, A. V. (2021). *DSM: A history of psychiatry's bible.* Johns Hopkins University Press.

Hyland, P., Karatzias, T., Shevlin, M., McElroy, E., Ben-Ezra, M., Cloitre, M., & Brewin, C. R. (2021). Does requiring trauma exposure affect rates of ICD-11 PTSD and complex PTSD? Implications for DSM–5. *Psychological Trauma: Theory, Research, Practice, and Policy*, *13*(2), 133–141. https://doi.org/10.1037/tra0000908.

Jalnapurkar, I., Allen, M., & Pigott, T. (2018). Sex differences in anxiety disorders: A review. *Journal of Psychiatry, Depression & Anxiety*, *4*(1), 1–9. https://doi.org/10.24966/PDA-0150/100011.

Lai, M. C., Lin, H. Y., & Ameis, S. H. (2022). Towards equitable diagnoses for autism and attention-deficit/hyperactivity disorder across sexes and genders. *Current Opinion in Psychiatry*, *35*(2), 90–100. https://doi.org/10.1097/YCO.0000000000000770.

Linehan, M. (1993). *Cognitive-behavioral treatment of borderline personality disorder.* Guilford Press.

Moran, M. (2022). Impact of culture, race, and social determinants reflected throughout new DSM-5-TR. *Psychiatric News*, *57*(3). https://doi.org/10.1176/appi.pn.2022.03.3.20.

Newhill, C. A. (1990). The role of culture in the development of paranoid symptomology. *American Journal of Orthopsychiatry*, *60*(2), 176–185. https://doi.org/10.1037/h0079170.

Pedersen, S. L., Lindstrom, R., Powe, P. M., Louie, K., & Escobar-Viera, C. (2022). Lack of representation in psychiatric research: A data-driven example from scientific articles published in 2019 and 2020 in the American Journal of Psychiatry. *The American Journal of Psychiatry*, *179*(5), 388–392. https://doi.org/10.1176/appi.ajp.21070758.

Perlman, G., Kotov, R., Fu, J., Bromet, E. J., Fochtmann, L. J., Medeiros, H., & Pato, C. N. (2016). Symptoms of psychosis in schizophrenia, schizoaffective disorder, and bipolar disorder: A comparison of African Americans and Caucasians in the Genomic Psychiatry Cohort. *American Journal of Medical Genetics Part B: Neuropsychiatric Genetics*, *171*(4), 546–555. https://doi.org/10.1002/ajmg.b.32409.

Salk, R. H., Hyde, J. S., & Abramson, L. Y. (2017). Gender differences in depression in representative national samples: Meta-analyses of diagnoses and symptoms. *Psychological Bulletin*, *143*(8), 783–822. https://doi.org/10.1037/bul0000102.

Schwartz, R. C., & Blankenship, D. M. (2014). Racial disparities in psychotic disorder diagnosis: A review of empirical literature. *World Journal of Psychiatry*, *4*(4), 133–40. https://doi.org/10.5498/wjp.v4.i4.133.

Sperry, L., & Sperry, J. (2020). *Case conceptualization: Mastering this competency with ease and confidence.* Routledge.

Sue, D. W. (2001). Multidimensional facets of cultural competence. *The Counseling Psychologist*, *29*(6), 790–821. https://doi.org/10.1177/0011000001296002.

Sue, D. W., & Sue, D. (2016). *Counseling the culturally diverse: Theory and practice* (7th ed.). Wiley.

Tapia, J. D., Sparber, A., Lopez, O., Martin, P., Graziano, P. A., Basu, H., Beaulieu, M. A., & Sibley, M. H. (2024). Racial and gender disparities in community mental health center diagnoses of adolescent ADHD and comorbidities: A mixed methods investigation. *Journal of Child and Family Studies*, *33*, 3472–3485. https://doi.org/10.1007/s10826-024-02857-4.

van der Kolk, B. A. (2015). *The body keeps the score: Brain, mind, and body in the healing of trauma.* Penguin Books.

Vanderminden, J., & Esala, J .J. (2019). Beyond symptoms: Race and gender predict anxiety disorder diagnosis. *Society and Mental Health*, *9*(1), 111–126. https://doi.org/10.1177/2156869318811435.

Weinberg, M. S., Williams, C. J., & Pryor, D. W. (1995). *Dual attraction: Understanding bisexuality.* Oxford University Press.

Yang, K. G., Flores, M. W., Carson, N. J., & Cook, B. L. (2022). Racial and ethnic disparities in childhood ADHD treatment access and utilization: Results from a national study. *Psychiatric Services*, *73*(12), 1338–1345. https://doi.org/10.1176/appi.ps.202100578.

Chapter 2

A Note on Cultural Diversity

Veronica Regueiro

In an ever more connected world, it is reasonable for mental health clinicians to accept that they will be expected to, and should be competent in, evaluating and treating diverse individuals. Diversity variables include a wide variety of factors including, but not limited to, race, ethnicity, cultural background, sex, gender, sexual orientation, age, health status, mental health status, socioeconomic status, faith tradition, religious practice, etc. For some individuals, occupation informs the process of identity formation in such a way that it, too, must be taken into account as a diversity variable, such as can be the case with members of the armed forces, law enforcement officers, medical professionals, clergy, etc. For mental health clinicians, understanding diversity is the foundation for creating a context in which patients can feel the unconditional positive regard and benign curiosity that Carl Rogers made so famous when he revolutionized the field of psychology by introducing the concept of person-centered psychotherapy. That foundation is crucial for the provision of inclusive and equitable mental health services, and yet it is impossible for any clinician to learn about every possible diversity variable with which a patient might present. Even if a clinician could learn about the infinite number of diversity variables evident in the human population, including how they all may intersect with one another, it would be a grave mistake to assume that the experience of any individual patient could represent the experiences of all patients with those same diversity variables. Indeed, the myth of cultural competence suggests that, in any particular culture, there is a core set of beliefs and values that remain unchanged over time (Lekas et al., 2020) and so, once a clinician has mastered that culture, there is nothing more to learn before conducting a clinical interview, conceptualizing a case, or developing a treatment plan for a patient from that particular culture. As noted by multiple authors (Kirmayer, 2012; Shepherd, 2019; Lekas et al., 2020) such an approach is problematic specifically because it can contribute to stereotypes and stigmatization over time. Potentially more problematically, such an approach can lead to implicit biases specifically because they it can lead to "othering" patients (Lekas et al., 2020)

DOI: 10.4324/9781003586531-3

rather than learning about the patient and reflecting on one's own potential biases and their impacts on case conceptualization and treatment. That, then, is why the concept of cultural humility is also crucial to the work being done by mental health professionals around the world.

Cultural humility, when applied in any mental health setting, acknowledges that no one clinician can fully understand the entirety of a patient's diversity variables and how those variables may interact with one another to constitute that particular patient's overall worldview. Developed by Drs. Melanie Tervalon and Jann Murray-Garcia in 1998, cultural humility emphasizes self-reflection, self-critique, and commitment to lifelong learning, all in the service of developing and maintaining mutually respectful relationships with both individual patients and communities. As Tervalon and Murray-Garcia (1998) acknowledge, it is, of course, important for clinicians to learn as much as possible about the individuals and communities they serve, but that knowledge acquisition must unfold alongside a simultaneous process of self-reflection and continuous learning. More specifically, cultural humility requires that clinicians explicitly acknowledge not only that they may not know everything they need to know about a particular demographic group but also that they are willing to learn (Lekas et al., 2020). Gottlieb (2020) noted that cultural humility requires that one be teachable. This, of course, means adopting a posture of openness and non-defensiveness, which often means listening to listen instead of listening to respond or defend. As Tervalon and Murray-Garcia (1998) acknowledge, such a process requires courage and honesty. It is fair to say that the practice of cultural humility also requires incredible integrity, specifically because it may lead clinicians toward identifying previously unacknowledged racism as well as other biases and prejudices, all of which have the potential to negatively impact patient care if left unexamined but which also have the potential to elicit shame in the clinician.

In the model of cultural humility proposed by Tervalon and Murray-Garcia (1998), acknowledging the power differential between clinicians and patients is also of pivotal importance. Rather than clinicians casting themselves in the roles of experts and authorities, cultural humility proposes that patients be considered the experts regarding their own lives and that clinicians consider patients to be fully capable partners in the therapeutic alliance (Tervalon & Murray-Garcia, 1998). While it may no longer seem novel in some settings to acknowledge that patients should serve as the experts regarding their own lives and experiences, such a concept is certainly contrary to the historically paternalistic practice of mental health professionals for much of the history of the fields of psychology and social work as well as other related fields. Not surprisingly, clinicians adopting a position of cultural humility has been correlated with positive outcomes for clients (Hook et al., 2013).

Developing the Practice of Cultural Humility

To fully appreciate the power of cultural humility, it is important to first understand humility. According to the *Merriam-Webster Dictionary* online (n.d.) humility is "freedom from pride or arrogance." The *Cambridge Dictionary* online (n.d.) defines humility as "the feeling or attitude that you have no special importance that makes you better than others; lack of pride." In her 2020 article, Gottlieb expands on these definitions by stating that humility requires acknowledgment that there are as many different ways of knowing as there are individual human beings. This expansion regarding the definition of humility is epistemologically sound as, in the field of epistemology, there are various ways of knowing including empirical knowledge, self-knowledge, intuition, divine knowledge, etc. (Audi, 2010). As Gottlieb (2020) states, each individual experiences the world in unique ways and it is the responsibility of the clinician in the therapeutic relationship to be open to both learning about and prioritizing alternative perspectives.

In their seminal 1998 article, Tervalon and Murray-Garcia make several recommendations regarding how clinicians may develop the practice of cultural humility, the first step being that they think consciously about their own multifaceted identities. Thinking consciously about one's own multifaceted identity requires serious consideration of how one's cultural background, including all that such a cultural background might entail (i.e., race, ethnicity, religion, sex, gender, age, etc.), shapes one's worldview, including how one perceives oneself and others. This includes assumptions made about the self and others, deeply held beliefs and values, biases, and more. Clinicians interested in beginning to explore their own multifaceted identities may begin by engaging in individual activities to help them understand the events, people, and variables that have influenced them and their worldviews. For example, a clinician may wish to draw an influence map. When creating an influence map, clinicians participating in the activity place themselves in the center by writing their names there or drawing a small self-portrait and then drawing lines connecting themselves to other names or small portraits included on the paper. For each name or event included, clinicians ask themselves, *What did this person/event teach me? How did this person/event influence who I am today?* A similar activity can be completed using a timeline that categorizes a clinician's life into early childhood, middle childhood, adolescence, college, professional training, etc., and then leaves space for information regarding the pivotal people, events, and experiences that shaped or influenced that portion of the clinician's life. Clinicians familiar with acceptance and commitment therapy (ACT) may wish to engage in a values-ranking activity and then journal about the people, events, and experiences that contributed to the development of their top 5–10 values. When completing these activities, clinicians may want to also consider how greater societal events, books, movies, songs, etc., may have contributed to their worldviews. It may go without saying, but because practicing cultural humility requires conscious consideration of one's own multifaceted identity, there is an underlying assumption that one's particular worldview may be unique and that it is therefore unjust to impose one's own particular worldview on others within the context of mental health practice. It is only with explicit exploration of worldviews and the factors that shape and influence them that a clinician can begin to ensure that it is cultural humility informing their practice instead of assumptions or, worse, bias. Additionally, it is important to note that while activities focused on individual reflection and explicit exploration of one's multifaceted identity can serve as valuable tools, cultural humility, by definition, requires lifelong learning on the part of the clinician and so, while potentially valuable, activities such as those listed above are not sufficient to produce a posture of cultural humility.

Clinicians wanting to engage more fully in the practice of cultural humility may also be served by engaging with trusted colleagues around issues related to diversity and cultural humility (Gottlieb, 2020). Gottlieb (2020) notes that, like the rest of the human population, clinicians are socialized beings and their first thoughts and/or reactions about particular patients or situations may be involuntary. Developing a network of trusted colleagues with whom these thoughts can be shared and received with a spirit of unconditional positive regard and benign curiosity is not only consistent with models of training, supervision, and consultation followed in the various professions that comprise the field of mental health but can also allow for trusted colleagues to bring into awareness and name previously unexamined biases as well as their potential for negatively impacting patient care. Sharing thoughts and reactions that may be experienced by others as racist, homophobic, prejudicial, etc., can be an extraordinarily vulnerable experience, so much so that clinicians would prefer to not engage in these conversations with peers, supervisors, and/or mentors. Practicing in isolation, however, and avoiding difficult conversations regarding the diversity factors that unfold during therapeutic encounters only robs clinicians of the support needed to address these variables and move forward to provide the truly excellent care patients deserve. The encouragement, therefore, is to create and participate in a safe and diverse exchange of ideas with trusted colleagues (Gottlieb, 2020), as such a space has the potential to serve both clinicians and patients. These conversations can occur in individual supervision, group supervision, in a consultation group setting, or even casually, over coffee or lunch with a colleague. Whether formal or informal in nature, the priority is that these conversations unfold. As noted above, no one activity, nor any one conversation, can be considered sufficient to produce a posture of cultural humility. Cultural humility requires lifelong learning and has no designated endpoint; rather, it is a way of being (Foronda et al., 2016) embodied by a clinician in service of a patient.

The Multidimensional Cultural Humility Scale

For the intrepid clinician, the Multidimensional Cultural Humility Scale (MCHS) developed by Gonzalez et al. (2021) may serve as a valuable tool. Initially consisting of 57 items but ultimately reduced to 15, all of which are scored on a six-point Likert scale, the MCHS assesses a clinician's openness, self-awareness, egolessness, supportive interactions, and self-reflection and critique (Gonzalez et al., 2021). Items include statements such as *I am comfortable asking my clients about their cultural experiences*, *I seek feedback from my supervisors when working with diverse clients*, *I enjoy learning from my weaknesses*, etc., (Gonzalez et al., 2021). While some items are reverse-scored, higher scores on the overall measure generally indicate higher levels of cultural humility. The MCHS is a self-report measure and while some items were found to have poor internal consistency (Gonzalez et al., 2021), it can still serve as a guide for clinicians wanting to evaluate themselves regarding their practice of cultural humility.

The MCHS was based, in part, on Foronda et al.'s (2016) concept analysis of cultural humility. In their paper, Foronda et al. (2016) reiterated and expounded upon the aspects of cultural humility originally identified by Teravalon and Murray-Garcia (1998), with their final list including openness, self-awareness, egolessness, supportive interactions, and self-reflection and critique as the five dimensions that represent cultural humility. Foronda et al. (2016) defined genuine openness as the ability to explore new ideas with others while remaining open to diverse worldviews and further stated that this kind of openness is a pre-requisite to the practice of cultural humility. They defined self-awareness as the ability to be aware of one's own worldview and presentation as well as one's own strengths and areas of growth (Foronda et al., 2016). Per Foronda et al. (2016), being egoless refers to a clinician's ability to acknowledge the inherent dignity of others and, potentially more importantly, work to mitigate power differences inherent in the therapeutic relationship. Foronda et al. (2016) defined supportive interactions as being positive and defined self-reflection and critique as the ability for a clinician to reflect on how his/her/their worldview could potentially impact interactional processes with others. Supportive interactions could include asking open-ended questions from a posture of benign curiosity and demonstrating respect for the cultural practices of others during the course of a conversation. Living in a manner consistent with the values of self-reflection and critique could be demonstrated by one recognizing the limitations of one's own cultural knowledge as well as worldview by being open to feedback from others and modifying one's behavior in a manner consistent with that feedback.

Gonzalez et al. (2021) suggest that the MCHS can be used by clinicians to evaluate their own levels of cultural humility. Such a practice is consistent with the principles of cultural humility, specifically, the principles of self-awareness and self-reflection and critique. Use of the measure can support clinicians in identifying their areas of strength as they pertain to cultural humility but, more importantly, can help clinicians identify areas of growth. Once areas of growth have been identified, clinicians can respond by seeking additional training and supervision specifically geared toward addressing areas of growth identified by the measure. For some clinicians, working with their own therapists may be helpful in either addressing areas of growth identified by the measure or exploring underlying etiologies contributing to areas of growth, such as resistance, defensiveness, etc. For clinicians interested in their patients' perceptions of how cultural humility is being practiced by the provider, the Cultural Humility Scale (CHS) can be administered to patients and also provide valuable feedback.

Cultural Formulation Interview

For clinicians seeking further guidance regarding how to begin conversations related to diversity with their patients, the Cultural Formulation Interview (CFI) included in the *Diagnostic and Statistical Manual* (Fifth Edition, Text Revision) can provide a concrete list of questions to explore with patients, either during intake sessions or as the need arises over the course of the therapeutic encounter. The CFI is a semi-structured interview that allows clinicians to seek information regarding how patients understand themselves and their symptoms within the context of a cultural framework. While not necessarily based on the principles of cultural humility, for some clinicians, perhaps especially student clinicians or less experienced clinicians, a concrete list of questions to which they can refer can be helpful in beginning important conversations. Some relevant questions from the CFI include: *For you, what are the most important aspects of your background or identity? Are there any aspects of your background or identity that are causing other concerns or difficulties for you?* and *Sometimes doctors and patients misunderstand each other because they come from different backgrounds or have different expectations. Have you been concerned about this and is there anything that we can do to provide you with the care you need?* Other questions in the CFI can support clinicians in understanding how their patients are understanding/making meaning of their mental health symptoms within the context of their cultures, including how perhaps their faith traditions, religious practices, ethnic practices, etc., help them make sense of their symptoms (APA, 2022).

The use of the CFI represents a shift from historical approaches to understanding psychopathology, which have generally been rooted in categorical understandings about both psychopathology and its origins as well as what might be helpful in addressing such psychopathology. The CFI instead emphasizes the importance of the subjective experiences of patients within their own cultures. As noted above, the CFI promotes the practice of cultural humility by providing a structure in which a clinician can engage respectfully with a patient's worldview. While some clinicians may experience the CFI as being too time-consuming to be useful in a clinical setting, and while additional knowledge and experience is needed to interpret the information gathered as part of the CFI, the structure provided is valuable and affirms the cultural imperative to approach questions pertaining to mental health through the lens of cultural humility.

Clinical Practice and Cultural Humility

The practice of cultural humility is essential to the practice of clinicians working in mental health settings and while good intentions and the CFI can serve as first steps, much more is needed to ensure patients receive the care they need and deserve. Ultimately, the practice of cultural humility requires both intentional changes implemented on the part of individual clinicians and institutional support. The following is a list of humble recommendations to support both individual clinicians and organizations in implementing and practicing cultural humility.

Because self-reflection is foundational to the practice of cultural humility, it is recommended that such self-reflection be actively incorporated into both supervision and peer consultation. Such active integration into already-scheduled conversations can support both clinicians and their trainees in examining both their own values and their assumptions regarding the patients presenting to their clinic. Such an approach has the potential to cultivate cultural humility by facilitating conversations regarding clinician positionality as well as patient positionality and how these positions may be interacting with one another in the clinical setting, including how they may be impacting care. For clinicians accustomed to focusing simply on symptoms and interventions, such a transition to a more narrative format could be a first step in exploring a patient's cultural context. Individual practices can also be encouraged, such as reflective journaling and identity mapping. In both reflective journaling and identity mapping, clinicians can explore their own identities, worldviews, and associated assumptions and how these may impact their clinical practice.

Creating a culture of psychological safety within a clinical setting can also facilitate the practice of cultural humility. Psychological safety refers to the concept that individuals should be able to speak openly and express uncertainty as well as limitations without fear of punishment or humiliation (Edmondson, 1999). Such permission to speak freely is fundamental to the practice of cultural humility and requires that all involved clinicians approach conversations from positions free of judgment and moralizing, which, of course, requires deep intentionality from all involved. Psychological safety can be especially challenging to foster in clinical settings that include students and trainees given the inherent evaluative approach supervising clinicians must take when training others to provide mental health services. Supervision is hierarchical and supervisors carry both power and responsibility – responsibility to ensure students and trainees are competent, which can sometimes require challenging conversations regarding clinical errors but also power to either advance a student or trainee or report to their academic institutions that they are not ready to advance. Such an environment can cause students and trainees (and potentially supervisors) to hide areas of uncertainty – but doing so can only promote the status quo as opposed to encouraging cultural humility.

Because clinical supervision is necessarily hierarchical and therefore can inhibit both openness and vulnerability, supervisors are encouraged to explicitly name power dynamics and imbalances as well as how they can impact psychological safety and cultural humility. Supervisors are also encouraged to check in with their students and supervisees, not just in terms of how clinical training is progressing but about how their lives are unfolding and how they may be feeling impacted by local, national, or global events. Supervisors are also encouraged to explicitly speak with students and supervisees regarding how supervision itself is going and to provide students and trainees with opportunities to provide anonymous feedback if needed. Training clinics can also find ways of explicitly affirming cultural identity by learning more about the clinicians, students, trainees, and administrative staff and inviting both the sharing of cultural experiences and the recognition of lived experiences as legitimate sources of knowledge. Finally, when ruptures occur in the supervisory relationship, clinical supervisors can invite conversations focused on repair and responsivity to feedback rather than paternalism and defensiveness. Such conversations can invite acknowledgement of both institutional and social privileges while inviting students and trainees to participate in creating clinical culture by participating in agenda-setting, learning needs, preferred feedback methods, etc. More importantly, intentionally discussing power dynamics in supervision can facilitate a more collaborative culture, which can in turn facilitate the development of psychological safety and cultural humility.

Collaboration with Others

As an additional note, because cultural humility necessarily requires that the voices and experiences of individuals other than clinicians be included in conversations pertaining to mental health and lived experience, a final recommendation is that clinics and their respective clinicians work to develop authentic community partnerships, especially with the diverse groups local to their particular areas. The inclusion of local community elders, faith leaders, and other community organizations can facilitate a truly collaborative approach to mental health services by incorporating the voices of the community members most likely to be influenced by the services offered in the clinic. The inclusion of such individuals in the service of cultural humility can help to address systemic exclusion of marginalized individuals, amplify their voices, and build trust in the community. Practically speaking, this inclusion can take the form of a community advisory council composed of community members and designed to partner with the clinic in terms of needed clinical services and educational programs. This can also take the form of clinicians, students, and trainees moving services out into the community by creating drop-in clinics at local schools, community centers, or places of worship or by offering educational workshops in such locations. Another approach might include working more collaboratively with the other helpers in a patient's life, such as a community elder, pastor, priest, rabbi, or imam, in the spirit of providing truly holistic support. Regardless of the form collaboration with others takes, equity in decision making, transparency, and accountability as well as respect for culturally defined hierarchies and methods are critical for success. Specifically, respect for culturally defined hierarchies and methods may require clinicians to acknowledge the value of practices with which they may be unfamiliar, such as traditional healing practices, prayer, fasting, confession, etc.

Conclusion

Ultimately, the practice of cultural humility is and should be an essential and ongoing endeavor for mental health professionals who aim to provide truly equitable, inclusive, and person-centered care. While developing cultural competence is important, recognizing the limitations of cultural competence and embracing the principles of openness, self-awareness, and lifelong learning associated with cultural humility allows clinicians to engage more authentically with the diverse identities and lived experiences of their patients as well as their own diverse identities and lived experiences and how these interact with one another during any therapeutic encounter. Tools like the MCHS and the CFI can offer valuable structure and reflection points, yet it is the internal posture of humility, not any single tool or checklist, that ultimately shapes the quality of care provided. Similarly, while conscious and explicit individual reflection on the part of the clinician is crucial to the development of cultural humility and while engagement with supportive colleagues can be foundational, neither are sufficient for truly developing a posture of cultural humility. It is only by committing to *continuous* self-exploration and approaching each therapeutic encounter with curiosity and respect that clinicians can begin to dismantle the barriers created by bias and power imbalances. In doing so, clinicians foster spaces where patients can be truly seen, heard, and supported – not in spite of their differences, but because of them, and it is the safety that such spaces can evoke that can ultimately create the opportunity for healing.

References

APA (American Psychiatric Association). (2022). *Diagnostic and statistical manual of mental disorders* (5th ed., text rev.). American Psychiatric Association.

Audi, R. (2010). *Epistemology: A contemporary introduction to the theory of knowledge* (3rd ed.). Routledge.

Cambridge. (n.d.). Humility. *Cambridge.org dictionary*. https://dictionary.cambridge.org/. Retrieved 24 April 2025.

Edmondson, A. (1999). Psychological safety and learning behavior in work teams. *Administrative Science Quarterly*, *44*(2), 350–385. https://doi.org/10.2307/2666999.

Foronda, C., Baptiste, D., Reinholdt, M., & Ousman, K. (2016). Cultural humility: A concept analysis. *Journal of Transcultural Nursing*, *27*(3), 210–217. https://doi.org/10.1177/1043659615592677.

Gonzalez, E., Sperandio, K. R., Mullen, P. R., & Tuazon, V. E. (2021). Multidimensional Cultural Humility Scale [Database record]. Retrieved from PsycTESTS. https://dx.doi.org/10.1037/t86469-000.

Gottlieb, M. (2020). The case for a cultural humility framework in social work practice. *Journal of Ethnic and Cultural Diversity in Social Work*, *30*(6), 463–481. https://doi.org10.1080/15313204.2020.1753615.

Hook, J. N., Davis, D. E., Owen, J., Worthington, E. L., & Utsey, S. O. (2013). Cultural humility: Measuring openness to culturally diverse clients. *Journal of Counseling Psychology*, *60*(3), 353–366. https://doi.org/10.1037/a0032595.

Kirmayer, L. J. (2012). Rethinking cultural competence. *Transcultural Psychiatry*, *49*(2), 149–164. https://doi.org/10.1177/13634615124446733.

Lekas, H.-M., Pahl, K., & Fuller Lewis, C. (2020). Rethinking cultural competence: Shifting to cultural humility. *Health Services Insights*, *13*. https://doi.org/10.1177/1178632920970580.

Merriam-Webster. (n.d.). Humility. *Merriam-Webster.com dictionary*. https://www.merriam-webster.com. Retrieved 24 April 2025.

Shepherd, S. M. (2019). Cultural awareness workshops: Limitations and practical consequences. *BMC Medical Education*, *19*, Article 14. https://doi.org/10.1186/s12909-018-1450-5.

Tervalon, M., & Murray-Garcia, J. (1998). Cultural humility versus cultural competence: A critical distinction in defining physician training outcomes in multicultural education. *Journal of Health Care for the Poor and Underserved*, *9*(2), 117–125. https://doi.org/10.1353/hpu.2010.0233.

Chapter 3

Schizophrenia Spectrum and Other Psychotic Disorders

David J. Machado

Disorders included in the chapter of the DSM-5-TR pertaining to schizophrenia spectrum and other psychotic disorders share features such as delusions, hallucinations, disorganized speech and/or behavior, and negative symptoms such as flat affect and avolition. While disorders included in this chapter of the DSM-5-TR vary considerably in terms of severity and duration, two particularly challenging diagnoses are schizophrenia and schizoaffective disorder, for which clinical vignettes are included below. Schizophrenia is characterized by a variety of concerning symptoms but must include at least one of the following: delusions, hallucinations, and disorganized speech (APA, 2022). It may also include disorganized or catatonic behavior and/or negative symptoms (APA, 2022). As with many of the disorders included in the DSM-5-TR, some level of impairment and/clinically significant distress must be evident for the disorder to be diagnosed. Schizophrenia generally manifests in late adolescence or early adulthood and can be experienced as episodic or chronic (APA, 2022). For many patients, long-term support is required. Schizoaffective disorder shares many symptoms with schizophrenia, such as delusions, hallucinations, disorganized speech and/or behavior, and negative symptoms, but also includes symptoms of a major mood episode (APA, 2022). The major mood episode could be either depressive or manic in nature and when either manic in nature or characterized by the emotional lability often associated with bipolar disorder, a specifier of bipolar type can be added. These mood symptoms are what distinguishes schizoaffective disorder from schizophrenia and other psychotic disorders. Similar to schizophrenia, schizoaffective disorder also tends to manifest in early adulthood but in some cases, can sometimes become apparent later in life (APA, 2022).

DOI: 10.4324/9781003586531-4

Clinical Case Vignette #1

Demographic Information and History

Name: Jonathan Harker.

Demographic Information: The patient is a 33-year-old Hispanic American who identifies as heterosexual, non-religious, with no visible or invisible disabilities.

Medical Diagnoses: Hyperlipidemia.

Reason for Referral: Harker is currently under Lanterman-Petris-Short (LPS) conservatorship. Jonathan Harker was transferred to an inpatient psychiatric hospital for treatment stabilization after multiple elopements and aggressive actions towards peers and staff from previous treatment facilities. Upon intake, Harker was observed to be responding to internal stimuli. When prompted, he stated, "I hear voices and see things, sometimes they tell me to do things." Harker was observed to have low acceptance of reality testing as supported by his delusional beliefs and statements, "I have died over 200 times." Harker reported that he was recently transferred to the current treatment facility due to absent without leave (AWOL) attempts and illicit drug use while at the previous facility. Harker demonstrates fair insight into his mental health symptoms, low acceptance of reality, limited engagement in activities of daily living, and drug-seeking behaviors. However, it should be noted that Harker may not be an accurate historian due to his presentation of delusional beliefs at the time of information gathering.

Clinical Interview Data

Interpreter Used: No.

Current Psychosocial Stressors: Harker is currently a resident at a locked inpatient hospital under LPS conservatorship with limited access to familial social support and restrictions to personal freedoms. Harker is also experiencing cravings/urges to use multiple substances (nicotine, cannabis, methamphetamine).

Protective Factors: Harker is in forced remission while at the treatment facility. Harker has been observed to have consistent familial support as well as access to nursing and programming staff to monitor and ensure safety.

Developmental History: Harker reported meeting all his developmental milestones within the expected timeframes. However, it should be noted that Harker may not be an accurate historian due to his presentation of delusional beliefs at the time of information gathering.

Academic History: Harker reported that he did not complete high school nor earn his GED credential. He also reported that he was unsure of when he stopped attending school.

Social History: Harker reported that he does not have many friends and reported being homeless for about 8 years from 2012 to 2020. However, he did report weekly visits from his mother while at the facility.

Household: Harker reported that he is an only child but has close contact with his mother.

Previous Psychiatric History: He has been held at multiple inpatient psychiatric facilities in the region, with hospitalizations noted during the following time periods: 10 October 2024–1 November 2024, 3 May 2024–10 October 2024, 22 February 2023–23 March 2023, 23 March 2023–3 May 2024. An additional 1-day hold at a detention center was noted on 14 November 2022 after an incident involving petty theft and assault.

Family Psychiatric History: No family psychiatric history was reported.

History of Self-Harm: Harker endorsed having been deceased for various periods of time due to acts of violence or suicide attempts. He reported an extensive history of self-injurious behavior and suicidal ideation. Harker reported having over 1,000 suicide attempts, by means of firearms, cutting wrists/throat, self-drowning, and self-strangulation. He denied current suicidal ideation.

Wellness Profile

Sleep: Harker reports that he averages 8–10 hours of sleep per night. However, he reports using sleep as a means to avoid his auditory hallucinations when they are more present.

Diet: Due to his diagnosis of hyperlipidemia, his diet consists of a low-fat/low-cholesterol diet with regular textures and a thin consistency. Harker reports enjoying various Mexican dishes. He has reported and has been observed to miss meals when his auditory command hallucinations occur; however, he typically participates in meal replacements.

Elimination: Harker has no reported concerns with elimination.

Technology: Harker has limited access to technology per the facility protocol; however, during the observed "tech-time" and various facility-led groups, he engages in about 1–2 hours of watching television and 1–2 hours of screen time on a mobile device.

Physical Activity: Harker reports minimal engagement in physical activity; however, he reports walking throughout the facility to pass time or engaging in sports activities a few times a week.

Substance Use/Abuse: Harker endorsed an extensive history of substance use; however, he is in forced remission while at the current treatment facility. Harker endorsed a history of multiple legal and illegal substances, including alcohol, nicotine, cannabis, heroin, opiates, cocaine, methamphetamine, and misuse of prescription drugs.

Pain: 0/10.

Current Psychiatric Symptoms

Depression: Harker denied any depressive symptoms. Staff have not observed depressive symptoms.

Anxiety: Harker reports feelings of anxiety and paranoia when he is experiencing auditory and visual hallucinations. Harker reports feeling "on edge," having racing thoughts, increased heart rate, irritability, and mistrust of others.

Panic: Harker denied any previous experiences of panic attacks.

Mania: Harker denied any previous experiences of mania or hypomania.

Psychosis: Harker was unable to recall the exact onset of his experiences of psychosis; however, he reported that since early high school, he began having command auditory hallucinations and visual hallucinations. On occasion, Harker has reported that the command auditory hallucinations instruct him to avoid social interaction, restrict meals, and harm himself. In terms of visual hallucinations, Harker has reported seeing himself die multiple times and his soul leave his body.

Eating Disorder: While Harker reports not wanting to eat due to his command of auditory hallucinations, he regularly participates in meal replacements when he misses meals. The treatment team has no concerns for an eating disorder at this time but will continue to monitor his eating habits.

Risky Behaviors/Sexual Activity: Harker is known to engage in impulsive behaviors relating to self-harm. He did not report any engagement in risky sexual activities.

Mental Status Exam

Appearance: Harker was appropriately dressed but presented as malodorous and with poor self-care and hygiene engagement.

Behavior: Harker was observed in a guarded and withdrawn disposition and was observed repeatedly scanning the room. He was cooperative and willing to discuss his personal history and share details when prompted.

Speech: Harker's speech was observed to be slow and slurred.

Mood: Harker's mood was observed to be stable with a broad range of emotions but limited affect.

Affect: Harker was observed to have a broad range of affect; however, his presentation of affect was rather blunted.

Thought Process: Harker's thought process was observed to be coherent when prompted; however, his thought process was circumstantial and would often return to his delusions of being deceased.

Thought Content: Harker denied current suicidal ideation, homicidal ideation, but was observed to have bizarre delusions, in which he believed he was deceased and had died over 200 times in the past. Additionally, he was observed to be responding to internal stimuli; when prompted with reality testing, he was able to identify that he was experiencing auditory and visual hallucinations.

Orientation: Harker was observed to be oriented to person, place, time, and situation when redirected/prompted; however, he maintained the belief that he had died multiple times previously.

Recent Memory: Harker's recent memory was intact.

Remote Memory: Harker's remote memory appeared to be impaired by his fixed belief that he had died multiple times in the past.

Attention/Concentration: Harker's attention and concentration were within normal limits; however, he required minimal prompting when he became preoccupied with internal stimuli.

General Knowledge: Harker's general knowledge was within normal limits.

Language: Harker's language was within normal limits.

Insight: Harker demonstrated poor insight as evidenced by his statements, "I don't belong here, I don't need treatment," low acceptance of reality, and denial of a mental health diagnosis.

Judgment: Harker demonstrated poor judgment, as supported by his states of drug-seeking behaviors, "I just want to get out so I can use again."

Answer Key #1

Diversity Considerations

Interventions should take into consideration Harker's Hispanic cultural background. Specifically, Hispanic values associated with the normalization of stoicism in the face of adversity may be impacting Harker's willingness to engage in mental health treatment (Sue et al., 2019), which may subsequently be impacting his repeated attempts to escape from the institutions attempting to hold him. Traditional Hispanic gender norms that encourage self-reliance and discourage emotional self-expression may also complicate Harker's relationship with both the individual clinicians and the institutions attempting to support him (Addis & Mahalik, 2003). Granted, Harker's symptoms of psychosis are likely also strongly driving his behaviors, but underlying cultural factors should not be discounted in the process of conceptualization.

Harker reported having a history of homelessness for about 8 years as well as very limited education, both of which highlight the socioeconomic disadvantages that Harker has experienced. Both housing instability and limited education are known social determinants of health that disproportionately impact members of marginalized groups, including Hispanic individuals, and which can therefore raise the risk of experiencing mental health issues in this population (Metzl & Roberts, 2014).

Ethical Considerations

Harker is being held under LPS conservatorship due to grave disability. In the state of California, where treatment is being attempted, LPS conservatorship is the mechanism through which mental health treatment services can be implemented without an adult patient's consent. While such mechanisms are sometimes necessary for the sake of keeping patients safe, keeping communities safe, and rendering aid in situations where mental health symptoms themselves negatively impact a patient's ability to consent to care, it is still important for clinicians to provide as much opportunity for autonomy as possible. This includes seeking assent whenever possible, providing appropriate information regarding diagnoses and treatment planning, allowing for choices regarding diet when medically appropriate, allowing for choices regarding attire and personal expression if not inconsistent with a facility's safety standards, etc. Even when a patient is being held under an LPS conservatorship, as much effort as possible in establishing a collaborative therapeutic relationship is recommended.

Harker has an extensive history of suicidal ideation, multiple suicide attempts, and multiple reports of self-injurious behavior. Although there is some question regarding the number of attempts reported, clinicians are still ethically required to regularly assess for safety concerns and respond appropriately to ongoing suicidal ideation and/or self-harm attempts. Additionally, because Harker was detained on at least one occasion due to reports of assault, clinicians should consider also regularly assessing for homicidal ideation as well as intent to harm others, patients or staff, at the facility where Harker is currently being held. The integration regarding law and ethics becomes evident in situations such as this, as in California, Tarasoff laws born out of the landmark 1976 case of *Tarasoff v. Regents of the University of California* requires that mental health clinicians notify identified potential victims that they might be at risk and also that clinicians take any additional necessary steps, such as involving law enforcement or restraining a patient, if needed.

Legal Considerations

Harker reported a legal history, for petty theft and assault, as mentioned above. Given Harker's overall presentation, his engagement in criminal behavior could have been the result of his current symptoms of psychosis or because of the influence of any substances he may have been utilizing at the time. It is important for clinicians to be aware of the intersection of mental health issues and judicial involvement and, as much as possible, avoid from engaging with patients punitively within the context of a mental health treatment environment. While information regarding potential additional legal issues related to the petty theft and assault are not available, clinicians should remain sensitive to any access Harker may need to the judicial system, such as time to visit with his attorney if needed. Clinicians should also remain aware that their documentation may be requested by the court if any attorneys involved in the situation deem it necessary to provide the court with documentation regarding Harker's mental health disorder. In such situations, consultation with a malpractice insurance provider is recommended to help clinicians balance patient privacy and confidentiality with local laws pertaining to subpoenaed documents.

Diagnostic Impressions and Justification

F20.9 Schizophrenia.

Harker experiences both positive and negative symptoms associated with schizophrenia. Harker's symptoms include active delusions in which he believes he has died multiple times, paranoia relating to social interactions, and somatic delusions in which he believes he has "beings" growing from his skin tags. Harker also experiences auditory command hallucinations, which instruct him not to eat and to isolate himself from others. He also endorsed visual hallucinations, which involve seeing shadows and seeing himself deceased. Harker has also been observed having disorganized, tangential, circumstantial, and perseverating speech and thought patterns. During heightened periods of active symptoms, Harker has demonstrated limited engagement with activities of daily living and can exhibit self-care deficits. Harker also demonstrates limited and blunted affect, loss of interest in socialization, anhedonia, and isolative tendencies.

Psychodynamic Case Conceptualization

Harker experiences auditory command hallucinations, visual hallucinations, and bizarre, somatic, and paranoid delusions, which can be conceptualized as defense mechanisms that serve the psychological function of alleviating unbearable anxiety rooted in intense self-criticism (Ruffalo et al., 2023). However, the positive symptoms of hallucinations and delusions ultimately end up causing more distress than benefit. For example, Harker may experience visual hallucinations in which he sees himself deceased to express his emotional distress and suicidal ideation. Similarly, Harker experiences auditory command hallucinations that instruct him to restrict meals, avoid social interactions, and engage in isolative behaviors. These experiences of voices may be a projection of early internalized experiences of criticism/self-criticism of being overweight, feelings of inadequacy, suspicion, and fear of judgment of others (Ruffalo et al., 2023). His psychotic symptoms – such as the delusional belief that he has died hundreds of times and his hallucinations of his soul leaving his body – may reflect fragmented self and object representations. These psychotic phenomena can be understood as failed attempts to reconcile deeply ambivalent internal objects, wherein annihilation fantasies emerge as symbolic representations of unintegrated aggression and profound object loss (Klein, 1946; Ogden, 1986). Taken together, Harker's presentation may be consistent with a self that is so fragmented that its only option for survival is to retreat into psychosis. Additionally, while Harker reported a close relationship with his mother, his father is not mentioned, nor does he appear to be visiting Harker in the facility where Harker is currently being held. Harker also reported not finishing high school and that he never completed his GED, which is rare in the United States, especially in

California. As such, there seems to have been some sort of developmental disruption, even if not disclosed, which could potentially help explain Harker's longstanding difficulties with reality testing and self-regulation.

Psychodynamic treatment goals could include improving Harker's reality testing so as to improve his ability to distinguish between internal and external realities. Understanding his childhood experiences and how they could potentially have impacted his functioning, such as through the internalization of himself and others would also be important. Developing a strong therapeutic alliance would be fundamental in working with Harker, as a strong therapeutic alliance could ultimately foster both corrective emotional experiences and transference interpretations, which could then in turn facilitate the development of a more integrated sense of self. Finally, understanding the symbolic meaning of Harker's delusions and hallucinations could bring awareness to his fragmented self-states, also supporting the eventual emergence of a more integrated and stable sense of self.

Psychodynamic treatment interventions could include establishing a safe and consistent therapeutic relationship which can then serve as a form of external structure that can be gradually internalized over time. Because Harker presents with poor insight and active symptoms of psychosis, early sessions should focus on affirming his strengths, supporting him with affective regulation, and minimizing regression. More interpretive interventions should be postponed until some evidence of consistent improvement emerges. This includes addressing transference by observing and naming it rather than immediately interpreting it. The clinician should encourage narrative elaboration throughout the course of treatment, specifically to support him in exploring both his suffering and the potential symbolic meaning of the psychotic material with which he is presenting. Similarly, the clinician should observe and name defense mechanisms as they become apparent in session, which may support Harker in becoming more aware of his overall presentation and functioning.

Cognitive Behavioral Conceptualization

Harker experiences thought distortions in relation to his delusional beliefs and auditory/visual hallucinations. Harker appraises the auditory command hallucinations as antagonistic, powerful, and judgmental. Due to Harker's appraisal of the auditory command hallucinations, his appraisal impacts and informs his behavioral and emotional responses (Spencer et al., 2020). Harker's cognitive appraisals of the auditory hallucinations as threatening, fear- and anxiety-inducing, and authoritative modify his behavioral responses. This results in increased meal restriction and isolative, self-harming behaviors. It is important to note that Harker's presentation could be rooted in schema-level distortions related to self-worth. Harker has developed maladaptive coping skills such as substance use as a behavioral response to stress and anxiety caused by his appraisal of his hallucinations and delusions (Spencer et al. 2020). Substance use can serve as an avoidance-based coping strategy for some individuals. This may be the case for Harker as he also reported engaging in other avoidance-based coping strategies, specifically, sleep. Poor insight and cognitive rigidity related to poor insight are likely maintaining his symptoms.

Appropriate CBT treatment goals could include increasing Harker's awareness of his psychotic symptoms while decreasing the amount of distress he is experiencing related to these symptoms. Increasing Harker's insight into the multidirectional relationship between cognitions, emotions, and behaviors would also be helpful. CBT could also support Harker in improving his emotional regulation by improving his ability to tolerate distress. Because Harker has a well-established history of substance abuse, any CBT-based plan should include relapse prevention as a goal. Psychoeducation regarding the role illicit substances can play in exacerbating symptoms of psychosis may also be helpful. Additionally, goals related to behavioral activation, social skills training, and safety planning would be appropriate.

Appropriate CBT interventions could include providing general psychoeducation regarding psychosis as well as normalizing symptoms of psychosis and the distress related to them. Cognitive restructuring can be utilized to support Harker in identifying maladaptive thoughts and beliefs while adaptive coping strategies grounded in mindfulness can improve overall emotional and behavioral regulations. Additionally, cognitive defusion, a clinical intervention grounded in acceptance and commitment therapy, can support Harker in creating distance between himself and his hallucinations. Behavioral activation can also be utilized to diminish dependence on avoidance-based coping strategies and promote a sense of agency, which can be pivotal for patients being held under LPS conservatorship. Finally, safety planning should be integrated into sessions as needed, with skills noted on the safety plan regularly practiced to facilitate fluency in using the skills should the need arise.

Biopsychosocial Conceptualization

Harker's presentation is being impacted by multiple factors, including, but not limited to, biological factors. His history of significant polysubstance use, particularly his use of methamphetamine, may have played a role in the development of his psychotic symptoms. Specifically, methamphetamine is strongly associated with the onset and exacerbation of psychotic symptoms particularly because of how it negatively affects dopamine (Glasner-Edwards & Mooney, 2014). As is often the case in patients with substance use issues, Harker's substance use may also be maintaining his symptoms. Harker's medical diagnosis of hyperlipidemia may negatively impact the medications available to Harker, as some antipsychotic medications are known to contribute to the development of metabolic syndrome. Additionally, because research has repeatedly demonstrated the likely genetic underpinnings of schizophrenia, a genetic predisposition cannot be ruled out. Harker's reports of having died over 200 times indicate severe disruptions in terms of self-concept, but may also represent an attempt to make meaning out his suffering. His history of suicide attempts and self-harm substantiate the notion that he is suffering significantly, as do his attempts to avoid his suffering by engaging in substance use and sleep. It is also important to consider the role Harker's environment has played regarding both the development and maintenance of his symptoms. He was likely exposed to violence and social rejection during the time he was homeless, not to mention being exposed to the elements, nutritional deficiency, and dehydration. Because he left school so early and has not reported any meaningful occupation or volunteer service, Harker has likely found his social environment lacking, which may be contributing to feelings of inadequacy as well as an underdeveloped sense of identity.

Treatment goals grounded in the biopsychosocial model could include providing support in managing both psychiatric and other medical symptoms and issues and planning for the discontinuation of illicit substance use after discharge. Improving overall distress tolerance while reducing both self-harm behaviors and suicide attempts should be prioritized. Because Harker has been hospitalized repeatedly, focus on successful community integration as well as housing stability are warranted.

From a biopsychosocial perspective, ongoing collaboration with psychiatry as well as with other medical providers could be considered appropriate so as to support Harker with compliance to the medication and other medical regimens prescribed to reduce symptoms of psychosis while improving overall physical health. Psychoeducation regarding the problematic effects of illicit substances would be appropriate. Because Harker has not reported any interest in reducing his use of illicit substances, motivational interviewing may be appropriate to increase change talk as well as change behaviors. Interventions curated from acceptance and commitment therapy as well as dialectical behavior therapy could be implemented to improve self-harm behaviors and reduce suicide attempts. Clinician may also wish to collaborate with Harker's mother as well as local and county-based resources to ensure Harker is able to function successfully once discharged back into the community. Referrals to both Alcoholics Anonymous (AA) and Narcotics Anonymous (NA) may be helpful. Finally, a referral to low-cost legal services is recommended if needed.

Clinical Case Vignette #2

Demographic Information and History

Name: Mina Murray.

Demographic Information: 52-year-old Caucasian female.

Medical Diagnoses: Restless leg syndrome, hypothyroidism, gastro-esophageal reflux disease without esophagitis.

Reason for Referral: Mina is currently under LPS conservatorship. Mina Murray was transferred to an inpatient psychiatric hospital for treatment stabilization after being transferred from a different locked inpatient treatment facility. Mina was transferred to assist with treatment stabilization, drug and alcohol rehabilitation, and support with psychotic symptoms.

Clinical Interview Data

Interpreter Used: No.

Current Psychosocial Stressors: Mina is currently a resident at a locked inpatient hospital under LPS conservatorship with limited access to familial social support and restrictions to personal freedoms. As per her delusions, Mina believes that her mother is stuck and lost in the middle of the woods, and that she, Mina, needs to get a helicopter to find her. Mina also believes that her medications are "poison" and struggles with medication compliance. However, it should be noted that Mina may not be an accurate historian due to her presentation of delusional beliefs at the time of information gathering.

Protective Factors: Mina reported that she identifies as a Protestant Christian and that her faith and connection with God are a source of strength and safety, though she is not active in a Church. Mina reported that her faith is a protective factor. Mina also reported having a good relationship with one of her cousins and that social support is a protective factor.

Developmental History: Mina reported meeting all her developmental milestones within normal limits.

Academic History: Mina reported completing high school.

Social History: Mina reported having few friends within the facility and remaining in contact with one of her cousins.

Household: Mina reports that she is an only child and does not currently have contact with her mother, but reports that she is in contact with a cousin she is close to. Mina believes that her mother is lost in the woods and needs to be rescued by a helicopter. Mina has not made any comments regarding her father or other familial support.

Previous Psychiatric History: Mina reported being previously hospitalized from 26 June 2024 to 14 August 2024. Mina was concerned about a "gunshot wound" to her breast, for which there was no medical or visual evidence, and she struggles with methamphetamine use. Mina reported that she had been in jail since 2021 before arriving at the treatment facility.

Family Psychiatric History: Mina reported no family psychiatric history. However, this may be due to Mina's inability to provide an accurate history.

History of Self-Harm: Mina has a history of suicidal ideation, with the last known attempt in 2006. She is documented to have a history of self-harm by means of head-banging.

Wellness Profile

Sleep: Mina reports that sleep has been observed, averaging 8–12 hours per night.

Diet: Due to her diagnoses of hypothyroidism and gastro-esophageal reflux disease without esophagitis, Mina's diet consists of a regular diet, with regular textures and thin consistencies.

Elimination: Mina reports frequent constipation issues.

Technology: Mina has limited access to technology per the facility protocol; however, during the observed "tech-time" and various facility-led groups, Mina reports engaging in about 2–4 hours of screen time daily.

Physical Activity: Mina reports minimal physical activity outside of routine daily tasks and occasional walks throughout the facility.

Substance Use/Abuse: As per documentation and self-report, Mina has a history of methamphetamine use and alcohol dependence. She has been in forced remission since the beginning of treatment at the current facility as of 14 August 2024.

Pain: 4–6/10. Mina reports increased pain in the chest/breast region when her somatic delusions of having a "gunshot wound" increase.

Current Psychiatric Symptoms

Depression: Mina denied any current depressive symptoms; however, staff have observed Mina to be more isolated and withdrawn. Staff have also observed Mina to have low mood, increased irritation, poor engagement with hygiene practices, self-care deficits, and changes in diet during cycles of depressive symptoms.

Anxiety: Mina reports frequent anxiety over her concerns about her mother being lost in the woods and needing a helicopter rescue. However, this is part of her delusional beliefs, and she is not amenable to reality testing. This has resulted in Mina attempting to AWOL from the facility as well as repeatedly calling emergency services to request a rescue crew search for her mother.

Panic: Mina has no reported history of panic attacks.

Mania: Mina denies any manic or hypomanic experiences; however, this is contrary to staff observation. Mina is documented and observed to have manic episodes in which her delusions and experiences of auditory command hallucination increase. Mina has been observed to regress in sleeping patterns and become medication non-compliant during these periods. During these periods, Mina has been observed to become easily agitated or aggressive with others, engage in impulsive behaviors, such as AWOL attempts, stealing from peers, and calling emergency services. These periods appear to occur about once every 4–6 weeks and can last up to 2 weeks per episode.

Psychosis: Due to Mina's presentation as an inaccurate history, the onset of psychotic symptoms is unknown. However, Mina's baseline consists of persistent delusional beliefs and auditory hallucinations. Mina frequently reports, as part of her delusional beliefs, that her mother is trapped in the woods and needs a helicopter rescue, resulting in anxiety for Mina. Mina reports that she has a "gunshot" wound in her breast region. However, upon consultation with medical staff, there is no evidence of the reported wound. Mina appears to demonstrate poor insight into her delusions and is not amenable to reality testing. Similarly, Mina denies having a mental health diagnosis and believes that her mother has held a job as a clerk at the post office for the last 15 years.

Eating Disorder: Mina reported no symptoms of an eating disorder.

Risky Behaviors/Sexual Activity: Mina has been observed engaging in impulsive and risky behaviors, which involve attempting to elope from the facility, engaging in drug-seeking behaviors, and has a documented history of heightened sexual activities and performing sexual favors in exchange for items, trading, and bartering.

Mental Status Exam

Appearance: Mina was appropriate; however, she frequently wears bizarre makeup (excessive eyeshadow on eyelids, under-eye area, and nose).

Behavior: Mina was cooperative; however, as the session progressed, she became more labile and irritable.

Speech: Mina's speech was within normal limits. However, as she becomes anxious, she can become hyperverbal. Similarly, during periods of mania, Mina has been observed to have pressured speech.

Mood: Mina's mood is generally stable and euthymic. However, she can be easily agitated and irritated when her concerns and demands about her mother are not met.

Affect: Mina's affect is typically congruent with a broad range of emotions.

Thought Process: Mina's thought process initially appears coherent and logical; however, in past superficial conversations, Mina's thought process appears tangential and circumstantial.

Thought Content: At this time, Mina denied suicidal ideation and homicidal ideation. However, Mina was observed responding to internal stimuli via thought blocking and endorsed delusional beliefs regarding her mother.

Orientation: Mina appeared to be oriented to person, place, and time, but not to her situation, as evidenced by her denial of a mental health diagnosis, need for treatment, and repeated endorsement of delusional beliefs that were not amenable to reality testing.

Recent Memory: Mina's recent memory appears to demonstrate slight impairments to her recent memory as supposed by her frequent endorsements of delusional beliefs.

Remote Memory: Mina's remote memory appears to demonstrate slight impairments to her recent memory as supported by her frequent endorsements of delusional beliefs of past events (i.e., having a gunshot wound).

Attention/Concentration: Mina's attention and concentration appear to be impaired, as supported by her circumstantial thinking patterns and preoccupation with thought blocking.

General Knowledge: Mina's general knowledge was within normal limits.

Language: Mina's language was within normal limits.

Insight: Mina's insight appeared to be poor, as evidenced by her repeated statements of not having a mental health diagnosis or needing treatment stabilization.

Judgment: Mina appeared to have poor judgment as evidenced by her repeated attempts to elope from the facility, impulsive behaviors, and medication non-compliance.

Answer Key #2

Diversity Considerations

Mina identifies as a Protestant Christian and reported her faith is protective even though she does not actively participate in a religious community. Respectful exploration of Mina's worldview and the protective elements of her faith tradition should be explored, with a focus on improving her access to the aspects of her faith tradition that feel particularly supportive or protective. Elements of her worldview could be utilized in conversations associated with meaning-making and she can be provided with increased opportunities to engage with sacred scripture, listen to worship music, etc.

Because Mina was previously incarcerated, attention should be given to the systemic inequalities often faced by those incarcerated, such as limited access to medical care and social stigma as well as how these factors may contribute to Mina's sense of self and interaction with others, including her non-compliance with providers.

Ethical Considerations

Mina is under LPS conservatorship due to grave disability. Because Mina is being held under LPS conservatorship due to grave disability, similar considerations as those associated with the previous patient must be taken into account. In the state of California, where treatment is being attempted, LPS conservatorship is the mechanism through which mental health treatment services can be implemented without an adult patient's consent. While such mechanisms are sometimes necessary for the sake of keeping patients safe, keeping communities safe, and rendering aid in situations where mental health symptoms themselves negatively impact a patient's ability to consent to care, it is still important for clinicians to provide as much opportunity for autonomy as possible. This includes seeking assent whenever possible, providing appropriate information regarding diagnoses and treatment planning, allowing for choices regarding diet when medically appropriate, allowing for choices regarding attire and personal expression if not inconsistent with a facility's safety standards, etc. Even when a patient is being held under an LPS conservatorship, as much effort as possible into establishing a collaborative therapeutic relationship is recommended.

Legal Considerations

Mian reported that she had been in jail for 3 years, prior to her first placement in a psychiatric treatment facility, but she was unable to provide details regarding her arrest. Similar to Harker, her engagement in criminal behavior leading to an arrest and incarceration could have been the result of her current symptoms of psychosis or because of the influence of any substances she may have been utilizing at the time. It is important for clinicians to be aware of the intersection of mental health issues and judicial involvement and, as much as possible, avoid engaging with patients punitively within the context of a mental health treatment environment. While information regarding potential additional legal issues is not available, clinicians should remain sensitive to any access Mina may need to the judicial system, such as time to visit with her attorney if needed. Clinicians should also remain aware that their documentation may be requested by the court if any attorneys involved in the situation deem it necessary to provide the court with documentation regarding Mina's mental health disorder. In such situations, consultation with a malpractice insurance provider is recommended to help clinicians balance patient privacy and confidentiality with local laws pertaining to subpoenaed documents.

Diagnostic Impressions and Justification

F25.0 Schizoaffective Disorder, Bipolar Type.

Mina meets the criteria for schizoaffective disorder, bipolar type, by demonstrating the following symptoms: Mina's baseline functioning includes persistent delusions of her mother being lost in the woods and in need of rescue. Mina's thought process is tangential and circumstantially related to her fixed beliefs. Mina has also been observed responding to internal stimuli and often presents as preoccupied due to thought blocking when prompted. Mina reports experiencing auditory and visual hallucinations. Mina also has recurrent manic episodes in which she demonstrates a lack of sleep, increased impulsive behaviors, and aggressive behaviors toward peers and staff. These periods appear to occur about once every 4–6 weeks and can last up to 2 weeks per episode. Mina has endorsed delusional beliefs outside of periods in which she is experiencing depressive or manic symptoms. Per staff observation, Mina also demonstrates periods of depressive symptoms in which she engages in isolative behaviors, poor self-care practices, and limited social engagement.

Psychodynamic Case Conceptualization

Mina's preoccupation with her delusional beliefs regarding her mother's need for rescue may be a projection of her internalized fear of abandonment, reliving past traumatic events, or avoidance of intrusive memories (Ruffalo et al., 2023). The anxiety stirred up by her belief that her mother is in distress contributes to her aggressive, impulsive, and maladaptive behaviors, such as elopement attempts, calling of emergency services, drug-seeking, and risky sexual behaviors. Similarly, Mina may use illicit substances and impulsive behaviors as defense mechanisms to avoid her emotional distress from her perception of her mother's suffering (Ruffalo et al., 2023). Mina also tends to report somatic symptoms over psychological distress and may use conversion as a means of downplaying her state of distress. This, as well as her substance use, may represent a desire to avoid overwhelming affect. At the heart of Mina's presentation may be distress stemming from maternal attachment as well as abandonment. It is possible that Mina's desire to rescue her mother is serving as a form of symbolic re-enactment associated with some sort of early relational rupture. In some cases, delusional beliefs can serve as a manner of organizing otherwise disorganized or fragmented experiences and internal states.

Psychodynamic treatment goals appropriate for Mina could include addressing her underlying unconscious conflicts as well as her emotional dysregulation and maladaptive behaviors. As with Harker, the initial approach to treatment should include the development of a safe, consistent therapeutic relationship. A safe, consistent therapeutic relationship ultimately supports the repair of disrupted attachment patterns. Exploring and modifying current problematic defense mechanisms are also goals relevant to the practice of psychodynamic psychotherapy and could ultimately support Mina into being able to articulate the psychological distress that has been somaticized. Overall, treatment should support Mina in developing the capacity to tolerate distress without needing to escape into impulsivity or psychosis.

Psychodynamic interventions designed to support Mina should be grounded in a primarily supportive approach that balances the historical interventions used in psychodynamic psychotherapy with the impairment caused by Mina's symptoms of psychosis. In psychodynamic psychotherapy, the use of a well-established therapeutic frame with good consistent boundaries is itself an intervention and can provide the space for Mina to eventually feel safe enough to begin exploring distressing internal material. Validating emotional distress while gently redirecting Mina to the present moment may be more supportive and effective, particularly at the beginning of treatment, than directly challenging delusional content or providing direct interpretations. That being said, as time progresses and Mina begins to stabilize, more direct interpretation of her defenses as well as of transference dynamics may become possible. Mina may also benefit from the mentalization-based interventions incorporated into mentalization-based therapy, which can support her in reflecting on her own mental states as well as the mental states of others. Increased reflection on her own mental states may subsequently reduce aggressive, impulsive behaviors.

Cognitive Behavioral Conceptualization

Mina experiences bizarre, non-bizarre, and somatic delusions, which are not amenable to reality testing. Her perception of the delusions as reality causes distress and impulsive behaviors (Spencer et al. 2020). Due to her perception that her mother is lost in the woods and in need of rescue, Mina engages in impulsive behavior such as attempting to elope from the treatment facility and calling emergency services to request a rescue crew. Alternatively, her cognitive appraisal of her delusional beliefs can lead to avoidance strategies, resulting in her drug-seeking and risky sexual behaviors as a means of coping with her emotional distress through maladaptive coping strategies. She is presenting with several cognitive distortions including catastrophizing, jumping to conclusions, and personalization, which are further amplifying her distress. She is also likely experiencing automatic thoughts that are contributing to her distress. Mina likely holds maladaptive core beliefs about herself as well as the people around, including beliefs that she herself is helpless while the people around her are dangerous. When her avoidance leads to short-term benefits, it can result in a cycle of maintained avoidance in which she does not address the root cause of her anxiety and distress but becomes fixed in her avoidant behaviors (Spencer et al., 2020).

Appropriate CBT-based treatment goals for Mina include improving her reality testing and cognitive flexibility as well as her medication compliance. Mina would also benefit from improved emotional and behavioral regulation skills to help manage impulsivity, especially impulsivity related to risky behaviors. Additionally, Mina would benefit from increased engagement in meaningful structured activities. Of fundamental importance would be improving safety.

Cognitive restructuring can be utilized to help Mina learn how to distinguish between her delusional beliefs and reality while reducing cognitive distortions. Motivational interviewing can also be used as an adjunct to CBT to improve medication compliance. Mina may benefit specifically from interventions grounded in mindfulness, as well as additional skills associated with dialectical behavior therapy. Such skills can be incorporated into a safety plan designed to reduce both elopement and self-harm behaviors, such as head-banging. If she struggles with engaging in the strategies outlined in her safety plan, coping cards can be utilized to support regular practice. Behavioral activation can be utilized to support Mina in developing a daily routine; behavioral activation could include increased involvement in activities related to her preferred religious tradition, given that she has identified her faith as being protective.

Biopsychosocial Conceptualization

Mina presents with multiple medical issues, including hypothyroidism, which is known to be associated with both cognitive and mood symptoms such as cognitive slowing and mood dysregulation, both of which can contribute to and/or exacerbate psychiatric symptoms (Joffe et al., 2007). Mina's use of methamphetamine is also problematic as methamphetamine use is implicated in the development of psychotic symptoms and cognitive impairment (Glasner-Edwards & Mooney, 2014), both of which can contribute to emotional and behavioral dysregulation. Additionally, Mina presents with poor insight and affective lability that is cyclical in nature, which is likely contributing to her impulsive behaviors, including the reported risky behaviors. Mina is also socially isolated given that she is currently residing in a locked psychiatric facility. Her judicial history and her history of substance abuse are both likely exacerbating her current presentation and may serve as barriers to successful community reintegration.

Appropriate treatment goals grounded in the biopsychosocial model include improving medication compliance, supporting compliance with medical interventions targeting her medical diagnoses, and reducing psychiatric symptoms. Increasing adaptive coping skills and reducing maladaptive coping as well as cognitive distortions will be helpful in reducing psychiatric symptoms. Creating a relapse prevention plan will be fundamental to Mina's success upon discharge. Equally important would be facilitating increased social connection, so that life in the community can maintained successfully upon discharge.

Psychoeducation, motivational interviewing, and building trust with providers within a relational context can all support medication compliance. Because Mina's medical diagnoses can impact her psychiatric presentation, appropriate referrals should be facilitated as needed. Specifically, referral to an endocrinologist can create the opportunity for Mina to receive the necessary medical screenings needed to determine if an underlying medical condition is causing her thyroid to underperform, which can subsequently allow for appropriate medical treatment. Additionally, restless leg syndrome is often caused by anemia, another condition associated with fatigue, and so referral to a primary care physician for routine blood work may also be indicated. Psychiatric symptoms can also be improved through the implementation of CBT-based interventions as well as religiously integrated interventions, given that Mina reported her faith as being a source of strength. Prior to discharge, increased contact and communication with Mina's cousin should be encouraged and facilitated, as well as connection with a local church of Mina's choosing. If needed, a referral to low-cost legal services can be generated, to support Mina with any lingering judicial issues associated with her incarceration.

Conclusion

Overall, schizophrenia spectrum and other psychotic disorders can be characterized by significant disruptions in perception and cognition, which subsequently affects emotional and behavioral regulation. Because of the overlapping symptoms common to both schizophrenia and schizoaffective disorder, differentiating between them during the conceptualization and diagnostic process can be challenging. Patients with schizophrenia and schizoaffective disorder present with psychotic features, including hallucinations and/or delusions and disorganized speech and/or behavior. Schizoaffective disorder, however, can be differentiated from schizophrenia by the prominent role mood symptoms play in the patient's presentation. The mood symptoms present in schizoaffective disorder can appear similar to those found in patients with major depressive disorder or patients with bipolar disorder, leading to the specifiers often paired with diagnoses of schizoaffective disorder. Ultimately, a comprehensive approach to conceptualization and treatment planning grounded in compassion is crucial when providing care to patients impacted by either schizophrenia or schizoaffective disorder.

References

Addis, M. E., & Mahalik, J. R. (2003). Men, masculinity, and the contexts of help seeking. *American Psychologist*, *58*(1), 5–14. https://doi.org/10.1037/0003-066X.58.1.5.

APA (American Psychiatric Association). (2022). *Diagnostic and statistical manual of mental disorders* (5th ed., text rev.). American Psychiatric Association.

Glasner-Edwards, S., & Mooney, L. J. (2014). Methamphetamine psychosis: Epidemiology and management. *CNS Drugs*, *28*(12), 1115–1126. https://doi.org/10.1007/s40263-014-0209-8.

Joffe, R. T., Levitt, A. J., & MacQueen, G. M. (2007). Thyroid dysfunction in patients with major depressive disorder: A clinical review. *Journal of Affective Disorders*, *103*(1–3), 1–6. https://doi.org/10.1016/j.jad.2007.01.004.

Klein, M. (1946) Notes on some schizoid mechanisms. *The International Journal of Psychoanalysis*, *27*, 99–110.

Metzl, J. M., & Roberts, D. E. (2014). Structural competency meets structural racism: Race, politics, and the structure of medical knowledge. *Virtual Mentor: American Medical Association Journal of Ethics*, *16*(9), 674–690. https://doi.org/10.1001/virtualmentor.2014.16.9.spec1-1409.

Ogden, T. H. (1986). *The matrix of the mind: Object relations and the psychoanalytic dialogue*. Jason Aronson.

Ruffalo, M. L. (2023). The psychotherapy of schizophrenia: A review of the evidence for psychodynamic and nonpsychodynamic treatments. *Psychiatry and Clinical Psychopharmacology*. https://doi.org/10.5152/pcp.2023.23627.

Spencer, H. M., Dudley, R., Freeston, M. H., & Turkington, D. (2020). What are the essential ingredients of a CBT case conceptualization for voices and delusions in schizophrenia spectrum disorders? A study of expert consensus. *Schizophrenia Research, 224*, 74–81. https://doi.org/10.1016/j.schres.2020.09.026.

Sue, D. W., Sue, D., Neville, H. A., & Smith, L. (2019). *Counseling the culturally diverse: Theory and practice* (8th ed.). Wiley.

Chapter 4

Depressive Disorders

Noel Cooper

Depressive disorders included in the DSM-5-TR are generally characterized by sad and/or irritable mood as well as cognitive and somatic symptoms that negatively impact an individual's ability to function across several domains of life including in academic, occupational, and social settings. While each depressive disorder differs from others due to differences in terms of onset and duration, all include disruptions in affective experience and expression.

Major depressive disorder, commonly referred to as MDD, is the flagship disorder included in this chapter of the DSM-5-TR and has been extensively studied. MDD is characterized by the presence of one or more major depressive episodes. A depressive episode is in turn defined a 2-week period wherein the patient experiences a depressed mood and/or anhedonia as well as somatic symptoms such as appetite and sleep changes (APA, 2022). Cognitive symptoms also present during this time can include difficulty concentrating and/or recurrent thoughts of death (APA, 2022). Persistent depressive disorder, previously referred to as dysthymia, is characterized by a depressive episode that impacts the patient for most of the day, more days than not, for at least two years (APA, 2022). In children and adolescents, these symptoms can last for just a year (APA, 2022). The symptoms of depression experienced as part of a persistent depressive episode can be less severe than those experienced as part of MDD but do result in impairment over time (APA, 2022). Additional depressive disorders outlined in the DSM-5-TR include disruptive mood dysregulation disorder, often referred to as DMDD and primarily diagnosed in children and adolescents, as well as premenstrual dysphoric disorder, often referred to as PMDD and primarily diagnosed in women. All individuals experience sadness from time to time and such experiences can and should be considered as part of the normal range of human emotions and experiences. Depressive episodes and the disorders associated with them can be distinguished from normative sadness due to the severity of the symptoms experienced as well the level of functional impairment.

DOI: 10.4324/9781003586531-5

Clinical Case Vignette #1

Demographic Information and History

Name: Julia Kao.

Demographic Information: 37-year-old Asian American female.

Medical Diagnoses: None.

Reason for Referral: Julia reported experiencing low mood, lack of energy, and loss of interest beginning approximately one year ago. She reported having trouble getting to sleep at night, which contributes to her fatigue. Julie said that she often feels overwhelmed by the demands of parenting her two young children (ages 2 and 4) and feels guilty that she is not a better mother. She specifically identified that she spends a lot of time cleaning up after them, picking up toys, monitoring and correcting their behavior, and taking them to age-appropriate classes (e.g., gymnastics, swim lessons, story time at the library). Julia reported that she has thought about suicide but has not considered a method or developed a plan.

Clinical Interview Data

Interpreter Used: No.

Current Psychosocial Stressors: At the time of her first child's birth four years ago, Julia left her high-paying career. While her husband works and there are no financial concerns, Julia reported that she misses her job.

Protective Factors: Julia is well educated, highly verbal, and self-reflective. She identified her sister as a significant source of support.

Developmental History: Julia reported no significant challenges in her developmental history.

Academic History: Julia has an MBA.

Social History: Julia reported that she has few friends that she keeps in regular contact with, citing her lack of free time as a significant barrier to socializing. She said that she has not kept in touch with any of her friends or colleagues from her previous job. Julia said that she sees her mother regularly, but they have a somewhat contentious relationship. Julia reported that her younger sister is her main source of social support, but that she lives two hours away. Julia and her husband have been married for ten years. She described him as supportive and helpful, but also very busy with his job. She said that in the past year they have had more conflict and distance in their relationship, which she attributes to her irritable mood and lack of interest in activities that they previously enjoyed together.

Household: Julia lives with her husband (age 43) and her two young children (ages 2 and 4).

Previous Psychiatric History: Julia reported experiencing an episode of depression and self-harm when she was 16. She said that her symptoms lasted for about a year and a half and improved when she left home for college. She said that she did not attend therapy or take medication at the time.

Family Psychiatric History: Julia reported that her mother has an undiagnosed history of anxiety but was unsure of other family members' psychiatric history because "mental health is not talked about in my family."

History of Self-Harm: From ages 16 to 18 Julia engaged in self-harm through cutting. Julia has not engaged in self-harm since that time. She reported currently experiencing thoughts of wishing she were dead, and that her family might be better off without her, but denied having a method or plan.

Wellness Profile

Sleep: Julia reported that she usually goes to bed around 11 pm but frequently has trouble falling asleep, often being awake until 1 am or later. She said that she drinks 1–2 glasses of wine at night to try to help herself fall asleep.

Diet: Julia reported that she typically has cereal, oatmeal, a bagel, or a smoothie for breakfast. She said that she usually has a sandwich or leftovers for lunch but sometimes misses lunch due to parenting demands. When that happens, she reported having more snacks (chips, fruit, granola bars) while she gives snacks to her children. She said that dinner is typically a family affair and that she plans a well-rounded meal (e.g., meat, starch, vegetables), though she is often distracted from eating because she is focused on getting her children to eat. She described her diet as "overall averagely healthy, but a bit sporadic due to the stresses of parenting."

Elimination: No concerns in this area.

Technology: Julia reported 1–2 hours per day of phone use, plus 1–2 hours of television viewing in the evenings with her husband. She said that she also watches 2–3 hours of television with her children.

Physical Activity: Julia described herself as "always on the go" but said that she rarely has dedicated time to work out and only gets to the gym about once a month.

Substance Use/Abuse: Julia reported drinking wine daily with dinner and in the evenings. She denied any other substance use.

Pain: 1/10 Julia reported mild muscle soreness from typical childcare and household tasks.

Current Psychiatric Symptoms

Depression: Julia reported depressed mood most of the day nearly every day, as well as irritability with her spouse and children. She said that she often feels unmotivated and does not enjoy most activities. She reported feeling fatigued nearly every day and has difficulty getting to sleep about half of each night. She reported feeling guilt about her ability to be a mother while feeling depressed and feeling like the things she does do not matter. She reported passive suicidal ideation but denied having a method or plan.

Anxiety: Julia reported feeling irritable most days, which she attributed to her fatigue, low mood, and the stresses of being a stay-at-home mother. She said that she will feel "stressed" by everything she has to do but denied feeling worried or anxious.

Panic: Julia reported no symptoms of panic.

Mania: Julia reported no symptoms of mania.

Psychosis: Julia reported no symptoms of psychosis.

Trauma: Julia denied any trauma history.

Eating Disorder: Julia reported no history of an eating disorder.

Risky Behaviors/Sexual Activity: Julia denied engaging in any risky behaviors.

Mental Status Exam

Appearance: Julia was dressed casually with appropriate hygiene.

Behavior: Julia was cooperative and engaged. She expressed some hesitancy about engaging in the therapeutic process due to it being outside her cultural norms.

Speech: Rate, articulation, volume, and coherence were all within normal limits.

Mood: Julia reported feeling depressed.

Affect: Julia's affect was congruent with her mood.

Thought Process: Julia's thought process was logical and linear.

Thought Content: Julia expressed passive suicidal ideation, no homicidal ideation, no auditory or visual hallucinations.

Orientation: Julia was oriented to person, place, and time.

Recent Memory: Julia's recent memory was intact.

Remote Memory: Julia's remote memory was intact.

Attention/Concentration: Julia did not demonstrate any deficits in attention or concentration.

General Knowledge: Julia's general knowledge was average.

Language: Julia's language was within normal.

Insight: Julia demonstrated good insight.

Judgment: Julia demonstrated good judgment.

Answer Key #1

Diversity Considerations

Julia has multiple intersecting identities that are having a cumulative effect on her expectations for herself and her subsequent feeling of failing to meet those expectations. Julia's Asian American background may include high standards for success and accomplishment, leading to a drive for perfectionism. The American standards for women and mothers also set a high standard for parenting and perfectionism, which leads to increased stress and anxiety for mothers (Henderson et al., 2016).

Ethical Considerations

Julia's suicidal ideation needs to be monitored closely and hospitalization considered if ideation becomes more severe.

It is essential that the clinician approach this case with curiosity and cultural humility to help Julia explore the role that her intersecting cultural expectations have played in how she views herself, her children, and her role as a mother. The clinician should be careful to make sure that their own cultural expectations and biases are not imposed upon Julia, either explicitly or implicitly. Treatment interventions should also be culturally sensitive and appropriate for an Asian American woman (Hall & Eap, 2007). Developing a strong working alliance is also important for overcoming any mistrust of therapy that Julia may have (Su-Kibricht, et al., 2024).

Legal Considerations

No relevant legal considerations.

Diagnostic Impressions and Justification

F32.1 Major Depressive Disorder, Moderate, Single Episode.

Julia reports depressed mood most of the day more days than not, loss of motivation and interest, insomnia, fatigue, feelings of guilt and worthlessness, and suicidal thoughts. These symptoms have been present for more than two weeks and are causing an impairment in functioning. Her symptoms are not attributable to substance use or a medical condition, and they are not better explained by another mental disorder. She has never had a manic or hypomanic episode.

Psychodynamic Case Conceptualization

Julia seems to be driven by an unconscious desire and expectation for perfection for herself as a mother. This has led to her developing an inferiority complex which she defends against by overcompensating and trying to meet all the possible expectations of a perfect mother (Abramson, 2015; Berezyuk et al., 2023).

Psychodynamic treatment would focus on exploring Julia's feelings of guilt, worthlessness, and inferiority to bring them into her conscious awareness by challenging her resistances and defenses and facilitating her expression of emotions. Julia's experiences of her own mother and childhood, which shaped her early attachment styles, are likely also shaping the expectations she has for herself as a mother and the ways that she parents her children (Jones et al., 2015). Gaining insight into her interpersonal patterns (e.g., with her mother, her partner, and her children) and how they impact her depression can help Julia alter some of those patterns.

Specific psychodynamic interventions could potentially include interpreting Julia's self-critical thoughts as internalized parental expectations as well as exploring the possibility that her passive suicidal ideation represents unconscious aggression turned inward toward herself. The clinician could also utilize both transference and countertransference to explore relational patterns and help Julia develop insight into both past and present interpersonal dynamics. Additionally, it might be helpful for the clinician to help Julia identify the defense mechanisms in which she engages, such as reaction formation and displacement. All psychodynamic interventions should, of course, be implemented within the context of a safe and consistent holding environment.

Cognitive Behavioral Conceptualization

Julia appears to be struggling with distorted beliefs related to accomplishments as a mother, as well as a core schema of "I must be perfect." These distortions cause her to downplay and discount the things she does, and her core schema holds her to an impossible standard that she is unable to meet.

The ultimate goal would be to help Julia restructure her inner cognitive world to be more balanced with less negative bias.

Julia's negative self-talk and rumination can be tracked with the use of a thought record, and her cognitive distortions and core schemas can be challenged with the use of a positive data log (Persons et al., 2001). These same cognitive techniques can also be used to explore and challenge Julia's thoughts of suicidal ideation, and a safety plan can help her implement alternative behaviors when she experiences suicidal ideation. In addition to her negative thinking, Julia also has fewer opportunities to engage in potentially enjoyable activities that might serve to counteract her low mood; activity scheduling and behavioral activation can help Julia have more opportunities to have positive experiences. Mindfulness activities (such as meditation, relaxation, present moment awareness, etc.) can also be helpful, but should be tailored to Julia's cultural background (Hall et al., 2011).

Biopsychosocial Conceptualization

Julia's depressive symptoms are accompanied by neurochemical changes that can be addressed by medication; she should consult with her doctor about the possibility of beginning an antidepressant medication. Although antidepressant medication is effective for many individuals (Cipriani et al., 2018) there are also concerns about potential side effects and adverse events from antidepressants (Jakobsen et al., 2020). Unhealthy behaviors related to exercise, sleep, and alcohol consumption also contribute to Julia's depressive symptoms as well as decreasing her overall health. Engaging in a regular exercise routine, utilizing appropriate sleep hygiene for better sleep, and decreasing her alcohol consumption will likely all have a positive impact on Julia's depressive symptoms as well as increasing her overall health. Exercise, in particular, has been shown to have a significant positive effect on decreasing depressive symptoms (Heissel et al., 2023). An increasing body of research is also highlighting the role of nutrition in the depressive process (Yeum et al., 2019); a focus on regular, nutritionally balanced meals will increase Julia's overall health and may also have a positive impact on her depressive symptoms. Additionally, Julia's depressive symptoms are maintained by a lack of engagement with her social support system, with a relative lack of involvement by her husband in childcare, a somewhat contentious relationship with her mother, and a lack of regular contact with friends for socializing.

Treatment goals grounded in the biopsychosocial approach include improving sleep hygiene, promoting nutritional stability, and decreasing alcohol use. Increasing physical activity would also be helpful for both mitigating symptoms of depression and supporting adequate sleep. Overall, Julia would benefit from improving symptoms of depression while increasing her repertoire of adaptive coping skills. She may also benefit from engaging in activities she deems meaningful.

To improve Juila's sleep, the clinician can encourage her to consistently go to bed and wake up at the same times each day while also implementing interventions designed to support sleep onset, such as relaxation training. A referral to a registered dietitian may be helpful in addressing difficulties around diet and nutrition while a referral to Alcoholics Anonymous (AA) may provide the support needed to reduce alcohol use. Using behavioral activation strategies, the clinician can support Julia in increasing her overall physical activity such as by taking daily walks or engaging in a local exercise class. To more directly address symptoms of depression, the clinician can implement interventions taken from CBT, such as challenging cognitive distortions. Clinical interventions taken from dialectal behavior therapy (DBT) as well as mindfulness-based stress reduction (MBSR) would also be helpful in improving both symptoms of depression and Julia's overall ability to maintain emotional and behavioral regulation. Julia may additionally benefit from engaging with former friends or colleagues, or by creating new opportunities for social engagement, such as by joining local parenting groups or attending community events with her husband and children. Finally, Julia may wish to engage in some form of volunteer work she finds meaningful. These ways of helping Julia engage more with her support system, both through recreational activities with her friends and her husband, as well as material support with childrearing duties, will also likely help reduce Julia's depressive symptoms.

Clinical Case Vignette #2

Demographic Information and History

Name: Aubriela Garcia.

Demographic Information: 12-year-old White Hispanic female.

Medical Diagnoses: None.

Reason for Referral: Aubriela's parents have brought her to therapy because of a recent drop in grades and withdrawal from the family. The mom also discovered that Aubriela had been engaging in self-harm (cutting). Aubriela stated that she only did that twice. Aubriela's parents reported that her symptoms started about three months ago, shortly after she started seventh grade. While previously she had been receiving mostly As with some Bs, her grades were all now Ds or Fs. Aubriela said that the reason her grades were low was because she does not finish her classwork and has trouble paying attention in class "because it's boring" and because she felt "tired" all the time. Aubriela had previously played the flute in the school band but had dropped out at the beginning of seventh grade. Aubriela reported that she liked to draw but had not done so recently. Aubriela's parents reported that Aubriela has become less engaged with the family – for example, not talking at dinner, not playing with her younger siblings, and expressing disinterest in joining family activities. They also reported that she seems to be spending less time talking to friends and seldom talks about her friends. Aubriela reported that she only has one "real" friend, though she used to have more. Aubriela's parents noted that she has become more irritable lately and often argues with her siblings and her parents. They also observed that she seems to be eating less than she used to, though they're not sure why.

Clinical Interview Data

Interpreter Used: No.

Current Psychosocial Stressors: Aubriela reported that two of her close friends moved away over the summer before seventh grade.

Protective Factors: Aubriela's parents reported that their family has typically been close and have enjoyed doing things together. Aubriela's parents reported that there is no significant conflict in their marriage.

Developmental History: Aubriela's parents reported that Aubriela had met her developmental milestones within normal limits. Aubriela had her first period about five months ago.

Academic History: Aubriela is in seventh grade. Her current grades (Ds and Fs) are a decline from her previous functioning (As and Bs). She does not have an individualized educational plan (IEP) or any identified learning challenges, though she describes social studies and math as being harder classes for her.

Social History: Prior to seventh grade, Aubriela and her parents reported that she had several friends that she would hang out with and talk to regularly. Aubriela reported that two of her closest friends moved away six months ago and she only talks to them occasionally now. She reported having a falling out with another close friend over the summer. She said that she only has one friend now, but they do not talk outside of school because her friend does not have a cell phone.

Household: Aubriela lives at home with her parents, her younger sister (age 9) and younger brother (age 7). Her maternal grandmother provides childcare for her and her siblings after school every day.

Previous Psychiatric History: Aubriela has no previous psychiatric history.

Family Psychiatric History: Parents reported no family psychiatric history.

History of Self-Harm: Aubriela reported that she had engaged in self-harm (cutting) twice after seeing videos about it online. She reported no prior self-harm and denied all suicidal ideation.

Wellness Profile

Sleep: Parents reported that Aubriela's bedtime is 9:00 pm, and they wake her up for school at 6:30 am; on the weekends she is allowed to stay up until 10:00 pm and sleep in until she wakes up (usually around 8:00 am). Aubriela said that she usually falls asleep by 10:00 pm on school nights, though she acknowledged that she "often" stays up later on her phone.

Diet: Parents reported that Aubriela usually has toast or cereal for breakfast, eats the school-provided lunch, has a snack (usually chips) after school, and eats dinner with the family (typically a well-balanced nutritious meal). However, they reported that she sometimes skips breakfast if she is running late and only eats about a third of what she is served for dinner. Aubriela reported that she often does not eat much of the school-provided lunch "because it's gross."

Elimination: No concerns.

Technology: Aubriela has her own cell phone. Prior to the start of her symptoms, Aubriela reported that she primarily used her phone to text and call with her friends, particularly while playing online games together. She reported that now she primarily uses her phone to watch videos, shows, and movies, 4–5 hours per day and 10+ hours per day on weekends.

Physical Activity: Aubriela reported that she has gym every day at school, but she participates at little as possible. Parents reported that she used to play soccer, but stopped when she started middle school, a little over a year ago. Parents reported no regular physical activity now.

Substance Use/Abuse: Aubriela denied any substance use and parents reported no concern regarding substances.

Pain: 0/10.

Current Psychiatric Symptoms

Depression: Aubriela and her parents reported depressed and irritable mood and diminished interest and enjoyment in activities. Aubriela's parents reported an apparent decrease in appetite. Aubriela reported fatigue and trouble focusing.

Anxiety: Aubriela denied any anxiety symptoms.

Panic: Aubriela denied any panic symptoms.

Mania: Aubriela denied any manic or hypomanic symptoms.

Psychosis: Aubriela denied any hallucinations or delusions.

Trauma: Aubriela and her parents denied any experience of trauma.

Eating Disorder: Aubriela's parents denied any evidence of an eating disorder, though they expressed concern about her apparent reduced appetite.

Risky Behaviors/Sexual Activity: Aubriela denied any sexual activity.

Mental Status Exam

Appearance: Aubriela was dressed casually, with appropriate hygiene.

Behavior: Aubriela was cooperative but withdrawn and stated that her parents "were making a big deal out of nothing."

Speech: Aubriela's speech was within normal limits.

Mood: Aubriela reported her mood as "fine" and stated that she usually "didn't really feel anything particularly."

Affect: Aubriela's affect was appropriate.

Thought Process: Aubriela's thought process was logical and linear.

Thought Content: Aubriela denied any suicidal ideation, homicidal ideation, delusions, or hallucinations.

Orientation: Aubriela was oriented to person, place, and time.

Recent Memory: Aubriela's recent memory was intact.

Remote Memory: Aubriela's remote memory was intact.

Attention/Concentration: Aubriela's attention and concentration were intact when she was actively engaged in session, but she appeared to "check out" while her parents were talking.

General Knowledge: Aubriela's general knowledge appeared to be within normal limits.

Language: Aubriela's language was within normal limits.

Insight: Aubriela exhibited relatively poor insight.

Judgment: Aubriela exhibited fair judgment.

Answer Key #2

Diversity Considerations

Aubriela's Hispanic heritage should be considered to the degree she finds it relevant, and treatment should be sensitive to the unique circumstances of Latina adolescents (Hooper et al., 2016). Adolescent females are more at risk for self-harm behavior, and the adolescent online culture related to self-harm behavior needs to be taken into account (Susi et al., 2023).

Ethical Considerations

No ethical considerations other than those noted as also being legal considerations below.

Legal Considerations

Although the parents maintain rights to client records and information, privacy for Aubriela should be encouraged in order to allow her the freedom to fully express herself. However, Aubriela should be aware that in questions of self-harm or other risky behavior, parents will be informed. Aubriela should provide assent to therapy and be aware of the limits of confidentiality (e.g., danger to self or others).

Diagnostic Impressions and Justification

F32.0 Major Depressive Disorder, Mild, Single Episode.
R45.88 Current Non-suicidal Self-Injury.

Aubriela reports having depressed mood (feeling "nothing") and/or irritability most of the day for more days than not, diminished interest and enjoyment in activities, decreased appetite, fatigue, and trouble concentrating. These symptoms are causing impairment in Aubriela's academic functioning and interpersonal relationships. The symptoms are not attributable to substance use or a medical condition and are not better explained by another disorder. Aubriela has not experienced a manic or hypomanic episode. Additionally, Aubriela has engaged in two instances of non-suicidal self-injury (cutting).

Psychodynamic Case Conceptualization

Aubriela appears to be defending herself against the losses of her recent friendships by withdrawing from and devaluing previously valued relationships and activities and shutting off her emotions (Marcacci, 2024); this withdrawal further exacerbates her interpersonal challenges and increases her depressive symptoms (Rudolph et al., 2008). Treatment will focus on increasing Aubriela's insight into her defenses and helping her develop healthier defense mechanisms, as well as enhancing her interpersonal engagement and effectiveness. Aubriela engages in self-harm because she is lacking in developmentally appropriate coping strategies to deal with the loss and the threat to her ego and identity (Gibbons, 2024). Facilitating her expression of emotions and unconscious motivations will help Aubriela develop healthier coping strategies. Additionally, Aubriela appears somewhat resistant to engaging in the therapy process. Resistance is a common focus in psychodynamic approaches (Abbass, 2015) and working through the resistance will be essential in order to help Aubriela engage successfully in treatment.

Appropriate psychodynamic treatment goals include strengthening Aubriela's ego functioning in order to help her improve her ability to tolerate difficult affective states without needing to resort to maladaptive coping strategies. Aubriela would likely also benefit from increased insight into any internal conflicts she may be experiencing as well as increased insight into any internalized self-criticism. Overall, it would be helpful for Aubriela to improve her affective identification and articulation skills so that she can better understand and integrate the various aspects of her emerging identity.

Psychodynamic interventions suitable for Aubriela should be grounded in a safe and consistent therapeutic environment. Transference dynamics should be interpreted, but carefully and in a developmentally appropriate manner, given her age. Similarly, exploring and interpreting the defenses in which Aubriela engages would be helpful, but, again, should be done in a developmentally appropriate manner. Because of her age, the clinician may want to consider the appropriateness of utilizing either play therapy or art therapy, but such a determination would need to be made based on Aubriela's preferences as well as her developmental stage (i.e., still playing with dolls and other toys or preferring talk therapy).

Cognitive Behavioral Conceptualization

Aubriela may be struggling with some negative core schemas as a result of the recent loss of her friends, such as the belief that relationships are unpredictable and unstable, or the belief that she is isolated from others, or that she is unlovable. As a result, she likely experiences several cognitive distortions related to interpersonal relationships, such as overgeneralization, mental filtering, catastrophizing, and discounting the positive. Aubriela's self-harm is an attempt to cope with the negative emotions that result from her negative cognitions.

A main focus of therapy will be restructuring her negative and distorted cognitions.

Her cognitive distortions and core schemas can be challenged with the use of a positive data log (Persons et al., 2001). Additionally, behavioral activation and activity scheduling can be used to help Aubriela intentionally engage with potentially enjoyable activities, including socializing with friends and family. Mindfulness-based approaches (e.g., relaxation, meditation, present-moment awareness, etc.) show promise as treatments for adolescent depression (Ćavar et al., 2025; K et al., 2025) In addition to cognitive restructuring of thoughts related to self-harm, the clinician should develop a safety plan to help Aubriela activate coping skills and engage in alternative self-regulation behaviors.

Biopsychosocial Conceptualization

Aubriela's depressive symptoms are accompanied by neurochemical changes that can be addressed by medication. Aubriela and her parents should consult with her physician regarding the possibility of beginning antidepressant medication. The research is mixed regarding the efficacy of antidepressants in adolescents, with some concerns about side effects and adverse events (Cipriani et al., 2016; Zhang et al., 2025). Aubriela's symptoms are primarily caused by the loss of her social network. Unhealthy behaviors such as poor nutrition, too much screentime, and lack of exercise contribute to her depressive symptoms. Though there is some debate, excessive screentime has generally been associated with decreased mental health, particularly if there is increased social media usage (Santos et al., 2023).

Appropriate treatment goals grounded in the biopsychosocial model include improving sleep as well as nutritional intake, especially given that poor sleep and poor nutritional intake can negatively impact both mental health and overall growth and development. Two additional goals that can also contribute to Aubriela's achieving both these goals are reducing screentime and increasing physical activity. It may also be helpful to support Aubriela in improving her ability to identify and articulate affective states. Of note, maintaining safety should be a priority through all steps of psychotherapy. Improving social support should also be incorporated as a treatment goal as social withdrawal is both a symptom of depression and a maintaining factor.

Treatment can utilize social skills training to help Aubriela expand and enhance her social connections (Nilsen et al., 2013). An increasing body of research is highlighting the role of nutrition in the depressive process (Yeum et al., 2019); a focus on regular, nutritionally balanced meals will increase Aubriela's overall health and may also have a positive impact on her depressive symptoms. Reducing screentime may have a direct positive effect on Aubriela's depressive symptoms but will also allow her time to take part in more actively engaging and social activities. Exercise has been shown to reduce depressive symptoms in adolescents (Wang et al., 2022) and should be a part of Aubriela's treatment plan. Improving sleep hygiene in adolescents is also an effective strategy in reducing depressive symptoms (Thibault et al., 2024). A comprehensive safety plan should also be implemented to support maintaining safety. Of note, because eating disorders can sometimes emerge during pre-adolescence and adolescence, the clinician may want to regularly monitor for potentially emerging symptoms.

Clinical Case Vignette #3

Demographic Information and History

Name: Richard Highsmith.

Demographic Information: 70-year-old Caucasian male.

Medical Diagnoses: Richard has been diagnosed with hypertension and Type II diabetes, as well as mild arthritis.

Reason for Referral: Richard reported that he has struggled with depression "since adolescence," but his symptoms have worsened since his retirement six months ago. Richard reported that he sleeps 12 or more hours per day, rarely leaves the house, and spends most of the day watching television or browsing the internet. Richard reported having a low mood most of the time. He said that he gets little enjoyment out of his hobbies (reading, playing the piano, and working in his garden) and often feels unmotivated to do activities. Richard denied suicidal ideation but acknowledged thinking often about death.

Clinical Interview Data

Interpreter Used: No.

Current Psychosocial Stressors: Richard recently retired from his job of 40 years. He reported that his wife still works, and they do not have any financial concerns.

Protective Factors: Richard is intelligent and educated. He reported that he has a good relationship with his wife. He reported that he regularly attends church and a small Bible study group. Playing the piano has been a source of enjoyment and some fulfillment in the past, though he said he has been playing less often in the last few months.

Developmental History: Richard reported no significant challenges in his developmental history.

Academic History: Richard reported having a master's degree in his chosen field. He said that he had often considered pursuing a doctoral degree but had never followed through on the plan due to self-doubt about his abilities. The lack of a doctoral degree held him back from promotion at his university, where he was an untenured lecturer for his whole career. Richard reported that he disliked teaching, but didn't think he could do anything else in his field without a doctorate.

Social History: Richard reported having casual friends at the university where he worked, but that he has not kept in touch with them since retiring. He said that he attends church and Bible study but is not a very active participant. He reported that he and his wife have a few couple friends that they have dinner with once or twice a week. Richard's mother is deceased, his father and two sisters live in another state. He reported that he sees them about once a year and talks to them occasionally.

Household: Richard lives with his wife (age 62) of 35 years. He has a stepson from his wife's first marriage; the stepson lives and works in another country. Richard and his wife were not able to have children.

Previous Psychiatric History: Richard reported that he has previously been diagnosed with major depressive disorder and has attended therapy multiple times, with minimal success.

Family Psychiatric History: Richard reported that his mother struggled with depression, and he had an uncle who he believed had schizophrenia, though it was never discussed openly in the family.

History of Self-Harm: Richard reported no history of self-harm or suicidal ideation.

Wellness Profile

Sleep: Richard reported that he falls asleep around midnight, typically sleeps until early afternoon, and when he wakes up he feels sluggish. He denied taking naps and said he does not have difficulty falling asleep.

Diet: Richard reported that he typically only eats one meal a day (dinner), with some snacking. He said that his dinner is typically a relatively balanced and healthy meal because his wife cooks, but he eats unhealthy snacks (e.g., chips, cookies, etc.).

Elimination: No concerns in this area.

Technology: Richard reported that he spends most of his day watching television or browsing the internet. He said that he likes to watch documentaries and sports; he reads news articles about current events and his academic topic of interest.

Physical Activity: Richard reported that he will occasionally take walks with his wife but generally engages in minimal physical activity.

Substance Use/Abuse: Richard reported that he will have an occasional glass of wine with dinner or one to two beers while watching sports. Richard reported no other substance use history.

Pain: 3/10 due to arthritis.

Current Psychiatric Symptoms

Depression: Richard reported depressed mood most days. He said that he doesn't enjoy his hobbies and finds himself less motivated to do things, often because he feels "tired." Richard reported getting 12+ hours of sleep per night. He reported that he ruminates often over what he feels was a failed career and struggles with feelings of worthlessness.

Anxiety: Richard reported some worry about whether or not he would ever be able to not feel depressed and be able to enjoy life.

Panic: Richard reported no panic symptoms.

Mania: Richard reported no symptoms of mania or hypomania.

Psychosis: Richard reported no symptoms of psychosis.

Trauma: Richard reported no history of trauma.

Eating Disorder: Richard reported that he is overweight but said that he has no motivation to try to lose weight, though it has been recommended by his doctor.

Risky Behaviors/Sexual Activity: Richard reported no risky behaviors.

Mental Status Exam

Appearance: Dress was appropriate and casual. Hygiene and grooming were appropriate.

Behavior: Richard was cooperative and engaged.

Speech: Richard spoke somewhat slowly, with pauses between sentences.

Mood: Richard reported his mood as depressed and hopeless.

Affect: Richard presented with flat affect.

Thought Process: Richard's thought process was logical and linear.

Thought Content: Richard's thought content was appropriate.

Orientation: Richard was oriented to person, place, and time.

Recent Memory: Richard's recent memory was intact.

Remote Memory: Richard's remote memory was intact.

Attention/Concentration: Richard did not demonstrate any deficits in attention or concentration.

General Knowledge: Richard's general knowledge was above average, and his knowledge in his academic domain was above average.

Language: Richard's language was within normal limits.

Insight: Richard demonstrated fair insight.

Judgment: Richard demonstrated fair judgment.

Answer Key #3

Diversity Considerations

Richard's spiritual and religious beliefs and community should be considered as possible sources of support. Spiritually integrated psychotherapy has been shown to be an effective therapeutic approach for clients from Christian backgrounds (de Abreu Costa & Rosmarin, 2021; Koenig & Pearce, 2021). Consideration should also be given to Richard's stage of life as an older man who is retired after several decades working in his chosen field.

Ethical Considerations

While Richard is not currently presenting with suicidal ideation, the possibility of suicidal ideation should always be monitored in clients with depression. Ethical practice also requires that Richard's diversity considerations be incorporated into treatment to the degree he requests.

Legal Considerations

None at this time.

Diagnostic Impressions and Justification

F34.1 Persistent Depressive Disorder.

Richard reports having a depressed mood for most of the day, more days than not, for more than 2 years. He reports hypersomnia, low self-esteem, and feelings of hopelessness. Richard reported that he has never been without these symptoms for more than two months at a time. Richard denied ever having a manic or hypomanic episode. Richard's symptoms are not better explained by another disorder and are not attributable to a substance or another medical condition. He is experiencing significant impairments in his quality of life.

Psychodynamic Case Conceptualization

Richard appears to be experiencing an inferiority complex stemming from lack of success early in his career (Abramson, 2015; Berezyuk et al., 2023). He compensated with the defense of withdrawal and refusal to engage. This caused him to avoid potential challenges (like pursuing a doctorate), which further deepened his sense of self-doubt and inferiority. His recent retirement has enabled him to withdraw even further and become more entrenched in his defenses. Treatment will focus on helping Richard gain insight into his defenses and avoidance and provide interpretations of his withdrawal and resistance. Richard's inability to father a child may also contribute to his sense of inferiority. His relationships with significant others in his life (e.g., mother, father, and wife) may also either exacerbate or diminish his sense of inferiority. Exploration of these interpersonal dynamics, as well as the interpersonal transference with the therapist, may ameliorate aspects of his depressive symptoms (Lemma et al., 2024).

Appropriate treatment goals grounded in psychodynamic theory include increasing Richard's insight into what appear to be longstanding internal conflicts associated with self-worth and both personal and professional identity.

This would include addressing maladaptive defense mechanisms potentially contributing to some emotional numbing as well as social disengagement. Finally, the clinician may want to include strengthening ego function as a treatment goal.

Exploring Richard's early childhood experiences may support him in learning how to articulate the relationship between his past experiences and current emotional states. It would also be appropriate to utilize interpretations to enhance his understanding of the way in which he may use intellectualization, repression, etc., to protect himself against feelings of shame and inadequacy. Interpretations can also be utilized to understand transference dynamics and their relevance to Richard's interpersonal way of being. Because there may be some grief associated with Richard's retirement as well as some potential loss of identity stemming from the retirement, offering the opportunity to work through these affective experiences would be important. Allowing Richard the opportunity to process through the cognitions and emotions associated with this unique life stage may ultimately facilitate the development of a more cohesive sense of self as well as the emergence of hope and potentially new directions for this period of his life.

Cognitive Behavioral Conceptualization

Richard appears to hold a core schema of "I'm not good enough," which leads to distorted beliefs about himself and those around him. Richard engages in a significant amount of negative self-talk and rumination regarding his self-doubt and feelings of hopelessness. Richard's lack of engagement with the world around him holds him back from experiencing potentially pleasurable activities, and when he does have those opportunities, his distorted thinking leads him to discount any positive feedback.

The ultimate goal is to help Richard restructure his inner cognitive world and his core schemas. His negative self-talk and rumination can be tracked with the use of a thought record, and his cognitive distortions and core schemas can be challenged with the use of a positive data log (Persons et al., 2001). Activity scheduling and behavioral activation can help Richard have more opportunities to have positive experiences of himself and others, while cognitive challenging can help restructure his automatic negative thoughts.

Biopsychosocial Conceptualization

Richard's depressive symptoms are accompanied by possible neurochemical changes and/or neural circuity abnormalities. Unhealthy behaviors related to exercise, sleep, and nutrition also contribute to Richard's depressive symptoms as well as decreasing his overall health.

Appropriate treatment goals grounded in the biopsychosocial model include improving Richard's sleep while supporting compliance to the diet and medical regimen that would best support both his psychological and physiological health. Increasing the amount of physical activity in which he is engaging daily would also be an appropriate goal as would mitigating symptoms of depression.

Medication in combination with psychotherapy can be successful for individuals with persistent depressive disorder (Kriston et al., 2014), while neuromodulation strategies such as electroconvulsive therapy (ECT), deep brain stimulation (DBS), vagus nerve stimulation (VNS), and transcranial magnetic stimulation (TMS) are highly successful treatments for treatment resistant depression (Conroy & Holtzheimer, 2021). Engaging in a regular exercise routine, utilizing appropriate sleep hygiene for better sleep, and improving his eating habits will likely all have a positive impact on Richard's depressive symptoms as well as increasing his overall health. Exercise in particular has been shown to have a significant positive effect on decreasing depressive symptoms (Heissel et al., 2023). An increasing body of research is also highlighting the role of nutrition in the depressive process (Yeum et al., 2019). Exercise and nutrition are of particular importance for Richard's health because of his hypertension, Type II diabetes, obesity, and arthritis. Richard's lack of connection with his support system further exacerbates symptoms. Planning regular times for socializing, including engagement with his religious community and practices, may help alleviate some of Richard's depressive symptoms.

Conclusion

Depressive disorders, as they are defined in the DSM-5-TR, are characterized by affective, cognitive, and somatic symptoms that impair functioning across multiple domains and cause distress, generally negatively impacting quality of life. While depressive disorders differ in terms of onset and duration of symptoms as well as severity, patient cognitions, affective states, and physiological presentations are all impacted. The clinical case vignettes provided in this chapter serve to demonstrate the manifestation of MDD and persistent depressive disorder across the lifespan, specifically, adolescence, adulthood, and late adulthood. When applying psychodynamic theory to such cases, conceptualization can include how unresolved internal conflict, maladaptive relational patterns, and difficult internalized states can contribute to the development of depressive symptoms. CBT can elucidate the manner in which cognitive distortions, underlying schemas, and maladaptive behaviors can both cause and maintain symptoms of depression. The biopsychosocial model, in its turn, can contribute relevant information regarding underlying neurobiological vulnerabilities as well as information pertaining to environmental and social stressors. By utilizing the information gleaned through accurate case conceptualization, regardless of the theoretical orientation used, clinicians can better support patients with depressive disorders in achieving meaningful recovery.

References

Abbass, A. (2015). *Reaching through resistance: Advanced psychotherapy techniques*. Seven Leaves Press.

Abramson, Z. (2015). The meaning of neurosis according to Adler. *The Journal of Individual Psychology*, *71*(4), 426–439. https://doi.org/10.1353/jip.2015.0036.

APA (American Psychiatric Association). (2022). *Diagnostic and statistical manual of mental disorders* (5th ed., text rev.). American Psychiatric Association.

Berezyuk, O., Filts, O., Hrabchak, V., & Sirko, R. (2023). The phenomenon of inferiority and depression. *Proceedings of the Shevchenko Scientific Society. Medical Sciences*, *2*(72). https://doi.org/10.25040/ntsh.

Ćavar, F., Mihić, J., & Milas, G. (2025). Exploring the effects of mindfulness on adolescent depression – Findings from a longitudinal study. *Healthcare*, *13*(8), 906. https://doi.org/10.3390/healthcare13080906.

Cipriani, A., Furukawa, T. A., Salanti, G., Chaimani, A., Atkinson, L. Z., Ogawa, Y., Leucht, S., Ruhe, H. G., Turner, E. H., Higgins, J. P. T., Egger, M., Takeshima, N., Hayasaka, Y., Imai, H., Shinohara, K., Tajika, A., Ioannidis, J. P. A., & Geddes, J. R. (2018). Comparative efficacy and acceptability of 21 antidepressant drugs for the acute treatment of adults with major depressive disorder: A systematic review and network meta-analysis. *The Lancet*, *391*(10128), 1357–1366. https://doi.org/10.1016/S0140-6736(17)32802-7.

Cipriani, A., Zhou, X., Del Giovane, C., Hetrick, S. E., Qin, B., Whittington, C., Coghill, D., Zhang, Y., Hazell, P., Leucht, S., Cuijpers, P., Pu, J., Cohen, D., Ravindran, A. V., Liu, Y., Michael, K. D., Yang, L., Liu, L., & Xie, P. (2016). Comparative efficacy and tolerability of antidepressants for major depressive disorder in children and adolescents: A network meta-analysis. *The Lancet*, *388*(10047), 881–890. https://doi.org/10.1016/S0140-6736(16)30385-3.

Conroy, S. K., & Holtzheimer, P. E. (2021). Neuromodulation strategies for the treatment of depression. *American Journal of Psychiatry*, *178*(12), 1082–1088. https://doi.org/10.1176/appi.ajp.2021.21101034.

de Abreu Costa, M., & Rosmarin, D. H. (2021). Spiritually integrated psychotherapy. In A. Moreira-Almeida, B. P. Mosqueiro, & D. Bhugra (Eds.), *Spirituality and mental health across cultures*. Oxford University Press.

Gibbons, R. (2024). The psychodynamics of self-harm. *British Journal of Psychiatry: Advances in Psychiatric Treatment*, 1–9. https://doi.org/10.1192/bja.2024.68.

Hall, G. C. N., & Eap, S. (2007). Empirically supported therapies for Asian Americans. In F. T. L. Leong, A. Ebreo, L. Kinoshita, A. G. Inman, L. H. Yang, & M. Fu (Eds.), *Handbook of Asian American psychology* (2nd ed.). Sage.

Hall, G. C. N., Hong, J. J., Zane, N. W. S., & Meyer, O. L. (2011). Culturally competent treatment for Asian Americans: The relevance of mindfulness and acceptance-based psychotherapies. *Clinical Psychology: Science and Practice*, *18*(3), 215–231. https://doi.org/10.1111/j.1468-2850.2011.01253.x.

Heissel, A., Heinen, D., Brokmeier, L. L., Skarabis, N., Kangas, M., Vancampfort, D., Stubbs, B., Firth, J., Ward, P. B., Rosenbaum, S., Hallgren, M., & Schuch, F. (2023). Exercise as medicine for depressive symptoms? A systematic review and meta-analysis with meta-regression. *British Journal of Sports Medicine*, *57*(16), 1049–1057. https://doi.org/10.1136/bjsports-2022-106282.

Henderson, A., Harmon, S., & Newman, H. (2016). The price mothers pay, even when they are not buying it: Mental health consequences of idealized motherhood. *Sex Roles*, *74*, 512–526. https://doi.org/10.1007/s11199-015-0534-5.

Hooper, L. M., Mier-Chairez, J., Mugoya, G. C. T., & Arellano, B. (2016). Depressive symptoms, assessments, and treatment in Latino/a adolescents: A brief review. *Current Psychiatry Reviews*, *12*(2), 150–162. https://doi.org/10.2174/15734005126661606 02114446.

Jakobsen, J. C., Gluud, C., & Kirsch, I. (2020) Should antidepressants be used for major depressive disorder? *BMJ Evidence-Based Medicine*, *25*(4), 130. https://doi.org/10.1136/bmjebm-2019-111238.

Jones, J. D., Cassidy, J., & Shaver, P. R. (2015). Adult attachment style and parenting. In J.A. Simpson & W.S. Rholes (Eds.), *Attachment theory and research: New directions and emerging themes* (pp. 234–260). Guilford.

K, J., K, N. R., Ashok, L., Manjula, M., J J, T. E., Mathias, E. G., & Krishnan, P. (2025). Mindfulness-based interventions for enhancing adolescent mental health and well-being: A scoping review. *Clinical Epidemiology and Global Health*, *32*, 101961. https://doi.org/10.1016/j.cegh.2025.101961.

Koenig, H. G., & Pearce, M. (2021). Christian-integrated psychotherapy. In J. R. Peteet, H. S. Moffic, A. Hankir, & H. G. Koenig (Eds.), *Christianity and psychiatry*. Springer. https://doi.org/10.1007/978-3-030-80854-9_13.

Kriston, L., von Wolff, A., Westphal, A., Hölzel, L. P., & Härter, M. (2014). Efficacy and acceptability of acute treatments for persistent depressive disorder: A network meta-analysis. *Depression and Anxiety*, *31*(8), 621–630. https://doi.org/10.1002/da.22236.

Lemma, A., Hepworth, M., Fonagy, P., Abrahams, D., & Luyten, P. (2024). *Brief dynamic interpersonal therapy: A clinician's guide* (2nd ed.). Oxford University Press.

Marcacci, T. (2024). Social withdrawal in adolescence: Psychodynamic reflections and clinical strategies. In R. Cassorla & S. Flechner (Eds.), *The astonishing adolescent upheaval in psychoanalysis*. Routledge.

Nilsen, W., Karevold, E., Roysamb, E., Gustavson, K., & Mathiesen, K. S. (2013). Social skills and depressive symptoms across adolescence: Social support as a mediator in girls versus boys. *Journal of Adolescence*, *36*(1), 11–20. https://doi.org/10.1016/j.adolescence.2012.08.005.

Persons, J. B., Davidson, J., & Tompkins, M. A. (2001). *Essential components of cognitive-behavior therapy for depression*. American Psychological Association.

Rudolph, K. D., Flynn, M., & Abaied, J. L. (2008). A developmental perspective on interpersonal theories of youth depression. In J. R. Z. Abela & B. L. Hankin (Eds.), *Handbook of depression in children and adolescents* (pp. 79–109). Guilford.

Santos, R. M. S., Mendes, C. G., Sen Bressani, G. Y., de Alcantara Ventura, S., de Almeida Nogueria, Y. J., de Miranda, D. M., & Romano-Silva, M. A. (2023). The associations between screen time and mental health in adolescents: A systematic review. *BMC Psychology*, *11*, Article 127. https://doi.org/10.1186/s40359-023-01166-7.

Su-Kibricht, L. P., Chen, H.-M., Guo, S., & Miller, R. B. (2024). Towards culturally sensitive care: Addressing challenges in Asian and Asian American mental health services. *Contemporary Family Therapy: An International Journal*, *47*, 202–215. https://doi.org/10.1007/s10591-024-09716-w.

Susi, K., Glover-Ford, F., Stewart, A., Bevis, R. K., & Hawton, K. (2023). Research review: Viewing self-harm images on the internet and social media platforms: Systematic review of the impact and associated psychological mechanisms. *The Journal of Child Psychology and Psychiatry*, *64*(8), 1115–1139. https://doi.org/10.1111/jcpp.13754.

Thibault, D., Derouin, A., Cain, L. A., Thibault, N. E., & Roberts, J. (2024). Sleep hygiene education as a treatment for depression in adolescents. *The Journal for Nurse Practitioners*, *20*(8), 105114. https://doi.org/10.1016/j.nurpra.2024.105114.

Wang, X., Cai, Z., Jiang, W., Fang, Y., Sun, W., & Wang, X. (2022). Systematic review and meta-analysis of the effects of exercise on depression in adolescents. *Child and Adolescent Psychiatry and Mental Health*, *16*, Article 16. https://doi.org/10.1186/s13034-022-00453-2.

Yeum, T.-S., Maggiolo, N. S., Gupta, C. T., Davis, B. J., Nierenberg, A. A., & Sylvia, L. G. (2019). Adjunctive nutrition therapy for depression. *Psychiatric Annals*, *49*(1), 21–25. https://doi.org/10.3928/00485713-20181205-02.

Zhang, Y., Gao, Y., Li, X., Zou, Y., Ye, Y., & Zou, Z. (2025). Antidepressant treatment of depression in children and adolescents: A systematic review and dose-response meta-analysis. *European Child and Adolescent Psychiatry*. https://doi.org/10.1007/s00787-025-02688-8.

Chapter 5

Anxiety Disorders

Lindsay Gonzalez

As a group, anxiety disorders are characterized by fear that is considered to be out of proportion to a patient's current situation, or excessive, and related emotional and behavioral symptoms. The DSM-5-TR includes several anxiety disorders, such as generalized anxiety disorder, social anxiety disorder, panic disorder, separation anxiety disorder, selective mutism, specific phobia, and agoraphobia (APA, 2022). While each anxiety disorder is distinct from the others, there is overlap in terms of symptom presentation and often include features such as worry and hypervigilance. Anxiety disorders are also known to frequently cause somatic distress, such as muscle tension. Anxiety disorders, as a group, constitute some of the most commonly diagnosed disorders in the DSM-5-TR. This chapter will provide clinical case vignettes related to generalized anxiety disorder, social anxiety disorder, and panic disorder.

Generalized anxiety disorder, commonly referred to as GAD, is characterized by persistent and excessive worry about a variety of issues and is typically accompanied by somatic symptoms such as fatigue and muscle tension as well as restlessness, difficulty concentrating, irritability, and sleep disturbance (APA, 2022). GAD's distinguishing feature is that it is not specific to any one item, experience, or situation but, rather, is pervasive across multiple settings, with the anxiety caused by a wide variety of stimuli.

Social anxiety disorder is more specific than GAD and specifically has to do with the intense fear of being scrutinized by others in social situations (APA, 2022). Individuals with social anxiety disorder often struggle to engage in typical social situations such as eating out in public but also struggle with more situationally specific tasks such as public speaking. To meet DSM-5-TR diagnostic criteria for social anxiety disorder, the actual fear experienced by the patient must be out of proportion to the actual danger or risk present in the situation and lead to avoidance behaviors or significant distress. Social anxiety disorder often first manifests in adolescence.

Panic disorder involves recurrent panic attacks, which are defined as sudden unexpected surges of intense fear (APA, 2022). Panic attacks involve both

DOI: 10.4324/9781003586531-6

cognitive and somatic symptoms, sometimes to the degree of causing a patient to feel as though a medical emergency is imminent. This is largely because symptoms of panic attack can include chest pain, heart palpitations, sweating, and dizziness (APA, 2022), which can cause one to feel as though a heart attack is imminent. Additional symptoms of a panic attack include derealization, fear of losing control, and/or fear of dying (APA, 2022). To meet DSM-5-TR diagnostic criteria for panic disorder (as opposed to an individual simply reporting having had a panic attack), at least one of the panic attacks experienced by the individual has to be followed by at least a month of persistent concern regarding experiencing additional panic attacks or maladaptive behaviors related to the panic attacks, such as avoiding potential stimuli.

Clinical Case Vignette #1

Demographic Information and History

Name: Anais Cortez.

Demographic Information: 24-year-old Mexican-American female.

Medical Diagnoses: None.

Reason for Referral: Anais self-referred for therapy because of her daily anxiety surrounding her performance at work, her health, and her father's health. Anais reported that each day of the week she has several episodes of racing thoughts that are distressing and distracting. She has a difficult time making the thoughts go away and has noticed that they are interfering with her abilities to get tasks done at work. Outside of work, Anais has noticed that anxious thoughts have kept her from enjoying social outings with friends and family. In extreme cases, worries about having anxiety have kept Anais from leaving the house at all. In addition to the distressing thoughts, she experiences muscle tension, sweating, chest pain, and shortness of breath during episodes of anxiety. Anais reported that she did not experience anxiety to this extent until around nine months ago when she started her first job after completing her bachelor's degree.

Clinical Interview Data

Interpreter Used: No.

Current Psychosocial Stressors: Anais had just taken on a new role at work that increased her responsibilities and overall workload. Anais's father has a history of cancer and is currently enduring medical concerns. He is scheduled to have an upcoming surgery in the next month. Anais herself has current medical concerns in that her red blood cell count was significantly higher than the normal range. She is currently attending various medical appointments to get answers about the causes and impacts.

Protective Factors: Anais identifies as a Christian. She finds her faith a source of relief and comfort during moments of emotional distress, especially her anxiety. Anais served as a volunteer at her church for various community events in the past but does not currently work as one. She has intentions about getting back into volunteering but worries that her anxiety will prevent her from being able to handle the role.

Developmental History: Anais reported meeting all her developmental milestones.

Academic History: Anais earned her bachelor's degree in business. She reported maintaining good grades throughout high school and college. While in high school, she was a student athlete on the swim team.

Social History: Anais has a couple of friends from high school and college who she sees every few months. She spends most of her social time with her siblings and cousins. Anais reported that when anxiety was not a problem, she would see her cousins several times a month. Anais also reported that she has a strong relationship with both her parents.

Household: Anais has two older siblings, one brother and one sister. She currently lives at home with her mother and father.

Previous Psychiatric History: No previous psychiatric history.

Family Psychiatric History: No family psychiatric history.

History of Self-Harm: No history of self-harm.

Assessment Data

Anais completed the Beck Anxiety Inventory (BAI) at the start of treatment. She received a total score of 42, which falls within the "severe levels of anxiety" range.

Wellness Profile

Sleep: Anais reported that she sporadically has insomnia when her anxiety is more elevated than typical. She indicated that she gets between 6 and 8 hours of sleep a night the majority of the time.

Diet: Anais reported that she eats three meals a day and does her best to eat balanced meals. She has snacks throughout the workday. Anais noted that she is exploring potential dietary changes once she gets feedback from her doctor about her high red blood cell count.

Technology: Anais reported that she has difficulty not checking her phone for work emails when she is out of the office, during vacation time, and on sick days. She denied any concerns surrounding other media and technology consumption.

Physical Activity: Anais reported that she tries to take walks after work at least three times a week. She noted that as her anxiety has intensified, she has become too fatigued after work to meet her walking goal.

Substance Use/Abuse: Anais denied past or current substance use.

Pain: Anais denied at complaints of pain.

Current Psychiatric Symptoms

Depression: Anais reported that she sometimes feels depressed about how severe her anxiety has gotten in recent months. She noted that it is not very often that she feels sad but has certain days where her anxiety makes her feel depleted and hopeless about the future.

Anxiety: Anais has recurrent worries about her performance at work. She endures racing thoughts about completing tasks correctly, how she sounds in emails, how she engages with her colleagues, and, overall, how she is perceived by others. Anais's episodes of racing anxious thoughts at work are generally accompanied by chest pains, shortness of breath, and sweating. In recent weeks, the anxious episodes have impacted Anais's ability to focus and complete tasks in a timely manner. In addition to work-related anxiety, Anais also reported recurring thoughts about the health of her father and herself. With her father's upcoming surgery, she finds herself getting into a "spiraling" pattern where she cannot stop the worried thoughts of the worst possible outcomes. Similarly, she endures the spiraling pattern when she becomes anxious about her own current health concerns. Anais has difficulty making the negative thoughts stop or go away. Additionally, she frequently worries about having anxiety while out with her cousins or when doing errands alone. She has anxious thoughts about how others might perceive her, which often leads her to avoid leaving the house.

Panic: Anais reported no symptoms of panic.

Mania: Anais reported no symptoms of mania or hypomania.

Psychosis: Anais reported no symptoms of psychosis.

Trauma: Anais reported no history of trauma.

Eating Disorder: Anais reported no symptoms of an eating disorder.

Risky Behaviors/Sexual Activity: Anais denied engaging in any risky behaviors.

Mental Status Exam

Appearance: Anais was dressed appropriately.

Behavior: Anais was cooperative and eager to participate.

Speech: Anais's speech was normal.

Mood: Anais described her mood as "nervous."

Affect: Anais's affect was congruent and appropriate.

Thought Process: Anais's thought process was logical and linear.

Thought Content: Anais denied suicidal ideation, homicidal ideation, delusions, or hallucinations.

Orientation: Anais was oriented to person, place, and time.

Recent Memory: Anais's recent memory was intact.

Remote Memory: Anais's remote memory was intact.

Attention/Concentration: Anais had sufficient attention and concentration.

General Knowledge: Anais's general knowledge was within normal limits.

Language: Anais's language was within normal limits

Insight: Anais demonstrated good insight.

Judgment: Anais demonstrated good judgment.

Answer Key #1

Diversity Considerations

Conceptualization and interventions should take into consideration the impact of Anais's Mexican-American heritage. Of note, because Anais specifically identifies as Mexican-American (not just Mexican and not just American, but both), it may be important to include an understanding of acculturative stress, which, for bicultural individuals, does include heightened experiences of anxiety, especially when there is conflict around expectations associated with work and family (Torres et al., 2012). It may be that Anais does not experience such tension but because she reported anxiety around both work and issues developing within her family, at least exploring the possibility would be recommended. Additionally, because Anais is, specifically, a Mexican-American woman, she may be struggling to navigate expectations regarding being both high-achieving and self-sacrificing, which can increase distress in Hispanic women (Cianelli et al., 2008). This is of note, because members of Hispanic communities often view mental health issues and mental health-related help-seeking behaviors, such as attending psychotherapy, with a certain amount of stigma. It may be important to evaluate any anxiety Anais might report regarding presenting for an intake session and whether not she will feel pressure to hide her participation in psychotherapy from her parents with whom she lives.

While in some cultures leaving home once the age of majority has been achieved is considered normative, in Hispanic families, many children continue to live with their parents, even after they begin working full-time. While Anais living at home might be representative of socioeconomic pressures, she may also simply be living with them because that is the custom in her culture. There may be both protective and difficult aspects of this living situation, especially if there are strong generational differences present between herself and her parents. Additionally, because family is often viewed as a key value in Mexican-American culture, it is important not to overpathologize Anais's worries and concerns regarding the health of her father.

Interventions should also consider the influence of Anais's faith as a source of coping.

Legal Considerations

There are no specific legal considerations related to this case.

Diagnostic Impressions and Justification

F41.1 Generalized Anxiety Disorder.

Anais has been experiencing excessive worry and anxiety on a daily basis for the past 9 months. Her anxiety is related to a number of different activities such as work performance, social situations, and the health of herself and others. Her anxiety and worry have caused significant distress in various settings, such as work and personal life. These symptoms are not attributable to any medical condition, substance use, or another mental disorder.

Psychodynamic Case Conceptualization

Anais's racing thoughts and physical symptoms of anxiety arise from internal conflicts between unacceptable unconscious wishes and the ego's efforts to repress or manage them. Her anxiety serves as a signal that these impulses are threatening to break into consciousness, further maintaining her distress. She may have, at some point, internalized a working model in which her value is contingent upon aspects of her behavioral presentation, such as meeting high expectations. It is interesting to note that Anais's symptoms emerged after she began her first job out of college, as beginning a first full-time job is often considered a milestone in adulthood. That her anxiety emerged at such a time might indicate that her internal conflicts specifically stem from unresolved issues related to autonomy and individuation, which become even more interesting to consider with the context of Anais's culture. Additionally, Anais appears to present with neurotic-level defenses such as intellectualization, overthinking, reaction formation, and projection, all of which are common in patients presenting with anxiety disorders (Vaillant, 1992).

Appropriate psychodynamic goals related to Anais's case include improving insight into internal conflicts, strengthening her observing ego, and improving her ability to articulate her affective experience. Addressing and modifying maladaptive defense mechanisms may also support Anais in replacing the intellectualization in which she currently engages with more adaptive coping strategies. Additionally, psychodynamic psychotherapy can support Anais in developing a more coherent and stable sense of self. For some patients, supporting individuation and differentiation from the family system might be an appropriate goal but given Anais's cultural background, additional consideration would need to be given to whether or not supporting such a goal would, specifically, be appropriate for her.

The general context of most psychodynamic care is free association, which refers to the patient's ability to set the agenda for each session, freely sharing their thoughts and feelings associated with their emotional needs. Free association within the context of a supportive therapeutic relationship can improve Anais's ability to be aware of her thoughts and feelings without becoming overwhelmed by them. Interpretation can be utilized when providing psychodynamic care to both highlight unconscious conflicts related to Anais's symptoms of anxiety while also exploring unfolding relational patterns. The use of interpretation as well as supportive confrontation may also support Anais in improving insight surrounding the defenses she currently deploys to avoid becoming overwhelmed by her affective state. Another clinical intervention associated with psychodynamic psychotherapy involves specifically interpreting transference reactions to both improve Anais's insight into her relational patterns and early caregiver relationships and also provide her with a corrective emotional experience.

Cognitive Behavioral Conceptualization

Anais experiences distressing cognitive distortions about the self, others, and the future. Her anxious thoughts often surround her competence at work, being judged by others, and her health. Collectively, her distortions and maladaptive behaviors maintain her anxious distress specifically because they shape her interpretations of daily events. Anais's work environment, home life, and social environments fuel her anxious thoughts. As a response, she often uses distraction and isolating at home to cope, which, in the moment, likely provides a brief respite but ultimately reinforces the notion that she is unable to tolerate anxiety.

Goals appropriate to CBT treatment include reducing the frequency and intensity of Anais's symptoms, improving overall emotional regulation, and increasing engagement in meaningful activities.

General psychoeducation regarding anxiety as well as the multidirectional relationship between cognitions, emotions, and behaviors would serve as an appropriate intervention. Use of a thought log or mood tracker, or a combination of the two, may help Anais to understand the relationship between her cognitions and her affective experiences. An emotions wheel or other visual tool could support Anais in learning the vocabulary needed to express her emotions, while strength-based exercises such as utilizing affirmations could help her develop a stronger and more resilient sense of self. Interventions incorporating mindfulness would support her emotional regulation, as well as simple grounding techniques she can use while at work or in the community. Cognitive structuring could be deployed to help Anais identify cognitive distortions. Behavioral activation can be used to increase Anais's engagement in meaningful activities as well as activities to support her overall mental and physical health. For example, when feeling anxious and overwhelmed, Anais might take a walk instead of isolating in her bedroom. She might also benefit from a lockbox for her phone, to prevent her constantly checking it. Finally, Anais might benefit from role-playing with her clinician to help build confidence for navigating challenging situations both at work and at home.

Biopsychosocial Conceptualization

Anais's generalized anxiety symptoms could be attributed to dysregulation of certain neurotransmitters such as serotonin, GABA, and norepinephrine, which can contribute to heightened anxiety. Additionally, she recently received irregular blood work results but there is no information available regarding why her results were abnormal. There could be an underlying medical issue contributing to her presentation and, even if there is not an underlying medical condition, the stress associated with not knowing the etiology for the elevated red blood cell count is likely affecting her. Anais reported pervasive distressing thoughts including cognitive distortions that are exacerbating both her psychological and physiological symptoms. Additionally, environmental factors such as health concerns within the family, work stress, and pressure to be successful may also play a role in elevating her experiences of anxiety. Additional stress could be coming from her recent transition into full-time employment.

Treatment goals grounded in the biopsychosocial model include reducing symptoms of anxiety, improving physical health, and increasing social support. The clinician may also want to support Anais in developing greater insight into the causes of her distress, including the role that major life transitions can play in exacerbating psychiatric symptoms.

Anais would likely benefit from clinical interventions to improve both her cognitive symptoms of anxiety and her somatic symptoms of anxiety. Mindfulness-based strategies would be appropriate to improve her symptoms. She should also be referred to a primary care provider and possibly a hematologist to discuss the abnormal results she received after her most recent blood draw. If cleared by a medical professional, Anais could be encouraged to engage in regular physical activity, as physical activity not only improves physical health but also serves as a protective factor when a patient is experiencing stress, regardless of the source of that stress. Interventions based in CBT would be helpful to address Anais's symptoms of anxiety, as would interventions stemming from solution-focused therapy. Because Anais has the tendency to isolate herself when overwhelmed, she may feel as though she is lacking much-needed social support. From a biopsychosocial perspective, it would be appropriate for the clinician to encourage her to connect and/or reconnect with family and friends and even to increase her participation in church activities, as long as the responsibilities of involvement do not become too overwhelming for her. Because Anais reported her faith to be a source of strength, religiously integrated interventions might be appropriate for use during the course of psychotherapy.

Clinical Case Vignette #2

Demographic Information and History

Name: Chris Turner.

Demographic Information: 37-year-old Caucasian male.

Medical Diagnoses: None.

Reason for Referral: Chris was referred to an intensive outpatient therapy program (IOP) by his primary psychotherapist because of depressive symptoms and elevated anxiety in social situations. Chris said that he stopped going to his taekwondo classes around 2 months ago after he started having anxious episodes during class. Chris reported that he began experiencing intrusive thoughts about embarrassing himself in front of his peers, having an anxiety attack during the class, and ultimately being judged. Chris said that in addition to the intrusive thoughts, he also endured sweatiness of the palms, chest pains, shortness of breath, and stomach aches. Shortly after the anxiety started occurring in his classes, Chris had an anxiety attack at class on one particular day in which his sparring partner asked him repeatedly if he was okay. Chris stated that he ended up leaving the class early and has not returned since. He stated that he felt a lot of shame and embarrassment about the situation and worried about another attack happening if he were to return to class. Additionally, Chris had started experiencing the same anxiety symptoms during work, resulting in a temporary leave of absence to participate in IOP treatment. Chris reported that he experienced similar anxiety symptoms during high school, but that they seemed to decrease during his years in college.

Clinical Interview Data

Interpreter Used: No.

Current Psychosocial Stressors: Chris is currently on leave of absence from work due to mental health concerns. He reported feeling anxious and shameful about having to step away from work to receive a higher level of treatment.

Protective Factors: Chris has a strong support system including his wife, brother, and friends. Chris reported that all his loved ones have been very supportive in his treatment journey. He utilizes his supports to help regulation anxiety, expressing himself, and receiving reassurance.

Developmental History: Chris reported meeting all his developmental milestones within normal limits.

Academic History: Chris earned a bachelor's degree in communications. He currently works in customer service for an appliance company.

Social History: Chris reported he spends the majority of his time with his wife. Additionally, he is close with his brother and frequently visits old friends (with whom he was in a band previously).

Household: Chris lives with his wife and dog.

Previous Psychiatric History: Chris reported previous depression and anxiety during adolescence, but he did not receive any formal diagnosis during that time. Chris began individual psychotherapy for the first time around six months ago.

Family Psychiatric History: No family psychiatric history.

History of Self-Harm: Chris has a history of self-harm by cutting. He reported engaging in cutting behaviors during high school.

Assessment Data

Chris completed the Beck Depression Inventory (BDI) and the BAI at the start of treatment. He received total scores of 17 and 51, respectively. His scores fall within the "mild depression" and "severe levels of anxiety" ranges.

Wellness Profile

Sleep: Chris denied any difficulties with sleep. He gets between 6 and 8 hours of sleep per night.

Diet: Chris reported that he regularly eats three balanced meals a day and some snacks.

Elimination: Nothing to report.

Technology: Chris reported that he frequently uses his phone as a coping and distraction tool whenever he is out in public and begins feeling anxious. He stated that being on his phone makes him feel more comfortable and less worried about what others might be thinking of him.

Physical Activity: Chris reported that his activity levels decreased significantly since leaving his taekwondo classes. He takes his dog on walks each morning.

Substance Use/Abuse: Chris denied past or current substance use.

Pain: 3/10. Chris reported more pain in the chest when he is experiencing an episode of anxiety.

Current Psychiatric Symptoms

Depression: Chris reported that he recently has become more depressed as a result of his struggle with anxiety. Chris stated that he often feels ashamed, sad, and hopeless when he thinks about how intense his anxiety has gotten. Chris feels particularly down about being afraid to return to his taekwondo classes, leaving work temporarily, and needing a higher level of care.

Anxiety: Chris reported that he worries on a daily basis about having anxiety in public spaces. When he is out doing errands or socializing in public, he experiences recurring intrusive thoughts about being judged, doing something embarrassing, and people noticing his anxiety. He frequently worries about people noticing his shakiness or sweaty hands. Prior to his leave from work, he often endured racing thoughts about how his co-workers did not like him or enjoy talking with him.

Panic: Chris reported no symptoms of panic.

Mania: Chris reported no symptoms of mania or hypomania.

Psychosis: Chris reported no symptoms of psychosis.

Trauma: Chris reported no history of trauma.

Eating Disorder: Chris reported no symptoms of an eating disorder.

Risky Behaviors/Sexual Activity: Chris denied engaging in any risky behaviors.

Mental Status Exam

Appearance: Chris was dressed appropriately.

Behavior: Chris was cooperative.

Speech: Chris's speech was soft spoken.

Mood: Chris described his mood as "uneasy."

Affect: Chris's affect was congruent.

Thought Process: Chris's thought process was logical and linear.

Thought Content: Chris denied suicidal ideation, homicidal ideation, delusions, or hallucinations.

Orientation: Chris was oriented to person, place, and time.

Recent Memory: Chris's recent memory was intact.

Remote Memory: Chris's remote memory was intact.

Attention/Concentration: Chris had sufficient attention and concentration.

General Knowledge: Chris's general knowledge was within normal limits.

Language: Chris's language was within normal limits.

Insight: Chris demonstrated good insight.

Judgment: Chris demonstrated good judgment.

Answer Key #2

Diversity Considerations

Interventions for Chris should consider the influence of masculinity norms associated with Western culture; it is worth asking Chris directly how he experiences mental health struggles as a cisgender male. It would also likely be beneficial to discuss professional identity with him, given that he had to step away from work, as well as how his family, friends, and colleague have responded to him being a man receiving treatment for anxiety.

Ethical Considerations

While it does not appear, based on the information provided, that Chris is participating in an IOP program related to his employer or at the request of his employer, clinicians would want to keep in mind that, if his employer is somehow involved in the psychotherapy process, appropriate information regarding their involvement would need to be included in the informed consent process and all relevant releases of information would need to be signed. Similarly, because Chris has an individual psychotherapist and has enrolled in the IOP program as an adjunct to his individual psychotherapy sessions, the informed consent process and any relevant releases of information would need to be modified if Chris would like his psychotherapist to be updated regarding treatment or if he would like his psychotherapist to provide information to the IOP program. While such communication would likely facilitate more comprehensive and continuous care, Chris would have to give permission for any such communication to occur. As an additional note, because Chris is now enrolled in an IOP program, which likely includes group therapy, clinicians should be sure to provide him, as well as other members of the group, with the informed consent information specific to group therapy settings, including the additional limits to privacy and confidentiality since clinicians are not able to control what group members share outside of the group.

Because Chris presents with a history of self-harm, clinicians would need to regularly evaluate for self-harm and suicidal ideations as well as self-harm behaviors, implementing a safety plan as needed and appropriate.

Legal Considerations

Because Chris is on leave from work specifically because of mental health concerns, the Family and Medical Leave Act (FMLA) may apply to his situation. It may be beneficial for the clinicians to remind him to speak with his human resources department at work, in the event that they are able to support him with additional considerations or resources.

Diagnostic Impressions and Justification

F40.10 Social Anxiety Disorder.

Chris experiences recurrent worry and anxiety about being in social situations where he is exposed to possible scrutiny or judgment by others. This anxiety occurs when having conversations with colleagues at work, during taekwondo classes, and being out in public by himself. Chris's anxiety has created significant disturbance resulting in him being on temporary leave from work, unable to go out in public comfortably, and unable to return to his taekwondo classes. These symptoms are not attributable to any medical condition, substance use, or another mental disorder.

Psychodynamic Case Conceptualization

Chris's anxiety in social settings is driven by unconscious feelings of shame, or a deep belief that he is inherently flawed or unacceptable. This could be attributed to a harsh critical inner voice (superego) formed from internalized parental or authority figures. As a response, Chris engages in self-monitoring and self-judgment in social interactions, creating intense anxiety about how he is being perceived. His history of engaging in self-harm behaviors does seem to suggest a pattern of internalized aggression as well as a longstanding history of difficulties with emotional and behavioral dysregulation that, while seemingly in remission for a prolonged period, have now re-emerged. Chris's overall anxiety in social situations, especially social situations where he may be exposed to scrutiny, reveals a potential internal conflict between his longing for approval and his fear of exposure or humiliation.

Appropriate treatment goals grounded in psychodynamic theory would include helping Chris develop insights into the unconscious conflicts contributing to his symptoms of anxiety as well as improving his ego function and emotional regulation. Part of this process would include helping Chris identify any internalized critical objects so he can work through them in later stages of therapy. It may also be worthwhile to help Chris repair any disruptions he has experienced to his (potentially) previously cohesive self. Another appropriate goal based in psychodynamic theory would be to help Chris modify any maladaptive defenses in which he may be engaging such as avoidance and distraction; there is evidence of some of these maladaptive defenses.

Interpretation, a classical psychodynamic intervention, can be utilized to support Chris in exploring the symbolic nature of his anxiety as well as the distressing cognitions associated with his anxiety. Interpretation could also eventually support Chris in recognizing his phone use as a maladaptive form of coping, i.e., avoidance of an affective experience that might otherwise feel overwhelming. Providing Chris with empathic and reflective listening, for the purpose of improving his own affective articulation skills, would also be helpful. The clinician could also support Chris in identifying repetitive relational patterns from his early childhood as well as high school and connect them to present experiences to better understand the grander relational themes of his life.

Cognitive Behavioral Conceptualization

According to CBT, Chris Turner's psychological suffering can best be explained by the interplay of physiological response, behavioral avoidance, and maladaptive thought patterns, all of which contribute to an ongoing cycle of anxiety and despair. Chris's presentation has become so severe that it seriously impairs his ability to function at his job, interact with others, and engage in worthwhile activities like taekwondo. In addition to contributing to a subsequent decline in mood, his cognitive and behavioral reactions to events that cause worry serve to reinforce his symptoms. Given that Chris has experienced a sudden revival of his likely basic schemas of vulnerability and social rejection, it seems possible they were never fully addressed and may have stayed latent until provoked by current circumstances. These maladaptive thoughts lead to somatic sensations like tightness in the chest, sweaty hands, and gastrointestinal distress, as well as strong emotional and physical responses like shame, anxiety, and anticipatory dread. Chris responds by avoiding his overwhelming emotional responses by using his phone in public places. Chris's symptoms are likely also being maintained by his disengagement from pursuits he finds meaningful.

Appropriate CBT-related treatment goals for Chris include identifying and reducing maladaptive automatic thoughts as well as overall psychological and physiological symptoms of anxiety. As therapy progresses, Chris may also benefit from gaining insight into the schemas that are underlying his overall presentation. Ultimately, the goal of CBT, like the vast majority of psychotherapy interventions, is to reduce distress *and* improve functioning; one of the goals of CBT would be to have Chris return to work as well as to the taekwondo classes he used to enjoy.

Thought records and Socratic questioning can be utilized to increase Chris's awareness of his automatic thoughts and how they are affecting him. Chris would likely benefit from learning mindfulness-based adaptive coping strategies. Exposure therapy, either completed in vivo or completed in person, might help desensitize Christ to the anxiety he experiences in social situations. Such an intervention could begin by first having Chris develop a fear hierarchy and then supporting him in progressing through it, from least anxiety-producing situation to most anxiety-producing situation. Behavioral experiments may also support Chris in working toward his goal of reducing psychological and physiological symptoms associated with anxiety. Once Chris has reached the point of being able to explore and articulate the schemas underlying his overall psychopathology, the downward arrow technique could prove useful. Self-compassion exercises and daily affirmations may also be helpful in rebuilding Chris self-esteem. Many of the interventions listed up until this point would support Chris in both returning to work and returning to the leisure activities he enjoys, but additional support for these goals could be implemented in the form of role plays as well as assertiveness training.

Biopsychosocial Conceptualization

Chris's social anxiety may be due to overactivity in the amygdala, which can cause heightened fear responses to social evaluation. It may also be attributed to neurochemical imbalances within serotonin and dopamine systems, which could impair emotion regulation and social reward processing. Chris's symptoms of anxiety are causing behavioral changes that are further exacerbating his symptoms as well as robbing him of the protective activities he previously enjoyed, such as taekwondo. Social isolation is a known risk factor for depression and anxiety maintenance (Cacioppo & Cacioppo, 2014) and so the bidirectional relationship between his distress and his behaviors is only worsening both. Cognitive distortions are likely contributing to his overall presentation, including his symptoms of depression, which is especially concerning given his history of self-harm. It is also important to note that Chris is likely not sleeping enough.

Treatment goals grounded in the biopsychosocial approach include reducing both psychological and physiological symptoms of anxiety while increasing physical activity to support both mental and physical health. Specifically, it seems reasonable to have Chris re-engage in his taekwondo classes, given how meaningful they were to him previously. An additional therapeutic goal appropriate for the biopsychosocial approach would be to support Chris in returning to work.

Mindfulness-based interventions such as diaphragmatic breathing and progressive muscle relaxation may be helpful for Chris, given that they can help reduce autonomic arousal. Additionally, other mindfulness-based interventions, such as the loving-kindness meditation may support Chris in reducing feelings of shame. Clinicians can encourage Chris to re-engage in his taekwondo classes and, if he presents as hesitant or resistant, implement motivational interviewing to explore his hesitations and engage him in change talk. Cognitive restricting would also be helpful in addressing the cognitive distortions contributing to his symptoms of anxiety. Thought records can be deployed in the service of this intervention to help improve Chris's insight into just how affected he likely is by these automatic thoughts. Similar to CBT, a fear hierarchy can be utilized to gradually expose Chris to anxiety-provoking situations. If Chris is amenable and gives permission, clinicians can collaborate with either his human resources department or his direct supervisor to implement a return-to-work plan that incorporates gradual exposure with adaptive coping strategies to help re-acclimate him to the work environment.

Clinical Case Vignette #3

Demographic Information and History

Name: Cassandra Daniels.

Demographic Information: 19-year-old African American bisexual female.

Medical Diagnoses: None.

Reason for Referral: Cassandra was referred to a partial hospitalization program (PHP) by her primary care provider due to complaints of panic attacks. Cassandra stated that in the past year she started having panic attacks increasingly. At one point, she reported having brief panic attacks each week for about 2 months straight. Cassandra stated that during attacks, she typically experiences rapid heart rate and palpitations, shortness of breath, chest pain, sweating, lost sense of control, and sometimes trembling or shaking. Once her panic attacks started becoming more frequent, Cassandra started falling behind in her college courses. She became unable to complete assignments and eventually stopped going to classes altogether due to fears of having panic attacks in front of her classmates. She is currently on a temporary leave from school due to the state of her mental health.

Clinical Interview Data

Interpreter Used: No.

Current Psychosocial Stressors: Cassandra has currently taken a temporary leave of absence from her university due to the current state of her mental health. The panic attacks and anxiety symptoms started interfering with her ability to attend classes and keep up with coursework. Currently, Cassandra feels lost in whether she wants to continue college or not. Not having a clear direction further exacerbates her anxiety symptoms. Cassandra is enrolled in a PHP program using the clinic's scholarship funds due to Cassandra's parents being unsupportive of mental health treatment. Cassandra has not informed her parents directly about receiving mental health treatment at the clinic.

Protective Factors: Cassandra reported that her friends and cousins serve as a strong support system for her. She is able to confide in her supports for comfort during moments of distress and sometimes during the midst of a panic attack. Cassandra also has a dog that she identifies as a source of comfort during moments of panic.

Developmental History: Cassandra reported meeting most of her developmental milestones within normal limits. Cassandra reported that she was delayed in speech and did not start consistently communicating until she was around 2 years old. She stated that her mother talks about how using sign language helped her communicate when she was unable to speak the words herself. Cassandra denied any noticeable issues with speech to date.

Academic History: Cassandra is currently enrolled at a local university with an undeclared major. She is currently on temporary leave due to mental health concerns. She is uncertain whether she wants to continue her education or not.

Social History: Cassandra identified a couple friends and her cousins as her primary support system. At times where her anxiety and panic attacks feel more manageable, Cassandra will go out and socialize with her friends or cousins at weekends. At points where anxiety has been especially difficulty, Cassandra has been unable to leave her house due to fears of having a panic attack.

Household: Cassandra currently lives at home with both parents and a younger brother.

Previous Psychiatric History: Cassandra reported having a couple of free counseling sessions at her university, but stopped going due to lack of motivation.

Family Psychiatric History: Cassandra reported that she believes her mother experienced postpartum depression after giving birth to her younger sibling, but her mother "does not believe in mental health issues." Cassandra stated that she does not observe any depressive symptoms in her mother currently.

History of Self-Harm: No history of self-harm.

Assessment Data to be Included as Needed

Cassandra completed the BDI and the BAI at the start of treatment. She received a total score of 12 and 49, respectively. Her scores fall within the "mild depression" and "severe levels of anxiety" ranges.

Wellness Profile

Sleep: Cassandra reported that she consistently has trouble falling asleep and frequent nights of insomnia due to racing thoughts and worry. After informing her PCP about her sleep difficulties, she was prescribed with trazodone and has not seen much of a difference.

Diet: Cassandra reported that she generally eats three meals a day, but sometimes skips meals when anxiety interferes and creates gastrointestinal issues such as stomach aches and nausea.

Technology: Cassandra reported that, since being off from school, she spends over 10 hours a day on her phone. Her primary activities include texting, scrolling on social media, and watching YouTube videos.

Physical Activity: Cassandra reported that she rarely exercises. She goes on a neighborhood walk around once a month.

Substance Use/Abuse: Cassandra reported that she occasionally smokes marijuana in social settings with friends. She stated that sometimes it eases her anxiety and other times it makes it worse.

Pain: Cassandra denied any pain-related concerns.

Current Psychiatric Symptoms

Depression: Cassandra reported that she experiences anxiety more than depression but acknowledged that she sometimes feels ashamed about her panic attacks. She stated that falling behind in school and being on temporary leave has made her feel sad and insecure, but that she feels stressed more than anything else.

Anxiety: Cassandra experiences worry on a daily basis about having a panic attack. Her anticipation of the "next" panic attack intensifies any time she leaves her house, worrying about what would happen if she experienced an unmanageable panic attack in public. She endures racing thoughts about panic attacks at least once a day.

Panic: Cassandra reports currently having multiple panic attacks each month. At the most elevated time, she reported having panic attacks every week for around two months. Her panic attacks include symptoms of rapid heart rate and palpitations, shortness of breath, chest pain, sweating, lost sense of control, and sometimes trembling. Her panic attacks do not last longer than 10 minutes. She has had panic attacks both at home and in public, but now actively avoids leaving her house as much as possible to prevent having attacks in front of others.

Mania: Cassandra reported no symptoms of mania or hypomania.

Psychosis: Cassandra reported no symptoms of psychosis.

Trauma: When asked about previous traumas, Cassandra reported that when she was in elementary school, she observed her parents arguing and fighting on a regular basis. At one point when Cassandra was around 7 years old, her father left the home for several months. Cassandra's parents never separated and eventually her father returned home. Cassandra's parents have been together since and a similar event has never taken place. Cassandra reported feeling devastated and anxious about her parents getting a divorce during that time. Additionally, she continued to feel anxious whenever her parents argued for years afterward, and she still feels somewhat anxious when she senses tension between her parents.

Eating Disorder: Cassandra reported no symptoms of an eating disorder.

Risky Behaviors/Sexual Activity: Cassandra denied engaging in any risky behaviors.

Mental Status Exam

Appearance: Cassandra was dressed appropriately.

Behavior: Cassandra was cooperative.

Speech: Cassandra's speech was within normal limits.

Mood: Cassandra described her mood as "very anxious."

Affect: Cassandra's affect was congruent.

Thought Process: Cassandra's thought process was logical and linear.

Thought Content: Cassandra denied suicidal ideation, homicidal ideation, delusions, or hallucinations.

Orientation: Cassandra was oriented to person, place, and time.

Recent Memory: Cassandra's recent memory was intact.

Remote Memory: Cassandra's remote memory was intact.

Attention/Concentration: Cassandra appeared distracted by a fidget toy that was on the table. She refrained from using any eye contact.

General Knowledge: Cassandra's general knowledge was within normal limits.

Language: Cassandra's language was within normal limits.

Insight: Cassandra demonstrated good insight.

Judgment: Cassandra demonstrated good judgment.

Answer Key #3

Diversity Considerations

Because Cassandra is 19, she is in a stage of life often referred to "emerging adulthood" or "transitional age youth" where stressors related to independent functioning, individuation, and identity exploration can become increasingly salient. While it is not clear how Cassandra and her family approach these issues, care should be given to the exploration of cultural values related to autonomy, relationships with extended family, etc. Conceptualization and interventions should especially take into account the impact of Cassandra's African American culture, including how Cassandra's family's beliefs toward mental health impact her current experience of treatment. Given that African American patients often experience barriers to accessing culturally congruent, equitable care, including when attempting to address mental health issues (Snowden, 2001), it may be important to explore whether Cassandra experiences her parents' refusal to support her search for services as an additional barrier. Because some African American families report associating mental health issues and seeking mental health services as weakness (Ward et al., 2009), Cassandra may have internalized some of her parents' approach to mental health services in a way that contributes to feelings of shame or isolation.

Because Cassandra is, specifically, a bisexual African American woman, the intersection of these identities may contribute to an internalized sense of invalidation and/or internalized stigma, contributing to her overall presentation and felt distress. While it is not known whether Cassandra has revealed her bisexual identity to her parents, clinicians should take family dynamics around these issues into account, especially if Cassandra is experiencing distress around having to keep such an important part of herself a secret from the family members with whom she lives. This is especially important within the context of her already keeping her enrollment in mental health services a secret.

Ultimately, Cassandra's overall presentation and her reported experiences, cognitions, and feelings must be understood through an intersectional lens that considers her race, gender, sexual orientation, and stage of life as well as whatever other diversity variables may present over the course of treatment to ensure that she is provided with the highest level of care possible (Crenshaw, 1991).

Ethical Considerations

Because Cassandra desires to keep her treatment undisclosed to her parents due to the harm of their mental health beliefs, the clinic had to consider options to make that possible. Going through Cassandra's health insurance was not an effective solution due to her not being the policyholder. Instead, the clinic decided that Cassandra was an appropriate candidate for their scholarship program, which funds certain patients to receive treatment due to various circumstances that prevent them from having financial coverage. Because treatment is being covered by the clinic's scholarship fund, there is an argument to be made for the fact that the clinic must now continue to pay for treatment until termination is clinically and ethically appropriate – treatment should not be discontinued simply because of funding limitations, especially if Cassandra feels unready to terminate treatment.

Legal Considerations

While cannabis is legal in many states and jurisdictions, it remains illegal in others. Adult use of illicit substances does not require a mandated report to any authority, however, Cassandra and clinician should both familiarize themselves with local and state laws related to cannabis use. The clinician should also be sure to provide Cassandra with information regarding the manner in which cannabis can exacerbate anxiety and recommend that she speak with her primary care provider (PCP) regarding any possible interactions between cannabis and her prescribed medication, i.e., trazadone.

Diagnostic Impressions and Justification

F41.0 Panic Disorder.

Cassandra experiences frequent, unexpected panic attacks during which she feels sudden intense fear or discomfort that reaches a peak within a couple of minutes. The symptoms she endures during a panic attack include rapid heart rate and palpitations, shortness of breath, chest pain, sweating, lost sense of control, and sometimes trembling. Cassandra also experiences intense worry about experiencing additional panic attacks, resulting in her inability to attend classes at her university. Due to the impact of her panic attacks and the distress surrounding anticipation of them, she has been placed on a temporary absence from school, is unable to find work, and has been unable to socialize with friends and family. These symptoms are not attributable to any medical condition, substance use, or another mental disorder.

Psychodynamic Case Conceptualization

Beneath Cassandra's recurring experiences of panic exists a fear of ego collapse, or a terror of losing her coherent sense of self. It is probable that Cassandra may have endured early experiences of overwhelming emotion, inconsistent caregiving, or trauma that made her vulnerable to this fear. The panic attacks themselves can be seen as eruptions of intense emotions that Cassandra has not been able to consciously process or symbolize. Cassandra's panic attacks may serve as defenses against deeper fears of rejection or inadequacy (Busch et al., 2009). It is possible that the conflict between Cassandra's parents when she was very young, with the subsequent temporary departure of her father, could have served as a profound disruption to her sense of security, enough for it to become a source of disrupted attachment. Because Cassandra reported that her parents are not supportive of mental health treatment, one can assume that they have historically been unsupportive of anything resembling a mental health issue, which could have caused Cassandra to learn how to repress her emotions even while struggling significantly. Given her now emerging symptoms of panic disorder, it is possible that whatever defenses Cassandra has used throughout her life have become ineffective during this time of increased stressors.

Psychodynamic treatment goals for Cassandra include increasing her awareness of the unconscious conflicts contributing to her distress as well as facilitating exploration of early family dynamics that may have contributed to her current presentation, especially the history of conflict between her parents and her subsequent fear that their marriage would fail. It would also be appropriate to help Cassandra identify and modify the maladaptive defense mechanisms in which she is currently engaging and improve her overall ability to tolerate distressing emotions. Finally, it may be important to support Cassandra in developing a more coherent sense of self.

Treatment interventions grounded in psychodynamic theory include using interpretation to help develop Cassandra insight into the relationship between her panic attacks and possible unconscious fears of abandonment and rejection rooted in early childhood experiences, as well as reflecting on how her early childhood experiences may have shaped her sense of emotional safety as a new adult. The psychodynamic frame would also require the clinician to maintain a safe therapeutic space in which both transference and countertransference could be interpreted and explored to help Cassandra develop insight into relational patterns.

Cognitive Behavioral Conceptualization

From a CBT perspective, it is likely that Cassandra's symptoms are being maintained by a self-reinforcing cycle of cognitive distortions and maladaptive behaviors. Her core beliefs are likely rooted in fears of abandonment as well as invalidation, exacerbated by the new stressors associated with being a college student and emerging adult. Her cognitive distortions regarding the somatic symptoms are likely catastrophic in nature as that is common in panic disorder, thereby leading to avoidance of situations she believes may activate her anxiety enough to cause panic attack. While avoiding such situations may be helpful in the short term, in the long run, it will only reinforce the notion that the environments that trigger her anxiety are actually threatening or dangerous.

CBT treatment goals would include mitigating the cognitive distortions, automatic thoughts and distorted beliefs contributing to Cassandra's distress as well as increasing involvement in meaningful activities that could provide her with a sense of competence and accomplishment. Specifically, re-introducing Cassandra to the academic environment may provide her with a sense of mastery if she is able to return to school successfully.

Cognitive restructuring would be helpful in challenging Cassandra's cognitive distortions as well as the maladaptive beliefs contributing to her presentation, but clinicians must be careful not to invalidate thoughts or feelings that are accurate and appropriate responses to racism or prejudice that she may have experienced as a bisexual African American woman. Psychoeducation would be helpful in providing general information about anxiety and panic attacks as well as more specific information about the cognitive triangle and the bidirectional relationship between the mind and the body. Behavioral activation as well as behavioral experiments could support Cassandra in both reducing the amount of time she is isolating herself from others and creating the opportunity for her to learn that she can engage with the social and academic environment without becoming too overwhelmed to function. Granted, gradual exposure will likely be the key to successful reintegration into these environments and can be guided using a fear hierarchy as well as virtual exposure before moving to in vivo exposure.

Biopsychosocial Conceptualization

While Cassandra presents with uncomfortable physiological symptoms associated with her diagnosis of panic disorder, no other medical history has been reported. Per her report, the trazadone prescribed to her has not been effective in mitigating sleep difficulties, resulting in ongoing difficulties with sleep. Cassandra reported occasionally utilizing cannabis, which is likely exacerbating her symptoms of anxiety, including those associated with her diagnosis of panic disorder (Crippa et al., 2009). Her psychiatric symptoms do appear to be worsening, as she is now on leave from school because of the symptom severity she is experiencing. It is likely she is experiencing cognitive distortions such as catastrophizing, as such cognitive distortions typically present as part of a panic disorder. Additionally, Cassandra is engaging in behavioral avoidance of potentially activating situations. Underlying fears of abandonment and emotional invalidation may also be contributing to her overall presentation given the familial discord she experienced as a young child along with ongoing feelings of invalidation related her family's overall approach to mental health. Cassandra lives with her family, which may be increasing her overall feelings of distress and isolation, as the overall family structure appears rejecting of mental health disorders and services for these disorders. While such an approach to mental health is not uncommon in African American families (Snowden, 2001; Boyd et al., 2011), it is likely contributing to her distress. It is unclear if Cassandra's parents know she is bisexual but if she is having to hide her sexual orientation, such a necessity would likely also negatively impact her. Because Cassandra is on leave from her university, she may be feeling lost and unmoored in comparison to her peers. Additionally, and very concerningly, Cassandra reported excessive technology use and sedentary behaviors. While she may feel that using her phone serves as a method of coping with her distress, so much screen-time, coupled with physical inactivity, is likely worsening her symptoms.

Treatment goals grounded in the biopsychosocial model include reducing the frequency of panic attacks Cassandra is experiencing as well as associated symptoms of anxiety. Additional goals include improving the quantity and quality of her sleep and reducing her cannabis use, even if it is only occasional. Cassandra would also benefit from reducing the amount of time she is spending on her phone and re-engaging with relevant social and academic environments. Increasing social support and working to get appropriate academic accommodations put into place would also be appropriate goals for a clinician utilizing the biopsychosocial model. The clinician may also wish to help Cassandra explore generational and/or cultural differences she has with her parents regarding mental health and maybe even sexuality. Such a goal should only be incorporated, however, if it is consistent with the manner in which Cassandra would like to approach treatment.

Appropriate interventions include providing psychoeducation about the bidirectional relationship between the mind and the body as well as psychoeducation regarding panic disorder and panic attacks. A referral to her PCP, or perhaps a psychiatrist, would be appropriate to address Cassandra's concerns regarding the trazadone she was prescribed, as she reports it is not effective. Speaking with her PCP or a psychiatrist would also provide Cassandra with the opportunity to ask about any possible interactions between the cannabis she utilizes and her prescribed medication. Cassandra would also benefit from mindfulness-based interventions such as diaphragmatic breathing and progressive muscle relaxation. CBTi, a modified form of CBT specifically developed to address symptoms of insomnia, could be helpful in mitigating Cassandra's sleep difficulties. Cassandra may not consider her cannabis use to be problematic as she only uses occasionally; if this is the case, motivational interviewing can be utilized to explore her ambivalence around cannabis use and increase her engagement in change talk. The clinician could also provide Cassandra with psychoeducation regarding the negative effects of screentime, including the manner in which it negatively impacts sleep. Additional exploration of the content Cassandra is consuming may be important, as she may be engaging with anxiety-provoking content. Gradual exposure to the academic environment could also be helpful, paired with relaxation training, to help Cassandra manage distress that might otherwise feel overwhelming. It might also be appropriate to refer Cassandra to her university office for students with disabilities or its equivalent to explore whether the university may be able to provide her with any accommodations. Cassandra may also find additional social support in on-campus groups or clubs. Her university may host a Black Student Union, a lesbian, gay, bisexual. transgender, and queer (LGBTQ+) organization, a club for students interested in mental health issues, etc. Participating in such an activity with supportive peers may help convert the university from an anxiety-provoking stimulus into a place where she can find the support and acceptance she lacks at home. If return to the university remains too overwhelming for Cassandra to attempt, enrollment in online classes may be an option, at least until she is able to return to in-person classes. If Cassandra chooses to incorporate a goal related to discussing mental health and/or her sexual orientation with her family, role-playing may serve as a support. More importantly, the clinician and Cassandra should work together to explore culturally informed strategies to navigate whatever generational or cultural conflicts may arise between Cassandra and her parents.

Conclusion

Anxiety disorders constitute one of the categories of disorders most commonly seen by clinicians due to the number of individuals who struggle with such disorders. As a group, anxiety disorders are categorized by the presence of emotional dysregulation, i.e., fear, and behavioral dysregulation that is objectively out of proportion to the situation that the patient reports. GAD, social anxiety disorder, and panic disorder each present with some distinct symptoms but the symptoms common to each disorder cause functional impairment and/or clinically significant distress. The functional impairment and/or clinically significant distress occur largely because of the maladaptive cognitions and avoidant behaviors that persist across anxiety disorders. The purpose of the clinical case vignettes included in this chapter is to demonstrate the disorders from within the category of anxiety disorders clinicians may be most likely to treat within their various clinical settings. It is only by truly understanding the distress experienced by individuals presenting with anxiety disorders that clinicians can truly provide competent and compassionate care.

References

APA (American Psychiatric Association). (2022). *Diagnostic and statistical manual of mental disorders* (5th ed., text rev.). American Psychiatric Publishing.

Boyd, R. C., Diamond, G. S., & Wintersteen, M. B. (2011). Emotional and behavioral functioning of offspring of African American mothers with depression. *Journal of Child and Adolescent Mental Health*, *23*(4), 259–270.

Busch, F. N., Milrod, B. L., Singer, M. B., & Aronson, A. C. (2009). *Panic-focused psychodynamic psychotherapy extended range: A manual*. Routledge.

Cacioppo, J. T., & Cacioppo, S. (2014). Social relationships and health: The toxic effects of perceived social isolation. *Social and Personality Psychology Compass*, *8*(2), 58–72. https://doi.org/10.1111/spc3.12087.

Cianelli, R., Ferrer, L., & McElmurry, B. J. (2008). Cultural beliefs and mental health treatment among Latinas. *Issues in Mental Health Nursing*, *29*(6), 531–548. https://doi.org/10.1080/01612840802048836.

Crenshaw, K. (1991). Mapping the margins: Intersectionality, identity politics, and violence against women of color. *Stanford Law Review*, *43*(6), 1241–1299.

Crippa, J. A., Zuardi, A. W., Martín-Santos, R., Bhattacharyya, S., Atakan, Z., McGuire, P., & Fusar-Poli, P. (2009). Cannabis and anxiety: A critical review of the evidence. *Human Psychopharmcology: Clinical and Experimental*, *24*(7), 515–523. https://doi.org/10.1002/hup.1048.

Snowden, L. R. (2001). Barriers to effective mental health services for African Americans. *Mental Health Services Research*, *3*(4), 181–187.

Torres, L., Driscoll, M. W., & Voell, M. (2012). Discrimination, acculturation, acculturative stress, and Latino psychological distress: A moderated mediational model. *Cultural Diversity and Ethnic Minority Psychology*, *18*(1), 17–25. https://doi.org/10.1037/a0026710.

Vaillant, G. E. (1992). *Ego mechanisms of defense: A guide for clinicians and researchers*. American Psychiatric Press.

Ward, E. C., Wiltshire, J. C., Detry, M. A., & Brown, R. L. (2009). African American men and women's attitude toward mental illness, perceptions of stigma, and preferred coping behaviors. *Nursing Research*, *58*(3), 185–194.

Chapter 6

Bipolar and Related Disorders

Lauren Elizabeth Ponce

In the DSM-5-TR, the chapter pertaining to bipolar and related disorders outlines a collection of conditions primarily characterized by disturbances in mood and activity levels (APA, 2022). These disorders include episodes of mania or hypomania that alternate with depressive episodes, and which sometimes can present with psychotic features (APA, 2022). Principle diagnoses include bipolar I disorder, bipolar II disorder, and cyclothymic disorder. Clinical case vignettes for bipolar I and bipolar II have been included in this chapter. Diagnostic criteria for bipolar I disorder include the patient having to have experienced at least one manic episode as well as episodes of hypomania or depression (APA, 2022). Diagnostic criteria for bipolar II disorder require that a patient experience at least one hypomanic episode and one depressive episode, but a manic episode does not need to have been experienced (APA, 2022). As is the case with most disorders included in the DSM-5-TR, impairment and/or clinically significant distress must be present, although hypomanic episodes are generally understood to be less impairing than manic episodes.

Characteristics shared across the disorders included in the bipolar and related disorders chapter include mood instability, changes in levels of activity, and disturbances in cognition (APA, 2022). Patients experiencing either mania or hypomania may present with elevated or expansive mood but some patients experiencing mania or hypomania present with increased irritability. It is during episodes of mania and hypomania that patients also present with increased energy levels as well as increased goal-directed activity. Patients experiencing major depressive episodes generally present with sad/low mood, anhedonia, and somatic symptoms (APA, 2022). For patients with particularly salient symptoms of anxiety, psychosis, etc., specifiers can be assigned, including "with anxious distress," "with psychotic features," etc. (APA, 2022). Bipolar disorders typically manifest in late adolescence or early adulthood, with genetic predispositions and environmental factors recognized in playing roles in the development and maintenance of these disorders (APA, 2022).

DOI: 10.4324/9781003586531-7

Clinical Case Vignette #1

Demographic Information and History

Name: Maria Mendoza.

Demographic Information: 25-year-old Hispanic female.

Medical Diagnoses: No relevant medical diagnoses.

Reason for Referral: Maria was referred to the student counseling center for therapy by her roommate, Grace. Grace noticed a change in Maria's baseline behavior over the past three weeks and reported that Maria exhibited an increase in energy levels. Grace expressed concerns about Maria's spending habits and worried Maria would not be able to afford to live on campus. Grace noted that Maria stays up all night and has been skipping classes, which is unusual for her. As a result, Maria is experiencing a decline in school performance.

Clinical Interview Data

Interpreter Used: Interpreter not needed.

Current Psychosocial Stressors: Maria recently moved away from her family to a new state to pursue graduate school.

Protective Factors: Strong academic performance, responsible.

Developmental History: Maria met all developmental milestones.

Academic History: Maria graduated with her bachelor's degree 2 years ago cum laude. She recently began her first semester of graduate school and is in the ninth week of the semester. She skipped classes over the past three weeks and failed to turn in assignments.

Social History: Maria is acquainted with her roommate and two classmates. Lately, Maria has been excessively social with neighbors and anyone with whom she crosses paths. Maria believes people want to talk to her because she is admirable. When conversing with others, she overshares personal information.

Household: Maria lives with one roommate at an apartment near her college. Her parents and brother live in another state.

Previous Psychiatric History: Maria has no prior psychiatric history.

Family Psychiatric History: Maria's father has a diagnosis of bipolar I disorder.

History of Self-Harm: Maria has no history of self-harm or prior suicide attempts. However, she reported having suicidal ideations after moving to college and away from her family.

Wellness Profile

Sleep: Over the past 3 months, Maria has experienced a decreased need for sleep. She reported occasionally not sleeping for 2 days, and when she does sleep, it is for only a few hours.

Diet: Maria reported she often forgets to eat because she is preoccupied with her racing thoughts and various activities.

Elimination: No issues reported.

Technology: Maria reported excessively using the internet for concerning periods of time. She was overspending by donating to various charities and placing multiple online orders for expensive items.

Physical Activity: Maria reported a persistent increase in energy over the past 2 weeks. She felt as if she must always be moving and rarely rested. For instance, she recently started working out and has been spending 3 hours at the gym nearly every day.

Substance Use/Abuse: Maria reported no substance use.

Pain: 0/10.

Current Psychiatric Symptoms

Depression: Maria reported the onset of depressive symptoms about 9 weeks ago but denied current symptoms of depression. Her previous symptoms included anhedonia, insomnia, poor concentration, fatigue, and suicidal thoughts.

Anxiety: Maria reported no symptoms of anxiety.

Panic: Maria reported no symptoms of panic.

Mania: Maria demonstrated symptoms of grandiosity, decreased need for sleep, impulsivity, distractibility, flight of ideas, racing thoughts.

Psychosis: Maria presented with grandiose delusions, disorganized speech.

Trauma: Maria reported emotional trauma in childhood from her father.

Eating Disorder: Maria has been unintentionally restricting meals and eating less often due to distractibility.

Risky Behaviors/Sexual Activity: Maria reported spending large amounts of money online and donating to multiple charities for the past three weeks. No report of risky sexual activity.

Mental Status Exam

Appearance: *Dress*: inappropriate. *Hygiene*: inadequate. Appeared stated age.

Behavior: Guarded, hostile.

Speech: *Rate*: rapid. *Articulation*: within normal limits. *Volume*: loud. *Coherence*: forceful, disorganized.

Mood: Maria reported feeling irritable, increased energy, euphoric.

Affect: Euphoric, inappropriate to content of interview.

Thought Process: Flight of ideas.

Thought Content: Positive for suicidal ideation.

Orientation: Oriented to person, place, situation, and time.

Recent Memory: Intact.

Remote Memory: Intact.

Attention/Concentration: Sufficient, distractible.

General Knowledge: Average.

Language: Disorganized.

Insight: Poor.

Judgment: Poor.

Answer Key #1

Diversity Considerations

The peak age for onset of bipolar I disorder is between 20 and 30 years old (APA, 2022). Since Maria is 25 years old, her age is something to consider when diagnosing her. Environmental factors, such as the stress of being away from family and being in graduate school, should also be considered, including financial stress she may be experiencing as a student and how this might impact her ability to access resources.

Hispanic women are less likely to be diagnosed with bipolar I disorder and are more likely to exhibit depressive symptoms (APA, 2022). The clinician working with Maria should be aware of any biases in the assessment and conceptualization process, as unconscious bias could cause Maria to be mistakenly misdiagnosed with depression due to her prior depressive symptoms. Additionally, given that there is some stigma associated with mental health issues and obtaining mental health treatment within the Hispanic community, the clinician may wish to explore Maria's overall expectations of mental health treatment as well as her affective response. It may also be important to address Maria's overall level of acculturation (i.e., does she identify more with traditional Hispanic values as they manifest in her culture, or does she identify more with mainstream American culture?).

Ethical and Legal Considerations

Since Maria was referred to therapy by her roommate, it is essential to obtain Maria's informed consent, specifically to ensure that she is aware that services are voluntary and confidential, as she may be anxious about how engagement with the counseling center could impact her academic trajectory.

The risk of suicide in those with bipolar I disorder is 20 to 30 times greater than in the general population, and about 5–6 percent die by a completed attempt (APA, 2022). As such, the clinician should be aware of this elevated risk and regularly monitor for suicidal ideation, the results of which may require the implementation of a safety plan, or, if Maria presents with intention, possible psychiatric hospitalization.

Diagnostic Impressions and Justification

F31.11 Bipolar I Disorder, Mild.

Bipolar I disorder involves recurring mood episodes and is diagnosed after the occurrence of a manic episode (APA, 2022). Manic symptoms must be present for at least 1 week, cause marked impairment in social or occupational functioning, and cannot be due to the ingestion of a substance (APA, 2022). Manic episodes are often preceded and followed by a hypomanic or major depressive episode; therefore, there are fluctuations in these mood episodes (APA, 2022).

Maria meets the criteria for a manic episode due to her symptoms of irritable mood and increased energy that occurred for the past 3 weeks, fulfilling Criterion A. Criterion B was met because Maria exhibited a decreased need for sleep, risky behavior due to her increased spending, being more talkative, flight of ideas, and signs of grandiosity. Maria's mood disturbance caused marked impairment in her occupational functioning due to missing school and not submitting assignments, meeting Criterion C. Lastly, Criterion D was met because Maria reported no substance use, and her symptoms were not a result of medication or a medical condition.

In addition to meeting manic episode criteria, Maria met diagnostic requirements for a major depressive episode. A major depressive episode must involve 5 or more depressive symptoms (APA, 2022). These symptoms must be present for at least 2 weeks and cause changes in baseline functioning (APA, 2022). At least one of the symptoms must be a depressed mood or loss of interest or pleasure (APA, 2022).

Maria reported symptoms of depression that occurred 9 weeks prior to the manic symptoms that fulfilled Criterion A for a major depressive episode. These symptoms included anhedonia, insomnia, poor concentration, fatigue, and suicidal thoughts. According to the American Psychiatric Association (APA, 2022), a depressive episode is often the first episode of bipolar I disorder, and its symptoms are the most frequent. Criteria B and D were met because Maria's insomnia impacted her occupational functioning, and her symptoms were not due to substance use or a medical condition. Although Maria is currently experiencing a manic episode, her history of major depressive episode justifies a diagnosis of bipolar I disorder.

Psychodynamic Conceptualization

Psychodynamic theory explains human behavior, including psychopathology, by investigating unconscious influences as well as childhood experiences (Deal, 2007). According to Ingram (2006), childhood experiences impact adult functioning and children who experience neglect, abuse, or mistreatment can grow up with underlying feelings of shame. This could contribute to unresolved internal conflicts as well as difficulty maintaining a stable sense of self. Maria's history of experiencing emotional abuse from her father during her childhood puts her at a higher risk of developing bipolar I disorder (APA, 2022). The mania with which Maria presents could be a defense against feelings of depression and vulnerability that she finds overwhelming.

From a psychodynamic perspective, treatment goals would include helping Maria improve her overall emotional and behavioral dysregulation as well as providing Maria with a reparative relationship. Treatment could also help improve ego strength which could in turn contribute to a more cohesive sense of self across mood states. Additional treatment goals might include increasing insight into defensive patterns and fostering object constancy.

Interventions would include engaging Maria in free association to explore childhood experiences with her father. Transference interpretations would also be utilized as needed to help Maria develop insight into her current behavior (Vandenbos et al., 2014). These transference interpretations may help Maria eventually to identify, explore, and correct relational difficulties stemming from past difficulties from her early caregivers or others (Vandenbos et al., 2014). Of course, maintaining therapeutic rapport throughout would serve as the foundation for providing a reparative relationship. When working with patients who present with bipolar disorder, it is important to modulate treatment so that it corresponds with the patient's affective state.

Cognitive Behavioral Conceptualization

The recent stressor of moving and Maria's interpretation of that stressor may have caused an increase in maladaptive thought patterns, which could be contributing to her emotional and behavioral dysregulation. Specifically, mood-congruent cognitive distortions may be manifesting as alternating symptoms of depression and mania. Additionally, exposure to too much screentime and consistently poor sleep are likely to maintain Maria's emotional and behavioral dysregulation. Her excessive spending is also likely being reinforced by whatever feelings of satisfaction she may be experiencing by donating money to charitable causes. Maria may also have internalized problematic schemas about herself, others, and the world around her.

Treatment goals might include increasing insight into emotional and behavioral patterns as well as establishing and maintaining regular daily routines. It would also be important to support Maria in preventing impulsive actions when in the midst of a manic episode.

Clinical interventions should include reframing dysfunctional thoughts. Additionally, targeting and restructuring negative schemas may help change maladaptive behaviors caused by them (Kazantzis et al., 2018). Clinical interventions should also focus on reducing the behaviors that are maintaining the psychopathology by helping Maria improve her sleep quantity and quality. Mood tracking might be helpful with this. Urge surfing could be taught as a method for managing impulsivity during manic episodes; and other adaptive coping strategies are likely to be helpful. Group cognitive therapy may be valuable once Maria has been stabilized. According to Lam et al. (2005a, 2005b), individuals experienced fewer manic episodes when in group cognitive therapy and developed healthy coping strategies to manage early signs of mania.

Biopsychosocial Conceptualization

Stress, circadian function, cognition, genetics, and environment all play a role in the development of mood disorders (Lugg, 2022). While biological factors can be inherited, environmental circumstances can activate a disorder. For instance, Maria likely has a genetic heritability of bipolar I disorder due to her father's bipolar I disorder diagnosis (APA, 2022). Additionally, Maria experienced a life stressor when she moved away for graduate school and is experiencing a lack of sleep. While Maria may have had a genetic predisposition for developing a bipolar or related disorder, her current stressor and sleep disturbance may have activated the disorder. Furthermore, Barlow

(2008) stated that major life changes can disrupt circadian rhythms, and manic episodes are typically a result of life events that alter sleeping habits (as cited in Malkoff-Schwartz et al., 1998). Cognitive distortions and stress reactivity might also play a role.

Appropriate treatment goals would include promoting medication compliance as well as an appropriate sleep schedule. Increasing Maria's motivation for treatment may also be an appropriate goal. Additionally, the clinician may wish to work towards improving Maria's emotional insight and adaptive coping skills. Managing environmental and social stressors, such as Maria's current distance from her family, would also be indicated.

Maria would benefit, in general, from psychoeducation regarding common triggers and warning signs of both manic and depressive episodes. Additionally, a referral for a medication evaluation would be warranted as there is ample evidence to suggest mood stabilizing medications are helpful for individuals with bipolar and related disorders. Additional intervention would include encouraging Maria to follow a structured schedule that allows for consistent meals throughout the day and adequate sleep. According to Gold and Sylvia (2016), sleep disturbance is common in those with bipolar disorder and has a negative impact on the course of illness. According to Han et al. (2024), electronic use is linked to decreased sleep; therefore, limiting Maria's screentime is essential. Since she reported excessive internet use, reducing screentime, especially 1 hour before bed, may promote better sleep. Maria might also benefit from a referral to a peer support group.

Clinical Case Vignette #2

Demographic Information and History

Name: Maya Collins.

Demographic Information: 26-year-old White female.

Medical Diagnoses: No relevant medical diagnoses.

Reason for Referral: Maya was asked to attend therapy by her co-worker, Melanie. Over the past 2 months, Melanie noticed unusual behaviors in Maya. For example, for 1 month, Maya appeared sad and tearful, lost in thought, had little interest in socializing with her work friends, and was easily agitated. Additionally, Melanie noted that Maya lost a considerable amount of weight. Maya returned to baseline after 1 month. However, as of 2 weeks ago, Maya began displaying other unusual behaviors. For instance, she appeared much happier when interacting with people. She occasionally skipped around the halls at work and was more talkative than usual. Maya was also noticeably more distracted and impulsive at work. For example, she occasionally skipped protocols and took on multiple tasks at once. Lastly, Maya was caught making unrealistic promises to patients and stated she was the most extraordinary nurse in the world. Of note, Maya stated during the intake that she has been struggling because she worked so hard to become a nurse, yet she is still struggling financially.

Clinical Interview Data

Interpreter Used: No.

Current Psychosocial Stressors: Maya's husband, John, recently lost his job, which has caused financial challenges and strain in their relationship. They recently bought a home and now struggle to afford their mortgage. They stay distant and often argue over finances.

Protective Factors: Maya has a great support system at work, and her parents live nearby.

Developmental History: Maya met all developmental milestones.

Academic History: Maya earned her bachelor of science in nursing 5 years ago with a 3.9 grade point average (GPA). She is now a registered nurse in California and has plans to pursue a master of science degree in nursing.

Social History: Maya has always been social with her co-workers, especially with Melanie. However, over the past 2 months, Maya's social behaviors have fluctuated. For 1 month, she was withdrawn during her shifts, easily agitated when people talked to her, and isolated herself at work by sitting alone on her lunch breaks. Maya's social behavior returned to baseline for about 2 weeks. Now, she is more energetic and more talkative than usual.

Household: Maya lives with her husband, John.

Previous Psychiatric History: Maya experienced a depressive episode during her undergraduate program.

Family Psychiatric History: Maya's mother and grandfather had bipolar II diagnoses.

History of Self-Harm: Maya has no history of self-harm or prior suicide attempts. However, she reported having suicidal ideation 3 weeks ago.

Wellness Profile

Sleep: Despite working overnight shifts and feeling exhausted, Maya struggles to fall asleep after work. When she does sleep, it is for about 5 hours, which she reported is tolerable.

Diet: During the first month of symptoms, Maya reported eating one meal daily due to a diminished appetite. However, during the last 2 weeks, Maya stated she forgets to eat because of her busy schedule. As a result, Maya has lost a noticeable amount of weight.

Elimination: No issues reported.

Technology: Maya reported binge-watching her favorite television shows after work since she is unable to fall sleep. She recently made multiple online purchases for items she does not necessarily need.

Physical Activity: Maya reported constant fatigue during the first month of symptoms. Recently, she has experienced an increase in energy and cannot sleep.

Substance Use/Abuse: Maya reported no substance use.

Pain: 0/10.

Current Psychiatric Symptoms

Depression: Maya demonstrated depressive symptoms 2 months ago, which included depressed mood, loss of interest, irritable mood, weight/appetite change, insomnia, worthlessness, and poor concentration. Depressive symptoms ended after 1 month; however, suicidal thoughts began 3 weeks ago.

Anxiety: Maya reported no symptoms of anxiety.

Panic: Maya reported no symptoms of panic.

Mania: As of 2 weeks ago, Maya demonstrated a decreased need for sleep, inflated esteem, flight of ideas, distractibility, and impulsivity.

Psychosis: Maya reported no psychotic symptoms.

Trauma: Maya's father passed when she was 12 years old.

Eating Disorder: Maya as no previous eating disorders. However, she lost a noticeable amount of weight due to her lack of appetite and forgetting to eat.

Risky Behaviors/Sexual Activity: Maya was caught skipping protocols at work and performing multiple tasks at once, which resulted in mistakes related to patient care. She did not report risky sexual activity.

Mental Status Exam

Appearance: *Dress*: appropriate. *Hygiene*: adequate. Appeared stated age.

Behavior: Cooperative, indifferent, slightly guarded.

Speech: *Rate*: slightly faster than normal limits. *Articulation*: within normal limits. *Volume*: slightly loud. *Coherence*: minimally disorganized.

Mood: Maria reported feeling happy and energetic.

Affect: Elevated affect, congruent to mood, inappropriate to content of interview.

Thought Process: Flight of ideas.

Thought Content: Positive for suicidal ideation.

Orientation: Oriented to person, place, situation, and time.

Recent Memory: Intact.

Remote Memory: Intact.

Attention/Concentration: Distractible.

General Knowledge: Average.

Language: Slightly disorganized.

Insight: Fair.

Judgment: Poor.

Answer Key #2

Diversity Considerations

According to the American Psychiatric Association (APA, 2022), the average onset for bipolar II disorder is the mid-20s. Maya is 26 years old; therefore, her age should be considered when making a diagnosis.

Maya's socioeconomic status should be taken into consideration. She reported that her husband lost his job and that they are struggling financially. Therefore, Maya could have limited access to treatment and mental health care. Of note, because Maya is nurse, there may be aspects of her identity tied to ideas about self-sacrifice and resilience that may cause her to place her own mental health needs last, as can often happen with clinicians working in the helping professions. Maya may also feel the stigma of seeking mental health care services as healthcare workers often perceive themselves as having to be strong or resilient, and seeking mental health care may conflict with that aspect of Maya's professional culture.

Ethical and Legal Considerations

The American Psychiatric Association (APA, 2022) states that impulsivity is a common feature of bipolar II disorder, creating an increased risk of suicide attempts and substance use disorders. Therefore, clinicians should monitor Maya's risk of suicide, especially given the onset of suicidal ideation within the past 3 weeks. Additionally, Maya is a nurse and therefore responsible for patient care. A clinician may therefore need to evaluate whether her mental health symptoms are interfering with her ability to carry out her work responsibilities safely. If it is determined that Maya's symptoms are impacting her ability to care for patients safely, the clinician would need to consult with the local psychology board as well as a professional liability consultant regarding local laws pertaining to managing impaired professionals in mental health settings.

Diagnostic Impressions and Justification

F31.81 Bipolar II Disorder.

Per the diagnostic criteria set forth by the American Psychiatric Association (APA, 2022), bipolar II disorder consists of both hypomanic and major depressive episodes. Therefore, to be diagnosed with bipolar II disorder an individual must meet the criteria for current or past hypomanic and major depressive episodes.

To meet the requirements for a hypomanic episode, there must be a distinct period of abnormally and persistently elevated, expansive, or irritable mood, as well as increased activity or energy levels that persist for at least 4 consecutive days (APA, 2022). These symptoms must also be present most of the day, nearly every day. If identified, Criterion A can be fulfilled. Criterion B of hypomania states that during the period of mood disturbance and increased energy, at least three of the following symptoms must be present: inflated self-esteem or grandiosity, decreased need for sleep, more talkative than usual, flight of ideas, distractibility, increase in goal-directed activity, and excessive involvement in activities that have a high chance of adverse consequences (APA, 2022). Per the APA (2022), Criterion C is met when an individual acts noticeably differently from their normal functioning when they have a hypomanic episode. Criterion D specifies that the mood disturbance and changes in functioning must be noticeable to others. Criterion E requires that the episode is not severe enough to cause marked impairment in social or occupational functioning (marked impairment would indicate the presence of a manic, rather than a hypomanic, episode) (APA, 2022). Lastly, Criterion F notes that the episode should not result from substance use or a medical condition (APA, 2022).

The second qualification for bipolar II disorder is a major depressive episode. To meet Criterion A of a major depressive episode, at least five of the following symptoms: depressed mood most of the day and nearly every day that is noticeable to others, losing interest or pleasure in most or all activities, noticeable weight loss or weight gain, insomnia or hypersomnia, moving noticeably more slowly, feeling extremely tired almost every day, feeling worthless or feeling excessive guilt, decreased ability to concentrate, think, focus, or make decisions; and having repeated thoughts about death, suicidal thoughts, or suicide attempts (APA, 2022). Additionally, these symptoms must occur during the same 2-week period, show an evident change in normal functioning, and one of the symptoms must be either depressed mood or loss of interest or pleasure (APA, 2022). Criterion B states that symptoms must cause clinically significant distress in social and occupational functioning (APA, 2022). Lastly, Criterion C specifies that the depressive episode should not be due to substances or a medical condition (APA, 2022).

Maya presents with symptoms of both a hypomanic and depressive episode. With regard to hypomania, Maya met Criterion A because she exhibited an elevated mood. For example, she skipped around the halls at work and seemed more joyful and energetic for over 2 weeks. Criterion B was established because Maya showed multiple hypomanic symptoms. For instance, she described herself as the "greatest nurse in the world," representing inflated self-esteem. Maya reported she could not sleep after work, demonstrating a decreased need for sleep. Maya became more talkative and social at work, which others noticed. Maya exhibited distractibility, and it was revealed that she skipped required protocols and procedures and took on multiple tasks at once, resulting in mistakes. Lastly, Maya engaged in risky activities by overspending online. Criterion C and D were met because Maya's co-workers, particularly Melanie, noticed an evident change in Maya's typical behaviors. Maya satisfied Criterion E because although her behaviors were noticeable and caused her to make mistakes at work, she was not impaired enough to require hospitalization. Lastly, Maya reported no substance use or relevant medical conditions. Therefore, she met Criterion F.

Maya met the criteria for a major depressive episode. For instance, she fulfilled Criterion A because she reported depressed mood, loss of interest in socializing, noticeable weight loss due to undereating, difficulty sleeping, exhaustion, difficulty concentrating, and suicidal ideations that began 3 weeks ago. Criterion B was met because Maya's symptoms caused clinically significant impairment at her job. For example, she isolated herself from others during lunch, and the quality of her work performance decreased due to her symptoms. Lastly, Maya reported no substance use or relevant medical condition, satisfying Criterion C.

Psychodynamic Conceptualization

Maya may have an internal working model that experiences others as unreliable and herself as unworthy, which can contribute to both hypomanic and depressive episodes. Overall, her ego may be fragile, which would make affective regulation challenging. Her hypomanic episodes may serve as a defense against symptoms of depression and feelings of vulnerability.

It would be appropriate to work toward helping Maya learn how to tolerate intense emotions without resorting to hypomanic states. It would also be appropriate to help Maya strengthen her overall sense of self as well as ego functions. It is unclear how being exposed to caregivers with diagnoses of bipolar II may have impacted Maya, but it would be appropriate to explore whether any maladaptive interpersonal patterns imported from her childhood are being re-enacted in her marital relationship.

Psychodynamic interventions may include interpreting Maya's defenses (i.e., her escape into hypomania as protection against difficult and/or overwhelming emotions). It may also be helpful to support Maya in processing any feelings of grief related to her husband's recent job loss. Additionally, interpretation and working-through of early relational dynamics would be helpful. Similar to bipolar I disorder, psychodynamic treatment of bipolar II disorder should be modulated based on the patient's emotional state.

Cognitive Behavioral Conceptualization

Maya may be influenced by deeply held core beliefs that impact both her cognitions and behavior. There seems to be some evidence of this in her statement about working so hard to be a nurse but still struggling financially. Similar to Maria, she may experience mood congruent cognitive distortions. Maya's maladaptive coping strategies, such as shopping when she is unable to afford to do so, may further reinforce problematic schemas about herself and the world around her.

Appropriate CBT treatment goals would including having Maya learn how to identify cognitive distortions, enhancing her affect regulation skills, and stabilizing her daily routine. It would also be appropriate to teach her how to manage impulsivity when hypomanic.

Maya may benefit from both mood tracking and thought tracking. Behavioral activation would be helpful when Maya finds herself in a depressive episode. Social rhythm techniques would be generally beneficial. It would also be appropriate for the clinician to provide Maya with psychoeducation as well as adaptive coping strategies she can implement to manage both hypomania and conflict with her husband.

Biopsychosocial Conceptualization

Biological factors, including genetic factors, play a role in the development of bipolar II disorder and it is known that Maya has a strong family history of the disorder. Because disruptions in circadian rhythm can both contribute to and maintain the symptoms associated with bipolar II disorder, it is likely her poor sleep habits are contributing to her overall presentation. Because interpersonal stressors often precipitate mood episodes, it is possible that Maya's conflict with her husband is also playing a role. Additional stressors, such as occupation stress and financial stress may have played a role. Maya admitted to the financial stress caused by her husband's job loss, but it is important to remember that she may also be experiencing occupational stress given that nursing is a fairly stressful profession.

Appropriate treatment goals when conceptualizing through the biopsychosocial perspective include improving Maya's sleep schedule, increasing physical activity as a holistic approach to managing mental health concerns, and encouraging medication compliance. Additional goals could include reducing negative cognitions and improving adaptive coping skills as well as improving access to social and community supports.

Biopsychosocial interventions could include monitoring medication adherence as well as side effects using either analog or digital trackers and psychoeducation regarding bipolar II disorder and its related symptoms. Many forms of CBT could be integrated into Maya's care to address maladaptive cognitions and behaviors as well as to help her improve adaptive coping skills.

Conclusion

Bipolar disorders, as categorized by the DSM-5-TR, constitute a class of disorders characterized by alternating patterns of mood elevation and depression, which often present as mood lability, fluctuations in activity levels, and cognitive changes, all of which can impair functioning and/or cause clinically significant distress. The clinical case vignettes included in this chapter serve to illustrate the difference between the two disorders – bipolar I being characterized by the presence of at least one manic episode and bipolar II being characterized by hypomania with no history of manic episodes. In clinical practice, the ability to distinguish between bipolar I and bipolar II is essential for providing accurate conceptualization and subsequent treatment, which is, of course, itself the bedrock of competent, compassionate care.

References

APA (American Psychiatric Association). (2022). *Diagnostic and statistical manual of mental disorders* (5th ed., text rev.). American Psychiatric Publishing.

Barlow, D. H. (2008). *Clinical handbook of psychological disorders: A step-by-step treatment manual* (4th ed.). Guilford Press.

Deal, K. H. (2007). Psychodynamic theory. *Advances in Social Work*, *8*(1), 99–113.

Gold, A. K., & Sylvia, L. G. (2016). The role of sleep in bipolar disorder. *Nature and Science of Sleep*, *8*, 207–214. https://doi.org/10.2147/NSS.S85754.

Han, X., Zhou, E., & Liu, D. (2024). Electronic media use and sleep quality: Updated systematic review and meta-analysis. *Journal of Medical Internet Research*, *26*, e48356. https://doi.org/10.2196/48356.

Ingram, L. B. (2006). *Clinical case formulations: Matching the integrative treatment plan to the client*. Wiley.

Kazantzis, N., Luong, H. K., Usatoff, A. S., Impala, T., Yew, R. Y., & Hofmann, S. G. (2018). The processes of cognitive behavioral therapy: A review of meta-analyses. *Cognitive Therapy & Research*, *42*(4), 349–357. https://doi.org./10.1007/s10608-018-9920-y.

Lam, D. H., Hayward, P., Watkins, E. R., Wright, K., & Sham, P. (2005a). Relapse prevention in patients with bipolar disorder: Cognitive therapy outcome after 2 years. *The American Journal of Psychiatry*, *162*(2), 324–329. https://doi.org/10.1176/appi.ajp.162.2.324.

Lam, D. H., McCrone, P., Wright, K., & Kerr, N. (2005b). Cost-effectiveness of relapse-prevention cognitive therapy for bipolar disorder: 30-month study. *The British Journal of Psychiatry: The Journal of Mental Science*, *186*, 500–506. https://doi.org/10.1192/bjp.186.6.500.

Lugg, W. (2022). The biopsychosocial model: History, controversy and Engel. *Australasian Psychiatry*, *30*(1), 55–59. https://doi.org/10.1177/10398562211037333.

Malkoff-Schwartz, S., Frank, E., Anderson, B., Sherrill, J. T., Siegel, L., Patterson, D., & Kupfer, D. J. (1998). Stressful life events and social rhythm disruption in the onset of manic and depressive bipolar episodes: A preliminary investigation. *Archives of General Psychiatry*, *55*(8), 702–707. https://doi.org/10.1001/archpsyc.55.8.702.

Vandenbos, G., Meidenbauer, E., & Frank-McNeil, J. (2014). *Psychotherapy theories and techniques: A reader*. American Psychological Association.

Chapter 7

Obsessive-Compulsive and Related Disorders

Noel Cooper

In the DSM-5-TR, the chapter pertaining to obsessive-compulsive disorder (commonly referred to as OCD) and related diagnoses encompasses a cluster of disorders characterized by the presence of obsessions, compulsions, or both, as well as related repetitive behaviors or mental acts that the individual feels driven to perform. These disorders share common features such as intrusive thoughts, ritualistic behaviors, and cognitive distortions related to control, symmetry, contamination, and/or harm avoidance (APA, 2022). OCD, which is the primary is disorder within this category, is distinguished by the presence of obsessions and/or compulsions. Obsessions are persistent, intrusive thoughts, urges, or images; compulsions are repetitive behaviors aimed at reducing the anxiety or distress that is generally associated with the obsessions. The behaviors associated with OCD are often time-consuming and interfere significantly with social, occupational, or other areas of functioning. Unlike other anxiety disorders, the compulsions in OCD are not always linked in a realistic way to the feared outcomes and are typically recognized by the individual as excessive or irrational (APA, 2022). Several other disorders that feature with OCD are included in the DSM-5-TR chapter and include body dysmorphic disorder, hoarding disorder, trichotillomania, and excoriation disorder. Body dysmorphic disorder is commonly associated with eating disorders, as it can present as part of an eating disorder, but it can also present as a stand-alone diagnosis. Body dysmorphic disorder is characterized by a preoccupation with one or more perceived defects or flaws in physical appearance that are not observable or appear slight to others (APA, 2022). Hoarding disorder is characterized by persistent difficulty discarding or parting with possessions, regardless of their actual value, which stems from a perceived need to save items as well as distress associated with discarding them, resulting in accumulation that congests living spaces (APA, 2022). Both trichotillomania and excoriation disorder involve recurrent body-focused repetitive behaviors, such as pulling hair or picking skin, leading to noticeable damage. OCD was grouped with anxiety disorders in previous versions of the DSM but advances in neurobiological and genetic research suggest different underlying mechanisms (Pauls et al., 2014).

DOI: 10.4324/9781003586531-8

Clinical Case Vignette #1

Demographic Information and History

Name: Amira Ahamad.

Demographic Information: 32-year-old Indian American female.

Medical Diagnoses: Irritable bowel syndrome (IBS).

Reason for Referral: Amira self-referred to therapy because of her compulsive behaviors, particularly around cleanliness. She reported that she spends more time than is necessary when washing her hands and showering, frequently cleans and wipes down surfaces in her house, and refuses to sit on her bed or couch after getting home from work until she has showered and changed her clothes. She noted that her hands are often chapped and dry because of excessive washing. She reported that her obsessive thoughts are all related to cleanliness and germs. Amira reported that she has experienced these symptoms for about 10 years, since she was in dental school, but they worsened during the COVID-19 pandemic 5 years ago.

Clinical Interview Data

Interpreter Used: No.

Current Psychosocial Stressors: Amira reported she is the primary caretaker for her elderly parents. Her mother has worsening dementia that causes challenges for Amira and Amira's father. Both parents have typical recurrent illnesses associated with old age.

Protective Factors: Amira reported that her Muslim faith is an important source of strength and reassurance for her, though she is not active in a local mosque. Amira reported finding her job meaningful and a source of satisfaction in her life.

Developmental History: Amira reported meeting all her developmental milestones within normal limits.

Academic History: Amira earned her doctorate of dental surgery (DDS) and currently works as a dentist. She reported that she succeeded academically all through school.

Social History: Amira reported that she has a few friends she spends time with a few times a month as well as some extended family members that she sees a few times per year. Her primary social support is her parents.

Household: Amira reported she is an only child. Her parents live with her, and she serves as a caregiver for them.

Previous Psychiatric History: No previous psychiatric history was reported.

Family Psychiatric History: No family psychiatric history was reported.

History of Self-Harm: No history of self-harm was reported.

Assessment Data

On the Yale-Brown Obsessive-Compulsive Scale (Y-BOCS), Amira identified experiencing obsessions in the contamination category and compulsions in the cleaning/washing category. On the obsessions subtotal she scored 10 (max = 20) and on the compulsions subtotal she scored 11 (max = 20).

Wellness Profile

Sleep: Amira reported that she has both trouble falling asleep and trouble waking up in the morning but generally gets 6–7 hours of sleep per night.

Diet: Amira reported that she generally tries to avoid foods that cause IBS flare-ups, but is not always able adhere to the diet she prefers because foods such as onion, garlic, and peppers are frequently part of traditional Indian cuisine.

Elimination: Amira reported that her IBS often causes diarrhea, which exacerbates her compulsions around washing.

Technology: Amira reported that she is not on social media but spends 1–2 hours a day "scrolling" on her phone and 2–3 hours each evening watching television with her parents.

Physical Activity: Amira reported that she tries to go to the gym once or twice a week but is not always consistent.

Substance Use/Abuse: Amira denied past or current substance use.

Pain: 3–7/10. Amira reported more pain when her IBS flares up.

Current Psychiatric Symptoms

Depression: Amira reported that she sometimes feels depressed or hopeless when her IBS symptoms flare up and the physical discomfort makes her more irritable. She reported experiencing sadness when she thinks about her parents' age and declining health.

Anxiety: Amira reported that she has recurrent worries about cleanliness and germs. She said these thoughts are present throughout the day but are particularly strong when she returns home from work. She reported that she washes her hands for 10 or more minutes after using the toilet and showers for 45 minutes to an hour twice a day.

Panic: Amira denied symptoms of panic.

Mania: Amira denied symptoms of mania or hypomania.

Psychosis: Amira denied symptoms of psychosis.

Trauma: Amira denied a history of trauma.

Eating Disorder: Amira denied symptoms of an eating disorder.

Risky Behaviors/Sexual Activity: Amira denied engaging in any risky behaviors.

Mental Status Exam

Appearance: Amira was dressed casually.

Behavior: Amira was cooperative.

Speech: Amira's speech was within normal limits.

Mood: Amira described her mood as "somewhat anxious but also hopeful."

Affect: Amira's affect was congruent and appropriate.

Thought Process: Amira's thought process was logical and linear.

Thought Content: Amira denied suicidal ideation, homicidal ideation, delusions, or hallucinations.

Orientation: Amira was oriented to person, place, time, and situation.

Recent Memory: Amira's recent memory was intact.

Remote Memory: Amira's remote memory was intact.

Attention/Concentration: Amira's attention and concentration were within normal limits.

General Knowledge: Amira's general knowledge was within normal limits.

Language: Amira's language was within normal limits.

Insight: Amira demonstrated good insight.

Judgment: Amira demonstrated good judgment.

Answer Key #1

Diversity Considerations

Interventions should take into consideration Amira's cultural background including both her Indian ethnicity (Chandra et al., 2016) and her Muslim faith. Her faith may be a potential supportive resource for therapy (Abu Raiya & Pargament, 2010). Additionally, as the daughter of immigrants (or possibly an immigrant herself), she may experience acculturative stress from navigating both Indian and American cultural norms (Sue et al., 2019). This tension can be amplified by expectations around filial responsibility, particularly in collectivist cultures where adult children, especially daughters, often serve as primary caregivers for aging parents (Chang & Subramaniam, 2008). These expectations may contribute to chronic stress and exacerbate OCD symptoms. It is important to note that while Amira's faith tradition may be protective, she reported that she is not currently active at her local mosque. While Islam promotes cleanliness as a spiritual virtue, there is a risk that religious practices surrounding ritual purification might become entangled with pathological compulsions, especially in individuals predisposed to OCD (Al-Adawi et al., 2015). It is crucial for clinicians to distinguish between normative religious rituals and dysfunctional behaviors that impair functioning.

Ethical Considerations

Curiosity and cultural humility are essential whenever a clinician is working with a client from a non-majority identity. Ethical practice requires that Amira's diversity considerations be incorporated into treatment to the degree that she requests.

Legal Considerations

No additional legal considerations noted at this time.

Diagnostic Impressions and Justification

F42.2 Obsessive-Compulsive Disorder.

Amira experiences both obsessive thoughts and compulsive behaviors that are time consuming and cause her distress. These symptoms are not attributable to a substance or a medical condition and are not better explained by another mental disorder.

Psychodynamic Case Conceptualization

Amira's obsessive thoughts and compulsive behaviors are likely driven by unconscious defenses (e.g., undoing or reaction formation) against psychologically threatening impulses or anxieties (King, 2017). These maladaptive efforts to cope become repetitive behaviors to try to diminish the anxiety and avoid the perceived harm of those threatening impulses. Her overdeveloped superego maintains the repetitive behaviors, which are further reinforced by a profession in the medical community that highly values cleanliness.

Psychodynamic treatment will focus on increasing Amira's insight into her inner conflicts and decreasing the rigidity of her superego.

The clinician should facilitate Amira's expressions of emotion and provide interpretations of her defenses and resistance.

Cognitive Behavioral Conceptualization

Amira experiences distorted thinking regarding her intrusive thoughts about contamination and cleanliness. These distorted cognitions elicit anxiety, which she attempts to alleviate through her compulsive behaviors, further reinforcing the cognitive distortion and the anxiety (Clark, 2003).

The ultimate goal of therapy will be to decrease the frequency, intensity, and duration of Amira's obsessive thoughts and compulsive behaviors (e.g., decreasing handwashing time after toileting from 8 minutes to 2 minutes).

One of the most strongly supported interventions for OCD, exposure and response prevention (ERP) (Foa et al., 2012) entails exposing the client to the feared stimuli (e.g., an unwashed countertop) and then preventing the completion of the associated response or ritual (e.g., excessive washing). This behavioral component can be accompanied by cognitive reappraisal and cognitive restructuring (Clark, 2003), as well as increasing overall coping skills and regulation skills for emotional distress. Identifying common triggers or exacerbating factors can help provide insight into the patterns of Amira's symptoms that can then be modified. Mindfulness-based therapies also demonstrate effectiveness in addressing obsessions and compulsions that are primarily mentalizing in nature, allowing the client to recognize the intrusive thought while not further engaging with it (Hale et al., 2012).

Biopsychosocial Conceptualization

Amira's obsessive and compulsive symptoms are accompanied by neurochemical changes that can be addressed by medication. Medication alone is generally not sufficient for remediation of symptoms, but psychotherapeutic interventions are often more successful with medication as an adjuvant intervention (Skapinakis et al., 2016). Amira's contamination obsessions and cleanliness compulsions are likely exacerbated by her work in the healthcare field, which exposes her to legitimate threats of contamination. While this is not a situation that she is likely to wish to change, it should be considered as a factor in her treatment. Amira's own health concerns with IBS also increase her exposure to sources of potential contamination.

Appropriate treatment goals grounded in the biopsychosocial model could include reducing the physiological consequences of her compulsive washing behaviors, such as dermatological irritation and physical fatigue, through behavioral regulation and the gradual introduction of tolerable changes in hygiene routines. Additionally, given Amira's diagnosis of IBS, treatment should prioritize the stabilization of her gastrointestinal symptoms. Improvement in sleep quality is another important goal the clinician and Amira should work towards. Treatment should also focus on developing distress tolerance skills as well as improving insight into the affective and cognitive patterns that sustain her anxiety, including internalized expectations related to caregiving and cultural norms. It may also be important to strengthen Amira's existing support system while fostering new opportunities for connection outside her immediate family.

There is also evidence that incidence of IBS and OCD are correlated, and improvement in one area can also induce improvement in the other (Turna et al., 2019; Grassi & Pampaloni, 2024), and so a focus on appropriate nutrition for individuals with IBS may be helpful. Additionally, there is evidence that regular exercise can have an ameliorative effect on obsessive-compulsive disorder (Bottoms et al., 2023). Increasing her engagement with her support system and having more time for socializing may help Amira manage the stress of being a caretaker for her parents, and increasing engagement with her local Muslim community may also be beneficial. Given that Amira reported difficulty waking even after sleeping for seven hours, she may wish to consult with a sleep specialist to determine whether undergoing a sleep study would be helpful.

Clinical Case Vignette #2

Demographic Information and History

Name: David Carrolli.

Demographic Information: 23-year-old Caucasian male.

Medical Diagnoses: None reported.

Reason for Referral: David reported that his girlfriend threatened to break up with him if he does not stop "obsessing" about his body, expressing concern that his preoccupation with his body is negatively impacting their relationship. David acknowledged that he spends a lot of time working to have a lean and muscular body, including going to the gym once or twice every day for at least an hour and monitoring his diet closely. He said that he does not take rest days because of concerns about "losing gains." David reported that he takes pictures and measurements of his body at the beginning and end of every day to track his goals, analyzing even the slightest change in muscle definition or body fat percentage, as well as tracking his calorie, water, and protein intake each day to meet certain macronutrient and calorie goals. He said that he often compares himself to fitness influencers and bodybuilders on social media. David acknowledged feeling distress when he perceives himself as looking "small" or "soft," even when he receives reassurance from others. David acknowledged that he spends quite a bit of money on nutritional supplements as well. He also acknowledged that although he appears very fit, he is constantly worried about maintaining his physique and doubts that he is actually as fit as he appears to be.

Clinical Interview Data

Interpreter Used: No.

Current Psychosocial Stressors: David reported that he recently started a new job as a personal trainer at an elite gym.

Protective Factors: David described himself as very disciplined and focused. He said that his girlfriend is very supportive of him.

Developmental History: David reported that he met all his developmental milestones within normal limits. He described himself as a "chubby kid" until he started to work out when in high school.

Academic History: David reported that he generally did pretty well in school. He recently graduated from college with a degree in kinesiology.

Social History: David reported that he was bullied in elementary and middle school for being "chubby and unathletic" which is part of what inspired him to start working out in high school. He said that he has a strong core group of friends, all of whom are also very involved with fitness and exercise. He said that he and his girlfriend have been dating for 2 years and he's thinking about proposing to her. David reported that he grew up with his parents, who are still married, two younger sisters who still live at home, and an older brother who is in the military. He reported having good relationships with all his family members.

Household: David reported living in an apartment with two roommates who are also close friends.

Previous Psychiatric History: David denied any previous psychiatric history.

Family Psychiatric History: David reported that his mother previously attended therapy for anxiety but was not aware of any details.

History of Self-Harm: David denied any history of self-harm.

Wellness Profile

Sleep: David reported that he is very intentional about getting 8 hours of sleep per night because of the impact on his health and fitness if he does not receive sufficient sleep. He reported that he goes to bed and wakes up at the same times every day, even if this means missing out or cutting short social activities.

Diet: David reported that his typical diet is as follows:

- *Breakfast*: One cup of oatmeal with one cup of berries and Greek yogurt *or* five eggs and one apple.
- *Lunch*: 4 ounces of salmon or tilapia with one cup of brown rice or quinoa and one cup of vegetables.
- *Dinner*: 4 ounces of chicken or turkey breast with one cup of brown rice or lentils and one cup of vegetables.
- *Snacks*: Throughout the day, these often include two protein shakes, one cup of almonds, one cup of cottage cheese, 3 ounces of tuna, and/or one cup of edamame. David also reported regularly drinking pre-workout.

Elimination: David denied concerns in this area.

Technology: David reported that he only occasionally watches movies with his girlfriend and sometimes plays video games with his roommates. He said that he uses his phone less than 1 hour per day but that during that 1 hour, he primarily consumes content created by fitness influencers and bodybuilders.

Physical Activity: David reported that he does weight training every day for at least 1 hour and also does cardio exercises for 1 hour 3 days per week. Of note, he reported spending 30–45 minutes in his gym's sauna after each workout.

Substance Use/Abuse: David denied any substance use. He said that although he has considered using anabolic steroids, he has learned too much about their negative effects and so avoids them.

Pain: 0/10.

Current Psychiatric Symptoms

Depression: David denied any depressive symptoms.

Anxiety: David reported that he gets anxious or irritable if he feels like he has not been able to work out enough in a day or if he has not been able to adhere to his diet.

Panic: David denied any panic symptoms.

Mania: David denied any symptoms of mania or hypomania.

Psychosis: David denied any symptoms of psychosis.

Trauma: David denied any history of trauma.

Eating Disorder: David denied any binging or purging. He said that he is careful to consume the "right" number of calories, neither too many nor too few, and to balance his macronutrients. Specifically, he stated that he ensures he consumes sufficient calories to maintain and/or increase muscle mass and that he has never attempted to "cut" or "shred."

Risky Behaviors/Sexual Activity: David denied any risky behaviors.

Mental Status Exam

Appearance: David was dressed casually in workout clothes. He appeared slim and fit, with well-defined muscles.

Behavior: David was cooperative with the intake but expressed extreme ambivalence about change.

Speech: David's speech was within normal limits.

Mood: David reported feeling "generally good" but "anxious" when he thinks about his girlfriend.

Affect: David's affect was congruent with his mood.

Thought Process: David's thought process was logical and linear.

Thought Content: David denied any suicidal ideation, homicidal ideation, delusions, or hallucinations.

Orientation: David was oriented to person, place, time, and situation.

Recent Memory: David's recent memory was intact.

Remote Memory: David's remote memory was intact.

Attention/Concentration: David demonstrated sufficient attention and concentration.

General Knowledge: David's general knowledge was within normal limits.

Language: David's language was within normal limits.

Insight: David demonstrated poor insight.

Judgment: David demonstrated fair judgment.

Answer Key #2

Diversity Considerations

The modern American cultural emphasis on physical appearance is likely having an impact on David and what he views as desirable physical expectations (Ganson et al., 2025). For men, this includes an emphasis on being slim and muscular, and being heavily involved in the fitness community reinforces these expectations (Underwood & Olivardia, 2022).

Ethical Considerations

Although David currently denies any suicidal ideation, suicidal ideation is common for individuals with body dysmorphia (Cuzzolaro, 2018), so the possibility should be monitored.

Legal Considerations

No additional legal considerations.

Diagnostic Impressions and Justification

F45.22 Body Dysmorphic Disorder, with Muscle Dysmorphia.
David is preoccupied with the size and appearance of his muscles and performs repetitive behaviors in response to these concerns. This preoccupation is causing distress or impairment in his relationship with his girlfriend. He does not meet criteria for an eating disorder as he denied binging and purging behaviors, consumes sufficient calories to meet his energy needs, and is not actively trying to lose weight.

Psychodynamic Case Conceptualization

David's symptoms may be a defense mechanism against the unconscious fear of experiencing himself as weak, shameful, or vulnerable. These fears often have their roots in early object relations and deficits in social relationships, perhaps with peers or his older brother; his relationship with his father is also a significant consideration (Woolridge, 2023). David's overdeveloped superego maintains his maladaptive defenses.

Treatment should focus on facilitating David's expression of emotions, including unconscious anxiety, and increasing his insight into his inner conflicts. Exploring his significant relationships, including early attachment with his father, will be important.

Through psychodynamic interpretations of his defenses and resistance, the goal will be to decrease the rigidity of his superego and develop a more balanced relationship to his body.

Cognitive Behavioral Conceptualization

David's symptoms are caused by cognitive distortions regarding his physical appearance which focus on minor flaws or discrepancies. These cognitive distortions elicit anxiety, which he attempts to alleviate through rigorous adherence to a strict diet and exercise regimen. David may experience a core schema of "I'm not good enough."

A CBT-focused treatment approach might focus on establishing more flexible eating patterns, reducing compulsive exercise, developing alternative emotional regulation strategies, and restructuring distorted cognitions related to body checking and comparison (Martenstyn et al., 2025). A successful treatment will address both the dysfunctional behaviors (excessive exercise, strict diet) and the dysfunctional and distorted thinking that drives those behaviors.

Appropriate CBT interventions could include cognitive restructuring as well as Socratic questioning to examine the evidence for his beliefs, such as the assumption that not adhering to his regimen will lead to catastrophic outcomes. Behavioral interventions would include establishing a balanced workout and rest schedule, as well as reducing excessive self-monitoring, such as taking daily measurements and photos, to minimize the reinforcing cycle of anxiety. David might also benefit from mindfulness and acceptance-based strategies to reduce anxiety when his body does not meet his standards.

Biopsychosocial Conceptualization

David's concerns about his body are likely strongly influenced by the cultural expectations regarding fitness and physique (Ganson et al., 2025), as well as what constitutes traditional masculinity. These are further reinforced by his work as a personal trainer, where these expectations are made more explicit (Underwood & Olivardia, 2022).

Appropriate biopsychosocial goals would include promoting a balanced and sustainable approach to physical fitness as well as reducing David's preoccupation with body image. Treatment goals should also include strengthening David's relationship with his girlfriend by addressing how his body preoccupation is impacting their dynamic, and fostering communication skills to help David navigate conflicts related to his fitness goals. Additionally, supporting David in expanding his self-concept beyond physical appearance and encouraging social interactions that are not focused on fitness could be essential to improving his overall quality of life.

Given David's ambivalence about change in this area of functioning, it is likely important to engage him in motivational interviewing to help him explore the possibilities for change (Rollnick et al., 2022). Helping David explore and challenge these cultural expectations may help him be more open to treatment. Consulting with a dietitian and a medical doctor regarding his eating and exercise habits, including frequent sauna use, may help challenge some of David's rigid thinking in this area and incorporate healthy changes.

Clinical Case Vignette #3

Demographic Information and History

Name: Hannah Watts.

Demographic Information: 29-year-old Caucasian female.

Medical Diagnoses: None reported.

Reason for Referral: Hannah is seeking therapy for self-described hoarding behavior. She described her studio apartment as "full of stuff" that she has trouble getting rid of. She said that food trash is the only thing she can dispose of, but that she keeps her all her mail, receipts, and other papers "just in case." She described herself as "obsessed" with getting things that are on sale or free, which has led to owning an excessive amount of clothing, shoes, household items, cleaning supplies, non-perishable food goods, beauty care items, and craft supplies. She reported presenting to therapy because she recently became engaged and after seeing her overfilled apartment for the first time, her fiancé stated that she would need to get rid of most of her belongings before they could move in together.

Clinical Interview Data

Interpreter Used: No.

Current Psychosocial Stressors: Hannah recently became engaged.

Protective Factors: Hannah is intelligent and insightful. She has strong friendships, and her fiancé is very supportive of her. Hannah reported being very engaged in her crafting hobbies. She reported that she became involved in a church in her early 20s and her spirituality is very important to her.

Developmental History: Hannah met her developmental milestones within normal limits. She reported that she was "in and out" of foster care beginning at age 6, with multiple foster home placements and reunifications with her biological parents on three occasions. She was placed permanently in a group home at age 16, from which she transitioned into a transitional housing program when she turned 18.

Academic History: Hannah reported that her grades were average, but academic work was challenging because she changed schools often. She reported that she graduated from high school and attended 2 years of community college to get her associate's degree in business. She said that she currently works as an administrative assistant for a local small business that specializes in high-end craft supplies.

Social History: Hannah reported that she has no contact with her parents and only occasional contact with her siblings. She said that she has several close friends she made through the crafting group and the Bible study group to which she belongs. She has been dating her fiancé for 3 years.

Household: Hannah reported living alone.

Previous Psychiatric History: Hannah reported that she was enrolled in psychotherapy multiple times after initially being placed in foster care. She said, "It was helpful to have someone to talk to just to keep me stable, but it never lasted." Hannah reported that she struggled with depression and anxiety when she was in foster care, but these symptoms improved when she received steady housing through a transitional housing program and started college. She also identified this period as a time when she began holding on to things "because it felt good that I had the space to finally keep everything I wanted."

Family Psychiatric History: Hannah reported that her parents had a history of substance abuse, and she suspected that they also had untreated mental illnesses but was unsure if they were ever formally diagnosed.

History of Self-Harm: Hannah denied any history of self-harm.

Wellness Profile

Sleep: Hannah reported that she typically sleeps 6–8 hours per night.

Diet: Hannah reported that she typically eats "more or less" balanced and nutritious meals.

Elimination: Hannah denied concerns in this area.

Technology: Hannah reported that she watches 1–2 hours of television per day, and spends 1–2 hours on her phone, mostly watching crafting videos.

Physical Activity: Hannah reported that she enjoys taking walks most days but does not have a regular exercise routine.

Substance Use/Abuse: Hannah reported that she occasionally used alcohol and other substances during her adolescence and early adulthood but denied any current use.

Pain: 0/10.

Current Psychiatric Symptoms

Depression: Hannah denied any current depressive symptoms.

Anxiety: Hannah reported that she feels anxious and agitated when she thinks about downsizing her possessions and worries that she will regret getting rid of belongings that are important to her.

Panic: Hannah reported that she had a panic attack the first time her fiancé tried to help her dispose of some belongings, which is what prompted her to seek therapy. She denied any previous history of panic attacks.

Mania: Hannah denied any symptoms of mania or hypomania.

Psychosis: Hannah denied any symptoms of psychosis.

Trauma: Hannah reported that she experienced neglect and verbal abuse when she lived with her biological parents. She attributed her ability to throw away food trash (in comparison to her inability to discard other objects) to the disgust she experienced at the "filth" at her family's home. She reported her experiences in foster care as "mixed," with some mild verbal, emotional, and physical abuse at various foster homes, but also some loving and supportive foster homes. Hannah described the transition between her biological family home and her first foster home as particularly difficult, as she had to pack her belongings in trash bags or grocery bags and she was not able to take all her toys or clothes with her. She said that she has very few pictures or mementoes from her childhood and still remembers many special things that were lost to her. Hannah reported that her foster families, doctors, and schools never seemed to have all her documentation and records, which caused delays and disruptions for her, particularly at school.

Eating Disorder: Hannah denied symptoms of an eating disorder.

Risky Behaviors/Sexual Activity: Hannah reported that she engaged in some risky behaviors during her adolescence but denied any current risky behaviors.

Mental Status Exam

Appearance: Hannah was dressed casually.

Behavior: Hannah was cooperative.

Speech: Hannah's speech was within normal limits except when she was anxious. When she was anxious, her speech became more rapid.

Mood: Hannah reported her mood as "generally good" but anxious and agitated whenever she thought about disposing of her belongings.

Affect: Hannah's affect was congruent with her mood.

Thought Process: Hannah's thought process was logical and linear. She acknowledged the illogic of her hoarding tendencies.

Thought Content: Hannah denied suicidal ideation, homicidal ideation, delusions, and hallucinations.

Orientation: Hannah was oriented to person, place, situation, and time.

Recent Memory: Hannah's recent memory was intact.

Remote Memory: Hannah reported some gaps in her memory of childhood prior to living in the group home at 16.

Attention/Concentration: Hannah's attention and concentration were sufficient.

General Knowledge: Hannah's general knowledge was within normal limits.

Language: Hannah's language was within normal limits.

Insight: Hannah exhibited good insight.

Judgment: Hannah exhibited fair judgment.

Answer Key #3

Diversity Considerations

Hannah's faith is a potential resource for therapy (de Abreu Costa & Rosmarin, 2021; Koenig & Pearce, 2021). Hannah's status as a former foster child gives her a unique set of experiences that influenced her early attachment and her psychosocial development (Fahlberg, 1991).

Ethical Considerations

Hannah's clinician should educate themselves on the experience of children in foster care in order to have a more complete understanding of the challenges of Hannah's childhood (Fahlberg, 1991; Badeau et al., 2010), while also exploring with Hannah the ways that her experiences were both similar to and different from others' experiences in foster care. Hannah's spiritual faith should be integrated into treatment to the degree that she prefers.

Legal Considerations

Hoarding disorder can affect the home environment in ways that may lead to violations of housing codes or other regulations, especially if living conditions become unsanitary or unsafe. If Hannah's behaviors interfere with her ability to maintain safe and sanitary living conditions, this could become a legal issue, particularly if it involves her landlord or housing provider. In extreme cases, hoarding behavior may result in legal actions related to eviction or property damage, especially if items create hazards (e.g., fire risks or sanitation violations).

Diagnostic Impressions and Justification

F42.3 Hoarding Disorder, with Excessive Acquisition.

Hannah experiences difficulty discarding possessions due to emotional distress, which results in her apartment being congested and cluttered. Her symptoms are beginning to interfere with her intimate relationships and cause her emotional and relational distress. Her symptoms are not attributable to a medical condition or another mental disorder.

Psychodynamic Case Conceptualization

Hannah's symptoms may be the result of disrupted object relations from her early years, which have been reinforced by repetitive experiences of loss and abandonment (Volkan, 2021; Mathes et al., 2020). The hoarding behavior could be a defense against further experiences of loss and a sense of inherent instability in the world. These traumas may have disrupted Hannah's sense of self, and her possessions may have become merged with her sense of self.

Treatment should focus on helping Hannah explore her inner psychic conflicts through facilitating emotional expression and providing interpretations of her defenses and resistance. Treatment may also focus on developing healthier object relations and differentiating her sense of self (Mathes et al., 2020).

Psychodynamic interventions could include free association and the exploration of her transference reactions as well as exploring Hannah's ambivalence about discarding possessions, which may reflect unconscious feelings of loss, abandonment, or fear of inadequacy.

Cognitive Behavioral Conceptualization

Hannah appears to experience cognitive distortions regarding her possessions, driven by anxiety about not having something that she needs in the future, not having adequate supplies, or accidentally discarding something that is emotionally important to her. Hannah may experience a core schema of inherent instability; her hoarding behavior could be an attempt to create an artificial sense of stability.

Appropriate CBT goals for Hannah might include addressing the maladaptive cognitions and behavioral tendencies that both contribute to and maintain her hoarding behavior. This might involve examining the core beliefs that underscore her hoarding tendencies, as well as gradually reducing the distress associated with discarding possessions. CBT goals would also include the development of more adaptive coping strategies for managing the anxiety related to hoarding, such as improving emotional regulation skills and finding healthier ways to fulfill the emotional needs that hoarding has served. Over time, the aim would be to increase Hannah's ability to make more adaptive decisions regarding possessions, decrease her excessive accumulation behaviors, and foster a greater sense of control over her environment and her life.

Challenging and restructuring Hannah's cognitive distortions (e.g., "Throwing away this possession is like throwing away a part of me") will enable her to engage in the necessary task of divesting herself of unneeded possessions (Wheaton, 2016). Hannah will likely need a broad range of emotional regulation and coping strategies for the distress that will accompany that task (Wheaton, 2016). Acceptance and commitment therapy, with a focus on tolerating distress and discontinuing experiential avoidance, may prove helpful (Eppingstall et al., 2020). Hannah may also need assistance developing appropriate decision-making skills regarding what to keep and what to throw away, a developmental and emotional skill that she may not have had the opportunity to acquire in her multiple foster placements.

Biopsychosocial Conceptualization

Hannah's social context and psychosocial history contributed to the start of her hoarding tendencies, which have been further enabled by the fact that she lives alone. Additionally, societal influences that promote overconsumption of material goods may be reinforcing her behaviors (Grisham & Timpano, 2024).

Appropriate goals grounded in the biopsychosocial model might be enhancing sleep hygiene, promoting balanced nutrition, and considering relaxation techniques to mitigate the physiological symptoms of anxiety that manifest when she contemplates discarding possessions. Hannah might also need support working through her unresolved trauma, especially the early childhood disruptions and experiences of neglect, which have influenced her attachment to objects. Additional treatment goals would focus on strengthening her relationships, particularly with her fiancé, by addressing the role hoarding plays in their interactions and improving her ability to engage in shared decision making and collaborative problem solving regarding her living situation.

As Hannah begins to make decisions about what to do with her possessions (e.g., keep, discard, donate, sell), she may find it helpful to engage with her values as a guide (e.g., donating some items to a local group home, selling items and donating the money to an organization that helps foster children). Hannah may also benefit from participation in a psychotherapy group specifically for individuals who engage in hoarding behaviors (Tolin et al., 2017; Bodryzlova et al., 2018). While regular exercise does not have a direct effect on hoarding disorder symptoms, it does have proven mood-boosting effects that may be beneficial to Hannah, as well as being helpful for physical health (Chen & Nakagawa, 2023).

Conclusion

OCD, body dysmorphic disorder, and hoarding disorder, are all characterized by the presence of obsessive, compulsive, or repetitive behaviors that significantly affect an individual's ability to function in various aspects of life, including intrusive thoughts, anxiety-driven rituals, and a perceived lack of control. With a growing understanding of the neurobiological and genetic underpinnings of these conditions, clinicians are better equipped to provide evidence-based interventions, which may include CBT, ERP, and other therapeutic approaches that aim to alleviate the distress and functional impairments associated with these disorders, within the context of competent, compassionate care.

References

Abu Raiya, H., & Pargament, K. I. (2010). Religiously integrated therapy with Muslim clients: From research to practice. *Professional Psychology: Research and Practice*, *41*(2), 181–188. https://doi.org/10.1037/a0017988.

Al-Adawi, S., Al-Sinawi, H., Al-Azri, F., Al-Maqbali, M., & Al-Balushi, N. (2015). Obsessive compulsive disorder in Islam: A critical review of the religious practices contributing to the presentation and treatment. *Journal of Obsessive-Compulsive and Related Disorders*, *6*, 99–105. https://doi.org/10.1016/j.jocrd.2015.07.001.

APA (American Psychiatric Association). (2022). *Diagnostic and statistical manual of mental disorders* (5th ed., text rev.). https://doi.org/10.1176/appi.books.9780890425787.

Badeau, S., Haralambie, A. M., & Duquette, D. N. (2010). A child's journey through the child welfare system. In D. N. Duquette & A. M. Haralambie (Eds.), *Child welfare law and practice: Representing children, parents, and state agencies in abuse, neglect, and dependency cases* (pp. 341–362). Bradford Publishing.

Bodryzlova, Y., Audet, J.-S., Bergeron, K., & O'Connor, K. (2018). Group cognitive-behavioural therapy for hoarding disorder: Systematic review and meta-analysis. *Health and Social Care in the Community*, *27*(3), 517–530. https://doi.org/10.1111/hsc.12598.

Bottoms, L., Pons, M. P., Fineberg, N. A., Pellegrini, L., Fox, O., Wellsted, D., Drummond, L. M., Reid, J., Baldwin, D. S., Hou, R., Chamberlain, S., Sireau, N., Grohmann, D., & Laws, K. R. (2023). Effects of exercise on obsessive-compulsive disorder symptoms: A systematic review and meta-analysis. *International Journal of Psychiatry in Clinical Practice*, *27*(3), 232–242. https://doi.org/10.1080/13651501.2022.2151474.

Chandra, R. M., Arora, L., Mehta, U. M., Asnaani, A., & Radhakrishnan, R. (2016). Asian Indians in America: The influence of values and culture on mental health. *Asian Journal of Psychiatry*, *22*, 202–209. https://doi.org/10.1016/j.ajp.2015.09.011.

Chang, H., & Subramaniam, M. (2008). Asian perspectives on caregiving. In M. G. Morrow & L. L. McCall (Eds.), *Health and Culture* (pp. 221–238). Routledge.

Chen, C., & Nakagawa, S. (2023). Recent advances in the study of the neurobiological mechanisms behind the effects of physical activity on mood, resilience, and emotional disorders. *Advances in Clinical and Experimental Medicine*, *33*(12), 937–942. https://doi.org/10.17219/acem/171565.

Clark, D. A. (2003). *Cognitive-behavioral therapy for OCD*. Guilford Press.

Cuzzolaro, M. (2018). Body dysmorphic disorder and muscle dysmorphia. In M. Cuzzolaro & S. Fassino (Eds.), *Body image, eating, and weight* (pp. 67–84). Springer.

de Abreu Costa, M., & Rosmarin, D. H. (2021). Spiritually integrated psychotherapy. In A. Moreira-Almeida, B. P. Mosqueiro, & D. Bhugra (Eds.), *Spirituality and mental health across cultures*. Oxford University Press.

Eppingstall, J., Xenos, S., & Yap, K. (2020). Acceptance and commitment therapy for hoarding disorder: A proposed treatment protocol for individuals. *Australian Psychologist*, *55*(3), 183–195. https://doi.org/10.1111/ap.12438.

Fahlberg, V. I. (1991). *A child's journey through placement*. Perspective Press.

Foa, E. B., Yadin, E., & Lichner, T. K. (2012). *Exposure and response (ritual) prevention for obsessive-compulsive disorder*. Oxford University Press.

Ganson, K. T., Testa, A., Fodgers, R. F., Murray, S. B., & Nagata, J. M. (2025). Exploring body ideal internalization, sociocultural pressures, and probably muscle dysmorphia in Canadian and American boys and men. *Eating Behaviors*, *56*, 101944. https://doi.org/10.1016/j.eatbeh.2025.101944.

Grassi, G., & Pampaloni, I. (2024). Gut microbiota and gastrointestinal symptoms in the global assessment of obsessive-compulsive disorder: A narrative review of current evidence and practical implications. *Brain Sciences*, *14*(6), 539. https://doi.org/10.3390/brainsci14060539.

Grisham, J. R., & Timpano, K. R. (2024). Nudging society toward more adaptive approaches to material possessions: Harnessing implicit approaches to reduce overconsumption and excessive saving. *Current Opinion in Psychiatry*, *60*, 101933. https://doi.org/10.1016/j.copsyc.2024.101933.

Hale, L., Strauss, C., & Taylor, B. L. (2012). The effectiveness and acceptability of mindfulness-based therapy for obsessive-compulsive disorder: A review of the literature. *Mindfulness*, *4*, 375–382. https://doi.org/10.1007/s12671-012-0137-y.

King, R. A. (2017). Psychodynamic perspectives on OCD. In C. Pittenger (Ed.), *Obsessive-compulsive disorder: Phenomenology, pathophysiology, and treatment* (pp. 65–74). Oxford University Press.

Koenig, H. G., & Pearce, M. (2021). Christian-integrated psychotherapy. In J. R. Peteet, H. S. Moffic, A. Hankir, & H. G. Koenig (Eds.), *Christianity and psychiatry*. Springer. https://doi.org/10.1007/978-3-030-80854-9_13.

Martenstyn, J. A., Russell, J., Tran, C., Griffiths, S., & Maguire, S. (2025). Evaluation of an 8-week telehealth cognitive-behavioural therapy (CBT) program for adults with muscle dysmorphia: A pilot and feasibility study. *Body Image*, *52*, 101842. https://doi.org/10.1016/j.bodyim.2024.101842.

Mathes, B. M., Timpano, K. R., Raines, A. M., & Schmidt, N. B. (2020). Attachment theory and hoarding disorder: A review and theoretical integration. *Behaviour Research and Therapy*, *125*, 103549. https://doi.org/10.1016/j.brat.2019.103549.

Pauls, D. L., Abramovitch, A., Rauch, S. L., & Geller, D. A. (2014). Obsessive-compulsive disorder: An integrative genetic and neurobiological perspective. *Nature Reviews Neuroscience*, *15*(6), 410–424. https://doi.org/10.1038/nrn3746.

Rollnick, S., Miller, W. R., & Butler, C. C. (2022). *Motivational interviewing health care: Helping patients change behavior* (2nd ed.). Guilford Press.

Skapinakis, P., Caldwell, D. M., Hollingworth, W., Bryden, P., Fineberg, N. A., Salkovskis, P., Welton, N. J., Baxter, H., Kessler, D., Churchill, R., & Lewis, G. (2016). Pharmacological and psychotherapeutic interventions for management of obsessive-compulsive disorder in adults: A systematic review and network meta-analysis. *The Lancet Psychiatry*, *3*(8), 730–739. https://doi.org/10.1016/S2215-0366(16)30069-4.

Sue, D. W., Sue, D., Neville, H. A., & Smith, L. (2019). *Counseling the culturally diverse: Theory and practice* (8th ed.). Wiley.

Tolin, D. F., Worden, B. L., Wootton, B. M., & Gilliam, C. M. (2017). *CBT for hoarding disorder: A group therapy program therapist's guide*. Wiley.

Turna, J., Kaplan, K. G., Patterson, B., Bercik, P., Anglin, R., Soreni, N., & Van Ameringen, M. (2019). Higher prevalence of irritable bowel syndrome and greater gastrointestinal symptoms in obsessive-compulsive disorder. *Journal of Psychiatric Research*, *118*, 1–6. https://doi.org/10.1016/j.jpsychires.2019.08.004.

Underwood, M., & Olivardia, R. (2022). "The day you start lifting is the day you become forever small": Bodybuilders explain muscle dysmorphia. *Health*, *27*(6), 998–1018. https://doi.org/10.1177/13634593221093494.

Volkan, K. (2021). Hoarding and animal hoarding: Psychodynamic and transitional aspects. *Psychodynamic Psychiatry*, *49*(1), 24–47. https://doi.org/10.1521/pdps.2021.49.1.24.

Wheaton, M. G. (2016). Understanding and treating hoarding disorder: A review of cognitive-behavioral models and treatment. *Journal of Obsessive-Compulsive and Related Disorders*, *9*, 43–50. https://doi.org/10.1016/j.jocrd.2016.02.006.

Woolridge, T. (2023). Boys and their muscles: The paternal object in muscle dysmorphia. *The Psychoanalytic Study of the Child*, *76*(1), 123–139. https://doi.org/10.1080/00797308.2022.2057773.

Chapter 8

Trauma- and Stressor-Related Disorders

Susan N. Purrington

Most individuals have heard of post-traumatic stress disorder, most often referred to as PTSD, but do not realize that the chapter of the DSM-5-TR that outlines the diagnostic criteria for PTSD actually includes a variety of other disorders also related to traumatic or stressful events. The unique feature shared by the disorders in the chapter is the requirement of each that an individual has been exposed to an identifiable stressor prior to the onset of symptoms. Without the presence of an identifiable stressor, psychopathology and associated symptoms can still develop, but the diagnosis will not be related to the chapter of the DSM-5-TR pertaining to trauma- and stressor-related disorders. Key disorders in the DSM-5-TR include PTSD, acute stress disorder, adjustment disorder, reactive attachment disorder, disinhibited social engagement disorder, and prolonged grief disorder, which is new to the DSM as it was not included prior to the DSM-5.

PTSD, the most well known of the diagnoses, is characterized by the development of cognitive and mood symptoms following exposure to actual or threatened death, serious injury, or sexual violence (APA, 2022). The exposure to the traumatic event can be direct, such as the threat or violence being perpetrated against the identified patient, or witnessed, such as the patient seeing the threat or violence being perpetrated against another (APA, 2022). Additionally, individuals who learn about the threat or violence indirectly, such as through repeated exposure to the details of traumatic events, could also qualify for the diagnosis (APA, 2022). In addition to the cognitive and mood symptoms associated with PTSD, symptoms of intrusion, avoidance, marked alteration, or negative alterations must be present for a patient to meet diagnostic criteria for PTSD. Intrusion symptoms include flashbacks and nightmares as well as intrusive, unwelcome memories (APA, 2022). Avoidance of reminders of the trauma presents as avoiding the people, places, conversations, etc., that may remind the patient of the trauma that occurred (APA, 2022). Negative alterations in cognition and mood can include persistent negative beliefs and also guilt or anhedonia (APA, 2022), which refers to an individual's diminished capacity to

DOI: 10.4324/9781003586531-9

enjoy previously pleasurable activities. Finally, marked alterations in arousal and reactivity refers to hypervigilance and exaggerated startle response as well as irritability (APA, 2022). It is important to note that patients with PTSD can also sometimes present with dissociative symptoms such as depersonalization or derealization (APA, 2022).

Adjustment disorder as a diagnosis represents the development of psychopathology in response to an identifiable stressor and includes both marked distress that is out of proportion to the stressor that occurred as well as significant impairment in functioning (APA, 2022). The DSM-5-TR includes multiple specifiers that can be added to the adjustment disorder diagnosis, including with depressed mood, with anxiety, with mixed anxiety and depressed mood, with disturbance of conduct, and with mixed disturbance of emotions and conduct. Somewhat self-explanatory, the specifiers associated with adjustment disorder help clinicians identify additional symptoms the patient may be experiencing, such as low mood and tearfulness ("with depressed mood" specifier), nervousness and worry ("with anxiety" specifier), etc. Unlike PTSD, adjustment disorder is generally time-limited with symptoms remitting once the stressor or its consequence has resolved (APA, 2022).

Prolonged grief disorder, new to the DSM-5-TR, reflects grief considered to be pathological specifically because it persists and intensifies over time in a manner inconsistent with the expectations of a patient's culture (APA, 2022). Prolonged grief disorder can be diagnosed when such criteria are met after the passing of a close relative and when the bereaved individual experiences additional symptoms associated with intense yearning for or preoccupation with their lost loved one (APA, 2022). In order to avoid pathologizing culturally and/or religiously normative responses to grief, clinicians must carefully evaluate that which is considered normative within the patient's culture and/or religious tradition.

Clinical Case Vignette #1

Demographic Information and History

Name: Karry Williamson.

Demographic Information: Female, heterosexual, 34-years old, unmarried.

Medical Diagnoses: Karry reported none.

Reason for Referral: Karry served in the military and was encouraged to start therapy by her roommates, who expressed concern about her isolation and mood. She reported nightmares, difficulty sleeping, flashbacks, and feeling "on edge." Karry agreed with her roommates' assessment that she has been more socially isolated and irritable since she returned. Karry is hoping for effective coping tools to deal with her symptoms.

Karry estimated that these symptoms started after she returned from deployment, 3 months ago. She added that she "can't stop thinking" about watching people in her unit killed by a hidden explosive device. To cope with this, she avoids watching movies or shows with themes of war, and she asks people not to talk about her time deployed.

Clinical Interview Data

Interpreter Used: No.

Current Psychosocial Stressors: Karry described her current stressors as acclimating back to civilian life, socially and occupationally.

Protective Factors: Karry feels supported by her roommates.

Developmental History: Karry reported an unremarkable developmental history and reaching expected milestones on time.

Academic History: Karry completed college and reported earning As and Bs throughout school.

Social History: Karry reported strong social networks with roommates, friends, and co-workers. Karry also feels connected to her church community.

Household: Karry lives with three roommates.

Previous Psychiatric History: No history reported.

Family Psychiatric History: No history was reported.

History of Self-Harm: Karry reported no suicidal ideation. She added that she feels guilt for surviving when many of her friends were killed and she often wonders how things would be different if she had been the one who died.

Wellness Profile

Sleep: Karry described sleeping 2 to 4 hours a night due to feeling restless, nightmares, and flashbacks.

Diet: Karry reported no concerns.

Elimination: Karry reported no concerns.

Technology: Karry described her engagement with technology as "average."

Physical Activity: Karry reported she walks her dogs once a day and goes the gym on average three times a week.

Substance Use/Abuse: Karry reported no substance usage.

Physical/medical concerns: Karry reported none.

Current Psychiatric Symptoms

Depression: Karry reported that she often feels sad about the friends she lost.

Anxiety: Karry described her anxiety symptoms as restlessness, trouble sleeping, mind racing, heartbeat increasing, and flashbacks of the explosion. She experiences these symptoms during the day and at night.

Panic: Karry reported her anxiety peaking into a panic attack on several occasions.

Mania: Karry reported none.

Psychosis: Karry reported no symptoms.

Trauma: Karry reported no trauma history prior to the most recent deployment.

Eating Disorder: Karry reported no symptoms.

Risky Behaviors/Sexual Activity: Karry reported no symptoms.

Mental Status Exam

Appearance: Karry was dressed comfortably, wearing sweats and a t-shirt.

Behavior: Karry was open and cooperative.

Speech: Karry's rate, volume, and coherence was within normal range.

Mood: Karry stated her current mood as stressed and disconnected.

Affect: Karry displayed restricted affect.

Thought Process: Karry's thought process seemed logical and linear.

Thought Content: Karry reported no suicidal ideation, homicidal ideation, delusions, or hallucinations.

Orientation: Karry was oriented to person, place, time, and situation.

Recent Memory: Karry's recent memory appeared intact.

Remote Memory: Karry's remote memory appeared intact.

Attention/Concentration: Karry's attention and concentration were within normal limits.

General Knowledge: Karry presented with average to above average intelligence.

Language: Karry's language was within normal limits.

Insight: Karry presented good insight.

Judgment: Karry displayed good judgment.

Answer Key #1

Diversity Considerations

It may be helpful to consider interventions that take into account Karry's faith and involvement in her local church. Such involvement could serve as a protective factor, but both negative religious coping and stigma toward mental health treatment within the church community could also negatively impact Karry; as such, clinicians should remain aware of the possible of presence of both these factors.

Because she is a woman who has served in the military, Karry may both experience and express trauma in a manner that differs from that of the civilian population. Specifically, women serving in the military are at greater risk for experiencing gender-based discrimination, marginalization, and difficulty managing their dual roles as women and solders (Street et al., 2009; Maguen et al., 2012). Women serving in the military are also at greater risk of having been sexually assaulted (Kimerling et al., 2007). While Karry did not necessarily report these forms of trauma, she may be underreporting for a variety of reasons, as can sometimes happen with victims of trauma in general. While it would be inadvisable for the clinician to make assumptions about her history, it would be wise for the clinician to remained attuned to subtle indicators of trauma and/or discrimination that may become apparent during sessions. Additionally, Karry may present with ambivalence or resistance during sessions even given that she voluntarily presented for treatment. This ambivalence or resistance could potentially be attributed to the internalized stigma toward mental health treatment that can sometimes stem from values associated with stoicism, emotional suppression, and self-sufficiency, all of which are values promoted in the military (Hall, 2011) and which may impact help-seeking behaviors. Rather than conceptualizing this potential ambivalence or resistance as pathological, clinicians are encouraged instead to consider this possible ambivalence or resistance as a potential manifestation of Karry's occupational identity.

Because Karry is experiencing a life transition that, for many, includes the need to reconstruct both personal and professional identity, she may experience additional stressors not yet disclosed. Specifically, veterans often report loss of identity and purpose following deployment (Demers, 2011) and some of Karry's reported distress may be related to those factors. Clinicians may wish to ensure they do not overpathologize Karry's presentation but instead conceptualize some aspects of her experience as representing normative transitional stages and their affective experiences.

Ethical Considerations

It is important for the clinician to continually assess concerns for potential suicidal ideation.

Legal Considerations

Because she is a veteran, Karry may be entitled to certain rights and benefits, such as access to both medical and mental health treatment through her local veteran's administration offices. While she is likely aware of these benefits, the clinician may wish to provide her with education regarding services available to her and how she can advocate for herself. While Karry did not report any ongoing involvement with her local veteran's administration office, the clinician should be aware that patient records could be requested and potentially even subpoenaed should any questions arise regarding disability status, discharge upgrade, etc.

Diagnostic Impressions and Justification

F43.1 Post-Traumatic Stress Disorder.

Karry witnessed a traumatic event by watching her friends in her unit killed or injured by an explosion. She tries to avoid content that might stimulate those memories and feelings. She experiences intrusive memories, nightmares, and flashbacks, and feels irritable.

Psychodynamic Case Conceptualization

Karry's presentation could be understood as the manifestation of unresolved internal conflicts associated with both the traumatic event she witnessed and ongoing variables related to identity and a sense of loss. The nightmares and flashbacks she reported experiencing could be evidence of a repetition compulsion, a mechanism by which the unconscious attempts to master trauma by re-experiencing it in different forms. Karry also reported engaging in defense mechanisms commonly employed by individuals who have experienced trauma, specifically, avoidance and emotional numbing (McWilliams, 2011).

Appropriate treatment goals grounded in a psychodynamic approach to treatment include increasing Karry's awareness of her unconscious internal conflicts and internalized guilt while improving her ability to tolerate distressing affective states without resorting to the use of maladaptive defenses.

When providing Karry with treatment grounded in psychodynamic theory, the clinician may wish to help Karry explore any fantasies associated with possible survivor's guilt by utilizing free association and empathic attunement with the use of empathic and reflective listening. Interpretation can also be used to help Karry develop insight into her unconscious internal conflicts as well as any transference dynamics that may arise.

Cognitive Behavioral Conceptualization

Karry is experiencing faulty thinking about her role in the explosion. Specifically, she is presenting with automatic thoughts and core beliefs that appear to be contributing to her symptoms. Some potential problematic core beliefs could be, "I am responsible for what happened," "No one understands what I have been through," "Life is never going to feel normal again," etc. These core beliefs could be contributing to automatic thoughts such as, "It should have been me," "I can't handle being back home," etc. Karry is also engaging in behaviors that are maintaining her distressing symptoms, including social withdrawal and avoidance of stimuli that remind her of her experiences serving in the military.

Appropriate treatment goals grounded in CBT include improving Karry's understanding of PTSD, restructuring her automatic thoughts, and reducing avoidance behaviors. Karry would also benefit from learning and practicing adaptive coping skills. Additionally, increasing in engagement would support Karry's overall mental health.

Treatment could potentially begin with the clinician providing Karry with psychoeducation about both PTSD and the multidirectional relationship between cognitions, emotions, and behaviors. Socratic questioning and thought records could support Karry in learning how to identify the automatic thoughts contributing to her distress. To support Karry in reducing avoidance behaviors, the clinician can help Karry draft a fear hierarchy and then help her work through the hierarchy both during sessions and also by assigning homework to her between sessions. Working through the fear hierarchy could include imaginal exposure, in vivo exposure, virtual reality exposure, or a combination of all three, depending on the resources available to the clinician. Teaching Karry adaptive coping skills prior to having her work through the fear hierarchy could support her overall success when finally engaging with the fear hierarchy. Additionally, behavior activation can be implemented through the use of activity scheduling to increase

Karry's involvement in meaningful and/or pleasurable activities, such as activities at her church and/or socializing with her roommates.

Biopsychosocial Conceptualization

While Karry did not report a significant medical history, she did report sleep disturbance and physiological arousal which could be consistent with hyperactivation of the hypothalamic-pituitary-adrenal axis (HPA axis), a common physiological response often associated with PTSD (Yehuda et al., 2013). Karry is being negatively affected by her PTSD symptoms including negative alterations in cognition and mood and in avoidance. She is also in the process of transitioning from military life to civilian life, which constitutes a major life transition that could result in identity disruption (Castro & Kintzle, 2014). She is struggling both socially and with regard to her ability to obtain and maintain meaningful occupation, which is likely also contributing to her distress.

Appropriate treatment goals grounded in the biopsychosocial model include improving sleep quantity and quality while reducing physiological hyperarousal. Karry would also benefit from the clinician helping her directly address and reduce her symptoms of PTSD while improving her distress tolerance and affective expression skills. An additional treatment goal would include supporting Karry in forming a narrative that helps her create meaning out of the traumatic experiences she endured. Finally, Karry would benefit from direct support with community reintegration as well as occupational stability.

Clinical interventions could include improving sleep hygiene by providing psychoeducation and helping develop a consistent sleep schedule. Appropriate sleep hygiene could include 20–30 minutes of exercise during the day before dinner as well as eliminating nighttime screen use. Interventions grounded in mindfulness-based interventions such as progressive muscle relaxation, diaphragmatic breathing, and guided imagery could improve sleep. Interventions stemming from CBT may also be helpful – for example, cognitive restructuring and Socratic questioning, or engagement in cognitive processing therapy. Interventions from dialectal behavior therapy (DBT) can also be incorporated into treatment. It would be appropriate to refer Karry to a support group or social group for veterans, especially if a local group specifically for women who have served in the armed forces can be found. Increased meaningful engagement with her church community may be helpful as well as some sort of mentoring program for veterans struggling to find and/or maintain employment. A local peer mentorship group, whereby veterans who have successfully transitioned into civilian life could provide mentorship and support would be especially helpful. Of note, because Karry reports being religious, explicit use of religiously integrated interventions may be appropriate. Karry may also benefit from referral to a chaplain or spiritual director who can support Karry in making meaning out of her traumatic experiences in the military through the lens of her particular worldview. A referral to grief counseling may also be appropriate.

Clinical Case Vignette #2

Demographic Information and History

Name: Oscar Rodriguez.

Demographic Information: Male, heterosexual, 45-years old, married.

Medical Diagnoses: Oscar reported none.

Reason for Referral: Oscar is self-referred to therapy. He is hoping to address his unresolved grief from losing his 16-year-old daughter to cancer 2 years ago. He stated that he still feels stuck and unable to cope with her gone. Oscar struggles with getting out of bed, and he spends most days sitting in his daughter's bedroom "longing for her to walk through the door again." Oscar feels responsible for her death and questions if he missed warning signs from the cancer. His persistent sadness, low energy, and feelings of hopelessness have not lessened since she was gone. Due to these difficulties, he lost his job and has struggled to maintain relationships with his family and friends.

Clinical Interview Data

Interpreter Used: No.

Current Psychosocial Stressors: Oscar is experiencing financial challenges due to his unemployment, and relational difficulties due to his isolation.

Protective Factors: Oscar attends church most Sundays with his family, and he described this community as "an anchor."

Developmental History: Oscar reported an unremarkable developmental history and reaching expected milestones on time.

Academic History: Oscar completed his doctorate in mathematics and earned a 4.0 throughout his schooling.

Social History: In the last two years, Oscar has struggled to maintain friendships and feels disconnected/isolated from family members.

Household: Oscar is married, and he has two teenagers living at home and one child in college.

Previous Psychiatric History: No history reported.

Family Psychiatric History: No history was reported.

History of Self-Harm: Oscar said he often feels hopeless about the future and does not see a "reason to keep going." While he denied self-harm or suicidal ideation, he said he often imagines seeing his daughter in Heaven one day.

Wellness Profile

Sleep: Oscar estimates that he averages approximately 5 hours of sleep a night since his daughter passed away.

Diet: Oscar stated that he does not usually feel hungry but makes himself eat two to three meals a day.

Elimination: Oscar reported no concerns.

Technology: Oscar estimated that his engagement with technology was significantly higher than prior to his daughter's death. Oscar stated that he spends between 5 and 6 hours a day "mindlessly scrolling" through social media posts or reading the news.

Physical Activity: Oscar reported no exercise activity.

Substance Use/Abuse: Oscar reported no substance usage.

Physical/medical concerns: Oscar reported none.

Current Psychiatric Symptoms

Depression: Oscar reported that he often feels depressed and guilty about losing his daughter.

Anxiety: Oscar reported no symptoms.

Panic: Oscar reported no symptoms.

Mania: Oscar reported none.

Psychosis: Oscar reported no symptoms.

Trauma: Oscar reported no symptoms.

Eating Disorder: Oscar reported historically eating an average amount (three meals and several snacks per day), but that he is numb to feeling hungry since his daughter passed away.

Risky Behaviors/Sexual Activity: Oscar reported no risky behaviors. He added that he has felt emotionally disconnected from his wife for 2 years, and that this has "significantly lowered" their sexual connection/activity.

Mental Status Exam

Appearance: Oscar seemed to have difficulty taking care of himself and would often arrive late for sessions. He often wore clothes that looked old and torn.

Behavior: Oscar was open but seemed to have low energy.

Speech: Oscar's rate, volume, and coherence was within normal range.

Mood: Oscar stated his general mood is feeling sad, hopeless, and guilty.

Affect: Oscar displayed restricted affect and often seemed disconnected to the emotional content. The main emotions Osar would express was sadness and hopelessness.

Thought Process: Oscar's thought process seemed logical and linear.

Thought Content: Oscar reported no suicidal ideation, homicidal ideation, delusions, or hallucinations.

Orientation: Oscar was oriented to person, place, time, and situation.

Recent Memory: Oscar's recent memory appeared intact.

Remote Memory: Oscar's remote memory appeared intact.

Attention/Concentration: Oscar often seemed distracted in session.

General Knowledge: Oscar presented with an above average intelligence.

Language: Oscar's language was within normal limits.

Insight: Oscar presented average insight.

Judgment: Oscar displayed average judgment.

Answer Key #2

Diversity Considerations

It may be helpful to consider interventions that take into account Oscar's faith and beliefs surrounding the afterlife. Religious beliefs can often provide a framework for understanding death, which can subsequently contribute to adaptive meaning-making (Pargament, 2007). An individual's beliefs supporting adaptive meaning-making after a loss is an example of positive religious coping that can be incredibly supportive for many individuals. At the same time, the clinician should be aware that negative religious coping, such as Oscar believing his daughter was taken from him as a form of divine retribution, could also become manifest and should therefore explore these considerations carefully.

Additionally, because Oscar is a Hispanic man, cultural values related to both family and grief may be salient to the overall case conceptualization. Oscar may specifically struggle with managing the depth of his grief and how much it has impaired him within the context of the pressure many Hispanic men feel to embody traditional masculine norms (such as emotional stoicism and fulfilling a provider role within his family). Some of these internal conflicts may be or may become especially profound given Oscar's specific occupational impairment. Additionally, given that strong intergenerational bonds and family cohesion are often emphasized in Hispanic culture, Oscar's feelings of disconnection from his wife and surviving children may be especially distressing to him as well as to the members of his family (Vasquez, 2007).

Ethical Considerations

It is important for the clinician to continually assess concerns for hopelessness and potential suicidal ideation.

Legal Considerations

No additional legal considerations.

Diagnostic Impressions and Justification

F43.8 Prolonged Grief Disorder.
Oscar lost his 16-year-old daughter to cancer 2 years ago. He has experienced persistent sadness, low energy, and feelings of hopelessness and guilt. Due to his arrested grief, Oscar was unable to perform at work and lost his job. He also isolates and has become disconnected from his children, wife, and friendships.

Psychodynamic Case Conceptualization

Oscar's overall presentation can be conceptualized as the result of complex unconscious internal conflicts as well as relational processes that have been activated as the result of the traumatic loss of his daughter following her battle with cancer. It is possible that guilt and recrimination are complicating the grieving process such that self-reproach has taken the place of actually grieving his loss, resulting in an arrested grief. As his grief has become arrested, his unconscious anger over his loss has become directed inward, resulting in self-punishment as well as the self-imposed isolation in which he is engaging (Blatt, 2004). Oscar also appears to be engaging ins several primitive defense mechanisms, including denial and idealization. Because parents often experience their children as extensions of themselves and because traditional masculinity often allows the space for men to identify as providers and protectors, the loss of his daughter may have resulted in a narcissistic injury profoundly negatively affecting Oscar's sense of self. Overall, Oscar's ego functioning appears to be significantly compromised. It is important to note that while it may not be reasonable to expect any parent to ever truly "get over" or "get past" the loss of a child, there is a way in which healthy grieving can allow the intense, overwhelming initial grief to wax and wane over time, so that even though the loss remains present, sometimes more strongly than others, functioning for the sake of a spouse and remaining children can be maintained.

Appropriate treatment goals grounded in psychodynamic theory could include supporting Oscar in grieving the loss of his daughter, first by helping him identify and articulate the guilt he appears to be feeling regarding her loss. Addressing his internalized guilt and blame would be important to an optimal therapeutic outcome as would improving ego strength and emotional regulation as well as repairing any experience of identity disruption.

The first step in providing Oscar with competent psychodynamic care would be to establish a safe, consistent holding environment that could eventually facilitate Oscar's experience of a corrective emotional experience. The clinician may wish to explore Oscar's perspective on fatherhood and how being a father has impacted the formation of his identity. Over time, the clinician might support Oscar in exploring internal representations of his daughter, including both idealized aspects and potentially unresolved aspects. Interpretations could eventually be utilized to help Oscar connect his symptoms of prolonged grief disorder with any unconscious internal conflicts related to loss. It may become important at some point during treatment to gently challenge Oscar's belief that he could have prevented his daughter's death, a belief that might be rooted in an unconscious fantasy about his own omnipotence.

Cognitive Behavioral Conceptualization

Oscar appears to be presenting with maladaptive core beliefs as well as negative automatic thoughts regarding his own failings as a father as well as his worthlessness without his daughter present in his life to give him a sense of identity and meaning. These maladaptive core beliefs are contributing to his affective experience of hopelessness and sorrow. He may also be experiencing conditional assumptions, such as, "If I don't grieve every day, it means I didn't love her," or "If I move on with my life, it means I am forgetting her." These problematic conditional assumptions can not only inhibit psychological recovery but also reinforce avoidance behaviors.

In Oscar's situation, CBT could be used to reduce symptoms of depression and improve overall daily functioning. Throughout treatment, the clinician could address Oscar's maladaptive cognitions, especially those related to guilt and self-blame. Oscar would also benefit from increasing his adaptive functioning skills, specifically to replace the rumination in which he is currently engaging.

Behavioral activation could be utilized to help Oscar re-engage with both activities of daily living (ADLs) and meaningful activities that engage his sense of pleasure and accomplishment. Socratic questioning and cognitive restructuring could be implemented to address the maladaptive cognitions contributing to his symptoms. If competent in the treatment modalities, the clinician could implement complicated grief therapy (CGT) to help Oscar integrate the loss of his daughter into the overall story of his life (Shear, 2015) or mindfulness-based cognitive therapy (MBCT) to increase awareness of the present moment rather than rumination on past events. Self-compassion activities and/or loving-kindness meditation may be particularly helpful. Another helpful treatment modality grounded in the principles of CBT that may be helpful to Oscar would be acceptance and commitment therapy (ACT). Implementation of ACT could help Oscar eventually accept the loss of his daughter, potentially in a manner consistent with his faith tradition, while helping clarify his values as a father, husband, and, overall, an accomplished Hispanic man.

Biopsychosocial Conceptualization

While Oscar did not report any history of medical or psychiatric illness, his current sleep dysregulation is likely negatively impacting both his physiology and psychology. Additionally, his reduced appetite may be causing him to consume fewer nutrients than he needs to maintain adequate energy levels throughout the day. Overall, the chronic stress associated with his grief may have disrupted Oscar's HPA axis, contributing to his depressive symptoms including anhedonia (Keller et al., 2017). Oscar's unresolved grief is interfering with ADLs in part because his loss was traumatic and in part because of the cognitions and behaviors maintaining his symptoms (Boelen et al., 2006). His occupational difficulties have also likely further undermined his sense of agency and identity, especially as he was so successful prior to the loss of his daughter. Because the loss of a child can severely strain family relationships, including marital relationships and parent/child relationships with surviving children, Oscar has also lost the safe harbor that could have been his wife and children.

Appropriate treatment goals grounded in the biopsychosocial model include improving sleep as well as other health maintenance behaviors such as adequate nutrition and physical activity. Mitigating symptoms of prolonged grief disorder and increasing social engagement would also be appropriate goals.

Psychoeducation regarding sleep hygiene, relaxation training, and, in general, having a much more structured daily routine would all be helpful in supporting increased participation in health maintenance behaviors. If competent in the treatment modality, the clinician could implement CGT or even CBT strategies as needed. A referral to couples' therapy, family therapy, or both, may be warranted given Oscar's report, but more information would be need prior to confirming such referrals. Re-engagement in his profession, even if at first that simply means reading the most recent academic peer-reviewed journals from his field, may be helpful. Additionally, the clinician should encourage Oscar to connect with one friend or colleague each week. Oscar may even benefit from participating in a support group specifically for parents who have lost children due to cancer, such as Padres Contra el Cancer, a group located in California that offers support services in both Spanish and English.

Clinical Case Vignette #3

Demographic Information and History

Name: Billy Martin.

Demographic Information: Male, heterosexual, 21-years old, unmarried.

Medical Diagnoses: Billy reported none.

Reason for Referral: Billy is starting counseling at the encouragement of his academic advisor. Billy moved from New York to Oregon 4 months ago for an internship. Within 2 months of the move, Billy started experiencing sadness, difficulty making friends, and performing in his internship duties. Billy added that he feels "homesick" and misses his family and friends. Although Billy is usually extroverted, he noticed he has withdrawn from social functions and rarely replies to family and friends back home. He doesn't believe it is worth the energy to make new friendships because his internship will end after a year.

Clinical Interview Data

Interpreter Used: No.

Current Psychosocial Stressors: Billy described his current stressors as being in a new state away from family and friends, and starting an internship.

Protective Factors: Billy stated his university has been supportive in his current struggles and helped him find a therapist.

Developmental History: Billy reported an unremarkable developmental history and reaching expected milestones on time.

Academic History: Billy is completing an internship requirement for his college degree, and described his academic history as mostly As and Bs with occasional Cs.

Social History: Billy reported a strong history of close connections with family and friends; however, he currently does not live near these individuals and has withdrawn from making new connections.

Household: Billy has two younger siblings living at home in New York. He currently rents a small apartment and lives by himself.

Previous Psychiatric History: No history reported.

Family Psychiatric History: Billy reported that his mother has a history of depression, although he did not know more specific details.

History of Self-Harm: Billy reported no suicidal ideation or self-harm history.

Wellness Profile

Sleep: Billy estimated that he averages 5–6 hours of sleep a night.

Diet: Billy noticed that he does not feel hungry and skips a meal several times a week.

Elimination: Billy reported no concerns.

Technology: Billy estimates that his screentime has increased since being away from home. He says he "gets lost" playing video games, averaging 4 hours a night after he gets home from the internship.

Physical Activity: Billy described his physical activity as minimal to none.

Substance Use/Abuse: Billy reported no substance usage.

Physical/medical concerns: Billy reported none.

Current Psychiatric Symptoms

Depression: Billy reported that he misses home. He added that he feels sad most days, often to the point of crying at night.

Anxiety: Billy reported no anxiety symptoms.

Panic: Billy reported no panic symptoms.

Mania: Billy reported symptoms of mania or hypomania.

Psychosis: Billy reported no symptoms of psychosis.

Trauma: Billy reported no symptoms of trauma.

Eating Disorder: Billy reported no symptoms. According to Billy, the occasional missed meals did not seem impactful.

Risky Behaviors/Sexual Activity: Billy reported no symptoms.

Mental Status Exam

Appearance: Billy was dressed casually and seemed disheveled at times.

Behavior: Billy was open and cooperative.

Speech: Billy's rate, volume, and coherence was within normal range.

Mood: Billy described his mood as withdrawn and unmotivated.

Affect: Billy displayed restricted affect.

Thought Process: Billy's thought process seemed logical and linear.

Thought Content: Billy reported no suicidal ideation, homicidal ideation, delusions, or hallucinations.

Orientation: Billy was oriented to person, place, time, and situation.

Recent Memory: Billy's recent memory appeared intact.

Remote Memory: Billy's remote memory appeared intact.

Attention/Concentration: Billy's attention and concentration were within normal limits.

General Knowledge: Billy presented with average intelligence.

Language: Billy's language was within normal limits.

Insight: Billy presented low to average insight. He could make connections between the new environment and his sadness, but he had difficulty understanding how his isolation behaviors were exacerbating his sadness.

Judgment: Billy displayed average judgment.

Answer Key #3

Diversity Considerations

Billy may be experiencing gender-based social pressures about if and how to express emotions and seek support. Specifically, as a young man, he may be influenced by internalized traditional gender roles that often discourage men from engaging in help-seeking behaviors or demonstrating any form of emotional vulnerability, which can lead to internalized stigma (Mahalik et al., 2003). Additionally, moving from New York to Oregon represents a significant geographical change, although this may depend on where in New York he grew up and where in Oregon he is now living. An argument can be made with regard to similarities between urban parts of New York and urban areas of Oregon, as well as between rural areas of New York and rural parts of Oregon, but a move from urban New York to rural Oregon may present as something of a culture shock.

Because he is 21 years old, Billy is currently in a stage of life often called emerging adulthood and might be considered a transitional age youth. This stage of life is often characterized by identity exploration, increasing independence, and significant social transitions, such as moving to obtain employment (Arnett, 2000). While these transitions can be considered normative, they are often experienced as stressful, specifically because the brains of most 21-year-olds are not fully developed and so deficits in executive functioning skills, adaptive living skills, and overall adaptive forms of coping can compound distress. Additionally, being an intern right out of college may reflect somewhat lower socioeconomic status, which points to the significance of the social determinants of health and barriers to care that Billy may experience as a result.

Ethical Considerations

None identified.

Legal Considerations

None identified.

Diagnostic Impressions and Justification

F43.21 Adjustment Disorder with Depressed Mood.

Billy moved to a new state for his internship, thereby leaving his support system, and the move serves as a clearly identifiable stressor. He feels disconnected from these relationships and has withdrawn socially. He has experienced symptoms of depression and has difficulty performing in his internship role. These symptoms started within the 3-month requirement for adjustment disorder.

Psychodynamic Case Conceptualization

Billy's recent life changes have destabilized him relationally and emotionally and may have activated past unresolved relational patterns and unconscious needs. To cope, Billy has turned to maladaptive defense mechanisms including regression into isolation, which suggests separation anxiety or potentially unresolved dependency needs. Billy may be struggling with internalized representations of attachment figures, potentially in the form of object loss. He is also likely experiencing unconscious internal conflicts associated with autonomy versus attachment and his symptoms of depression may serve as a way of remaining emotionally close to or even loyal to the family he left behind. Billy also appears to depend on primitive defense mechanisms including avoidance, intellectualization, denial, and regression to protect himself from potentially more overwhelming affective states. Of note, because Billy can be considered an emerging adult currently processing through a developmental transition, his emotional regression could represent a development arrest, i.e., a retreat into dependency due to overwhelming challenges associated with individuation.

Appropriate psychodynamic treatment goals include increasing conscious awareness of affective states and internal conflicts, while decreasing dependence on maladaptive defense mechanisms. Billy may also benefit from the opportunity to modify internalized objects. Finally, Billy might benefit from support in transitioning through the developmental stage in which he has found himself as well as strengthening his ego functions.

Free association would be an important clinical intervention in order to allow Billy the space to learn how to articulate the affective states he currently finds overwhelming. Clarification and confrontation can also be utilized to support Billy in developing insight into the discrepancies between what he says and how he reports feeling. Interpretations can also be utilized to bring awareness to the ways in which maladaptive defense mechanisms may be protecting Billy from more overwhelming affective states. Additionally, interpretations of transference dynamics can help improve Billy's insight into how past relationships have impacted him and may even be re-enacted in present relationships. Supportive techniques can be utilized to facilitate developmental tasks and exploration into themes pertaining to autonomy and individuation. Throughout the therapeutic encounter, the therapeutic alliance and holding environment should provide the context for healing.

Cognitive Behavioral Conceptualization

Billy may be interpreting his current situation with a critical and discouraging lens. His belief that it is not worth the effort to make new friends is causing him to withdraw and isolate, exacerbating his depressive symptoms and reducing his ability to perform in his internship. Specifically, he may hold core beliefs centered on themes of helplessness and worthlessness as well as impermanence. Certain intermediate beliefs and/or assumptions pertaining to failure and loneliness are likely exacerbating his symptoms, as are automatic thoughts pertaining to belongingness as well as the lack thereof. Additionally, Billy's behaviors, such as avoiding social connectedness and engaging in excessive screentime, as well as skipping meals, are likely maintaining his symptoms.

Goals consistent with CBT would include improving Billy's mood while decreasing his symptoms, especially his symptoms of depression, through the implementation of adaptive coping skills. CBT could also support Billy in restructuring his automatic thoughts while increasing his insight into how his behaviors are maintaining his symptoms. Additionally, CBT can support Billy in increasing his social engagement and social support.

Behavioral activation can be utilized to support Billy in developing a structured schedule that creates opportunities for meaningful engagement. Mood tracking can be utilized throughout to track progress and implement treatment modifications as needed. Cognitive restructuring, Socratic questioning, and thought logs can all be utilized to help Billy identify cognitive distortions, such as catastrophic and/or dichotomous thinking, while helping him gather evidence for more adaptive thoughts he can later implement. Graded exposure and social skills training can support Billy in gradually re-engaging in social activities while developing the skills to feel confident when engaging in social interactions. Psychoeducation and cost-benefit analysis may be crucial throughout the therapeutic process. Teaching, practicing, and reinforcing adaptive coping strategies will also be supportive throughout treatment.

Biopsychosocial Conceptualization

Billy may have a genetic disposition to depression, especially since he believes his mother has a history of depression. Additionally, his irregular meals may serve as both a symptom and a contributor to the symptoms he is reporting. His inadequate sleep is likely also contributing to his emotional dysregulation. He is also withdrawing from connection, which is limiting his social support, while increasing his screentime, which is likely providing him with some short-term relief but overall exacerbating his symptoms. Cognitive distortions are playing a role in Billy's overall presentation as well as his difficulty adjusting to a normative developmental task. Billy's psychosocial context plays a significant role in his overall presentation: being in a geographically and potentially culturally new environment, far from his support system consisting of family and friends, is serving as both the activating issue and the major maintainer of his difficult symptoms.

Appropriate treatment goals grounded in the biopsychosocial model include improving sleep, nutrition, and physical activity, all in service of improving and supporting Billy's physical and mental health. Additional goals could include mitigating symptoms of depression and increasing engagement in social activities.

Billy would benefit from psychoeducation regarding sleep hygiene as well as a course of cognitive behavioral therapy for insomnia (CBTi) to improve the quantity and quality of his sleep. Billy would also benefit from general education about the mind-body connection, including how appropriate nutrition can support both adequate energy throughout the day as well as a better, more balanced affective experience. If needed, Billy could be referred to a registered dietitian for additional education and monitoring. Behavioral activation could be utilized to increase Billy's level of engagement in physical activities as well as social engagement. Graded exposure could be used to increase engagement in both physical activities and social activities, with positive reinforcement being provided as warranted. The clinician can also engage Billy in cognitive restructuring and/or mindfulness-based stress reduction activities. Billy should also be encouraged to maintain connection with his family at home as they may serve as valuable supports during this transitional period.

Conclusion

Trauma- and stressor-related disorders, as they are defined in the DSM-5-TR, represent a unique category of disorders primarily identified by the presence of an identifiable stressor at the outset of the disorder. While PTSD is the best known disorder currently included in this particular diagnostic category, the category itself contains several disorders meant to capture the nuanced impact of significant stressors, including trauma, on human functioning. The clinical case vignettes included in this chapter highlight the necessity for individualized assessment as well as treatment planning completed within the context of cultural humility. While keeping diagnostic criteria in mind is crucial to the conceptualization and treatment process, clinicians must also be willing to explore the subjective meaning of the stressor itself to the affected individual in order to avoid overpathologizing potentially normative responses to loss and change.

References

APA (American Psychiatric Association). (2022). *Diagnostic and statistical manual of mental disorders* (5th ed., text rev.). American Psychiatric Association. https://doi.org/10.1176/appi.books.9780890425787.

Arnett, J. J. (2000). Emerging adulthood: A theory of development from the late teens through the twenties. *American Psychologist*, *55*(5), 469–480 https://doi.org/10.1037/0003-066X.55.5.469.

Blatt, S. J. (2004). *Experiences of depression: Theoretical, clinical, and research perspectives*. American Psychological Association.

Boelen, P. A., van den Bout, J., & de Keijser, J. (2006). Traumatic grief as a distinct disorder: A rationale, consensus criteria, and a preliminary empirical test. *Clinical Psychology: Science and Practice*, *13*(2), 135–155. https://doi.org/10.1111/j.14682850.2006.00013.x.

Castro, C. A., & Kintzle, S. (2014). Suicides in the military: The post-modern combat veteran and the Hemingway effect. *Current Psychiatry Reports*, *16*(8), 460. https://doi.org/10.1007/s11920-014-0460-1.

Demers, A. (2011). When veterans return: The role of community in reintegration. *Journal of Loss and Trauma*, *16*(2), 160–179. https://doi.org/10.1080/15325024.2010.519281.

Hall, L. K. (2011). The importance of understanding military culture. *Social Work in Health Care*, *50*(1), 4–18. https://doi.org/10.1080/00981389.2010.513914.

Keller, J., Gomez, R. G., Williams, G., Lembke, A., Lazzeroni, L., Murphy, G. M., & Schatzberg, A. F. (2017). HPA axis in major depression: Cortisol, clinical symptomatology and genetic variation predict cognition. *Molecular Psychiatry*, *22*(4), 527–536. https://doi.org/10.1038/mp.2016.120.

Kimerling, R., Gima, K., Smith, M. W., Street, A., & Frayne, S. (2007). The Veterans Health Administration and military sexual trauma. *American Journal of Public Health*, *97*(12), 2160–2166. https://doi.org/10.2105/AJPH.2006.092999.

Maguen, S., Luxton, D. D., Skopp, N. A., & Madden, E. (2012). Gender differences in traumatic experiences and mental health in active duty soldiers redeployed from Iraq and Afghanistan. *Journal of Psychiatric Research*, *46*(3), 311–316. https://doi.org/10.1016/j.jpsychires.2011.11.007.

Mahalik, J. R., Burns, S. M., & Syzdek, M. (2003). Masculinity and perceived normative health behaviors as predictors of men's health behaviors. *Social Science & Medicine*, *64*(11), 2201–2209. https://doi.org/10.1016/S0277-9536(02)00450-3.

McWilliams, N. (2011). *Psychoanalytic diagnosis: Understanding personality structure in the clinical process* (2nd ed.). Guilford Press.

Pargament, K. I. (2007). *Spiritually integrated psychotherapy: Understanding and addressing the sacred.* Guilford Press.

Shear, M. K. (2015). Complicated grief treatment: Theoretical foundations and treatment procedures. *Journal of Loss and Trauma*, 20(2), 98–109. https://doi.org/10.1080/15325024.2013.819491.

Street, A. E., Vogt, D., & Dutra, L. (2009). A new generation of women veterans: Stressors faced by women deployed to Iraq and Afghanistan. *Clinical Psychology Review*, *29*(8), 685–694. https://doi.org/10.1016/j.cpr.2009.08.007.

Vasquez, M. J. T. (2007). Cultural difference and the therapeutic alliance: An evidence-based analysis. *American Psychologist*, *62*(8), 878–885.

Yehuda, R., Daskalakis, N. P., Desarnaud, F., Makotkine, I., Lehrner, A. L., Koch, E., Flory, J. D., Buxbaum, J. D., Meaney, M. J., & Bierer, L. M. (2013). Epigenetic biomarkers as predictors and correlates of symptom improvement following psychotherapy in combat veterans with PTSD. *Frontiers in Psychiatry*, *27*(4), 118.

Chapter 9

Dissociative Disorders

Jessie Lowell

Disorders included in the chapter of the DSM-5-TR pertaining to dissociative disorders are characterized by disruptions or breakdowns in memory, identity, perception, sense of self, behavior and/or awareness of one's reality. They have the potential to disrupt every area of mental functioning. There are three primary disorders included in this section of the DSM-5-TR: dissociative identity disorder (DID), dissociative amnesia, and depersonalization/derealization disorder (DPDR) (APA, 2022). Unspecified dissociative disorders and other specified dissociative disorders are also included. This chapter focuses on dissociative identity disorder and depersonalization/derealization disorder. These disorders have in common a disconnection between thoughts, feelings, behaviors, sensations, and other mental processes that is severe enough to impact functioning.

Dissociative identity disorder is considered the most severe of the dissociative disorders and involves the presence of two or more distinct personality states that control behavior. There is a marked discontinuity in sense of self and it is accompanied by alterations in affect, consciousness, memory, perception, cognition and/or sensorimotor functioning. There must be a presence of at least one "alter," or distinct, personality state, in addition to the host. The symptoms may be self-reported or observed by others. The person with DID will also have gaps in memory of everyday events and important personal information. The symptoms must cause distress or impairment in functioning and cannot be a normal part of a broadly accepted cultural or religious practice. For children, the symptoms cannot be better explained by imaginary playmates or fantasy play. These dissociative states also cannot be attributed to physiological effects of a substance or other medical condition.

Dissociative amnesia is a dissociative disorder in which a person experiences an inability to recall important autobiographical information that is inconsistent with normal forgetting. This is often related to traumatic or stressful events. This must cause clinical distress or impairment and not be attributable to the effects of a substance, neurological condition, or other medical condition. Dissociative amnesia can occur in the context of dissociative identity disorder and is not diagnosed as a separate disorder in those cases.

DOI: 10.4324/9781003586531-10

Depersonalization/derealization disorder is a dissociative disorder characterized by persistent and distressing episodes in which the person experiences feelings of unreality and detachment from their own self and surroundings. Depersonalization is an alteration of perception and a feeling of the self as strange or unreal or a feeling of being detached from, or as an outside observer of, one's thoughts, feelings, sensations, body, or actions. Derealization is defined as the perception of other people, objects, or the world as strange or unreal. Most people will experience minor and fleeting moments of depersonalization and derealization over their lifespan. Those with DPDR experience persistent episodes of depersonalization or derealization or both and have resulting functional impairment.

Clinical Case Vignette #1

Demographic Information and History

Name: Samantha Silverton.

Demographic Information: A 26-year-old Caucasian female.

Medical Diagnoses: Samantha is healthy with no previous significant medical issues. She has had previous bouts of sexually transmitted infections but reports that she has never been sexually active.

Reason for Referral: Samantha was encouraged by her parents to request an assessment. Samantha, admits that she may have some memory and organization challenges, but only agreed to an assessment to prove to her parents that "nothing is wrong with her." She acknowledges that she is forgetful, has a hard time maintaining employment, and struggles with social relationships, but feels that her parents exaggerate the problem and make up stories. She indicates that she is shy, has difficulty trusting others, and prefers to spend time alone.

Clinical Interview Data

Interpreter Used: No.

Current Psychosocial Stressors: Samantha lives at home with her parents because she reports having a string of bad luck. She has attempted to maintain employment, but has been dismissed from her last few jobs. She believes that, because she is reluctant to engage with people at her jobs in a social manner, they dislike her. This leads people to make up stories or place blame on her for things she did not do. She wants to live independently because she feels the same way at home. Her parents are often accusing her of misbehavior or being disrespectful, but she does not understand why. She finds it stressful in the home but cannot leave without a more stable income.

Protective Factors: Samantha presents as intelligent and functional. She is financially supported by her parents and although there seem to be disagreements between her and her parents, they seem to care about her well-being. Samantha reported herself to be an evangelical Christian and places great importance of this in her life.

Developmental History: Samantha reported meeting all her developmental milestones within the expected timeframes. She does not recall ever needing services in school, but that she was taken to many professionals over the years. She believes her parents have felt that something was wrong with her since she was around 9 or 10 years old, but she was never diagnosed with any condition.

Academic History: Samantha completed high school but felt too unsure of herself to go to college. She was overwhelmed by the idea. She often regrets not earning a degree and wonders if she would be able to be more successful in a career than in the types of jobs she has worked at. She worked hard, but did not do well in school. She thinks her memory was an issue back then as well. She paid attention but often missed assignments and was unprepared for tests. She also reported that teachers did not like her. She did not understand why they would indicate she was disrespectful when she hardly spoke at school. She was tested for learning and attention problems when she was in middle and high school but was never given services.

Social History: Samantha reported that she does not have any friends. She has always struggled socially. She has often wondered if she has something like an autism spectrum disorder. From an early age, Samantha thought people were her friends, but then they would be angry with her or would stop talking to her. Other times people she did not know would treat her like they were friends or they knew each other. She has questioned whether she really understands people and social relationships. She reports finding it more enjoyable to be alone than try to understand other people. She says her mother and father are who she spends time with when she does not want to be alone. She has never been in a relationship and identifies as heterosexual. She knows it is unusual and has tried to explain to her physician that she not been sexually active, but feels her medical provider and parents do not believe her.

Samantha desires to find a church community but has also experienced issues at a number of churches. After being at a church for some time, church members will either accuse her of misconduct, try to pray for her for sins she has not committed, or people start to exclude her from events. Her own mother at times has said she thinks Samantha is possessed. She finds that she connects with God best on her own through reading her Bible, prayer, and devotion.

Household: Samantha lives at home with her parents and has never lived independently. She reported that she is an only child. She said a maternal uncle lived with them when she was younger, but she has not seen him since she was about 9 years old. Her parents refuse to speak about him, and they have no contact with extended family members.

Previous Psychiatric History: Samantha has seen a number of psychiatrists and psychologists over the years trying to convince her parents that she does not have a mental health issue. At times in her life she thought maybe something was wrong with her, but after all these evaluations she convinced that maybe is more of a neurological issue instead like her memory. Samantha did admit that she has woken up once or twice in a hospital and not been sure why. She would stay a couple days and then they would let her go home. It never really made sense to her, but this only encouraged her parents to be more certain something was wrong.

Family Psychiatric History: Samantha does not have much information about her family history as her parents do not talk about their families. She does not remember ever meeting her father's family. She remembers, when she was younger, her mother's family was very active in her life but has no current contact and her mother refuses to talk about them. Although her parents have not told her of any psychiatric history sometimes, she wonders if her mother has paranoia or a condition that makes her create stories or lies.

History of Self-Harm: Samantha reports at no time has she ever thought about harming herself and has no thoughts of suicide. She has read in her medical charts, however, especially the hospital reports, that she has indicated suicidal intent, but she does not really trust medical professionals. She reported that she believes they mix up clients, tests, and charts all the time. She believes this is why they think she has had sexually transmitted infections when she has not ever been sexually active.

Wellness Profile

Sleep: Samantha reports that she sleeps well. She can easily sleep a whole day or two, but since she does not have a job or much to do in a day anyway, she feels that if her body needs the sleep, she allows herself to sleep. She is often tired even after sleeping long periods at a time.

Diet: Samantha reports that she eats healthy meals and has no concerns regarding her diet.

Elimination: Samantha has no reported concerns with elimination.

Technology: Samantha indicated that she prefers to read over watching television or movies. She enjoys jigsaw puzzles and word searches. This has, however, been another example of how she seems to lose focus because she will sometimes start a puzzle and come back to it being finished with no recall of having worked on it. She has a cellular phone but has little use for it except for her calendar; because she tends to be so forgetful, she relies on her phone's calendar. She does not have any social media as she is convinced that the technology is used by the government to track people. She knows they have access because she will get notifications for social media accounts that she does not even subscribe too and will find the applications on her phone even after she has deleted them.

Physical Activity: Samantha enjoys working out at the gym, although she does not like the way men there talk to her as though she knows them. She finds them vulgar and inappropriate. She goes to the gym most days but prefers to walk outside alone or with her mother.

Substance Use/Abuse: Samantha, despite her mother's accusations, does not drink alcohol, use any substances, or smoke cigarettes. She has no history of any these although her mother does not believe her. Samantha says that if you ask her mother, she would say that Samantha drinks alcohol to the point of blacking out and often comes home under the influence of substances, but that is not true.

Pain: 0/10.

Current Psychiatric Symptoms

Depression: Samantha denied any depressive symptoms.

Anxiety: Samantha reports feelings of anxiety at times because she never knows what to expect from people. She has had too many situations where people confront her unexpectedly or she is mistaken for someone else. She feels like she is unsure of her mother's mood on a daily basis.

Panic: Samantha denied any previous experiences of panic attacks.

Mania: Samantha denied any previous experiences of mania or hypomania.

Psychosis: Samantha did disclose that at times she has had experiences that she could only describe as feeling like she is watching herself. That these started in elementary school. She also has very vivid dreams and sometimes cannot tell the difference between a memory and a dream. In her dreams she is a different version of herself. She reported that sometimes she likes to go to sleep to see what this other version of herself is doing, almost like a movie. She has never experienced any visual or verbal hallucinations.

Eating Disorder: No reports of a history of disordered eating.

Risky Behaviors/Sexual Activity: Samantha reports that she is generally a very cautious person who likes to follow the rules. She reports being accident-prone as she often has bruises and other injuries she does not even remember getting.

Mental Status Exam

Appearance: Samantha was appropriately dressed and groomed. She was dressed conservatively and appeared her age.

Behavior: Samantha was observed to be cooperative and willing to discuss her personal history, although she was markedly timid. She often had her arms crossed into her body and her leg shook often as she spoke.

Speech: Samantha speech was appropriate although very quiet and almost whispered.

Mood: Samantha's mood was stable with a broad range of expressed emotions.

Affect: Samantha was observed to have a broad range of affect; however, she would appear uncomfortable after displaying affective responses.

Thought Process: Samantha's thought process was observed to be coherent.

Thought Content: Samantha's thought content was appropriate, although it appeared that at times she was confused or lacked detail that she could not explain, but this did not appear to distress her.

Orientation: Samantha was observed to be oriented to person, place, time, and situation; however, she often referred to her cellular phone's clock and date as though to assure herself.

Recent Memory: Samantha's recent memory was intact.

Remote Memory: Samantha's remote memory had a number of gaps and unexplained situations.

Attention/Concentration: Samantha's attention and concentration were excellent; especially for someone who reports this to be a concern.

General Knowledge: Samantha's general knowledge was within normal limits and she appeared to be very bright which does not correlate with her current situation.

Language: Samantha's language was within normal limits.

Insight: Samantha demonstrated what appeared to be good insight, but at other times in the interview it was clear she was not able to fully explain areas of her life that, given her level of knowledge and presentation, she should be able to explain.

Judgment: Samantha seems to avoid or dismiss anything that she cannot explain, which was more frequent in the interview than would be expected. She often indicated that others are mistaken or incorrect.

Answer Key #1

Diversity Considerations

Interventions should take into consideration Samantha's religious background. Specifically, some religions and cultures may describe Samantha's presentation as being the result of possession, as is the case with Samantha's mother. While Samantha's religious tradition and spiritual practices seem to be a source of strength for her, she has also experienced some interpersonal conflict with the members of her religious community which may contribute to spiritual struggle, specifically because of potential experiences with spiritual stigmatization. Samantha is also a woman, which may bring societal expectations of how to behave in addition to possible gender roles promoted from the perspective of a conservative religious tradition. Additionally, if Samantha's reports of social interactions are credible, she has experienced repeated experiences of gender-based discrimination and harassment, both by members of the general public such as men at the gym as well as medical professionals who seem suspicious of her self-reports. These experiences likely contribute to an overall feeling distrust when engaging with professionals and may also hamper help-seeking behaviors. Further evaluation is warranted.

Ethical Considerations

Although the information is not a clear history, there seems to be a history of suicidal ideation and/or attempts given her medical record. As the clinician in this case, it is vital to regularly assess for safety concerns and respond appropriately to ongoing suicidal ideation and/or self-harm attempts if needed. Because Samantha reported a long history of interactions with the mental health and medical symptoms, almost always at the insistence of her parents, it will also be important to ensure she is not being coerced to enter treatment, especially as she is financially dependent upon them, causing a more significant power differential than she might be comfortable with.

Legal Considerations

Legal guidelines would prompt further assessment in this case in two areas. The first area that should be noted and followed up on is possible abuse as a child. Samantha's history suggests that there was an uncle in the home until she was around 9 years old, at which time there was a rupture in the family and no contact has been made with the uncle. Given her symptoms, a more thorough assessment of possible early trauma, especially sexual trauma is warranted. As she is an adult, if a discovery is made of abuse, a mandated report would be necessary if the perpetrator is still known to have access to children. In this case, she has no contact with him and therefore a report should be thoughtfully considered. Additionally, while additional evaluation is warranted, Samantha reported multiple instances of unexplained injuries, testing positive for sexually transmitted diseases without a reported history of sexual activity, and concerning hospitalizations. While she does not currently appear to meet the criteria for being considered a dependent adult, it would be reasonable for the clinician to be concerned about ongoing abuse in the home as well as possible sexual exploitation. Should Samantha at any point be found to meet the definition of a dependent adult and should ongoing abuse of any kind be substantiated within the home, the clinician should inform Adult Protective Services (APS). As part of this ongoing assessment, the clinician should consider whether Samantha meets criteria for grave disability – consultation is recommended should the clinician require support with making such a determination.

While there is no indication at this time that Samantha's parents would wish to inappropriately inset themselves into treatment, she does live with them and she is financially dependent upon them. The clinician might then correctly assume that they are paying for treatment and might therefore feel the right to access Samantha's information. It will be important for the clinician to maintain appropriate and clear boundaries, including not disclosing any information to anyone with Samantha's express written consent.

Diagnostic Impressions and Justification

F44.81 Dissociative Identity Disorder.

Although this case would need further assessment to verify this diagnosis, the presentation suggests the possibility of dissociative identity disorder. Samantha appears to be presenting as her main personality, but describes a history of having the presence of a distinct personality state that has sharp discontinuities from her normal state that would satisfy Criterion A. She reports others having experienced her as someone who presents and behaves differently. Her alter appears to be more social, sexually active, expressive, and impulsive. Evidence also suggests her alter may experience suicidal ideation or attempts and abuses alcohol and substances.

Samantha also provides evidence of Criterion B by describing memory lapses, evidence of time loss, and unusual interactions with friends, family, and strangers. She has indicated dissociative fugue episodes (dissociation related to travel or wandering) as well as amnesia for everyday events, which she downplays or rationalizes. She has been having issues with peers, teachers, and parents for years that she is unaware of. She has been dismissed from jobs and hospitalized without clear rationale. Even though she appears to be functioning well, she is unable to maintain employment, has conflict with her family, and lacks community, all indicating that she meets Criterion C.

Although it appears she drinks alcohol to the point of blacking out when in her alter state, it does not appear that that alone is explaining the symptoms. She also does not appear to have any other medical or religious or cultural explanation for the dissociative experience (Criteria D and E).

It should be noted that the majority of individuals with DID are undiagnosed and even clinicians might not recognize the presence of alters for some time. DID most often has roots in childhood and subtle symptoms can be noted in children; it is most often diagnosed in adulthood. This case has a good justification for a diagnostic impression of DID, although assessment would need to continue.

Psychodynamic Case Conceptualization

The case suggests that Samantha experienced some sort of traumatic experience (possible abuse) as a young child. Dissociation can be conceptualized as a response to overwhelming traumatic experience that offers a psychic escape when there is no physical escape. From a psychodynamic perspective, DID is explained as a defense mechanism against trauma. It can be hypothesized that Samantha was unable to cope with the emotional pain of an abusive situation or the family's response to reporting abuse, that she fragmented her sense of self into distinct personalities to protect herself. The alternate personalities serve to compartmentalize different aspects of her identity, memories, and emotions and are made inaccessible to each other. Samantha, the primary personality, is rule-oriented, quiet, reserved, introverted, religious, and respectful. This would be the one protected from the abuse, which is why she is not recalling her history. The alter is the one who experienced the abuse and is more emotionally dysregulated. Her alter is more promiscuous, impulsive, defiant, and emotionally expressive. The formation of alters and the experience of dissociation is an unconscious process, which is why the clinician meeting Samantha (the primary personality) would have to deduce the dissociative symptoms from her history, as her primary personality will not have access to the memories or personality of the alter.

Psychodynamic treatment goals could include reintegrating the fragmented self. This would include bringing the dissociated memories, especially that of the childhood trauma, back into her conscious awareness. She could then process the underlying trauma and reassign blame, removing any responsibility from herself. The early traumatic experience during childhood disrupted her ego development and a goal of treatment would be to strengthen the ego's capacity to manage internal conflicts. Further treatment goals could be to develop healthier coping mechanisms for the future.

Psychodynamic treatment interventions could include establishing a safe and consistent therapeutic relationship, which can then serve as a form of external structure that can be gradually internalized over time. A comprehensive, long-term psychotherapy that addresses the underlying trauma is going to be most effective from a psychodynamic perspective. Free association, interpretation, and confrontation will aid Samantha in meeting her treatment goals by understanding unconscious conflicts and developing a more unified sense of self.

Cognitive Behavioral Conceptualization

From a cognitive behavioral perspective, dissociative symptoms are learned in childhood as a means of coping with traumatic events. Samantha's traumatic experience (possible abuse) as a young child altered her information processing. In addition, her cognitive appraisals of the world and others were shifted to threatening, fear-and-anxiety-inducing, and authoritative, modifying her behavioral responses and leading to dissociation. Samantha could have also experienced schema-level distortions related to self-worth and therefore created alters who are viewed as more acceptable or less vulnerable to the threats of the world. Maladaptive coping skills such as denial are also being utilized.

Appropriate CBT treatment goals could include identifying Samantha's underlying schemas regarding her view of self, world, and others. Bringing to Samantha's awareness her alter and the amount of distress she is experiencing related to her past can be introduced slowly. Increasing her insight into the multidirectional relationship between cognitions, emotions, and behaviors would also be helpful in allowing her to understand her condition and address negative thought patterns. CBT could also support Samantha in improving her emotional regulation and distress tolerance and coping with her trauma history. Additionally, goals related to social skills training and safety planning would be appropriate.

Treatment of DID from a CBT perspective would begin with psychoeducation that explores the nature of how the human mind and body are connected. Therapy would then focus on facilitating the processing of her trauma, including confronting trauma-related memories and challenging negative thoughts and beliefs that contribute to their symptoms, such as any belief that she was to blame as a young child for her experience. CBT can also work to improve Samantha's emotion regulation capabilities. More specific treatments such as trauma-focused CBT or dialectical behavioral therapy could be employed as well.

Biopsychosocial Conceptualization

DID is complex and considered to have multiple factors related to its development. Early traumatic experiences and family and sociocultural factors point to a psychosocial etiology, whereas the neurobiological response to the trauma is biological in nature, as are biologically derived traits and epigenetic mechanisms that create a vulnerability in a person and lead them to experience dissociation when faced with developmental trauma. There is evidence of structural anomalies in persons with DID, however it is not verified if these are causes or consequences of DID. For example, early research found those with DID to have increased cerebral blood flow in the amygdala, insular cortex, somatosensory areas in the parietal cortex, and the basal ganglia (Reinders et al., 2003). The "orbitofrontal model" for DID suggests that the orbitofrontal cortex plays a critical role in the development of distinct mental states (i.e., dissociative identities) due to its inhibitory functions (Hanson et al., 2010). There is also a genetic link to dissociation (Wolf et al., 2014). In Samantha's case, it could be conceptualized from a biopsychosocial perspective that her identity alterations are trauma-related intrusion and avoidance. Her alter is a break in consciousness between her distinct identities. Her assumed experience with some sort of abuse by her uncle and the possible response by her parents could cause contradictory internal working models of a caregiver who is both safe and dangerous. In her early years, Samantha would try to protect herself from the same relationship where she is seeking safety. It can be assumed that Samantha may not have received the necessary relational support of her parents to help her to process the abuse appropriately and constructively, which could have impacted her ability to make sense of the trauma. Thus, the memories of the abuse would remain isolated from her integrated self. Then other experiences and further isolation could have prevented her from developing an ordinary sense of self-in-relation-to-others, based on a coherent narrative that includes her abuse experience. As a result, dissociative identities may have begun to form (Sar et al., 2017). Her biological vulnerabilities and her psychosocial experiences made way for distinct identities to form and be maintained.

Treatment goals from the biopsychosocial model would consider the biological, psychological, and social factors that are contributing to her presentation. Her treatment would be focused on establishing safety, stabilizing symptoms, processing traumatic memories, and ultimately integrating her identities into a cohesive sense of self. Goals may also include improving communication, social skills, and creating a stable environment.

Treating Samantha from a biopsychosocial perspective would be a holistic approach that would involve potential collaboration with her medical providers to support Samantha in addressing her medical needs. Individual therapy that addresses her trauma and dissociation would be vital. Family therapy may also help her to communicate better with her family who appear to be her support system and create a stronger supportive network. Local and community-based resources may be beneficial to aid her in maintaining employment and supporting her independence.

Clinical Case Vignette #2

Demographic Information and History

Name: Mei Huang.

Demographic Information: 23-year-old Chinese American female.

Medical Diagnoses: No significant medical history.

Reason for Referral: Mei is currently in nursing school and was referred by one of her clinical proctors due to concerns about her performance. Mei agreed with the referral as she reports that she feels like she is "losing her mind." She has worried for some time that she has some kind of brain impairment but has been afraid to acknowledge it. She has not sought help before her proctor referred her because she has difficulty even explaining her experiences. She reports what she calls episodes in which she is watching herself. These have happened for a few years, but are increasing in frequency, particularly when she is at the hospital for her clinicals. She explains that during the episodes she is in a dream-like state where the world does not seem real. But then she starts to feel distressed and disoriented because she cannot feel anything or wake herself up. At times, after these episodes, she can pull herself together, but other times she panics and escapes. This has caused her to be at risk of failing her clinical rotation. She has also experienced it when she goes home to her parents' house. Even though she grew up there, when she walks in it feels unfamiliar and she feels she does not belong there. She will also see herself interact with her family as though she is no longer there. Her parents say she seems distant and emotionless causing her family concern as well as her proctor. Mei reports that the first time she experienced an episode was at the age of 17, when there was an active shooter at her school. She was hiding in a classroom with her peers and a teacher. She still has a hard time believing the incident happened and remembers it like a dream. She had a bird's eye view of the classroom as though she was watching from above. She said the rest of that day and week she felt numb, as though she had no sensations at all. Since then, she has been getting these episodes. She also reports anxiety (anticipating and fearing these episodes), general fatigue, and having trouble sleeping.

Clinical Interview Data

Interpreter Used: No.

Current Psychosocial Stressors: Mei is in the second term of her first year of nursing school, which she reports has been incredibly stressful. Her first term classes were challenging and many of her cohort failed out, which the school said was typical. She worked hard and was able to pass her classes and exams. She started her clinical rotation this term which has added even more stress. She felt she adapted well to moving to a new city for school but does report that it has been a change to live more independently and balance family expectations back home.

Protective Factors: Mei reported that her family is Buddhist, but she does not identify with any religion and does not see herself as a spiritual person. Mei reported having a good relationship with her family and has a group of friends back home, but she does not spend much time with them currently because of school keeping her busy. Mei indicated that her cohort in nursing school is a source of support because they all help each other to succeed. Overall, Mei is goal-oriented and wants to succeed.

Developmental History: Mei reported meeting all her developmental milestones within normal limits.

Academic History: Mei graduated high school and then attended a local emergency medical technician (EMT) program as a way to help her get into nursing school. She had always done well in school and planned to go to college directly from high school, but after the incident at school in her junior year she struggled. She reports that she felt detached and foggy. She stayed often home from school, telling her parents that she felt light-headed and fatigued. She started to have less frequent episodes later in her senior year, but it was too late to get into the colleges she had desired and so she decided on this path. She did well her first term of nursing school, but she also started to have the episodes a bit more frequently and had a harder time as the term went on feeling as though the whole experience was unreal.

Social History: Mei reported having a good network of friends back home, but that being away at nursing school allows her to have some space as she deals with this problem. Mei indicated that she has connected with her cohort on an academic level, but does not feel close to them socially. She knows they think she does not reveal much about herself, but Mei reported feeling as though she does not know herself, even though she knows that does not make sense.

Household: Mei is the oldest sibling and has two younger brothers. One recently started college, and the other is still in high school. Both live at home with their parents in their childhood home and she is the first child who has moved out. She currently lives alone in an apartment near her campus.

Previous Psychiatric History: Mei received counseling services following the incident at her school at the age of 17. She reported that she attended about 10 sessions at school before the school year ended, but her parents did not look into other services even though she asked. She thinks her parents were disturbed by the incident at school but also wanted to move on from it. Her mother took her to an acupuncturist and offered herbs and teas. Mei was willing to try anything to help her gain control of her thoughts after the incident.

Family Psychiatric History: Mei reported no family psychiatric history that she was aware of.

History of Self-Harm: There has been no history of self-harm or suicidal ideation.

Wellness Profile

Sleep: Mei reported that she does suffer from insomnia. She has trouble falling asleep and staying asleep. She reports that she experiences frequent nightmares. Even when she does sleep, she often feels fatigued.

Diet: Mei reports that she eats well, but probably less nutritiously than she should since living on her own. Her diet consists of more convenience food than she would like.

Elimination: No concerns reported.

Technology: Mei reported that she is on her computer for at least 8 hours a day because of schoolwork and studying for exams. She indicated that she does have social media but scrolls on it without engaging.

Physical Activity: Mei reports minimal physical activity. She does walk to and from campus from her apartment for classes and walks around the hospital for her clinicals.

Substance Use/Abuse: Mei does not have a history of or current use of alcohol or substances.

Pain: 0/10.

Current Psychiatric Symptoms

Depression: Mei denies any current depression symptoms, although she indicated that she rarely feels emotions overall.

Anxiety: Mei reports frequent anxiety over her concerns about having an episode. She reports that she was an anxious child. She never received services, but she felt she worried and stressed more than her peers. She was an overachiever and likes to be in control, which is why these episodes cause her a high level of distress.

Panic: Mei does not report panic attacks, but during her episodes she feels panicked and tries to escape.

Mania: Mei denies any manic or hypomanic experiences.

Psychosis: None reported or observed.

Eating Disorder: Mei reported no symptoms of an eating disorder.

Risky Behaviors/Sexual Activity: Mei did not report any risky behaviors and is not sexually active.

Mental Status Exam

Appearance: Mei was dressed and groomed appropriately. She presented in scrubs and is within normal limits for height and weight.

Behavior: Mei was highly cooperative; however, she was overly apologetic that she had difficulty explaining her experience.

Speech: Mei's speech was within normal limits.

Mood: Mei's mood was stable and appropriate.

Affect: Mei's affect was congruent with a broad range of emotions. She appeared with less affect than would be expected overall, especially when discussing her experience in the school shooting incident.

Thought Process: Mei's thought process appeared coherent and logical; however, at times she had difficulty forming her thoughts in terms of how to explain her experiences. She has developed terms and ways of thinking to rationalize her experience.

Thought Content: Mei's thought content was appropriate. Some evidence of rumination that seemed consistent with trying to understand her experience.

Orientation: Mei was oriented to person, place, time, and situation. Her reality testing was not impacted.

Recent Memory: Mei's recent memory appears to be intact.

Remote Memory: Mei's remote memory appears impacted in some ways. She reports difficulty in recalling memories vividly and owning them as personal. It is as though she is telling stories about experiences she has observed rather than experienced. She also has trouble connecting emotions to the memories. This is observed in the way she reported her history but was not reported by Mei.

Attention/Concentration: Mei's attention and concentration were within normal limits.

General Knowledge: Mei's general knowledge was within normal limits.

Language: Mei's language was within normal limits.

Insight: Mei's insight was good.

Judgment: Mei appeared to have good judgment.

Answer Key #2

Diversity Considerations

Mei is an American of Chinese descent, which suggests she may be navigating dynamics associated with holding bicultural values as well as acculturative stress. Mei would likely consider herself as living within two cultures and it will be important to explore how this impacts her worldview. Because she is of Chinese descent, her limited affect may be more representative of learned emotional restraint consistent with her culture rather than the flat or blunted affect indicative of psychiatric disorder. Her family appears to prefer Eastern medicine practices, which should be considered and possibly integrated into her treatment plan. It will also be important to keep in mind that Mei may experience some ambivalence with regard to engaging in psychotherapy due to the shame with which some Chinese families consider mental illness as well as mental health-seeking behaviors.

Mei's cultural background may also be a factor in her desire to excel as she is the eldest child coming from a collectivistic culture. She expressed that it is challenging to balance her school and family responsibilities. At the same time, as an Asian American student preparing for a challenging career in a competitive academic setting, Mei may experience some internalized pressure associated with the model minority myth, a stereotype characterized by high achievement to the point of perfectionism and emotional control. Of note, Mei also experiences ambivalence regarding mental health issues and help-seeking behaviors as she may fear the impact struggling with a mental health issue may have on her future nursing license. At the same time, because her academic program appears to value academic rigor and professional gatekeeping, her educational setting may itself be contributing to her psychological distress.

Mei does not identify with a religion or spiritual practice but grew up in a Buddhist home. This is another area that can be explored and considered in her conceptualization and treatment plan.

Legal Considerations

While these concerns may not be relevant at this particular moment, Mei's presentation may become problematic once she is working as a nurse, or even engaging in clinical rotations, as her symptoms may raise questions about fitness for duty, especially in a healthcare setting, where patient safety needs to be considered. Depending on the severity of her symptoms and whether the clinical proctor reported concerns to Mei's academic institution, she may ultimately require some sort of clearance to progress in her training. Additional issues may arise in the future, however, with her respective licensing board if issues continue once she is ready to be licensed and clinicians will need to balance patient privacy with any mandatory reporting laws that may exist in their state related to professional impairment. She may also, however, be entitled to reasonable accommodations under the Americans with Disabilities Act (ADA) if her symptoms qualify her for such accommodations due to a psychiatric disability.

Additionally, releases of information (ROIs) might be required if Mei's family members (for example, her parents) wish to become involved in treatment. While family member involvement in treatment is not only acceptable but considered normative in many cultures, appropriate documentation must still be completed prior to disclosing information to family members. Although Mei denies any suicidal ideation, this should continually be assessed as well.

Diagnostic Impressions and Justification

F48.1 Depersonalization/Derealization Disorder.
Mei meets the criteria for depersonalization/derealization disorder as she is experiencing ongoing and recurring episodes of both depersonalization and derealization. In terms of depersonalization she is experiencing perceptual distortions, an unreal sense of self, emotional detachment, the feeling of being an outside observer, and numbness. She reports familiar places like her family home feeling strange and unknown. Regarding derealization, she is experiencing dissociation for the environment as she describes her life seeming surreal or dreamlike. She also reported feeling lightheadedness which is a common associated feature. Mei is aware of these episodes, and her reality testing is unaffected. She is also experiencing fatigue and anxiety around the symptoms. The symptoms are causing her significant distress. She has had her family concerned, but now it is also putting her at risk of not being successful in nursing school. Even though she can maintain relationships, it has impacted her ability to make friends in her new cohort. As Mei does not use alcohol, substances, and is not on any prescription medication, the disruption cannot be attributed to a substance's physiological effects. Although post-traumatic stress disorder can be considered, because the start of the disturbance can be linked to her traumatic experience of the school shooting, her symptoms align more with DPDR, and this provides a better explanation for her presentation.

Psychodynamic Case Conceptualization

From a psychodynamic perspective, dissociation is typically viewed as a sense of unreality about the outside world as a defense mechanism to protect the individual from the anxiety that can arise from a traumatic situation. Mei was an anxious child, suggesting that she already was susceptible to her unconscious drives breaking through and the use of ineffective defense mechanisms. It may be because of her high desire to succeed or an experience of her parents only loving her if she meets expectations, but Mei as a child likely developed a stronger superego and a low tolerance of her unconscious drives. Any themes or ideas that stem from the unconscious that went against Mei's view of her ideal self was likely to cause anxiety. When she experienced the traumatic school shooting incident, she was completely out of control and likely dissociated as a way to protect herself from the unmanageable anxiety. Dissociation can serve as a manner of organizing otherwise disorganized or fragmented experiences and internal states, and a split occurs between the person and their mental activity. The stress of nursing school likely exacerbated her unmanageable unconscious fears and thoughts, once again increasing her episodes of depersonalization and derealization.

Psychodynamic treatment goals appropriate for Mei could include addressing her underlying unconscious conflicts as well as her maladaptive defense mechanism of dissociation. The initial approach to treatment should include the development of a safe, consistent therapeutic relationship. A safe, consistent therapeutic relationship will allow her to explore and modify current problematic defense mechanisms and allow Mei to articulate the psychological distress that has led to dissociation. Overall, treatment should support Mei in developing the capacity to tolerate distress and stress without needing to escape into dissociation.

Psychodynamic interventions designed to support Mei will aim to reveal the hidden parts of the self and the disturbances to her stable identity. The exploration of the unbearable, namely Mei's traumatic experiences and feelings of potential failure, will diminish the tension that causes dissociation. The deeper the understanding that she gains and the acceptance of her inner life, the less she will feel the intensity of the depersonalization. In psychodynamic psychotherapy, the use of a well-established therapeutic frame with good consistent boundaries is itself an intervention and can provide the space for Mei to eventually feel safe enough to begin exploring distressing internal material. Validating emotional distress while gently redirecting Mei to the present moment may be more supportive and effective.

Cognitive Behavioral Conceptualization

A cognitive-behavioral conceptualization of Mei's presentation would start with the assumption that everyone experiences transient symptoms of depersonalization and derealization. This is even more common in traumatic situations. Mei's experience of the school shooting incident and the depersonalization and derealization she felt in that moment and the days following, were misinterpreted as indicative of brain dysfunction due to the maladaptive cognitive distortion of catastrophic appraisal. This created a vicious cycle of increasing anxiety and consequently increased depersonalization and derealization symptoms. Her behavioral responses, such as avoidance, maintained the disorder by increasing awareness of the symptoms and heightening the perceived threat, and preventing disconfirmation of the maladaptive catastrophic thoughts. Once she entered nursing school and again experienced the depersonalization and derealization symptoms due to the stress, she engaged in thinking biases and processes such as focusing on her symptoms and ruminating about them. She experienced anxiety (negative emotion) followed by behavioral changes of avoidance. She is also likely experiencing automatic thoughts that are contributing to her distress such as "I am losing my mind," and "Something is wrong with my brain." Mei likely holds maladaptive core beliefs about herself, such as she is only accepted if successful or that lack of control is indicative of failure.

Appropriate CBT-based treatment goals for Mei include altering her detrimental thought patterns and behaviors and developing better adaptive coping strategies for stressful situations. Mei should gain understanding of the beliefs that are leading to her behavior and gain a cognitive understanding of why she is engaging in these behaviors. Other goals should focus on changing her maladaptive schemas and allowing her to develop new beliefs about herself. Finally, behavioral goals can include helping her develop behavioral alternatives by reinforcing non-symptom related behaviors.

Cognitive behavioral therapy would begin with psychoeducation in order to help her understand the nature of her symptoms so that she can understand that her brain is not damaged. Emotional exposure can be utilized to allow Mei to confront and process distressing emotions. Cognitive restructuring could then be employed to help change her thought patterns and reduce anxious thoughts. Self-monitoring techniques, somatic experiencing, and mindfulness-based interventions will be beneficial to ground her and be present, address the feelings of detachment, and encourage Mei to fully engage with her surroundings and develop a sense of reality and presence. This will also help her become more attuned to her emotions during moments of high arousal that potentially lead to her dissociate. Alternative therapeutic approaches such as acceptance and commitment therapy can help her accept herself and her experiences, improve her emotional regulation skills, and address negative thought patterns. Self-compassion will allow her to reduce self-criticism and enhance overall well-being while decreasing dissociation. Dialectical behavior therapy has also been shown to be beneficial for treatment of DPDR as it has a focus on emotional regulation and stress mitigation.

Biopsychosocial Conceptualization

The biopsychosocial model would consider the multiple factors that contribute to and maintain Mei's symptoms. Although the exact cause of depersonalization and derealization is unknown, traumatic experiences, childhood anxiety, stress, depression, and panic attacks have been identified as triggers. Mei's experience of psychosocial stressors, including early high expectations and family dynamics, may have contributed to childhood anxiety. Then a traumatic experience at school left her even more vulnerable and contributed to her symptoms. Nursing school and moving away from home could be further current triggers for her symptoms.

In terms of biological factors, chronic stress causes our nervous system to become overwhelmed. This can lead to dorsal vagal shut down. Derealization then is seen as connected to our fight-or-flight response. When Mei experienced the school shooting incident the stress went beyond her capacity and she went to a freeze mode, shutting down and leaving her feeling emotionally and mentally immobilized. This led her feeling distant and disconnected from her surroundings. This then became her way of coping and it persisted into a disorder. Several neurotransmitter systems have also been implicated in dissociation including glutamate NMDA (N-methyl-D-aspartate) receptor antagonists, cannabinoids, hallucinogens, and opioid receptor agonists. There is evidence that neurobiological mechanisms are at play in DPDR, including a significant association between brain regions involved in emotional perception and memory. Alterations in activities of brain areas like the amygdala, hippocampus, and middle/superior temporal gyrus, along with white matter and other cortical regions, are linked with DPDR (Murphy 2023). Studies have also revealed that a family history of anxiety disorders and psychiatric and dissociative disorders may lead to an increased genetic susceptibility and higher environmental risk of being exposed to parents with anxiety disorders. Although Mei does not use any substance and did not report a family history of psychiatric disorders, it is still possible the neurotransmitters or genetic vulnerability may be part of the etiology of her disorder.

Appropriate treatment goals for depersonalization/derealization disorder grounded in the biopsychosocial model include a multifaceted approach encompassing therapeutic, pharmacological and lifestyle goals. Therapeutic goals would include increasing adaptive coping skills and reducing maladaptive coping as well as cognitive distortions will be helpful in reducing symptoms. Developing self-compassion and acceptance of self as a whole will be beneficial. Evaluating the need for medication management should be included as a goal. Improving sleep and physical activity should also be considered for a holistic approach.

Treatment from a biopsychosocial model should start with referrals to appropriate providers such as a psychiatrist. Pharmacologically, selective serotonin reuptake inhibitors (SSRIs) and serotonin-norepinephrine reuptake inhibitors (SNRIs) are prevalently used, especially for DPDR. In addition to psychotherapy, stress reduction techniques and assuring a healthy lifestyle, characterized by regular physical activity, adequate sleep, and balanced nutrition, is essential for the holistic management of those with DPDR.

Conclusion

Dissociative disorders represent a generally misunderstood category of psychiatric diagnoses, differentiated from other psychiatric diagnoses by the disruption of conscious states, which impacts identity, affective states, behaviors, etc. Overall, dissociation can be understood as the mind's attempt to distance itself or escape from overwhelmingly distressing events, whether those events be external or internal in nature. Each dissociative disorder presents with distinct diagnostic features, but all include some sort of fragmentation within the self. DID is considered to be the most severe form of dissociation, but other diagnoses categorized as dissociative in nature can be as impairing. Successful, competent, compassionate care of patients presenting with any dissociative disorder requires clear and nuanced understanding of consciousness and trauma, including the roles that consciousness and trauma play in identity formation.

References

APA (American Psychiatric Association). (2022). Dissociative disorders. In *Diagnostic and statistical manual of mental disorders* (5th ed., text rev.). American Psychiatric Association.

Hanson, J. L., Chung, M. K., Avants, B. B., Shirtcliff, E. A., Gee, J. C., Davidson, R. J., & Pollak, S. D. (2010). Early stress is associated with alterations in the orbitofrontal cortex: A tensor-based morphometry investigation of brain structure and behavioral risk. *Journal of Neuroscience*, *30*(22), 7466–7472. doi: 10.1523/JNEUROSCI.0859-10.2010.

Murphy, R. (2023). Depersonalization/derealization disorder and neural correlates of trauma-related pathology: A critical review. *Innovations in Clinical Neuroscience*, *20*, 53–59.

Reinders, A., Nijenhuis, E., Paans, A., Korf, J., Willemsen, A., Den Boer, J. A. (2003). One brain, two selves. *Neuroimage*, *20*(4), 2119–2125. doi: 10.1016/j.neuroimage.2003.08.021.

Şar, V., Dorahy, M.J., & Krüger, C. (2017). Revisiting the etiological aspects of dissociative identity disorder: A biopsychosocial perspective. *Psychology Research and Behavior Management*, 10, 137–146. doi: 10.2147/PRBM.S113743.

Wolf, E. J., Rasmusson, A. M., Mitchell, K. S., Logue, M. W., Baldwin, C. T., & Miller, M. W. (2014). A genome-wide association study of clinical symptoms of dissociation in a trauma-exposed sample. *Depression and Anxiety*, *31*(4), 352–360. doi: 10.1002/da.22260.

Chapter 10

Somatic Symptom Disorder and Related Disorders

Matthew Heidl

Patients presenting with somatic symptom disorder and its adjacent disorders tend to be referred to mental health professionals by other healthcare providers, typically primary care physicians, due to the presentation of their symptoms. Many of these individuals will have already undergone an extensive medical workup related to their various complaints and they are likely to be frustrated or anxious about their unclear results. This is not to say that these symptoms are "in their heads"; these patients are reporting their genuine suffering from their somatic or neurological symptoms, even if the etiology is primarily psychological in nature. However, this poses a unique challenge to many clinicians to learn how to apply psychological theory to help an individual who is mainly complaining of pain, stomach issues, or other physiological symptoms in the therapy room. It is thus important to remember that, regardless of modality, the clinician is attempting to help them learn how better to handle their anxieties and fixations on their symptoms to reduce the amount of suffering in their daily lives.

Somatic symptom disorder is a relatively common disorder that occurs in approximately 5–7 percent of the population, with the majority of these patients being women (approximately 10:1 ratio of women to men) (APA, 2022; Kurlansik & Maffei, 2016). In order for an individual to be diagnosed with this disorder, three criteria outlined in the DSM-5-TR must be met, including one or more somatic symptoms that are distressing or result in significant disruption of daily life and excessive thoughts, feelings, or behaviors related to the somatic symptoms or associated with health concerns. The first and third criteria are fairly straightforward to understand: the patient must be experiencing some type of physical distress that is causing difficulties in their life, and these symptoms must have been present for an extended period of time. The second criterion is a little more nuanced as what is a disproportionate concern or time spent on these physical symptoms can be challenging to parse out. Some research suggests that if an individual spends approximately 4 hours of their day focusing on their symptoms, then this may be an objective way to meet Criterion B; the majority of studies that have evaluated this criterion, however, recommend

DOI: 10.4324/9781003586531-11

using clinical judgment to determine if a patient meets this criterion (Löwe et al., 2021). Clinicians should focus on the level of preoccupation their patient has with their somatic symptoms and the impact this preoccupation has on their life; people's symptoms are likely to cause a decrease in the quality of life, but it is necessary to observe if their focus on their distress is amplifying an already existing problem (APA, 2022). It is important to note that these symptoms may or may not be related to another medical condition that the patient has, but it is the perseveration of their symptoms that is greatly impactful (APA, 2022). Of note, patients with vertigo and dizziness symptoms tend to have higher levels of illness anxiety, so these patients are possibly at higher risk of developing somatic symptom disorder (Löwe et al., 2021).

Illness anxiety disorder can appear to be quite similar to somatic symptom disorder due to the high levels of stress and anxiety that these patients will have regarding their health and potential symptoms. With a prevalence of approximately 3 percent throughout the healthy population, this disorder occurs with similar frequency in both men and women, with typical onset of the disorder occurring in adulthood (APA, 2022). The DSM-5-TR criteria for this disorder include preoccupation with having or acquiring a serious illness, significant anxiety about health status, and engagement in excessive health-related behaviors. Somatic symptoms may or may not be present but, if present, might be only mild in intensity, with the amount of anxiety experienced disproportionate to the actual situation. As noted by the criteria, the major difference between this disorder and somatic symptom disorder is the presence of the somatic symptoms themselves; the DSM-5-TR provides examples of mild somatic symptoms such as getting dizzy when standing up too quickly, brief episodes of ringing in the ears, or more frequent belching (APA, 2022). Diagnosis of this disorder should primarily be based on the anxiety about the potential danger to the patient's health versus the actual symptoms or concerns that they have; patients with illness anxiety tend to frequently be over-attuned to potential bodily threats (Wolters et al., 2022). There is some research that suggests that both illness anxiety and somatic symptom disorder can be a result of the individual being overly tuned to bodily sensations with interoceptive accuracy being abnormal for them; these individuals perceive small bodily sensations and interpret through the lens of their disorder making them feel like they are signs of impending bodily disaster (Wolters et al., 2022).

Factitious disorder may be the trickiest of the somatic symptom and related disorders to be able to be successfully identified, due to the nature of the disorder being rooted in deception. It is for this reason the DSM-5-TR states that it is unclear what the prevalence rate of the disorder is, although there is some data that suggests approximately 1 percent of psychiatric consultations involve this disorder, and potentially up to 5 percent of all physician encounters may be related to a factitious disorder (APA, 2022; Jafferany et al., 2018). The DSM-5-TR criteria for the disorder actually has two variants based on whether the disorder is being imposed on oneself or another person. "Factitious Disorder Imposed on the Self" requires falsification of physical or psychological signs or symptoms, or induction of injury or disease, associated with identified deception. "Factitious Disorder Imposed on Another" requires falsification of physical or psychological signs or symptoms or induction of injury or disease in another, associated with identified deception, *and* the patient presenting another individual to others as ill, impaired, or injured. These individuals, like many patients with somatic related disorders, will likely present in a medical setting when they are first being evaluated as they will be falsifying symptoms that they will want medically evaluated (APA, 2022). It will be notable that experiencing their symptoms will be a conscious decision, unlike the somatization of somatic symptom disorder or functional neurological symptom disorder; these individuals are creating their own symptoms, sometimes even inflicting wounds or lesions on themselves or ingesting substances to create abnormal lab results (Jafferany et al., 2018; APA, 2022). For this reason, there has been some evidence to suggest that healthcare professionals are more likely to present with a factitious disorder as they understand how to present to a medical setting for treatment (Krahn et al., 2003). The other key criteria to consider are that there appear to be no external rewards for their illness, no legal liability or lawsuits that would be impacted by their illness, attempting to falsify for disability, drug-seeking behavior, or other forms of secondary gain (APA, 2022). There is still motivation for creating their symptoms, but it is typically more psychological in nature and can vary from a sense of control to seeking out thrills in a medical setting (Jafferany et al., 2018). Hence, factitious disorder is a complex disorder to identify and will typically require an interdisciplinary team to help identify the deception and be able to develop an appropriate treatment plan for the patient.

Functional neurological symptom disorder, often also referred to as conversion disorder, can be characterized as a rare disorder occurring approximately in every 4–12/100,000 people and can manifest in a myriad of neurological symptoms (APA, 2022). DSM-5-TR criteria for this disorder include one or more symptoms of altered voluntary motor or sensory function, clinical findings providing evidence of incompatibility between the symptom and recognized neurological or medical conditions, and that the symptom or deficit is not better explained by another medical or mental disorder. Of note, this disorder should be considered as a diagnosis of exclusion versus a primary diagnosis of the patient's symptoms. These patients will typically be seen initially in an inpatient medical setting due to their concerning neurological symptoms, such as numbness, motor weakness, seizure-like activity, or even severe sensory loss, such as reported blindness (APA, 2022). However, medically speaking, these neurological deficits will be found to be inconsistent with known neurological pathways or patterns; this does not make these deficits any less debilitating, though, and these patients will still need specialty care to be treated properly (Tsui et al., 2017; APA, 2022). The onset of functional neurological symptom disorder is typically understood as being attributed to a stress response, usually to a severe stressor in a patient's life, and so it is highly recommended that a thorough history be taken for these patients in order to elucidate the possible cause of their neuropsychological symptoms (Keynejad et al., 2018). Thus, evaluating for history of abuse and maladaptive emotional coping strategies is going to be vital in both diagnosis as well as treatment of individuals with this particular disorder (APA, 2022).

Clinical Case Vignette #1

Demographic Information and History

Name: Jennifer Wales.

Demographic Information: 45-year-old White female.

Medical Diagnoses: History is relevant for fibromyalgia, which was diagnosed 5 years ago, on Flexeril nightly.

Reason for Referral: Jennifer presents after being referred to the clinic by her PCP due to Jennifer experiencing significant, chronic discomfort that has currently had a negative medical workup. Jennifer has been dealing with diffuse muscular pain and fatigue for the past 5 years, which has been impacting her ability to work as a mechanical engineer. She is gravely worried that her symptoms mean that she is going to die soon and that no one is taking her symptoms seriously. Jennifer has been to multiple medical specialists and has spent a large amount of her savings attempting to resolve her symptoms.

Clinical Interview Data

Interpreter Used: No.

Current Psychosocial Stressors: Her husband is currently considering divorce due to the financial strain her condition has placed on the family.

Protective Factors: Jennifer is highly self-motivated for therapy and appears hopeful for the process. Reports having a hobby of painting that regularly soothes her.

Developmental History: Jennifer reported meeting all of her developmental milestones.

Academic History: Jennifer has completed her bachelor's degree in mechanical engineering.

Social History: Jennifer reports having a few work colleagues that she will occasionally eat dinner with or see outside of work, but she otherwise notes that many of her close friends are out of state since moving for a better job. She does occasionally attend a community art workshop to improve her skills.

Household: Jennifer with her husband and teenage son in their home.

Previous Psychiatric History: Jennifer does report a previous diagnosis of generalized anxiety disorder for which she has been taking buspirone for several years without changes.

Family Psychiatric History: Jennifer reported that her father was diagnosed with depression when she was a child.

History of Self-Harm: Denies self-injury or suicidal ideation.

Wellness Profile

Sleep: Jennifer reports that it is difficult to sleep until she takes her Flexeril but otherwise notes that she can sleep 6–7 hours nightly. Does note that she naps frequently when her feelings of fatigue become more intense.

Diet: Jennifer reports that she eats two meals (breakfast and dinner) while cooking for the entire family and otherwise eats snack foods throughout the middle of the day. She does make sure that her diet does not contain ingredients that will reportedly trigger her symptoms.

Elimination: Occasional bouts of diarrhea she relates to her symptoms.

Technology: Jennifer reports that for work, she is frequently on her computer; however, with the severity of her symptoms, she now feels that she spends much of her time on the computer researching different facets of fibromyalgia.

Physical Activity: Jennifer reports that she used to be more active prior to her symptoms starting but states that she now just spends most of her time inside.

Substance Use/Abuse: Jennifer regularly drinks a glass of wine during the evening. No smoking or other substance was reported.

Pain: 10/10.

Current Psychiatric Symptoms

Depression: Jennifer does report feeling more "down" since her symptoms began but is still able to enjoy her hobbies when she is not dealing with her concerns. She does feel that it is harder to focus at times since her symptoms frequently distract her.

Anxiety: Jennifer reports multiple anxious symptoms, such as being unable to control her worry about her symptoms, fatigue, anxiety regarding her situation, persistent muscle tension, and difficulty concentrating due to her pain.

Panic: Jennifer does report some concerns about her symptoms causing her to die young, but she is mainly worried that people are not taking her seriously, which causes her anxiety to be even more intense.

Mania: No manic symptoms present.

Psychosis: No reported psychotic symptoms.

Trauma: No reported traumatic events, although Jennifer does report that her parents were rarely available in her life and were only present when she was sick.

Eating Disorder: No concerns for eating disorder reported.

Risky Behaviors/Sexual Activity: Jennifer reports that she has not been sexually active with her husband in 2 years. No risky behaviors were reported.

Mental Status Exam

Appearance: *Dress*: appropriate. *Hygiene*: adequate. Appeared stated age.

Behavior: Appropriate, cooperative.

Speech: *Rate*: within normal limits. *Articulation*: within normal limits. *Volume*: within normal limits. Coherence: within normal limits.

Mood: "Worried."

Affect: Full, congruent to mood, appropriate to the content of the interview.

Thought Process: Logical, linear, goal directed.

Thought Content: Denied suicidal ideation, homicidal ideation, delusions, and hallucinations.

Orientation: Oriented to person, place, situation, and time.

Recent Memory: Intact.

Remote Memory: Intact.

Attention/Concentration: Sufficient.

General Knowledge: Average.

Language: Receptive and expressive skills within normal limits.

Insight: Fair.

Judgment: Fair.

Answer Key #1

Diversity Considerations

Women's pain can be considered to be exaggerated by medical providers, and medical providers may favor more psychological resources, so keeping this in mind during treatment will be crucial to avoid a rupture by possibly playing out a similar pattern to the one that has been occurring since her diagnosis (Schäfer et al., 2016). Fibromyalgia can be heavily stigmatized as a disease due to its unknown mechanisms of causing distress and due to its psychological components. Many physicians and others in her life may just experience her symptoms as "all in her head," especially as a woman, so considering this is also important (Quintner, 2019). Complicating the situation is Jennifer's age and life stage – she may be perimenopausal and symptoms associated with the perimenopause could complicate the diagnostic process.

Ethical and Legal Considerations

The main ethical consideration is to ensure that she is following with her PCP regarding new symptoms that may develop over the course of treatment. While somatic symptom disorder is psychologically treatable, these symptoms may be indicative of an underlying medical issue as well and so should always be taken seriously. Fatigue regarding her symptoms is likely to occur, so it will be important for the physician to be self-evaluating.

Diagnostic Impressions and Justification

F45.1 Somatic Symptom Disorder, Moderate, Persistent.

For more than 6 months, Jennifer has been experiencing somatic symptoms that are greatly disrupting her life, which is markedly amplified by her persistent focus on figuring out how to resolve these symptoms. She spends an excessive amount of time researching her symptoms and attempting to find ways to resolve her symptoms, which is greatly impacting her life. Additionally, her anxiety regarding the severity of her symptoms is quite high, with her being consistently tense in her muscles and frequently worrying about her prognosis. It is also important to note that fibromyalgia itself is already considered a functional somatic disorder, so this diagnosis can be indicative that a patient may likely be experiencing a somatic symptom disorder (Tak et al., 2011).

Psychodynamic Case Conceptualization

Somatization, from a psychodynamic perspective, is seen as a primary defense used by individuals who are unable to express their emotions in a typical manner, and, thus, their unexpressed affect comes out in somatic symptoms (McWilliams, 2011). Jennifer's history suggests that her parents were likely emotionally neglectful and did not provide her with the necessary emotional skills to express her needs adequately. This has led to her being in another situation where her emotional needs are being unmet by her family, and she is struggling to be able to express these feelings, which could be resulting in her increased focus on her somatic symptoms as a way to express that she needs help. Her somatic symptoms, however, are likely only increasing her overall distress as these potential emotional signals are being completely missed by her husband and son, which is likely causing her to experience and focus on her symptoms even more intensely in a bid to receive the care that she desperately needs. It is likely that she will view the therapist with hope for fulfilling some of these needs in her life, but it is also likely that she will struggle to express her affect, which could be seen as frustrating and will require the therapist to spend adequate time managing the frustration that is likely to occur (McWilliams, 2011). In sum, disrupted attachment stemming from early life experiences and repressed affect are likely contributing to her presentation, allowing her to express internal pain that may otherwise feel intolerable.

The main goal of treatment for this individual is to help Jennifer learn how to express her emotions better and potentially provide her with both the necessary language and the ability to recognize her own emotional state. This ideally will help with her overall somatic symptoms, although complete cessation of symptoms is unlikely. Allowing Jennifer to gain insight into her somatic symptoms, her relationships with significant others, and the interaction between the two, will be a further treatment goal. Strengthening ego functions and improving Jennifer's capacity for symbolic thought may also be important treatment goals.

Overall, treatment and interventions should strongly focus on reflective comments and deepening of affect throughout treatment; focusing on the underlying emotions will be vital for her. Interpretations with Jennifer will likely take even more time than normal in order to build the proper rapport, since patients with somatic symptom disorder tend to struggle with alexithymia, as well as people viewing their symptoms as "all in their head" (McWilliams, 2011). Jennifer would also benefit from the opportunity to explore the symbolic meaning of her symptoms as well as how internalized relationships may be impacting both her experience of her body and her self-concept. Specifically, dynamic interpersonal therapy focusing on the use of secondary attachment figures (the somatic symptoms) and difficulty mentalizing would likely to be greatly beneficial to Jennifer (Luyten et al., 2019).

Cognitive Behavioral Conceptualization

Somatic symptom disorder is regularly treated with CBT due to the focus on being able to help the individuals understand the cognitive distortions that they hold about their symptoms. Using the standard ABC model of CBT, the activating event for these individuals is, typically, experiencing some type of physical symptom or pain that starts their cascade of thoughts and beliefs regarding their situation. These thoughts may involve ideas such as, "Here's my awful disease again," "I am unable to do anything while I am feeling this way," or "I should just stop doing anything because of the pain." This then leads to the behavioral consequences of the individual staying inside their house, focusing on their symptoms, and becoming increasingly anxious regarding their symptoms as their thoughts focus all their attention on the sensations that they are feeling. It is clear that Jennifer is suffering from multiple cognitive distortions that are impacting her behavior, which include selective attention on her bodily sensations to the point where this is consuming all her focus, rumination on her symptoms, and catastrophizing her symptoms (Orzechowska et al., 2021). These common distortions of somatic symptom disorder likely play into an underlying schema that she, Jennifer, is powerless to change her situation and is a victim of this disease, making her feel overall helplessness in her current situation, which is only reinforced by her frequent medical visits and her family.

Treatment goals for Jennifer would be, first, to help identify an alternate way of viewing her disease in a psychological manner in order to help improve her cognitive distortions regarding her fibromyalgia (Orzechowska et al., 2021). The clinician should also help to identify her underlying schemas regarding her focus on her symptoms and allow her to be more mindful of the actions that she takes when she feels those activating symptoms. The clinician may also wish to address the potentially dysfunctional beliefs Jennifer holds about herself and her body while reducing her fear response to pain.

Initial treatment should involve empathic psychoeducation that explores the nature of how the human mind and body are connected. This psychoeducation may include information regarding the gate-control theory of pain. The clinician may also wish to provide various worksheets in order to help Jennifer identify the thoughts that lead to her isolating herself and spending the day worrying about her symptoms and weighing the costs and benefits of these actions. Schema work is likely to be beneficial once her initial cognitive distortions are better regulated in order to help her better understand what she wants from these behaviors. Behavioral activation as well as activity pacing may serve as valuable interventions. Helping Jennifer create days where she is able to minimize the stress of her disorder and increase enjoyable activities such as painting helps reduce the overall number of "bad days" (Sharma & Manjula, 2013). Mindfulness-based stress reduction combined with CBT therapy is likely to help reduce overall distress related to a patient's somatic symptoms (Fjorback et al. 2012). Teaching relaxation techniques to help minimize overall physiological activation reduces the likelihood of symptoms (Fjorback et al., 2012; Sharma & Manjula, 2013). Additionally, providing behavioral experiments to help Jennifer identify when she may be catastrophizing her symptoms allows her to make better health decisions for her body and mind (Sharma & Manjula, 2013).

Biopsychosocial Conceptualization

Somatic symptoms are still not fully understood from a neurobiological perspective, but some key areas do appear to be impacted. It is suggested that certain somatic disorders cause chronic activation of the hypothalamic-pituitary-adrenal (HPA) axis, eventually resulting in less cortisol throughout the body due to chronic psychological stress, which gives rise to various somatic symptoms (Tak et al., 2011; Çetin & Varma, 2021). Additionally, Jennifer's increased stress in her life due to financial and family issues is likely causing chronic inflammatory changes in her body that are also likely to increase her chances of experiencing the symptoms that caused her to present in the first place (Çetin & Varma, 2021). Jennifer is also struggling to have her family understand her struggles and pain, which is likely adding additional stress; seeking treatment is possibly the only way to express her pain and receive some care for it. This appears to cause her husband to pull away further in their marriage, which then only increases her stress further, likely amplifying her symptoms again, which then increases the level of strain in their relationship. Essentially, Jennifer is trapped in a feedback loop where her somatic symptoms and stress cause difficulties in her life, which leads to more stress due to her family and social support not responding well, which then leads her to begin to worry and focus on her symptoms, as she believes that she is the only person who is going to take them seriously.

Treatment goals should focus primarily on reducing her overall levels of stress and improving her relation to stress to help minimize the impact on her somatic symptoms. Focusing on the likely root cause of her symptoms will be critical due to the prolonged nature of her symptoms. Additionally, enhancing physical functioning, improving sleep, and decreasing physiological preoccupation are all appropriate goals. Working toward these goals would also require Jennifer to address cognitive distortions and improve adaptive coping skills.

Lastly, from a biopsychosocial perspective, care should be taken to reduce the amount of interpersonal conflict Jennifer in experiencing, especially within her marriage, as a result of her symptoms.

From a biopsychosocial perspective, collaboration with Jennifer's medical team would be appropriate to treat her mental health disorder but also to provide comprehensive pain management for her diagnosis of fibromyalgia, including non-pharmacological interventions. Referrals to physical therapy and a registered dietitian may be needed if Jennifer's symptoms begin to contribute to deconditioning but also to support her in following a diet and engaging in exercises that reduce inflammation. Mindfulness-based exercises may be helpful in reducing both pain and psychological distress, but the clinician should also focus on challenging cognitive distortions as well as other maladaptive cognitions. Jennifer and her husband may benefit from couple's counseling. Additionally, Jennifer may benefit from attending a support group for patients with chronic illnesses, while her husband may benefit from joining a support group for the loved ones of patients with chronic illness. Finally, given the financial issues reported in the home, referral to a financial planner or accountant may be helpful.

Clinical Case Vignette #2

Demographic Information and History

Name: Robert Nguyen.

Demographic Information: 37-year-old Vietnamese male.

Medical Diagnoses: None.

Reason for Referral: Robert presents to the outpatient clinic referred to by his PCP due to his persistent anxiety related to developing cancer. Robert's various cancer screening labs have all been negative; however, he has still been calling their medical office every week over "some new sign or symptom" that he is convinced is an early sign of cancer. These frequent calls and medical checkups have been occurring for approximately a year at the time of referral, and the PCP believes that psychological treatment is likely to benefit Robert. Robert himself does not believe that he needs to be seeking therapy at this time and believes that he is here simply because his PCP pawned him off (as the PCP did not want to continue doing the work to find the cancer that he knows is there).

Clinical Interview Data

Interpreter Used: No.

Current Psychosocial Stressors: Robert reported being in a car accident about a year ago, which, while destructive to his car, ultimately left him only with mild contusions at that time. He further noted that he has had to figure out how to handle his grandparents' declining health and what appropriate care he needs to be able to provide for them, which has increased as his brother's wife is now pregnant.

Protective Factors: Robert is strongly religious and believes that God will help him through his disease, and he reports having good social support at church. He also personally practices various mindful breathing techniques regularly to help him cope with his stress when it becomes intense.

Developmental History: All developmental milestones were met.

Academic History: Robert has completed his bachelor's degree in computer science. He was noted to have concerns regarding attention during his elementary school years but stated that his parents never formally tested him.

Social History: Robert regularly visits his church community and noted that he leads a men's group at church. He said he does not enjoy dating and has avoided entering into a romantic relationship despite his family and friends attempting to set him up on various dates. Further, Robert reported that he is pretty close to his brother and that the family regularly go on vacation together.

Household: Robert is currently single and lives in a three-bedroom house with his brother, his brother's wife, and grandparents. He takes turns caring for his grandparents with his brother. Additionally, his family is concerned that he is "wasting" money receiving extensive medical workups for his symptoms, which has led to increased tension in the household.

Previous Psychiatric History: None.

Family Psychiatric History: Robert reports that he is unsure, as he noted that both of his parents passed away in their early 40s from cancer. He stated that his grandfather is currently suffering from Alzheimer's dementia but has no other psychiatric history.

History of Self-Harm: None.

Wellness Profile

Sleep: Robert reports sleeping in 4-hour intervals throughout the night due to needing to care for his grandfather, who regularly wakes up in the middle of the night. He stated that his sleep is not the most restful and worries that this may increase his odds of disease.

Diet: Robert reports attempting to switch over to the Mediterranean diet for cancer prevention reasons but noted that it has been difficult to do so since his family does not enjoy these meals. He stated that he eats three meals regularly and typically does not snack.

Elimination: No concerns reported.

Technology: Robert reports that he is on his computer for at least 8 hours in the day and that it is primarily related to his job as a programmer. He stated that he will use his computer to research the latest trends in cancer prevention and treatments as well as find potential new specialists to visit. No social media usage was reported.

Physical Activity: Robert stated that he is unable to exercise regularly due to work and caring for his family but does attempt to go on walks during the evening when he can.

Substance Use/Abuse: Robert is a former hookah smoker and heavy drinker but stated that he has been sober of both substances for the past 5 years.

Pain: 2/10.

Current Psychiatric Symptoms

Depression: Irritable mood.

Anxiety: Restlessness, fatigue, irritability, sleep disturbance.

Panic: Fear of death, fear of not being taken seriously.

Mania: None.

Psychosis: None.

Trauma: Robert reported that he witnessed both of his parents slowly die from cancer when he was 8 and 10 years old, respectively; he noted that he spent a lot of his childhood in and out of hospitals. No abuse from his parents or the grandparents that he lived with afterward.

Eating Disorder: Robert regularly checks facts about his food in order to ensure that it is not a carcinogen.

Risky Behaviors/Sexual Activity: Robert previously smoked and drank heavily, but no risky behaviors reported currently.

Mental Status Exam

Appearance: *Dress*: appropriate. *Hygiene*: adequate. Appeared stated age.

Behavior: Appropriate, guarded.

Speech: *Rate*: within normal limits. *Articulation*: within normal limits. *Volume*: within normal limits. *Coherence*: within normal limits.

Mood: "Annoyed."

Affect: Full, congruent to mood, appropriate to content of interview.

Thought Process: Logical, goal directed, tangential regarding concerns about cancer.

Thought Content: Denied suicidal ideation, homicidal ideation, delusions, and hallucinations.

Orientation: Oriented to person, place, situation, and time.

Recent Memory: Intact.

Remote Memory: Intact.

Attention/Concentration: Distractible.

General Knowledge: Average.

Language: Within normal limits.

Insight: Fair.

Judgment: Fair.

Answer Key #2

Diversity Considerations

Due to Robert being a Vietnamese male, it should be considered that he may process his anxiety and worry as being related more to his concern for others and ensuring that he is able to continue to care for his familial obligations (Tran, 2017). Filial piety is important in Vietnamese culture and Robert might feel shame about prioritizing or wanting to prioritize his needs when he is in a caregiving role. Acculturative factors must also be considered in order to understand whether Robert's worldview incorporates more Western or more Eastern perspectives regarding health, illness, the medical establishment, etc. Culturally informed gender roles and expectations and how they might contribute to both Robert's health-seeking behaviors and his affective presentation might also be important to consider.

Because Robert is deeply religious, further exploration of his religious tradition and spiritual beliefs is warranted. While religion and spirituality are generally considered protective, it is important to note that individuals can leverage both religion and spirituality in adaptive or maladaptive manners. Specifically, it might be important to note whether Robert engages in positive religious coping or negative religious coping and how his religious perspective contributes to his understanding of illness (i.e., as punishment from God, as a blessing to join in the suffering of Christ, etc.).

Of note, males who are diagnosed with anxiety disorders tend to be more prone to substance abuse as a method of self-medication and have a higher potential for an undiagnosed ADHD diagnosis (McLean et al., 2011). It is important to note that illness anxiety tends to behave more as an anxiety disorder than a somatic symptom related disorder, and so literature that delves into anxiety disorders may provide additional insight for Robert (Kikas et al., 2024).

Ethical and Legal Considerations

The main ethical consideration that a clinician will need to be able to balance is ensuring that they are focused on validating Robert's emotions related to his illness anxiety but not colluding with him regarding his symptoms. Additionally, the clinician would likely need to do some background research into what may be concerning versus not concerning symptoms in order to ensure that potential concerns are explored appropriately by a medical provider.

Legally, the clinician will likely need multiple releases of information for Robert in order to obtain collateral information from medical providers, mainly Robert's PCP, so they can understand the full scope of what Robert is experiencing. Additional ROIs might be required if Robert's family members (for example, his brother) wish to become involved in treatment. While family member involvement in treatment is not only acceptable but considered normative in many cultures, appropriate documentation must still be completed prior to disclosing information to family members.

While Robert did not require an interpreter for the clinical interview, it is unclear how long he has been in the country and his legal status is also uncertain. While it is inadvisable for clinicians to make assumptions regarding the legal status of a patient, immigration status can often impact patient access to care; as such, the clinician should remain present to any potential barriers to care Robert reports so that appropriate, timely resources can be provided.

Diagnostic Impressions and Justification

F46.21 Illness Anxiety Disorder, Care-Seeking Type.

Robert's diagnosis can be justified by his significant preoccupation regarding his perceived symptoms, which, objectively, do not appear to be present. Robert is noted to be highly anxious regarding his health and is perceiving various mild physical symptoms as indicators that he is going to develop a severe disease. He is spending money and time excessively on his symptoms, with all evidence indicating that there is no likely physiological etiology contributing to his perceived symptoms; Robert is noted to be spending hours on his computer looking up symptoms as well as changing his entire diet due to his concerns. Robert's anxiety has been present for over the 6-month threshold for the diagnosis and is clearly causing him significant distress and disrupting his life in a manner that is disproportionate to the actual threat to his life. Lastly, Robert's anxiety appears to be solely focused on his health status and thus makes it more unlikely that he is suffering from another form of anxiety disorder at this time; lack of significant mood symptoms also provides evidence that there is not likely a co-morbid diagnosis.

Psychodynamic Case Conceptualization

There are multiple ways to conceptualize Robert's illness anxiety disorder from a psychodynamic perspective, as his early experiences with his family could be expressed in various ways. The loss of both parents at such a young age could constitute a profound developmental trauma. It is possible that he has internalized a fear of illness from watching his parents pass away from cancer themselves, and, after a recent non-dangerous but potentially life-threatening incident, he is having these old issues recur unconsciously. Robert's anxiety about his health may be serving as alternative focus to the increased stress caused by his accident and caring for his grandfather. These stressors threaten to bring into awareness Robert's fear of death and being left alone. His anxiety is thus displaced from its true source (loss of significant others) to something less psychologically threatening (his own potential illness) (Cramer, 2015). This lack of support and understanding from his family may be an unconscious indication that he is attempting to reach out for support from his family and bid for attention in a manner that he is familiar with due to the "attention" he likely saw his parents receive during the course of their illness. In short, these psychic defenses may help Robert protect his ego from the reality of feeling his difficult emotions of loneliness, grief, and fear of death by unconsciously focusing on perceived external signs of illness to create a safer reality (Cramer, 2015).

As with many of the somatic disorders, the main goal will be to help Robert gain appropriate insight into the nature of his symptoms and learn how his emotional states can result in his anxiety about their illness. An important goal is to focus on improving the defense mechanisms being used to help Robert cope with his anxiety and to create more adaptive defenses so that he is better able to handle the stressors in his life (Cramer, 2015). Insight-based work should also help Robert to be able to process his emotions regarding the death of his parents as well as his recent car accident so that he can gain deeper insight into the sources of his anxiety. Ultimately, the goal of psychodynamic treatment for Robert will be to reduce his dependence on somatization as a defense against overwhelming emotions.

Treatment should focus primarily on developing rapport and creating a safe therapeutic alliance for Robert that is able to help contain his anxiety in the therapy space; maintaining the frame will be crucial for him during this time. Interpretations regarding the defense that Robert is using should be offered gently in order to help him understand the underlying emotional anxiety and need for care being present whenever he starts to experience his illness anxiety symptoms (Petraglia et al., 2017). Processing Robert's affect in session after gaining insight into his symptoms should allow Robert to develop his own better coping strategies and defenses against his anxiety. The clinician can also support Robert in mentalizing his internal states. Of note: the clinician should be wary of accidentally causing Robert to begin intellectualizing his symptoms during interpretations, as it is likely that, due to his extensive time researching symptoms, this would be a way for him to continue avoiding his unconscious affect (Petraglia et al., 2017). Focusing primarily on Robert's underlying anxiety about death, as well as receiving care from his family and interpreting and processing this affect, will be crucial as illness anxiety disorder tends to be related to anxiety versus the somatic symptoms themselves (Kikas et al., 2024). Finally, improving Robert's attachment to God through mindfulness-based prayers may allow him to better connect to his own sensations as well as increase his chances of seeking out social support and care, which could improve his symptoms (Hoge et al., 2013).

Cognitive Behavioral Conceptualization

Illness anxiety disorder is another disorder that is classically considered appropriate for treatment with CBT as it relates to cognitive distortions in a similar manner to generalized anxiety disorder (GAD) but is more focused on rumination regarding a specific illness. Following the standard ABC model once again for this disorder, the activating event tends to be some form of bodily sensation that is likely mildly painful or uncomfortable or may be related to an intrusive thought regarding a health threat (Arnáez et al., 2021). This triggers belief that these are signs of a severe illness and the subsequent anxious thoughts related to such a belief, which can lead to various behaviors such as researching various treatments, frequent doctor visits, and changing multiple aspects of the individual's life in order to help quell this anxiety. In the case of Robert, it is possible that his beliefs are shaped by his very real concern about cancer, given his family history, but he then begins to overly ruminate on these thoughts, causing him distress. It is likely that he begins to overestimate the threat to his life and begins to engage in cognitive fusion with his thoughts, leading to his numerous visits to his PCP as well as becoming more irritable and upset with people in his life, as he feels that there is a severe threat to his life that no one is taking seriously (Arnáez et al., 2021). This may all be stemming from a schema that views the world as ultimately dangerous and unpredictable due to the deaths of Robert's parents and may be causing him to view minor bodily threats as major predictors of death.

Overall, treatment goals should be focused on reducing the impact of these cognitive distortions on Robert's life and increasing tolerance of distress that occurs whenever he experiences something that triggers his anxiety. Ideally, helping Robert change his dysfunctional beliefs will allow him to experience a decrease in anxiety and healthcare-seeking behaviors that are causing him distress in his life (Weck et al., 2012). Another goal of treatment would be to help Robert reduce the behaviors that are maintaining his anxiety, in this case, his frequent visits to medical professionals as well as the time spent searching the internet for information regarding his physiological symptoms. Of note, improving Robert's sleep hygiene will also be important, but this goal may need to wait until later in treatment as Robert's current sleep disturbance is related to his caregiving role within his family.

Interventions should begin with gentle psychoeducation regarding the nature of his condition that allows for challenging his cognitive distortions in later therapy (Weck et al., 2012). Decreasing reactive behaviors to his activating events and focusing on mindfulness interventions for his hypervigilance towards his bodily sensations will help Robert respond to the situation appropriately. Later work can also concentrate on underlying schemas that may be causing these activating events to be so triggering for Robert, with the goal of challenging his core beliefs about the world being unsafe. Thought records and Socratic questioning might be particularly helpful for Robert as well as behavioral experiments designed to help him gather data regarding the impact on his person of *not* searching the internet regarding his symptoms. Exposure-based CBT may be beneficial for Robert in reducing his anxiety symptoms regarding potential illness; focusing on exposure to activating stimuli that are ultimately unlikely to cause cancer can help reduce symptoms (Hedman et al., 2016). Because Robert is deeply religious, religiously integrated forms of mindfulness could be incorporated into his current mindfulness practice.

Biopsychosocial Conceptualization

The neurobiological research regarding illness anxiety disorder is relatively limited at this point in time, although there appears to be a small amount of evidence suggesting that there is increased amygdala activity and anterior cingulate cortex activity in response to words related to body-symptoms (Kikas et al., 2024). This would indicate that these individuals may have an underlying difficulty with cognition and emotional regulation when stress concerning bodily functioning is involved and this could potentially lead to dysfunctional cognitions surrounding their health (Kikas et al., 2024). Additionally, Robert's family history of cancer and exposure to a perceived life-threatening event may result in him being biologically activated with potential brain changes that make it difficult to regulate this, causing his anxieties about his health to increase (APA, 2022). Socially, the lack of validation Robert receives from his family regarding his concerns about his health is particularly painful for him when his illness anxiety behaviors are conceptualized as maladaptive forms of care-seeking behavior during difficult times (Kikas et al., 2024). Robert's repeated internet searching during this time could also be understood as a way to be able to relieve the tension that he is feeling regarding his heightened perceptions about his body and concerns about cancer (Kikas et al., 2024; Singh et al., 2016). This use of the internet is also likely to provide short-term reassurance at times about his symptoms but may also amplify his own uncertainty regarding his own health in the long term, especially as it may lead him to recall his interactions with his parents as they died of cancer (Singh et al., 2016). Coupled with a personality that appears to be more isolative and worry-prone, Robert can be viewed as an individual who was primed to develop an illness anxiety disorder during a period of high stress related to his body.

The treatment's primary goal should be to help Robert reduce the overall impact that stress has on his body and mind and improve adaptive coping strategies to reduce the likelihood of his symptoms occurring. Working with Robert to enable him to recognize the chain of events and emotions that lead to his illness anxiety symptoms so that he is better able to identify the biopsychological cascade would also be helpful. It may be impactful to help Robert understand how the death of his parents has affected him and essentially taught him to respond in the way that he is during periods of anxiety and stress related to disease and death (Kikas et al., 2024) Developing improved social support for Robert so he is once again able to cope with the stress in his life should also help to reduce his illness anxiety. Additionally, treatment should improve sleep and insight into the bidirectional relationship between psychological distress and physiological discomfort.

Initial treatment should focus on developing a strong therapeutic alliance, as this has been demonstrated to be vital for the treatment of those experiencing significant health anxiety; a major part of this will be showing competence to Robert during the course of therapy (Weck et al., 2015). Mindfulness-based interventions should help Robert gain awareness of when he is becoming more active so that he can better regulate his emotions at that moment. Additionally, it will be important to focus on re-learning anxiety responses regarding Robert's health and help him become better at reaching out to social support so that he can develop new coping strategies to decrease illness anxiety symptoms. Sleep hygiene training would also be appropriate when Robert is ready to engage in such an intervention. Finally, "cyberchondria" should be reduced by promoting a reduction of time spent on the computer in order to improve overall health outcomes and provide more time for other activities that Robert enjoys (Tyrer, 2018).

Of note, some research has indicated that fluoxetine and paroxetine (SSRIs) were helpful for the previous diagnosis of hypochondriasis, which illness anxiety disorder replaced; therefore, psychiatric evaluation for medications may benefit Robert (Kikas et al., 2024).

Clinical Case Vignette #3

Demographic Information and History

Name: Alexis Miller.

Demographic Information: 28-year-old Black woman.

Medical Diagnoses: None.

Reason for Referral: Alexis was admitted to the neurology department as an inpatient at the hospital due to concerns about seizures and tremors. An extensive neurological and medical workup was performed for Alexis, which yielded inconclusive evidence, with imaging and labs being negative, as well as an EEG (electroencephalogram) showing no seizure-like activity. Psychiatry and neurology have since cleared the Alexis. However, Alexis's non-epileptic seizures and tremors have remained persistent, so psychology was consulted for evaluation. Alexis herself states that she has had these symptoms over the past week and that they have been progressively worsening to the point where she is struggling to walk and is fearful of moving around the house due to concern that she will have a seizure and fall down. Of note, Alexis reports that her symptoms started around the time that she lost her job and was unable to make a rent payment due to this fact.

Clinical Interview Data

Interpreter Used: No.

Current Psychosocial Stressors: Her most notable recent stressors include losing her job and working in marketing. This loss in income made her late on her last rent payment, and she has been using credit debt to get through this time.

Protective Factors: Alexis appeared to have difficulty stating her strengths, although she noted that she is proud of her previous job and feels that she has found her calling. She reported developing good friendships from her previous job and that they have been supportive. Otherwise, she reported being Christian and that prayer has been beneficial to her in the past.

Developmental History: Alexis was born prematurely at 31 weeks and required a short stay in the neonatal intensive care unit. There were no reported complications from this time. She stated that she had met her developmental milestones otherwise.

Academic History: She stated that she received Bs and Cs in high school and college but graduated without significant difficulty with a bachelor's degree in marketing. No history of academic accommodations or learning disabilities was reported.

Social History: Alexis reports that she is close to a few previous co-workers and that they regularly spend time with each other. She otherwise reports a tenuous relationship with her current roommate, but overall, they are able to co-exist well. During the interview, Alexis appeared hesitant to discuss her family but mentioned that she was neglected severely as a child but that social services were never called. Alexis has since moved away from her parents and extended family and is currently living several states away.

Household: Alexis is currently living in a two-bedroom apartment with a female roommate who is similar in age; Alexis describes her as "too cold." She reiterated that she intentionally lives far away from any immediate or extended family.

Previous Psychiatric History: Alexis suspects that she has been depressed since her childhood years but has never sought out mental health treatment.

Family Psychiatric History: Alexis is unsure about any mental health diagnoses, although she noted that her parents were both polysubstance abusers.

History of Self-Harm: Alexis noted that she used to cut her inner thighs with a razor in order to feel better as an adolescent and does occasionally feel the desire to do so in adulthood whenever she feels stressed. No suicide attempts were reported.

Assessment Data

Magnetic resonance imaging (MRI), video-electroencephalogram (vEEG), and blood work were all reported to be negative. Neurological assessment and physical exam, per neurology, were negative for acute deficits.

Wellness Profile

Sleep: Alexis's sleep schedule was reported to be quite regular before losing her job, and she stated that she slept 6–8 hours a night. Noted that, since her tremors and seizures started, she would be awoken by these symptoms, and so she has been only sleeping 2–4 hours a night for the past week.

Diet: Alexis stated that she tries to eat healthily when she can but noted that she tends to rely on fast food whenever she is stressed as a way to comfort herself. She said that she usually eats a light breakfast and lunch, followed by a heavier dinner.

Elimination: No concerns about this were reported. No incontinence was reported during seizure activity.

Technology: Alexis reports that she used her computer regularly at work to answer emails and has since been spending multiple hours online either looking up her symptoms or attempting to find a new job. Stated that she is otherwise watching animated shows on TV in order to relax.

Physical Activity: Reported that she occasionally takes walks to stay in shape but otherwise noted a more sedentary lifestyle.

Substance Use/Abuse: She stated that she smokes cigarettes regularly but adamantly denied any history of alcohol or other drugs.

Pain: 3/10.

Current Psychiatric Symptoms

Depression: Depressed mood, anhedonia, insomnia, psychomotor agitation, loss of energy, feelings of worthlessness.

Anxiety: Restlessness, fatigue, irritability, muscle tension, sleep disturbance, difficulty controlling worry.

Panic: Shaking, shortness of breath, paraesthesias.

Mania: None reported.

Psychosis: None reported or observed.

Trauma: Alexis reported witnessing her parents using multiple substances as a child and that they would regularly forget to feed her to the point that she was cooking for herself at age 7. Stated that her parents rarely, if ever, responded to her while intoxicated; noted a time when she was injured and severely stressed due to bullying and that they barely acknowledged her. No direct physical or sexual abuse was reported.

Eating Disorder: None reported.

Risky Behaviors/Sexual Activity: None reported.

Mental Status Exam

Appearance: *Dress*: Alexis was in a clean hospital gown. *Hygiene*: Alexis has been maintaining good hygiene during her workup. Noted to have a tremor in her hands that was distractible.

Behavior: Appropriate but guarded.

Speech: *Rate*: within normal limits. *Articulation*: within normal limits. *Volume*: within normal limits. *Coherence*: within normal limits.

Mood: "Tired."

Affect: Constricted, congruent to mood, appropriate to content of interview.

Thought Process: Logical, linear, goal directed.

Thought Content: Denied suicidal ideation, homicidal ideation, delusions, and hallucinations.

Orientation: Oriented to person, place, situation, and time.

Recent Memory: Intact.

Remote Memory: Impaired regarding her family.

Attention/Concentration: Sufficient.

General Knowledge: Average.

Language: Within normal limits.

Insight: Poor.

Judgment: Fair.

Answer Key #3

Diversity Considerations

The intersection of Alexis's identity as an African American woman and a Christian may have caused a sense of being unable to express her distress in a verbal manner due to certain underlying sociocultural beliefs, and thus may be a possible area of exploration into her presentation (Schwartz et al., 2001). Specifically, cultural expectations regarding strength and resilience might contribute to internalization of the "strong Black woman" schema and thus serve as a deterrent for certain help-seeking behaviors. It is essentially more acceptable for Black Christian women to express physical complaints than psychological concerns, making it easier for them to present with these types of symptoms (Lara-Cinisomo et al., 2020). African American women are more likely to experience somatization of depressive symptoms more frequently than White women, so exploring how Alexis's recent stressors may be contributing to her depressive symptoms may yield insight into her neurological concerns (Lara-Cinisomo et al., 2020). Because Alexis identifies as a Christian, her religious tradition and faith may serve as an important source of support. She may also, however, engage in negative religious coping, which may in turn exacerbate her symptoms.

It is important for clinicians to keep in mind both the current systemic barriers to care for Black patients as well as the historical atrocities perpetuated on Black patients and how the confluence of these factors may contribute to patient distrust of the medical system, especially in a situation where a patient's physiological concerns are being attributed to a psychological etiology. Alexis's current financial instability as well as the recent loss of her job (and therefore, in all likelihood, her insurance benefits) may serve as additional barriers to care.

Ethical and Legal Considerations

Ensuring that the medical workup for Alexis is thorough so as to ensure that a major neurological condition is not being missed is vital (Tsui et al., 2017). It is also important to ensure that Alexis's symptoms are taken seriously, even if, when diagnosed, etiology is considered to be psychological, as her tremors and seizures are likely causing objective impairment to her life during a stressful period, even if they are not purely neurological in nature. An adequate explanation of Alexis's symptoms is likely necessary so that she can fully understand the full course of treatment that will need to take place, especially during a period of financial strain in her life; she may require more intensive outpatient services for her symptoms (Schwartz et al., 2001). Financial instability as well as likely recent loss of health insurance benefits must be taken into consideration when providing Alexis with referrals and resources.

Diagnostic Impressions and Justification

F44.7 Functional Neurological Symptom Disorder with Mixed Symptoms, Acute Episode.
Rule Out F34.1 Persistent Depressive Disorder, Early Onset, Moderate.
Alexis is being primarily evaluated due to her neurological complaints, which she is reporting as tremors and seizures with reported numbness during her physical exam. Her workup is medically negative, and her symptoms are inconsistent with a typical neurological distribution. Additionally, the onset of her symptoms appears to have occurred due to a significant life stressor, and she is in the usual age range for the onset of a functional neurological disorder (APA, 2022). The persistent depressive disorder is more challenging to assess, as Alexis remains guarded about symptoms outside of her neurological complaints, but it appears that, based on her report, she has had a depressed mood for several years with associated anhedonia, fatigue, and feelings of worthlessness. It is possible that, upon helping the Alexis adjust to her functional neurological symptom disorder, her depressive symptoms may become more prominent.

Psychodynamic Case Conceptualization

Similar to the case with somatic symptom disorder, the resulting symptoms of tremors and pseudoseizures likely represent the use of the defense mechanism of somatization as the mind attempts to process an emotion unconsciously (McWilliams, 2011). In the case of Alexis, it is likely that she is essentially experiencing a "panic attack without panic," as she is unable to process her high levels of anxiety and panic consciously and, thus, her body begins to process the affect from which she is dissociated (Jungilligens et al., 2022). Psychodynamic theory views emotions as the way people experience the world, so being consciously disconnected from these emotions can result in a patient's body still experiencing the world through those emotions, even if they are unaware of this fact (Frederickson et al., 2018). Alexis herself, being the victim of childhood neglect, likely never learned how to process her own emotions through her parents and thus may be bereft of the necessary ability to process difficult emotions consciously. This, coupled with her tendency to self-harm with the likely goal of relieving tension within herself, leads to the conclusion that she is unable to process her own emotional world appropriately, and that she lacks the support to be able to develop healthy relationships that could help model emotional regulation. Alexis is thus a woman who likely does not trust her own affective states due to them never being acknowledged by her family, and, thus, when a severe stressor enters her life, she is unable to process the emotions of panic within herself, resulting in her body somatizing the affect unconsciously for her.

Treatment goals should first focus on helping Alexis improve her affective expression skills so that she is able to learn how to process emotions in a way that does not rely on somatization. The other main goal that should be addressed is helping Alexis process her underlying history of neglect, also allowing her to process her emotions regarding this and gain an appropriate insight into how this is likely impacting her life in the present. Additionally, addressing how her depressive symptoms will be important during treatment and helping to reduce overall unconscious conflict will likely benefit the functional neurological symptoms as well (Feinstein, 2011). Treatment should also focus on improving Alexis's insight into how conversion is being used as a defense against both residual distress from childhood neglect and current stressors. The clinician should also leverage the therapeutic alliance in providing Alexis with a reparative relationship.

The treatment should heavily focus in the early stages on developing relational capital and providing reflections toward statements in order to help Alexis gain the emotional language to describe what she is feeling. Helping Alexis gain direct insight into the primary gain of reducing unconscious conflict with her emotions as well as secondary gains, potentially receiving care and concern, will be necessary during the treatment process for her to understand better what is leading to her functional neurological symptoms (Feinstein, 2011). Similar to somatic symptom disorder, interpretations will likely be provided to a patient later on in the process, due to these patients needing strong rapport in order to build trust and safety for reflecting on their childhood neglect (McWilliams, 2011). Managing countertransference will be vital to ensure that if Alexis does develop new neurological symptoms, they are evaluated appropriately and not dismissed, in order to avoid missing an important diagnosis (Espay et al., 2018). Some evidence has suggested that hypnotherapy may be effective for patients suffering from functional neurological disorders in order to bring awareness of and reduce symptoms (Tsui et al., 2017). Focusing on the defense mechanisms being used with Alexis and interpreting her need for support, as well as a tendency to attempt to dissociate from emotional needs through her seizure-like activity, will likely provide the emotional insight that she needs (Tsui et al., 2017; Jungilligens et al., 2022).

Cognitive Behavioral Conceptualization

By conceptualization using the cognitive theory that underlies CBT, functional neurological symptom disorder can be understood as a patient having real symptoms but having dysfunctional cognitions regarding how those symptoms present (Stone et al., 2016). In the case of Alexis, her non-epileptic seizures are likely a result of experiencing an activating event that increases high levels of emotional or autonomic arousal, triggering beliefs about how threatening these feelings can be and thoughts of being unable to handle the current threat, leading to Alexis being unable to inhibit the seizure-like activity (Reuber & Brown, 2016). The cognitive model would view her seizure-like activity and tremors as a behavior that is helping her avoid the high levels of arousal caused by her anxious thoughts, which are likely influenced by her core beliefs that no one will come to help her during difficult situations, due to the neglect she experienced as a child (Reuber & Brown, 2016; Goldstein, 2006). CBT then similarly views functional neurological symptoms, especially non-epileptic seizures, as also being "panic without the panic attack," as these symptoms tend to be more related to dissociative episodes so that Alexis does not have to experience her distressing thoughts and emotions regarding her life situation (Goldstein, 2006). Thus, Alexis is likely experiencing multiple anxious cognitions regarding her stressful life situation, which is causing her to experience high levels of emotional and autonomic arousal. This is leading her to have further thoughts about being overwhelmed and unable to handle her situation. Thus, without an effective strategy to handle these feelings, Alexis begins to experience the seizure-like activity as her body begins to panic, which then reinforces her own thought pattern about being unable to handle her situation.

Treatment goals will be more behavioral at first, as they should focus on helping Alexis perform behaviors that can help reduce her arousal and identify triggers that can lead to her seizure-like activity. It will also be important to address Alexis's cognitions to make them more functional for her, allowing her to relate to her symptoms and life situation, with the goal of helping to reduce her automatic arousal to situations (Stone & Carson, 2010). Additionally, focusing on treating Alexis's core schema of being unlovable and helpless will be necessary in order to reduce the impact of her anxious cognitions overall. Of note: Alexis should work toward increasing the number of hours she is sleeping each night.

Treatment should begin with psychoeducation in order to help Alexis understand the nature of her symptoms so that she can understand that her nervous system is "not damaged" but also, at the same time, it is not working correctly (Stone & Carson, 2010). Cognitive restructuring exercises should then be used to help Alexis better understand her symptoms as treatable and challenge her anxious thoughts to make them more functional for her life (Stone & Carson, 2010). Treatment should build on self-monitoring techniques and help Alexis develop improved social support in order to help her notice her high stress levels and cognitions around this, while developing a support system to help with these symptoms (Tsui et al., 2017). Mindfulness-based interventions will likely be beneficial as well so that Alexis will be able to become more attuned to her emotions during moments of high arousal that potentially lead to her functional neurological symptoms and be able to notice and experience her emotions instead of dissociating (Goldstein, 2006). Cognitive behavioral therapy for insomnia (CBTi) techniques may also be helpful. Additionally, ensuring that there is a relapse plan being developed toward the end of treatment in order to help Alexis feel ready for what to do should her symptoms recur. Finally, providing Alexis with religiously integrated psychotherapy interventions may support her in leveraging her faith in a manner that supports recovery.

Biopsychosocial Conceptualization

From a neurobiological perspective, Alexis is at a greater risk for the development of psychiatric disorders due to her premature birth, which may be manifesting in her depressive symptoms (Shaw et al., 2023). This, coupled with a history of neglect, has likely made her susceptible to developing a functional neurological symptom disorder related to the moderate-high stress event that occurred in her life recently, conceptualized using a stress-diathesis model (Keynejad et al., 2018; APA, 2022). It is likely that her HPA axis has resulted in a chronic level of cortisol being present in her body due to her family history, frequent financial stress, and limited support system, which has caused her to be more susceptible to functional neurological symptoms (Keynejad et al., 2018; Çetin & Varma, 2021). As a result, it is likely that Alexis is feeling psychologically overwhelmed by her current situation and feels unable to handle her situation, which is causing her already existing vulnerabilities to psychological disorders to become more prominent. Her restricted affect shows that Alexis is likely unable to fully express the necessary emotions regarding her situation, which may now be presented in the form of her tremors and non-epileptic seizures. Similar to the case with somatic symptom disorder, Alexis is becoming trapped in a feedback loop of feeling increased stress due to her symptoms, causing her greater difficulties during an already stressful period of life, which can then lead to further symptoms.

The main treatment goal is to help Alexis reduce her overall levels of stress in her life and develop new coping skills that will enable her to handle new stressors in the future. Additionally, Alexis will need to be able to process her co-morbid depressive symptoms and be able to understand the underlying processes that are leading to her functional neurological symptoms being present. Additional goals include improving sleep, reducing physiological symptoms, and reducing nicotine dependence, as well as addressing current financial instability.

Treatment should initially focus on psychoeducation regarding Alexis's symptoms, such as by providing information regarding psychogenic seizures and seizure thresholds, and on ensuring that she understands the intent behind interventions focusing on reducing the levels of stress in her life. This time providing psychoeducation should also include exploring the impact of her parents' neglect, in order for both clinician and Alexis to gain a better understanding of how this may still be impacting her symptoms. Physical rehabilitation may be necessary should her tremors or paresthesias impair motor functioning for a prolonged period of time in order to help potential muscular atrophy (Tsui et al., 2017); as such, appropriate referrals should be considered.

Helping Alexis create a home environment that minimizes the chances of a high level of arousal may help reduce the overall seizure-like activity (Jungilligens et al., 2022). Assisting Alexis in returning back to her previously healthy sleep schedule will also likely benefit her, and collaborating about how to attempt this with her current symptoms will be crucial. CBTi may be helpful in this regard. With the help of physiotherapy, the clinician can assist Alexis in having a less sedentary lifestyle in order to help combat overall fatigue in her life, which can improve symptoms (Jungilligens et al., 2022). Nicotine cessation can be attempted and motivational interviewing utilized if Alexis is not amenable to incorporating this health-promoting behavior. Lastly, increasing social support to find people who can help during difficult times will likely help reduce the overall impact of stressful events in the future and can help prevent symptoms from relapsing.

Clinical Case Vignette #4

Demographic Information and History

Name: Stephanie Smith.

Demographic Information: 32-year-old White female.

Medical Diagnoses: No previous medical history was reported.

Reason for Referral: Stephanie was referred for psychological treatment by her PCP due to concerns about recent hospital visits and medical findings. It has been noted that, over the past 3 months, Stephanie has presented to the emergency department (ED) multiple times for abdominal pain and has been reported to have hematemesis during these visits. Stephanie's history has been vague regarding her symptoms and, when confronted about metallic objects being present in her stomach on imaging, she has denied any knowledge of how these metallic shards ended up in her stomach. Stephanie has been noted to change her story regarding her symptoms multiple times and was reportedly witnessed attempting to unscrew a lightbulb in her inpatient bathroom, which she denied– she said she was "simply trying to kill a bug." Stephanie's blood loss has been mild so far, but her PCP and ED physicians are concerned about her continuing to induce hematemesis in herself by ingesting harmful objects and so have sent her for psychological treatment.

Clinical Interview Data

Interpreter Used: No.

Current Psychosocial Stressors: Stephanie has been reprimanded multiple times at her nursing job due to missing calls and is currently on her final warning at work. Additionally, Stephanie was recently informed that her son is failing middle school and she reported going through a "difficult parent-teacher conference." She also noted that she is currently going through a divorce but refused to share details about what led to the divorce.

Protective Factors: Stephanie is fairly disciplined and she regularly sets aside time for studying and exercise despite her busy schedule. It is noted that she is quite diligent in these things and appears to be motivated toward growth and improving her quality of life.

Developmental History: Stephanie reported meeting all of her developmental milestones. Stephanie's mother gave birth to her (and was delivered vaginally) at 39 weeks.

Academic History: Stephanie reported that she has her bachelor's in nursing and is in the process of obtaining her master's degree in nursing as she wants to be more qualified. She stated that she is struggling somewhat but is still able to maintain regular Bs in the program.

Social History: Stephanie reports that her main social support comes from her friends, who she met in nursing school, as well as her work colleagues. She stated that they would regularly have parties and enjoy meals together outside of work. It was noted that Stephanie became much more guarded when discussing her parents, although she reported that her parents were good for pushing her to be as successful as she is today. She reported that she does not see her parents often despite them living in a nearby city.

Household: Stephanie lives at home with just her 11-year-old son, who she reported as acting out lately since the divorce occurred. She reported that she has split custody with the father and has her son every other week.

Previous Psychiatric History: Stephanie reported that she was diagnosed with "depression" in her adolescent years and reportedly was in therapy for a few sessions before her parents pulled her out of therapy. She stated that she feels that this never entirely went away but noted that she thinks that she should be able "to pull herself together."

Family Psychiatric History: Stephanie reported no known psychiatric history in her family, although she suspects that her father likely struggles with "some form of mental illness" as he would have periods of staying up for days and would frequently spend a lot of their money.

History of Self-Harm: Stephanie reported having passive suicidal ideation in the past and self-harming as an adolescent and young adult. She stated that neither of these has occurred since she gave birth to her son.

Assessment Data

Bloodwork showed mild anemia, likely due to recurrent hematemesis. Imaging consistent with metallic objects located in the stomach.

Wellness Profile

Sleep: Stephanie admitted that her sleep schedule had been more disrupted as she is currently the lowest priority for scheduling among nurses and so is regularly switching between night and day shifts. She stated that she will get anywhere from 3–8 hours of sleep depending on how her shifts go and whether or not she has her son at home.

Diet: Her morning meal is typically some form of frozen meal that she can heat up in the microwave. She stated that she normally eats fast food for dinner as she feels too tired after work to cook. She does report high levels of caffeine intake due to drinking 2–3 energy drinks per shift.

Elimination: Stephanie did report some episodes of melena but otherwise is not having issues with urination or bowel movements.

Technology: Stephanie spends 1–2 hours on social media daily, stating that she mainly views nursing reels and attempts to learn how to be more successful in her career.

Physical Activity: Stephanie does report that her job requires her to be constantly on her feet and moving around. She also reports doing some light yoga using a phone app at home, as well as lower back stretches to help with the regular strain of moving patients.

Substance Use/Abuse: Stephanie reported that she does not smoke, drink, or use drugs regularly. She did, however, note that she will have "several drinks" during social events with friends or co-workers and occasionally will use marijuana or cocaine during this time.

Pain: 7/10 abdominal pain.

Current Psychiatric Symptoms

Depression: Depressed mood, irritable mood, feelings of worthlessness/guilt, decreased concentration and difficulty making decisions, fatigue.

Anxiety: Fatigue, irritability.

Panic: Abdominal distress, fear of losing control.

Mania: Heavy focus on goal directed activities.

Psychosis: None reported or observed.

Trauma: Stephanie initially denied abuse in her life; however, she noted that both her husband and her parents tended to yell at her frequently. She reported that she felt that if she made any mistake that was not excused, she would be harshly punished and berated by them. She stated that her son was never exposed to these incidents, as far as she knows.

Eating Disorder: Suspected eating of metallic and glass objects per physician report.

Risky Behaviors/Sexual Activity: Stephanie has reported having multiple sexual partners and unprotected sex over the course of the past year since the divorce. She reported that typically this occurs at a party where she is drinking and using either marijuana or cocaine; noted that this only happens once or twice every couple of months.

Mental Status Exam

Appearance: *Dress*: appropriate/inappropriate. *Hygiene*: adequate/inadequate. Appeared stated age.

Behavior: Appropriate and cooperative except for becoming guarded during certain topics as noted above.

Speech: *Rate*: within normal limits. *Articulation*: within normal limits. *Volume*: within normal limits. *Coherence*: within normal limits.

Mood: “Fine.”

Affect: Constricted, congruent to mood, appropriate to content of interview.

Thought Process: Logical, linear, goal directed.

Thought Content: Denied suicidal ideation, homicidal ideation, delusions, and hallucinations.

Orientation: Oriented to person, place, situation, and time.

Recent Memory: Intact.

Remote Memory: Intact.

Attention/Concentration: Distractible.

General Knowledge: Average.

Language: Within normal limits.

Insight: Poor.

Judgment: Poor.

Answer Key #4

Diversity Considerations

The rarity of factitious disorder being diagnosed makes the literature on diversity concerns quite sparse, although it should be noted that Stephanie is likely to be quite averse to receiving this diagnosis due to it being quite similar to malingering, and her nursing background may make it so that she already holds strong negative feelings towards these types of patients, making it particularly difficult for her to accept this diagnosis (Jafferany et al., 2018; Sinha & Smolik, 2021). That being said, diversity variables associated with being a woman, being a single mother, and being a nurse might intersect and influence both help-seeking behaviors and potential overidentification with both sick and caregiving roles.

Ethical and Legal Considerations

Non-compliance with treatment is something that is to be expected in this patient population, as well as concerns about litigation from the patient. Clinicians should be prepared to work with a multidisciplinary team and ensure careful documentation when working with this population (Sinha & Smolik, 2021). Consulting or referring to a specialist regarding Stephanie will likely be necessary as many therapists are likely not trained in treating these types of patients (Sinha & Smolik, 2021). Clinicians who find themselves as members of such interdisciplinary teams may wish to consult with both their malpractice insurance providers and their organization's legal counsel.

While this disorder can be dangerous and potentially life-threatening, most states do not view factitious disorder as grounds for an involuntary psychiatric hold. That being said, clinicians should still regularly assess for patient safety issues. Managing one's countertransference in these cases is vital to ensure that the patient's rights are not infringed (Sinha & Smolik, 2021). These patients invoke a lot of countertransference due to the nature of being deceived, so clinicians will need to be extra careful in managing their countertransference (Sinha & Smolik, 2021).

Additional ethical and legal considerations involve Stephanie's role as a nurse as well as her role as a mother. Stephanie may be using her training and education as a nurse to falsify symptoms, which may lead to legal repercussions in some states if her behavior leads to unnecessary hospitalizations, medical procedures, or use of emergency services. Questions may also arise regarding her ability to practice safely as a nurse, especially given the multiple reprimands she has already received at work. Additionally, while her mental health concerns and substance use may not necessarily indicate that she is neglecting her son – after all, she may be engaging in substance use when he is with his father – careful evaluation of her parenting practices may be warranted to ensure the child is safe and not being abused or neglected. Discovery of the child being abused and/or neglected may warrant a report to child protective services.

Diagnostic Impressions and Justification

F68.10 Factitious Disorder Imposed on Self.
F34.1 Persistent Depressive Disorder, Early Onset.
Stephanie's presentation is most consistent with a factitious disorder at this time, with an underlying co-morbid diagnosis of persistent depressive disorder that has likely contributed to her symptomology. She has been noted to be clearly inducing her physical symptoms by ingesting foreign materials and appears to be attempting to deceive the hospital team regarding the true nature of her symptoms. Stephanie is also presenting for the purpose of being identified as sick and has been demonstrating her hematemesis in order to receive care. Her mental status exam also supports factitious disorder, as, while her insight and judgment are markedly poor, there does not appear to be evidence of active psychosis or negative symptoms at this time, which could be another possibility for her symptoms. Additionally, there appears to be no tangible gain for Stephanie to be inducing her somatic symptoms, which makes malingering much less likely. As for her depressive symptoms, these have been persistent for several years (since her adolescence) and do not appear to be severe enough at the time to indicate major depressive disorder. Depressive symptoms and factitious disorder have a tendency to be co-morbid with one another, so it is possible that Stephanie's low energy, difficulty in making decisions, and depressed mood have contributed to the development of her factitious disorder.

Psychodynamic Case Conceptualization

This particular patient, as with many of the other patients discussed, suffers from an inability to resolve her intrapsychic conflicts in an adaptive manner. It is evident that Stephanie is currently undergoing multiple high-stress situations in her life, which she likely perceives as at least partially related to her failure as a mother and a nurse. Her family history demonstrates that she likely was never taught how to handle failure and therefore she likely views failure as significantly threatening to her ego and self-esteem. Additionally, it is possible that she holds an unconscious desire to be validated and to be treated with care during these times, but, in a similar vein, likely views being taken care of during times of failure as an impossibility. In this way, her factitious disorder symptoms can be viewed as her displacing her desire for emotional care into physical care by inducing symptoms to elicit care and sympathy from other people (Özdemir, 2020; Jafferany et al., 2018). Coupled with her already existing depression symptoms and taxing of her psychological resources, there is a possibility that her inducing these symptoms may also be a form of intrapsychic defense to protect herself from the guilt that she is likely feeling regarding the recent failures in her life; her ego is strongly influenced by her identity as a nurse, and so becoming quite sick can help assuage those injuries to the ego (Jafferany et al., 2018). Her guilt may also be activating potential underlying masochistic personality traits, and she may be inflicting these injuries on herself in order to relieve tension related to her guilt (Özdemir, 2020). Stephanie is likely working at a borderline level of functioning, and these actions have been her coping strategies, maladaptive as they are; she may feel that she must do something to get care and avoid falling apart (Özdemir, 2020). In sum, Stephanie is remarkably complex and likely has multiple intrapsychic components all contributing to her current presentation, but the core of the issue is that she is unequipped to handle the emotions related to failing at things in her life and unable to ask for help in order to have her emotional needs met.

The main goal of psychodynamic care for Stephanie is to help her gain insight into the emotional needs that are clearly unfulfilled so that she can acknowledge her need for help and care in a manner that is not destructive to her sense of self. Having Stephanie able to acknowledge her symptoms and cease deception is another goal of treatment and is also demonstrative of a good prognosis of treatment if she is able to acknowledge (Galli et al., 2017). Helping Stephanie develop a healthier attachment in the therapeutic alliance and begin to develop healthier defense mechanisms for future incidents will also be vital in order to stop a relapse of symptoms from occurring (Özdemir, 2020). Additional goals include exploring and examining early attachment disruptions as well as helping her develop a more fully integrated and stable sense of self.

Treatment will primarily involve empathic reflections and supportive interventions for several months of treatment as the clinician will need to build significant relational capital to move forward in treatment; rejection rates of treatment in this disorder are remarkably high (Jafferany et al., 2018; Krahn et al., 2003). This patient, in particular, will need steady boundaries to be maintained due to her various attachment injuries sustained and to help provide a regulating influence in therapy. Exploration into her early trauma and uncovering some of the emotional needs that were not met during her formative years will likely be beneficial to help Stephanie gain the insight necessary to improve (Özdemir, 2020). Interpretations should focus on pointing out her potential desire to suffer because of her mistakes as well as gentle confrontations that she may be acting in this way in order to reach out and seek the care she so desperately wants (Özdemir, 2020; Jafferany et al., 2018). Confrontation of the Stephanie's deception will likely be necessary for progress to proceed at some point and it is suggested that it is indirect in nature and focused on bringing awareness that there do appear to be factitious symptoms present (Özdemir, 2020).

Of note, working with the interdisciplinary team to help them provide empathic care will be necessary as countertransference can occur in the physicians caring for such a patient and can increase the risk of non-compliance with medical treatment (Krahn et al., 2003).

Cognitive Behavioral Conceptualization

Factitious disorder is conceptualized by CBT as being a behavioral byproduct of maladaptive core beliefs that are related to early childhood experiences; the abuse that Stephanie suffered as a child has meant she has created schemas about the world and herself that result in her deceptive and self-harm behavior (Kinsella, 2001; Comacchio et al., 2024). Stephanie likely has core beliefs where she views asking for help and vulnerability as dangerous, and so events that leave her in a situation where she would need help are likely highly activating for these cognitions (Kinsella, 2001). There is also likely another core belief that evaluates failure as making her unworthy of love and deserving of punishment, which likely makes the recent events in her life much more activating for her. Once the distressing emotions from her recent events and beliefs occur, it is unsurprising that Stephanie listens to her beliefs that receiving emotional care is dangerous and leaves her vulnerable, and thus cognitions focusing on receiving physical care coupled with her nursing background lead her to ingest dangerous materials to elicit this "safer care." Additionally, lying and illness may have been one of the few ways that she avoided psychological abuse, and so she has developed strategies that involve using these techniques during periods of high distress (Kinsella, 2001). These strategies are only reinforced by the care that Stephanie has been receiving during her hospitalization as she is finally receiving the attention and kindness during a difficult period that she has likely always been craving from others. At the moment, this allows her to cope better with those distressing emotions of being vulnerable and afraid, as the care that she receives likely does provide some immediate relief of her emotional distress (Kinsella, 2001). Stephanie can be understood then as a woman who has deep-seated maladaptive schemas that push her far away from seeking emotional or social support during this distressing time but also in desperate need of care, leading to harmful and deceptive behaviors in order to gain access to the care that she desires.

The initial goal of CBT for Stephanie is to reduce the dangerous behaviors in which Stephanie is engaging to minimize the risk to her life. Related to this goal, another goal will be to help Stephanie develop better adaptive coping strategies for stressful situations so that she can learn to engage in alternative behaviors that are significantly less harmful. Once the immediate danger to Stephanie has been improved, goals can shift to helping her understand the beliefs that are leading to her behavior and help her gain a cognitive understanding of why she is engaging in these behaviors (Kinsella, 2001). Later goals should focus on changing Stephanie's maladaptive schemas and allowing her to develop new beliefs about herself (Kinsella, 2001). Finally, behavioral goals can include helping Stephanie develop behavioral alternatives by reinforcing non-symptom-related behaviors.

Treatment should initially focus on maximizing engagement, gaining an in-depth understanding of Stephanie's cognitions, and evaluating if direct confrontation of her symptoms is appropriate for this Stephanie (Hausteiner-Wiehle & Hungerer, 2020; Kinsella, 2001). Providing coping strategies for the stressors in her life, such as mindfulness-based techniques, should be initiated early in treatment to help her relieve the stress and reduce the impact of the activating events in her life (Hausteiner-Wiehle & Hungerer, 2020). Addressing Stephanie's more harmful schemas and core beliefs will also be necessary to avoid relapse in the future and to help her understand and adjust her beliefs regarding herself and the world (Kinsella, 2001). Specifically, directly addressing dysfunctional goals and beliefs regarding her life and career may help Stephanie identify potential cognitive distortions that are driving attitudes and beliefs that may result in her factitious disorder symptoms from occurring again (Hausteiner-Wiehle & Hungerer, 2020).

Biopsychosocial Conceptualization

While the biological underpinnings of factitious disorder are likely quite complex and still not well understood, some abnormal perceptions appear to be present in such patients (Galli et al., 2017). Amygdala and motor area regions, such as the basal ganglia, have been noted to have decreased activity in these patients, suggesting that there may be neurodevelopmental concerns making patients such as Stephanie inherently more susceptible to cognitive abnormalities that lead to the factitious disorder (Galli et al., 2017). Additionally, Stephanie's previous history of depressive symptoms continues to put her at an elevated risk for developing symptoms as these disorders tend to be co-morbid with one another (Yates & Feldman, 2016; Comacchio et al., 2024). This, coupled with her medical knowledge as a nurse, gives Stephanie the knowledge base to induce symptoms that would be highly concerning to other people in healthcare in order to receive the care that she is seeking from her symptoms (Krahn et al., 2003; Yates & Feldman, 2016). Based on her family history, it is likely that she underwent significant emotional abuse as a child, which has continued with her ex-husband, placing additional stress and pressure on Stephanie, making her even more susceptible to her innate vulnerabilities (Galli et al., 2017; Yates & Feldman, 2016). Incidents of failure appear to have always been met with rebuke and emotional abuse, making her recent failings in her career particularly difficult and likely to be the psychosocial stressor that resulted in Stephanie inducing her symptoms. The evidence suggests that Stephanie became highly stressed, to the point that her emotional processing was impaired and she induced her symptoms as a cry for help. This indirect method was less emotionally vulnerable for her, protecting her from the emotional distress that she would expect from direct requests, given her previous experiences of responses to her moments of failure.

The main goal of treatment is first to ensure the overall safety of Stephanie to stop her from continuing these dangerous behaviors; these behaviors can have dangerous repercussions and can even lead to death in some cases (Krahn et al., 2003). Once the immediate threat to her life has been resolved, treatment goals should be focused on providing Stephanie with better ways to respond to high-stress situations and the clinician should collaborate with Stephanie on how to handle better future failures that may occur in her life in order to avoid a relapse of symptoms. Additional treatment goals can include reducing substance use, improving overall emotional and behavioral regulation, increasing engagement in adaptive forms of social support, mitigating occupational concerns, and improving quantity and quality of sleep.

From a biopsychosocial perspective, the recommended treatment plan should initially focus on working with the interdisciplinary team to help build rapport with Stephanie to ensure that she is amenable to opening up about the nature of her symptoms. Additionally, working with an interdisciplinary team throughout the treatment to ensure that Stephanie's physical health remains stable is vital; she needs to be regularly evaluated, and her hemoglobin levels, in particular, need to be closely monitored in the event that she does not disclose the full levels of her symptoms (Galli et al., 2017). Direct confrontation regarding Stephanie's deception will likely be unhelpful in the early stages, so developing a strong empathic connection with her will be vital to help reduce her self-injurious behaviors (Krahn et al., 2003; Galli et al., 2017). Potentially, focusing on Stephanie's depressive symptoms first may help her be more engaged in her therapy and open the door for expressing her factitious disorder diagnosis in the future (Comacchio et al., 2024; Galli et al., 2017). Treatment can then begin to focus on more mindfulness-based interventions to help Stephanie manage her stress levels as well as help her to develop healthier forms of social support in order to provide better adaptive coping mechanisms during distressing periods of life (Galli et al., 2017). Addressing Stephanie's sleep schedule as a nurse may be vital to help reduce physiological stress and decrease the overall activation of a chronic stress response present in the body (Galli et al., 2017; Sun et al., 2018). CBTi can be useful in helping Stephanie address problematic sleep.

Additionally, it will be important to collaborate with Stephanie to help reduce her overall caffeine intake and improve her sleep schedule to reduce stress responses within the body further; this should also allow her to better regulate her feelings during stressful periods. Finally, Stephanie should be provided with psychoeducation regarding the negative physiological and psychological consequences of cannabis and cocaine use. Motivational interviewing can be utilized if necessary. This information could potentially be provided within the context of Stephanie's occupational difficulties as well as showing how her substance use might negatively impact her parenting. If appropriate, Stephanie can be referred to parent support groups, 12-step programs, or resources that could specifically support her occupationally, such as her employer's employee assistance program.

Of note: antidepressants have been found to help improve symptoms of factitious disorder when depressive symptoms are co-morbid with it, so consulting with psychiatry regarding the appropriateness of medication will likely be crucial in this case (Comacchio et al., 2024).

Conclusion

Somatic symptom disorder and related disorders are generally characterized by the presence of somatic complaints and/or neurological deficits for which no underlying physiological cause can be identified. Somatic symptom disorder and related disorders are uniquely challenging specifically because of the diagnostic difficulty inherent for these disorders, which often requires thorough medical evaluations that mental health clinicians practicing outside of medical settings are unable to request and/or complete. Key to identifying somatic symptom disorder and related disorders is the ability to differentiate between genuine somatic distress, the etiology of reported anxiety, and the believability of a patient's report. While psychodynamic, CBT, and biopsychosocial frameworks can all be helpful in conceptualizing somatic symptom disorder and related disorders and developing appropriate treatment goals and plans, the need for medical evaluation and to understand a patient's medical history does seem to highlight the unique utility of the biopsychosocial approach when working with patients presenting with these particular disorders. Ultimately, successful treatment of these disorders is dependent on accurate conceptualization, but it also depends on a deep empathy for the suffering of patients and the ways in which that suffering can contribute to deeply problematic behavioral presentations. Ethical, competent, and compassionate treatment is, as is often the case, the most effective approach to alleviating suffering in patients presenting with diagnoses from this often-misunderstood class of disorders.

References

APA (American Psychiatric Association). (2022). Somatic symptom and related disorders. In *Diagnostic and statistical manual of mental disorders* (5th ed., text rev.). American Psychiatric Association.

Arnáez, S., García-Soriano, G., López-Santiago, J., & Belloch, A. (2021). Illness-related intrusive thoughts and illness anxiety disorder. *Psychology and Psychotherapy: Theory, Research and Practice*, *94*(1), 63–80. DOI:10.1111/papt.12267.

Çetin, Ş., & Varma, G. S. (2021). Somatic symptom disorder: Historical process and biopsychosocial approach. *Psikiyatride Guncel Yaklasimlar: Current Approaches in Psychiatry*, *13*(4), 790–804. https://doi.org/10.18863/pgy.882929.

Comacchio, C., Misca, D. M., Bortoletto, R., Palese, A., Balestrieri, M., & Colizzi, M. (2024). Prevalence and risk factors for depression in factitious disorder: A systematic review. *Frontiers in Psychiatry*, *15*. https://doi.org/10.3389/fpsyt.2024.1355243.

Cramer, P. (2015). Understanding defense mechanisms. *Psychodynamic Psychiatry*, 43(4), 523–552. https://doi.org/10.1521/pdps.2015.43.4.523.

Espay, A. J., Aybek, S., Carson, A., Edwards, M. J., Goldstein, L. H., Hallett, M., LaFaver, K., LaFrance, W. C., Lang, A. E., Nicholson, T., Nielsen, G., Reuber, M., Voon, V., Stone, J., & Morgante, F. (2018). Current concepts in diagnosis and treatment of functional neurological disorders. *JAMA Neurology*, *75*(9), 1132. https://doi.org/10.1001/jamaneurol.2018.1264.

Feinstein, A. (2011). Conversion disorder: Advances in our understanding. *Canadian Medical Association Journal*, *183*(8), 915–920. https://doi.org/10.1503/cmaj.110490.

Fjorback, L. O., Arendt, M., Ørnbøl, E., Walach, H., Rehfeld, E., Schröder, A., & Fink, P. (2012). Mindfulness therapy for somatization disorder and functional somatic syndromes: Randomized trial with one-year follow-up. *Journal of Psychosomatic Research*, *74*(1), 31–40. https://doi.org/10.1016/j.jpsychores.2012.09.006.

Frederickson, J. J., Messina, I., & Grecucci, A. (2018). Dysregulated anxiety and dysregulating defenses: Toward an emotion regulation informed dynamic psychotherapy. *Frontiers in Psychology*, *9*. https://doi.org/10.3389/fpsyg.2018.02054.

Galli, S., Tatu, L., Bogousslavsky, J., & Aybek, S. (2017). Conversion, factitious disorder and malingering: A distinct pattern or a continuum? *Frontiers of Neurology and Neuroscience*, 72–80. https://doi.org/10.1159/000475699.

Goldstein, L. H. (2006). Ictal symptoms of anxiety, avoidance behaviour, and dissociation in patients with dissociative seizures. *Journal of Neurology Neurosurgery & Psychiatry*, *77*(5), 616–621. https://doi.org/10.1136/jnnp.2005.066878.

Hausteiner-Wiehle, C., & Hungerer, S. (2020). Factitious disorders in everyday clinical practice. *Deutsches Ärzteblatt International*. https://doi.org/10.3238/arztebl.2020.0452.

Hedman, E., Axelsson, E., Andersson, E., Lekander, M., & Ljótsson, B. (2016). Exposure-based cognitive-behavioural therapy via the internet and as bibliotherapy for somatic symptom disorder and illness anxiety disorder: Randomised controlled trial. *The British Journal of Psychiatry*, 209(5), 407–413. https://doi.org/10.1192/bjp.bp.116.181396.

Hoge, E. A., Bui, E., Marques, L., Metcalf, C. A., Morris, L. K., Robinaugh, D. J., Worthington, J. J., Pollack, M. H., & Simon, N. M. (2013). Randomized controlled trial of mindfulness meditation for generalized anxiety disorder: Effects on anxiety and stress reactivity. *The Journal of Clinical Psychiatry*, 74(8), 786–792. https://doi.org/10.4088/JCP.12m08083.

Jafferany, M., Khalid, Z., McDonald, K. A., & Shelley, A. J. (2018). Psychological aspects of factitious disorder. *The Primary Care Companion for CNS Disorders*, *20*(1). https://doi.org/10.4088/pcc.17nr02229.

Jungilligens, J., Paredes-Echeverri, S., Popkirov, S., Barrett, L. F., & Perez, D. L. (2022). A new science of emotion: Implications for functional neurological disorder. *Brain*, *145*(8), 2648–2663. https://doi.org/10.1093/brain/awac204.

Keynejad, R. C., Frodl, T., Kanaan, R., Pariante, C., Reuber, M., & Nicholson, T. R. (2018). Stress and functional neurological disorders: Mechanistic insights. *Journal of Neurology Neurosurgery & Psychiatry*, *90*(7), 813–821. https://doi.org/10.1136/jnnp-2018-318297.

Kikas, K., Werner-Seidler, A., Upton, E., & Newby, J. (2024). Illness anxiety disorder: A review of the current research and future directions. *Current Psychiatry Reports*, *26*(7), 331–339. https://doi.org/10.1007/s11920-024-01507-2.

Kinsella, P. (2001). Factitious disorder: A cognitive behavioral perspective. *Behavioural and Cognitive Psychotherapy*, *29*(2), 195–202. https://doi.org/10.1017/s135246580 1002065.

Krahn, L. E., Li, H., & O'Connor, M. K. (2003). Patients who strive to be ill: Factitious disorder with physical symptoms. *American Journal of Psychiatry*, *160*(6), 1163–1168. https://doi.org/10.1176/appi.ajp.160.6.1163.

Kurlansik, S. L., & Maffei, M. S. (2016). Somatic symptom disorder. *American Family Physician*, *93*(1), 49–54.

Lara-Cinisomo, S., Akinbode, T. D., & Wood, J. (2020). A systematic review of somatic symptoms in women with depression or depressive symptoms: Do race or ethnicity matter? *Journal of Women's Health*, *29*(10), 1273–1282. https://doi.org/10.1089/jwh.2019.7975.

Löwe, B., Levenson, J., Depping, M., Hüsing, P., Kohlmann, S., Lehmann, M., Shedden-Mora, M., Toussaint, A., Uhlenbusch, N., & Weigel, A. (2021). Somatic symptom disorder: A scoping review on the empirical evidence of a new diagnosis. *Psychological Medicine*, *52*(4), 632–648. https://doi.org/10.1017/s0033291721004177.

Luyten, P., De Meulemeester, C., & Fonagy, P. (2019). Psychodynamic therapy in patients with somatic symptom disorder. In *Elsevier eBooks* (pp. 191–206). https://doi.org/10.1016/b978-0-12-813373-6.00013-1.

McLean, C. P., Asnaani, A., Litz, B. T., & Hofmann, S. G. (2011). Gender differences in anxiety disorders: Prevalence, course of illness, comorbidity and burden of illness. *Journal of Psychiatric Research*, *45*(8), 1027–1035. https://doi.org/10.1016/j.jpsychires.2011.03.006.

McWilliams, N. (2011). *Psychoanalytic diagnosis: Understanding personality structure in the clinical process*. Guilford Press.

Orzechowska, A., Maruszewska, P., & Gałecki, P. (2021). Cognitive behavioral therapy of patients with somatic symptoms: Diagnostic and therapeutic difficulties. *Journal of Clinical Medicine*, *10*(14), 3159. https://doi.org/10.3390/jcm10143159.

Özdemir, D. F. (2020). Psychodynamic aspects and clinical approach to the concepts of factitious disorder/factitious disorder imposed on another: a review. *Journal of Clinical Psychiatry*. https://doi.org/10.5505/kpd.2020.29291.

Petraglia, J., Bhatia, M., & Drapeau, M. (2017). Ten principles to guide psychodynamic technique with defense mechanisms: An examination of theory, research, and clinical implications. *Journal of Psychology & Psychotherapy*, *07*(01). https://doi.org/10.4172/21610487.1000288.

Quintner, J. (2019). Why are women with fibromyalgia so stigmatized? *Pain Medicine*, *21*(5), 882–888. https://doi.org/10.1093/pm/pnz350.

Reuber, M., & Brown, R. J. (2016). Understanding psychogenic nonepileptic seizures henomenology, semiology and the integrative cognitive model. *Seizure*, *44*, 199–205. https://doi.org/10.1016/j.seizure.2016.10.029.

Schäfer, G., Prkachin, K. M., Kaseweter, K. A., & De C Williams, A. C. (2016). Health care providers' judgments in chronic pain: The influence of gender and trustworthiness. *Pain*, *157*(8), 1618–1625. https://doi.org/10.1097/j.pain.0000000000000536.

Schwartz, A. C., Calhoun, A. W., Eschbach, C. L., & Seelig, B. J. (2001). Treatment of conversion disorder in an African American Christian woman: Cultural and social considerations. *American Journal of Psychiatry*, *158*(9), 1385–1391.

Sharma, M. P., & Manjula, M. (2013). Behavioural and psychological management of somatic symptom disorders: An overview. *International Review of Psychiatry*, *25*(1), 116–124. https://doi.org/10.3109/09540261.2012.746649.

Shaw, R. J., Givrad, S., Poe, C., Loi, E. C., Hoge, M. K., & Scala, M. (2023). Neurodevelopmental, mental health, and parenting issues in preterm infants. *Children*, *10*(9), 1565. https://doi.org/10.3390/children10091565.

Singh, K., Fox, J. R. E., & Brown, R. J. (2016). Health anxiety and internet use: A thematic analysis. *Cyberpsychology Journal of Psychosocial Research on Cyberspace*, *10*(2). https://doi.org/10.5817/cp2016-2-4.

Sinha, A., & Smolik, T. (2021). Striving to die: Medical, legal, and ethical dilemmas behind factitious disorder. *Cureus*. https://doi.org/10.7759/cureus.13243.

Stone, J., & Carson, A. (2010). Functional neurologic symptoms: Assessment and management. *Neurologic Clinics*, *29*(1), 1–18. https://doi.org/10.1016/j.ncl.2010.10.011.

Stone, J., Carson, A., & Hallett, M. (2016). Explanation as treatment for functional neurologic disorders. *Handbook of Clinical Neurology*, 543–553. https://doi.org/10.1016/b978-0-12801772-2.00044-8.

Sun, Q., Ji, X., Zhou, W., & Liu, J. (2018). Sleep problems in shift nurses: A brief review and recommendations at both individual and institutional levels. *Journal of Nursing Management*, *27*(1), 10–18. https://doi.org/10.1111/jonm.12656.

Tak, L. M., Cleare, A. J., Ormel, J., Manoharan, A., Kok, I. C., Wessely, S., & Rosmalen, J. G. (2011). Meta-analysis and meta-regression of hypothalamic-pituitary-adrenal axis activity in functional somatic disorders. *Biological Psychology*, *87*(2), 183–194. https://doi.org/10.1016/j.biopsycho.2011.02.002.

Tran, A. L. (2017). Neurasthenia, generalized anxiety disorder, and the medicalization of worry in a Vietnamese psychiatric hospital. *Medical Anthropology Quarterly*, *31*(2), 198–217. https://doi.org/10.1111/maq.12297.

Tsui, P., Deptula, A., & Yuan, D. Y. (2017). Conversion disorder, functional neurological symptom disorder, and chronic pain: comorbidity, assessment, and treatment. *Current Pain and Headache Reports*, *21*(6). https://doi.org/10.1007/s11916-017-0627-7.

Tyrer, P. (2018). Recent advances in the understanding and treatment of health anxiety. *Current Psychiatry Reports*, *20*(7). https://doi.org/10.1007/s11920-018-0912-0.

Weck, F., Neng, J. M. B., Richtberg, S., & Stangier, U. (2012). Dysfunctional beliefs about symptoms and illness in patients with hypochondriasis. *Psychosomatics*, *53*(2), 148–154. https://doi.org/10.1016/j.psym.2011.11.007.

Weck, F., Richtberg, S., Jakob, M., Neng, J. M., & Höfling, V. (2015). Therapist competence and therapeutic alliance are important in the treatment of health anxiety (hypochondriasis). *Psychiatry Research*, *228*(1), 53–58. https://doi.org/10.1016/j.psychres.2015.03.042.

Wolters, C., Gerlach, A. L., & Pohl, A. (2022). Interoceptive accuracy and bias in somatic symptom disorder, illness anxiety disorder, and functional syndromes: A systematic review and meta-analysis. *PLoS ONE*, *17*(8), e0271717. https://doi.org/10.1371/journal.pone.0271717.

Yates, G. P., & Feldman, M. D. (2016). Factitious disorder: A systematic review of 455 cases in the professional literature. *General Hospital Psychiatry*, *41*, 20–28. https://doi.org/10.1016/j.genhosppsych.2016.05.002.

Chapter 11

Feeding and Eating Disorders

Sabrina Zuniga

Feeding and eating disorders, as characterized in the DSM-5-TR, constitute a group of psychiatric conditions with primary symptomology related to abnormal eating behavior associated with distress or impairment. Feeding and eating disorders often, but not always, include some sort of disturbance associated with body weight and/or shape. While most individuals think of either anorexia nervosa or bulimia nervosa when they think of an eating disorder (EDO), feeding and eating disorders encompass a wide range of conditions. Anorexia nervosa is characterized by a patient's restriction of energy intake relative to requirements, ultimately leading to a significantly low body weight (APA, 2022). More simply, patients with anorexia nervosa do not consume as many calories as they should, given their levels of physical activity and, thus, they lose weight. Patients diagnosed with anorexia nervosa often experience extreme fear associated with gaining weight even when underweight. There are two subtypes associated with anorexia nervosa – the restricting type, whereby patients limit food intake as a means of losing weight, and the binge-eating/purging type, where patients engage in cyclical bingeing and purging (APA, 2022). Due to the medical complications associated with anorexia nervosa, patients with this condition are at significantly higher risk of mortality than patients diagnosed with other disorders in the DSM-5-TR (APA, 2022). Bulimia nervosa, often confused with anorexia nervosa, is also characterized by cyclical bingeing and purging behaviors, specifically to prevent weight gain. The primary difference between the two disorders, however, is that while patients diagnosed with anorexia nervosa often present as underweight, sometimes significantly so, patients diagnosed with bulimia nervosa often present as being at a weight normative for their heights and genders, and sometimes a little bit overweight. Patients diagnosed with binge-eating disorder engage in binge-eating but not in the compensatory behaviors associated with purging as in bulimia nervosa or the binge-eating/purging type in anorexia nervosa.

Less well-known feeding disorders include avoidant/restrictive food intake disorder, pica, and rumination disorder. Avoidant/restrictive food intake

DOI: 10.4324/9781003586531-12

disorder, most often known as ARFID, is a feeding disorder characterized by the avoidance and restriction of nutritional intake, but without associated concerns pertaining to weight loss or body image (APA, 2022). ARFID can include a fear of choking or vomiting and/or limited food preferences and/or a lack of interest in food (APA, 2022). Pica is characterized by the compulsive consumption of non-nutritive substances such as dirt, rocks, hair, etc., and is most often diagnosed in children and individuals with neurodevelopmental disorders (APA, 2022). Finally, rumination disorder is characterized by the repeated regurgitation of food which is subsequently re-chewed and then either reswallowed or spat out (APA, 2022).

Feeding and eating disorders have underlying biological, psychological, and sociocultural factors, all of which can contribute to and maintain symptoms of feeding and eating disorders. Research suggests that genetic predispositions, neurotransmitter imbalances, and hormonal disruptions can all contribute to the development of feeding and eating disorders (APA, 2022). Additionally, the combination of personality traits such as perfectionism and maladaptive coping strategies appears to be a risk factor for developing a feeding or eating disorder (APA, 2022). Finally, the sociocultural context can facilitate the development of eating disorders, especially in societies where media messages promote thin bodies as the ideal (APA, 2022).

Clinical Case Vignette #1

Demographic Information and History

Name: Maira Kali.

Demographic Information: 16-year-old Indian American female.

Medical Diagnoses: Sinus bradycardia, amenorrhea.

Reason for Referral: Maira was referred for inpatient eating disorder treatment by her primary care physician due to intentional restricting, overexercising, sinus bradycardia, amenorrhea, dizziness, and significant weight loss starting about 4 months prior to hospitalization. She reported significant fear of weight gain, body distortions (i.e., views herself as significantly overweight), and food guilt. Maira reported exercising about 1 to 2 hours per day every day, while engaging in restrictive eating patterns. Maira denied engaging in purging other than exercising. She reported engaging in eating disorder behaviors a few months prior to hospitalization, though she has had negative body image and self-esteem for most of her life.

Clinical Interview Data

Interpreter Used: No.

Current Psychosocial Stressors: No significant social determinants of health were indicated as barriers to treatment. Maira and her family immigrated from India when she was a child, and both Maira and her parents expressed acculturative stress.

Protective Factors: Maira reported using art as a primary coping skill. Furthermore, Maira is emotionally expressive and insightful in therapy.

Developmental History: Maira's parents reported that she met all developmental milestones within normal limits.

Academic History: Maira is in 8th grade and currently earns all As. She described herself as academically driven and high achieving.

Social History: Maira describes herself as shy and reserved, having a few friends but no emotionally deep relationships.

Household: Maira reported that she is an only child and lives with her two parents. Most of her extended family live in India.

Previous Psychiatric History: Maira has not received psychiatric services prior to hospitalization; however, Maira reported suspecting a history with obsessive-compulsive disorder and suicidal ideation.

Family Psychiatric History: No family psychiatric history was reported.

History of Self-Harm: No history of self-harm was reported.

Assessment Data

Maira was administered the Children's Yale-Brown Obsessive Compulsive Scale (CY-BOCS) and scored a 33; this suggests clinically significant extreme obsessive-compulsive symptoms. Her target symptoms for obsessions include excessive concern with body parts or aspects of physical appearance, fear harm will come to others, concern with dirt, germs, and certain illnesses (past), and forbidden and perverse sexual thoughts, images, and impulses (past). Her target symptom list for compulsions include ritualized eating behavior, other self-damaging/self-mutilating behaviors, washing/cleansing (past), and difficulty throwing things away (past).

Wellness Profile

Sleep: Maira reported difficulty falling asleep and staying asleep and gets about 5 hours of sleep per night.

Diet: Maira reported skipping breakfast and lunch most days. She said she will usually eat dinner because of her parents "nagging her," and that dinner usually consists of a bowl of vegetable soup or a small salad as well as a piece of fruit.

Elimination: Maira reported bowel movements about 1–2 times per week, which was attributed to restricted food intake.

Technology: Maira reports spending a significant amount of time on YouTube watching exercise videos and food/diet videos.

Physical Activity: Maira reported engaging in excessive movement about 1–2 hours per day every day per week.

Substance Use/Abuse: Maira denied current or past substance use.

Pain: 0/10.

Current Psychiatric Symptoms

Depression: Maira reported feeling worthless and of excessive guilt almost every day. She reported significant isolation from her family due to feeling fatigued and exercising. She expressed feeling depressed often. She reported having some suicidal ideation about once per week, in which she would overdose on prescription medication at home. Maira has no previous suicide attempts. She related her suicidal ideation to her eating disorder.

Anxiety: Maira reported experiencing physical anxiety symptoms (e.g., chest tightness, rapid heart rate, difficulty breathing) and cognitive anxiety (e.g., racing thoughts, fear of judgment, spiraling) at least once a day. She describes her anxiety as primarily related to eating and social issues.

Panic: Maira denied full-blown panic symptoms.

Mania: Maira denied symptoms of mania or hypomania.

Psychosis: Maira denied symptoms of psychosis.

Trauma: Maira denied any significant trauma history.

Eating Disorder: Maira reported restricting intake significantly with no signs of bingeing. She consumes significantly below the recommended intake for her gender and age group.

Risky Behaviors/Sexual Activity: Maira denied engaging in any risky behaviors.

Mental Status Exam

Appearance: Maira was dressed casually.

Behavior: Maira was cooperative.

Speech: Maira's speech was within normal limits.

Mood: Maira described her mood as anxious or depressed.

Affect: Maira's affect was congruent and appropriate.

Thought Process: Maira's thought process was logical and linear, at times ruminative.

Thought Content: Maira denied homicidal ideation, delusions, or hallucinations. She reported suicidal ideation about once per week, in which she thinks about a method of overdosing on prescription medications. She denied intent or a plan. Her access to means has been restricted by her parents. She reported her suicidal ideation as moderate and primarily uses distractions and social support as coping.

Orientation: Maira was oriented to person, place, time, and situation.

Recent Memory: Maira's recent memory was intact.

Remote Memory: Maira's remote memory was intact.

Attention/Concentration: Maira's attention and concentration were within normal limits.

General Knowledge: Maira's general knowledge was within normal limits.

Language: Maira's language was within normal limits, though usually presenting with a soft voice.

Insight: Maira demonstrated fair insight.

Judgment: Maira demonstrated fair judgment.

Answer Key #1

Diversity Considerations

Maira reported that she is Indian American, which may play a role in the development of her symptoms. Specifically, research has shown that immigrants can often experience acculturative stress and that the acculturative stress can manifest in many ways, including identity confusion, emotional dysregulation, and psychosomatic symptoms (Berry, 2006). While eating disorders have historically been considered to be a White Western phenomenon, emerging literature indicates that the prevalence rates of eating disorders are rising among adolescents who belong to racial and ethnic minorities, especially those living in Western societies (Rodgers et al., 2018). Of note, for Maira, the internalization of White Western ideals of thinness as beautiful could potentially be exacerbated by racialized expectations regarding femininity, appearance, and desirability (Chaudhary & Sanghvi, 2022). Another diversity consideration associated with Maira's South Asian culture is the stigma surrounding mental illness often found in such groups. In many South Asian cultures, mental illness is often seen as a moral failure, which can lead patients to either minimize or conceal their symptoms (Arora et al., 2016). Finally, Maira is an adolescent, a stage of life often characterized by identity exploration and formation as well as peer comparison (both in vivo and via social media channels). This combination of factors could exacerbate symptoms of disordered eating (Fardouly & Vartanian, 2016).

Ethical Considerations

No additional ethical considerations.

Legal Considerations

While participation in normative academic activities is often disregarded when a child or adolescent is admitted to a psychiatric facility, hospitalization for children and adolescents with eating disorders can sometimes last significantly longer than other forms of medical or psychiatric hospitalization. Because admission to a medical or psychiatric facility does not preclude a minor's right to access education, accommodations may need to be considered to ensure Maira retains this right. Many school districts are willing to partner with medical and psychiatric facilities to offer "home hospital school," which consists of a modified curriculum a patient can access while being out of school. Upon Maira's return to school, a 504 plan or individualized education plan might be appropriate if her psychiatric symptoms either impair her academic performance or require that she receive additional accommodations.

Diagnostic Impressions and Justification

F50.013 Anorexia Nervosa, Restricting Type, Severe.

Maira engages in restrictive food intake, which has resulted in a low body weight (body mass index (BMI) <15). She expresses an immense fear of weight gain and experiences significant body distortions related to her body shape. She denied compensatory behaviors other than excessive exercise.

Psychodynamic Case Conceptualization

Maira's overall presentation, including her symptoms of anorexia nervosa, are likely indicative of unconscious internal conflicts. Specifically, her perfectionistic tendencies suggest the presence of a harsh superego. Additionally, her symptoms of anorexia nervosa likely represent a maladaptive attempt to exert control over the environment as well as manage overwhelming affective experiences. Maira likely presents with unresolved attachment needs as well as split internal objects and a fragile ego.

Appropriate goals grounded in psychodynamic theory include facilitating ego integration and supporting the development of a cohesive sense of self. Psychodynamic psychotherapy may also serve to strengthen Maira's ego functions (McWilliams, 2011). Psychodynamic treatment can also facilitate Maira improving her capacity to tolerate ambivalence and articulate the affective contributors that underlie her behavioral presentation.

Psychodynamic treatment can begin by establishing a stable and predictable therapeutic alliance that can serve as the space in which Maira can explore unconscious material utilizing free association. Interpretations can be used to help her develop insight into the relationship between her early relational experience, affective states, and current circumstances. Interpretations related to the transference that emerges in the therapeutic relationship may be especially helpful. Confrontation can also be utilized to address maladaptive defense mechanisms, including intellectualization, displacement, and compulsion.

Cognitive Behavioral Conceptualization

Maira's overall presentation is likely the result of maladaptive cognitions and behavioral avoidance. She appears to present with rigid cognitive distortions related to body image, self-worth, and control. Her problematic beliefs are likely reinforced by safety behaviors such as excessive exercise, restrictive eating, and compulsive rituals. Her perfectionistic tendencies may be further evidence that she believes her value depends upon high performance and self-control.

Appropriate treatment goals for Maira may include reducing disordered eating behaviors by modifying the cognitive distortions that both cause and maintain them. Maira would also benefit from restructuring her core beliefs and intermediate assumptions, both of which contribute to her disordered eating and compulsive behaviors. Targeting symptoms of depression would also be recommended as well as improving Maira's ability to tolerate distress.

Cognitive-behavioral therapy interventions could begin by first providing Maira with psychoeducation regarding the CBT triangle and the mind-body connection, including how factors explained by both could contribute to the development and maintenance of an eating disorder. Using thought records could support Maira in developing awareness of her automatic thoughts and cognitive distortions. Additionally, cognitive restricting can be utilized to help Maira develop cognitive flexibility. Her maladaptive core beliefs could be addressed using the downward arrow and behavioral activation can be used to mitigate symptoms of depression.

Biopsychosocial Conceptualization

Maira's overall presentation is being significantly affected by her symptoms of anorexia nervosa. Specifically, she is presenting with sinus bradycardia and amenorrhea, both symptoms of extreme calorie deficiency. Because nutritional deficits impact serotonin and dopamine pathways implicated in mood regulation and executive functioning, Maira's cognitive rigidity and significant anxiety may be symptomatic of the neurobiological effects of malnutrition (Kaye et al., 2013). Maira also presents with significant cognitive distortions as well as compulsive rituals and obsessive thoughts that may somehow serve to contain her affect. It is important to note that Maira reported a history of low self-esteem prior to the onset of her eating disorder, which suggests that her presentation represents an underlying vulnerability exacerbated by the developmental challenges often associated with adolescence (Stice et al., 2000).

Treatment goals grounded in the biopsychosocial model could include improving Maira's nutritional status, supporting her in gaining weight, re-establishing normal eating patterns, and mitigating the physiological consequences of the malnutrition Maira has experienced. The clinician could also work with Maira to improve cognitive distortions related to weight and body shape while also improving distress tolerance. Given that recovery from an eating disorder can take a significant amount of time and that most adolescents complete at least some aspect of their recovery at home with their families, another appropriate goal would be to improve Maira's family's understanding of her disorder as well as how they may be able to continue to support recovery once she is home.

Collaborative work with a registered dietitian could be implemented to support nutritional rehabilitation, while collaboration with a physician could be implemented to ensure progress is being made toward treatment goals. The clinician could also provide psychoeducation regarding sleep hygiene as well as the negative effects of malnutrition on the brain and other body systems. In terms of manualized, evidence-based treatment modalities, either CBT or DBT could be considered appropriate. Art therapy, however, could also be helpful. Maira and her family may benefit from implementation of family-based treatment (FBT) – specifically, the Maudsley model (Lock & Le Grange, 2015). Finally, Maira and her family may benefit from attending acculturation-focused counseling together to support them in exploring intergenerational expectations as well as bicultural adaptation strategies (Hwang & Ting, 2008).

Clinical Case Vignette #2

Demographic Information and History

Name: Sandra Hays.

Demographic Information: 16-year-old White female.

Medical Diagnoses: Amenorrhea.

Reason for Referral: Sandra was referred by another behavioral health partial-hospitalization program to an eating disorder treatment facility due to daily restrictive eating, bingeing, and purging that started about 5 months prior to the current hospitalization. Sandra reportedly restricts her meals to 1,000 calories a day or less and engaged in self-induced vomiting or laxative use after bingeing a few times per week for the past 5 months. She expressed feeling out of control (i.e., unable to stop) when she binges and then engages in purging afterwards in response to guilt. She reported frequent feelings of dizziness, difficulty concentrating, stomach problems, and constipation. Sandra reported not having a period for the past 3 months due to restricting and bingeing/purging. She expressed feeling ashamed about her body shape for most of her life, though not developing eating disorder behaviors until 5 months ago. Notably, she also reported a history with major depressive disorder and generalized anxiety since the age of 10 years. She reported a history of non-suicidal self-injury by cutting, for which she entered treatment at a behavioral health partial-hospitalization program a month before the present hospitalization. She reported passive suicidal ideation about once per week.

Clinician Interview Data

Interpreter Used: No.

Current Psychosocial Stressors: Sandra and her family reported significant risk for food insecurity and transportation need. She and her family recently moved to a smaller dilapidated house in a rural town.

Protective Factors: Sandra reported emotional closeness with her extensive family. Sandra is emotionally expressive in individual therapy and listed artistic activities and games as a primary adaptive coping skill.

Developmental History: Sandra met all developmental milestones at appropriate times.

Academic History: Sandra is currently homeschooled and receives As and Bs.

Social History: Sandra reported feeling isolated due to being homeschooled. She reported missing friends due to her recent move. She also reported feeling little social support from her immediate family, though she expressed feeling emotionally supported by her extended family who live a few hours away.

Household: Sandra reported living in a three-generation household with seven individuals. She described their physical house as small and dilapidated.

Previous Psychiatric History: Sandra was diagnosed with generalized anxiety disorder and major depressive disorder at the age of 10. She entered a behavioral health partial-hospitalization program a month ago due to non-suicidal self-injury by cutting.

Family Psychiatric History: Sandra's mother reported being diagnosed with bipolar disorder as a teenager. Sandra reports substance use in her extended family.

History of Self-Harm: Sandra reported self-harming by cutting her wrists on three occasions in the last 5 months, one resulting in a need for stiches and a subsequent admission to a behavioral health partial-hospitalization program.

Wellness Profile

Sleep: Sandra reported difficulties staying asleep and wakes up frequently throughout the night. She reportedly gets about 6 hours of sleep per night.

Diet: Sandra reported attempting to restrict calorie intake to about 1,000 calories daily. She reported bingeing on average three times per week and engaging in compensatory behaviors (e.g., self-induced vomiting, laxatives) about five times per week.

Elimination: Sandra reported frequently feeling constipated.

Technology: Sandra reported frequently using social media to stay connected with friends, though this also can result in Sandra feeling lonely and triggers comparison.

Physical Activity: Sandra reported exercising by walking 3 miles almost every day.

Substance Use/Abuse: Sandra denied any substance use.

Pain: 0/10.

Current Psychiatric Symptoms

Depression: Sandra reported experiencing low self-worth, frequent feelings of guilt, low motivation to complete daily activities and pleasurable activities, isolation, and suicidal ideation. She was diagnosed with MDD at the age of 10.

Anxiety: Sandra reported experiencing anxiety symptoms (e.g., racing thoughts, chest tightness, sweating) primarily in social situations. She reported intense fear of judgment from others.

Panic: Sandra denied any panic symptoms.

Mania: Sandra denied any symptoms of panic or mania.

Psychosis: Sandra denied any symptoms of psychosis.

Trauma: Sandra reported witnessing intimate partner violence between her biological parents.

Eating Disorder: Sandra reported in restrictive eating, bingeing, and purging multiple times per week. Sandra expressed basing much of her self-worth on physical appearance and frequently feels guilty after eating.

Risky Behaviors/Sexual Activity: Sandra denied any risky behaviors.

Mental Status Exam

Appearance: Sandra appears normal and appropriately groomed during sessions.

Behavior: Sandra is cooperative and appropriately expressive in therapy.

Speech: Sandra's speech is within normal limits.

Mood: Sandra's mood typically presents as dysthymic or attentive.

Affect: Sandra's affect is typically blunted.

Thought Process: Sandra's thought process is primarily logical and linear, though ruminative at times.

Thought Content: Sandra denied any homicidal ideation, delusions, or hallucinations. Sandra endorsed passive suicidal ideation about once per week.

Orientation: Sandra is oriented to person, place, time, and situation.

Recent Memory: Sandra's recent memory is intact.

Remote Memory: Sandra's remote memory appears intact.

Attention/Concentration: Sandra demonstrates sufficient attention and concentration.

General Knowledge: Sandra's general knowledge is within normal limits.

Language: Sandra's language is within normal limits.

Insight: Sandra demonstrates fair levels of insight.

Judgment: Sandra demonstrates fair judgment.

Answer Key #2

Diversity Considerations

Gender plays a significant role in the development and maintenance of eating disorders, especially for girls, who are at increased risk of developing an EDO due to gender-based socialization that promotes objectification and thinness (Fredrickson & Roberts, 1997; Smolak & Levine, 2015). It is also important to consider the role that socioeconomic status (SES) plays in Sandra's overall presentation, especially as she reported experiencing food insecurity. For some patients, inconsistent food availability can reinforce binge-restrict cycles (Becker et al., 2019). Additional financial constraints may serve as barriers to engagement in the specialized services sometimes needed to treat EDOs, either because of insufficient insurance coverage, difficulty managing co-payments, difficulty arranging transportation, etc. Because Sandra lives in a rural area, her geographic area may also serve as a barrier to appropriate mental health care services. Finally, because Sandra is in an important developmental period, developmental tasks related to adolescence should be considered throughout the treatment process. Because peer belonging is considered to be a core developmental task of adolescence (Erikson, 1968), the social isolation she reported may be inhibiting the unfurling of normative adolescent processes, further exacerbating EDO symptoms.

Ethical Considerations

Because Sandra reported passive suicidal ideation, it is incumbent upon clinicians to regularly assess and maintain safety, which may require the development and implementation of a safety plan.

Legal Considerations

Sandra reported having witnessed intimate partner violence within her home, which in some locations, such as California, requires mandated reporters to contact local child protective services. Clinicians should be aware of the legal statutes pertaining to the locations where they practice so as to determine whether witnessed intimate partner violence necessitates a report in their locales. Because members of the extended family engage in substance use and because of the food and housing instability evident in Sandra's report, clinicians may also need to further evaluate and/or consider whether a mandated report regarding neglect may also be warranted.

While participation in normative academic activities is often disregarded when a child or adolescent is admitted to a psychiatric facility, hospitalizations for children and adolescents with eating disorders can sometimes last significantly longer than other forms of medical or psychiatric hospitalization. Because admission to a medical or psychiatric facility does not preclude a minor's right to access education, accommodations may need to be considered to ensure Sandra retains this right. Many school districts are willing to partner with medical and psychiatric facilities to offer home hospital school, which consists of a modified curriculum a patient can access while being out of school. Upon Sandra's return to school, a 504 plan or IEP might be appropriate if her psychiatric symptoms either impair her academic performance or require that she receive additional accommodations. Granted, because Sandra is homeschooled, these considerations may be inconsequential, but because it is unclear where her curriculum comes from or who is instructing her, due consideration to the accessibility of her education is warranted.

Diagnostic Impressions and Justification

F50.2 Bulimia Nervosa, Moderate.
F32.1 Major Depressive Disorder, Recurrent Episode, Moderate.
F41.1 Generalized Anxiety Disorder.

Sandra engages in binges (i.e., eating unusually large amounts of food accompanied with a feeling of being out of control) and purges (e.g., self-induced vomiting, laxatives) several times per week for about 5 months. She reported feeling significant amounts of shame related to her body shape and fears weight gain. As diagnosed when 10 years old, Sandra still meets criteria for MDD due to difficulties sleeping, persistent feelings of guilt, low motivation to complete daily and pleasurable activities given her excessive worry about various topics (e.g., food, social situations, academics), and difficulty controlling her anxiety.

Psychodynamic Case Conceptualization

Sandra's EDO, MDD, and GAD symptoms can all be conceptualized as expressions of unconscious internal conflicts rooted in her early relational experiences as well as in her emerging identity. Her disordered eating behaviors may serve as an attempt to exert control over her internal world given the chronic instability characteristic of her external world. Her disordered eating behaviors could also be manifestations of internalized self-criticism as well as an effort to manage overwhelming affective experiences. Taken together, Sandra's symptoms may be representative of an overdeveloped superego shaped by both familial and sociocultural socialization.

Appropriate psychodynamic treatment goals might include fostering a greater capacity for affect regulation, strengthening ego functioning, and promoting the development of a more cohesive sense of self. Generally speaking, the goal in psychodynamic psychotherapy is to bring unconscious conflicts into conscious awareness, so as to improve insight into the relational patterns of her life as well as the unconscious internal conflicts she has been experiencing. All treatment goals should be fostered within the context of a safe and consistent therapeutic relationship.

Psychodynamic treatment interventions could include establishing a consistent holding environment where Sandra can engage in the process of free association without fear of criticism or judgment. Interpretation can be used to help Sandra work through the defense mechanisms she is currently employing, especially as they relate to her body image and feelings of self-worth. Clarification and confrontation can both be utilized to address unmet dependency needs as well as transference dynamics that may manifest over the course of the therapeutic relationship.

Cognitive Behavioral Conceptualization

Sandra's overall presentation is likely being maintained by a combination of dysfunctional cognitions and reinforcement cycles associated with body image, control, and self-worth. Her purging behaviors specifically likely serve as negative reinforcement to reduce guilt following binge episodes. Additionally, cognitive distortions related to dichotomous thinking and catastrophizing are likely further exacerbating Sandra's symptoms. Finally, Sandra's history of non-suicidal self-injurious behaviors (NSSI) can be understood as a maladaptive coping mechanism.

Treatment goals stemming from CBT could include addressing maladaptive cognitions, modifying problematic behavioral patterns, and improving overall engagement in adaptive coping strategies. Additional goals could include reducing reliance on avoidance and NSSI as maladaptive forms of coping.

CBT treatment interventions could include psychoeducation and the implementation of self-monitoring tools such as food logs and thought records, although the implementation of a food log should only be considered if keeping track of what she is eating does not serve to support Sandra' overall psychopathology. Cognitive restructuring could be utilized to identify and modify both automatic thoughts and core beliefs while behavioral experiments could be used to challenge avoidance behaviors. Behavioral activation can be implemented to mitigate symptoms of depression and anxiety while mindfulness-based adaptive coping strategies can be incorporated to replace their maladaptive counterparts, such as purging and NSSI.

Biopsychosocial Conceptualization

Sandra's overall presentation is consistent with what might be expected in a patient with disordered eating. The physiological symptoms she reported are generally consistent with the disruption of both neuroendocrine and gastrointestinal (GI) systems often noted in patients with EDOs (Treasure et al., 2020). Additionally, Sandra's dysregulated sleep and reduced caloric intake are likely exacerbating her emotional dysregulation while depressing cognitive function. It is important to note that Sandra also reported a family history significant for mental illness, which could indicate that she herself may carry a genetic predisposition for various mental health issues. There is likely a multidirectional relationship between Sandra's symptoms of EDO, MDD, and GAD with cognitive distortions ultimately maintaining the symptomology associated with both her emotional dysregulation and disordered eating. Finally, it is important to note that Sandra presents with several risk factors that might negatively impact treatment outcomes, including food insecurity and possible transportation issues (Hudson et al., 2007). Additionally, the isolation she reported associated with homeschooling and living in a rural location has likely significantly reduced Sandra's opportunities for normative social experiences, causing her to become overly reliant on social media as a source of connection, without her being aware of how negatively her use of social media has affected her (Fardouly & Vartanian, 2016).

Treatment goals grounded in the biopsychosocial model might include restoring physical health, normalizing eating patterns, and improving sleep. Treatment goals could also include reducing passive suicidal ideation and NSSI while improving overall ability to tolerate potentially overwhelming affective experiences. Finally, clinicians may wish to address the reported food insecurity and transportation barriers while increasing opportunities for normative social engagement.

When treating patients with EDOs, coordination with medical professionals is strongly encouraged to ensure physiological symptoms are being both monitored and managed. Collaboration with a registered dietitian is also recommended to support nutritional rehabilitation. It is recommended that the clinician provide Sandra with psychoeducation pertaining to sleep hygiene to improve overall sleep. The clinician may also wish to implement interventions taken from either CBT or DBT, such as cognitive restructuring or chain analysis. Sandra may also benefit from the opportunity to engage in art therapy to facilitate the process of self-expression. It is recommended that the clinician provide Sandra and her family with information regarding local food banks and nutrition programs while also connecting them with a social worker who might be able to facilitate enrollment in programs for low-income families. In California, for example, Sandra and her family may benefit from enrollment in the CalFresh program. If Sandra's homeschool program is not part of a cooperative, then enrollment in a homeschooling co-op is recommended to increase opportunities to engage with same-age peers. Sandra would also benefit from engagement with local community events and programs, including opportunities for volunteering, as volunteering for a meaningful cause may improve Sandra's overall sense of self-efficacy. Finally, a comprehensive safety plan should be developed and implemented as needed.

Clinical Case Vignette #3

Demographic Information and History

Name: Erik Lane.

Demographic Information: 10-year-old White boy.

Medical Diagnoses: None reported.

Reason for referral: Erik was referred for partial hospitalization treatment by his primary care physician based on limited food intake and nutrition deficiency due to restricted brands, textures, and temperature foods. Erik and his parents reported that he does not eat fruits or vegetables, and he reportedly avoids foods that are not of a specific brand or made at home. Furthermore, Erik reported aversion to nutritional supplements (e.g., Ensure). Erik denies any negative self-evaluation based on weight or body shape as well as fear of weight gain.

Clinical Interview Data

Interpreter Used: No.

Current Psychosocial Stressors: None reported.

Protective Factors: Erik expressed a significantly close relationship with his parents and grandparents. Erik's parents reported that Erik performs well in school, though not being able to finish his lunch in time along with other kids.

Developmental History: Erik met all developmental milestones within normal limits.

Academic History: Erik attends a public school and receives As and Bs.

Social History: Erik reported experiencing some bullying at school, though noting that he has two close friends.

Household: Erik is an only child and lives with his two parents.

Previous Psychiatric History: Erik was diagnosed with GAD at the age of 8 years.

Family Psychiatric History: Erik and his parents denied any significant family psychiatric history.

History of self-harm: Erik reported at times banging his head against the wall or slapping himself when frustrated. Erik denied any suicidal ideation.

Wellness Profile

Sleep: Erik and his parents reported that Erik tends to receive about 8 hours of sleep a night.

Diet: Erik reported aversion to foods outside of his preferred temperature and will only eat brand-specific foods. He reported taking about an hour or more to eat each meal. Erik reported aversion to nutritional supplements and shakes.

Elimination: Erik and Erik's parents denied concerns in this area.

Technology: Erik reported frequently using technology for video games for hours at a time. Erik's parents reported that Erik may use technology for up to 5 hours per day.

Physical Activity: Erik reports enjoying playing outside 1–2 times per week.

Substance Use/Abuse: Erik and Erik's parents denied substance use.

Pain: 0/10.

Current Psychiatric Symptoms

Depression: Erik denied any depressive symptoms.

Anxiety: Erik was diagnosed with GAD at the age of 8 years due to frequent shaking, worrying, crying, and racing thoughts. Erik reported still experiencing significant anxiety about "anything."

Panic: Erik denied panic symptoms.

Mania: Erik denied manic symptoms.

Psychosis: Erik denied any symptoms of psychosis.

Trauma: No trauma history was reported.

Eating Disorder: Erik restricts food intake due to texture and sensory-related purposes. He denied fear of weight gain and intentional weight loss.

Risky Behaviors/Sexual Activity: Erik denied any risky behavior.

Mental Status Exam

Appearance: Erik appeared appropriately groomed for his age.

Behavior: Erik was primarily attentive, but at times appeared hyperactive.

Speech: Erik's speech was within normal limits.

Mood: Erik frequently reported feeling "fine" though appearing tense. Erik reported "bottling emotions up."

Affect: Erik's affect appeared blunted.

Thought Process: Erik's thought process was generally logical and linear, but at times tangential.

Thought Content: Erik denied suicidal ideation, homicidal ideation, delusions, and hallucinations.

Orientation: Erik was oriented to person, place, situation, and time.

Recent Memory: Erik's recent memory appeared intact.

Remote Memory: Erik's remote memory appeared intact.

Attention/Concentration: Erik appeared primarily attentive, though at times appearing hyperactive and distractible.

General Knowledge: Erik's general knowledge appeared within normal limits.

Language: Erik's language was within normal limits.

Insight: Erik exhibited fair insight.

Judgment: Erik exhibited fair judgment.

Answer Key #3

Diversity Considerations

Because Erik is only 10 years old, his overall presentation must be interpreted through a developmental lens so as to avoid overpathologizing him. Clinicians must also ensure that all interventions are implemented in developmentally appropriate ways that utilize concrete language and support the development of both autonomy and emotional expression. Additionally, because Erik is only 10, parental involvement in treatment should be strongly considered. Finally, Erik reported "bottling up" emotions and also presented with a blunted affect, both of which may reflect internalized gender norms with which boys are usually raised (Mahalik et al., 2003).

Ethical Considerations

None at this time.

Legal Considerations

It seems possible that Erik's feeding challenges may be interfering with his ability to engage in his academic setting, i.e., being unable to successfully complete a meal during his scheduled lunch, being unable to focus in class due to nutritional deficiencies, etc. If this does indeed turn out to be the case, Erik may be eligible for the implementation of either a 504 plan or an IEP, depending on his stage of residence, to provide accommodations for his diagnosed mental health condition as well as its medical sequelae. For example, Erik may qualify for extended lunch breaks, additional snack breaks during the day, a modified diet if he receives school lunch, etc.

Diagnostic Impressions and Justification

F50.82 Avoidant/Restrictive Food Intake Disorder.
Erik displayed an aversion to various types of food based on sensory and texture-related factors, such that Erik's primary care physician noted nutritional

deficiency and recommended nutritional supplements. Erik denied any significant evaluation of self, based on weight and body shape. However, his refusal to take supplements due to sensory factors suggests a diagnosis of ARFID.

Psychodynamic Case Conceptualization

Erik's restricted food intake, sensory sensitivities, and anxieties may be representative of developmental arrest as well as a maladaptive attempt to assert autonomy and control (McWilliams, 2011). His NSSI may represent primitive affect regulation strategies due to underdeveloped ego functions.

Psychodynamic treatment goals may include improving Erik's capacity for affective expression while facilitating ego development. The clinician may also wish to support Erik in understanding the relationship between his ARFID symptoms and underlying anxieties and/or relational patterns. Additionally, because Erik is age 10, it may be appropriate to support autonomy within the parent-child relationship while helping him modify internalized objects.

Because of Erik's age, he may benefit most from play therapy, which has its roots in psychodynamic theory. Only a clinician appropriately trained in the implementation of play therapy should engage young patients in this particular intervention as nuanced knowledge regarding the application of psychodynamic theory to play is required for effective treatment. Affect identification and containment may be helpful as well as gentle interpretation of Erik's eating behaviors and transference dynamics that emerge in the therapeutic alliance to support Erik in developing insight.

Cognitive Behavioral Conceptualization

Erik seems to be presenting with cognitive distortions such as dichotomous thinking and catastrophizing as well as limited expression of affect and avoidance of challenging foods. While this is facilitated by his parents, he also engages in a significant amount of screentime as a way of avoiding distress.

CBT treatment goals might include increasing Erik's food repertoire as well as decreasing his symptoms of anxiety while promoting increased emotional and behavioral regulation.

An exposure hierarchy may be helpful in establishing which foods Erik is most like to avoid and why while creating a structured plan through which anxiety-producing foods could be slowly introduced. When introducing anxiety-provoking foods, food experimentation could be encouraged to test potentially catastrophic beliefs about new foods. Cognitive restructuring may also be helpful but should be implemented in a developmentally-appropriate manner such as through the use of visual aids. Cartoon characters with thought bubbles, comic strips, the use of super hero characters and monsters, etc., could all serve as developmentally-appropriate ways of implementing cognitive restructuring for a 10-year-old. Erik would also benefit from learning adaptive coping skills in a developmentally appropriate manner, such as by using coping cards to remind him to engage in simple strategies such as deep breathing. Emotion wheels and mood thermometers could also be utilized to support increased affect regulation skills.

Biopsychosocial Conceptualization

Erik's ARFID diagnosis places him at significant risk for nutritional deficiencies that could impact his growth and development, especially given his aversion to nutritional supplements that might counteract some of the negative impact of his diagnosis. Additionally, because he is 10 years old, he requires more than eight hours of sleep each night. Overall, his lifestyle appears to be sedentary in nature with excessive exposure to screentime, which likely both exacerbates emotional and behavioral dysregulation and suppresses appetite. Erik's limited affective expression skills coupled with generally maladaptive coping and cognitive rigidity is likely also exacerbating his overall presentation. While Erik appears to benefit from a secure relationship with his parents, their accommodation of food avoidance while being overly reliant on technology is likely maintaining Erik's symptoms.

Treatment goals grounded in the biopsychosocial model could include improving Erik's nutritional intake, diversifying his diet, improving sleep, increasing physical activity, and reducing technology use. Additional treatment goals could include decreasing symptoms of anxiety while increasing knowledge of and engagement in adaptive coping skills. Erik would also benefit from learning how to better address the bullying and teasing he is experiencing at school. Finally, maintaining safety would be a key goal.

Collaboration with both a registered dietitian and a pediatric occupational therapist competent in sensory-based forms of intervention are warranted to provide Erik with person-centered, holistic care. Erik and his parents would benefit from psychoeducation regarding how much sleep a 10-year-old needs as well as detailed information regarding sleep hygiene. Erik and his parents would also benefit from psychoeducation regarding the problematic nature of excessive technology use and support in implementing a plan to reduce use. Erik should be encouraged to participate in more physical activity such as organized sports or playtime with friends at a park or indoor gym for children. Increased physical activity would both support improved mood and potentially stimulate appetite so that even if Erik's food repertoire remains limited, he consumes more calories. Developmentally appropriate strategies from CBT and DBT may be helpful in improving overall mental health status while teaching Erik how to manage anxiety at mealtimes when confronted with anxiety-provoking foods. Emotion identification tools such as emotion wheels, cartoon faces, mood thermometers, etc., may be helpful in teaching Erik how to identify and express affect. Zones of Regulation, in particular, may be a helpful, structured intervention that Erik's parents and teachers could use at home and/or at school to promote both Erik's awareness of his affective state and his ability manage it. Social skills training and assertiveness training may be helpful in reducing interpersonal issues occurring within the school environment. Finally, Erik can be taught how to replace unsafe behaviors such as head-banging with other sensory-based strategies that might promote affective and behavioral regulation, such as weighted blankets and sensory toys.

Conclusion

Feeding and eating disorders are complex, multifaceted conditions that impact a wide range of patients and families and include far more than the commonly recognized diagnoses of anorexia nervosa and bulimia nervosa. Feeding and eating disorders may or may not be related to concerns about weight or physical appearance but generally do cause a sequelae of medical concerns, some of which can be life-threatening. Because feeding and eating disorders can present with significant associated medical consequences, treatment by a multidisciplinary team of professionals, including physicians, psychologists, registered dietitians, occupational therapists, etc., is necessary for achieving optimal outcomes.

References

APA (American Psychiatric Association). (2022). *Diagnostic and statistical manual of mental disorders* (5th ed., text rev.). American Psychiatric Association.

Arora, P. G., Metz, K., & Carlson, C. I. (2016). Attitudes toward professional mental health services: Gender, acculturation, and stigma among Asian Americans. *Asian American Journal of Psychology*, *7*(3), 230–240. https://doi.org/10.1037/aap0000055.

Becker, C. B., Middlemass, K., Taylor, B., Johnson, C., & Gomez, F. (2019). Food insecurity and eating disorder pathology. *International Journal of Eating Disorders*, *52*(9), 1035–1039. https://doi.org/10.1002/eat.23090.

Berry, J. W. (2006). Acculturative stress. In *Handbook of multicultural perspectives on stress and coping* (pp. 287–298). Springer.

Chaudhary, S., & Sanghvi, R. (2022). Cultural constructions of body image and identity among South Asian American women. *Body Image*, *42*, 145–153. https://doi.org/10.1016/j.bodyim.2022.03.008.

Erikson, E. H. (1968). *Identity: Youth and crisis*. W. W. Norton.

Fardouly, J., & Vartanian, L. R. (2016). Social media and body image concerns: Current research and future directions. *Current Opinion in Psychology*, *9*, 1–5. https://doi.org/10.1016/j.copsyc.2015.09.005.

Fredrickson, B. L., & Roberts, T. A. (1997). Objectification theory: Toward understanding women's lived experiences and mental health risks. *Psychology of Women Quarterly*, *21*(2), 173–206.

Hudson, J. I., Hiripi, E., Pope, H. G., & Kessler, R. C. (2007). The prevalence and correlates of eating disorders in the National Comorbidity Survey Replication. *Biological Psychiatry*, 61(3), 348–358. https://doi.org/10.1016/j.biopsych.2006.03.040.

Hwang, W. C., & Ting, J. Y. (2008). Disaggregating the effects of acculturation and acculturative stress on the mental health of Asian Americans. *Cultural Diversity and Ethnic Minority Psychology*, *14*(2), 147–154. https://doi.org/10.1037/1099-9809.14.2.147.

Kaye, W. H., Wierenga, C. E., Bailer, U. F., Simmons, A. N., & Bischoff-Grethe, A. (2013). Nothing tastes as good as skinny feels: The neurobiology of anorexia nervosa. *Trends in Neurosciences*, *36*(2), 110–120. https://doi.org/10.1016/j.tins.2013.01.003.

Lock, J., & Le Grange, D. (2015). *Treatment manual for anorexia nervosa: A family-based approach* (2nd ed.). Guilford Press.

Mahalik, J. R., Burns, S. M., & Syzdek, M. (2003). Masculinity and perceived normative health behaviors as predictors of men's health behaviors. *Social Science & Medicine*, *64*(11), 2201–2209.

McWilliams, N. (2011). *Psychoanalytic diagnosis: Understanding personality structure in the clinical process* (2nd ed.). Guilford Press.

Rodgers, R. F., Berry, R., & Franko, D. L. (2018). Eating disorders in ethnic minorities: An update. *Current Psychiatry Reports*, *20*(10), 90. https://doi.org/10.1007/s11920-018-0944-0.

Smolak, L., & Levine, M. P. (2015). *The Wiley handbook of eating disorders*. Wiley-Blackwell.

Stice, E., Schupak-Neuberg, E., Shaw, H. E., & Stein, R. I. (2000). Relation of media exposure to eating disorder symptomatology: An examination of mediating mechanisms. *Journal of Abnormal Psychology*, *109*(3), 438–444. https://doi.org/10.1037/0021-843X.109.3.438.

Treasure, J., Stein, D., & Maguire, S. (2020). Medical complications of eating disorders. In W. H. Kaye, J. E. Mitchell, & D. M. L. Peat (Eds.), *Handbook of Eating Disorders* (pp. 219–238). Wiley-Blackwell.

Chapter 12

Gender Dysphoria

Emily Longfellow

The DSM-5-TR includes diagnostic criteria for gender dysphoria as it manifests in adults, adolescents, and children. In order to diagnose an adult or adolescent with gender dysphoria, the patient must report experiencing a significant discrepancy between the gender assigned at birth and his/her/their expressed or experienced gender, as manifested by at least two of the criteria included in the DSM-5-TR. These criteria include incongruence between one's expressed or experienced gender and one's primary and/or secondary sex characteristics, the desire to be rid of one's primary and/or secondary sex characteristics, a desire to acquire the primary and/or secondary sex characteristics of the opposite gender, the desire to be of the opposite gender or some alternative gender, the desire to be treated as though one is of the other gender or some alternative gender, and/or the conviction that one has the typical feelings and reactions of the opposite gender (APA, 2022). Similar to many disorders included in the DSM-5-TR, these symptoms must be present for at least 6 months and must cause clinically significant distress and/or impairment. The list of diagnostic criteria for gender dysphoria in children differs and children must meet at least six of the criteria *and* must have a strong desire to be of the other gender (APA, 2022). The diagnostic criteria for children include a preference for wearing clothing typical of the opposite gender, a preference for cross-gender roles when engaging in imaginative play, a preference for engaging in activities in which the opposite gender typically engages, a preference for playmates of the opposite gender, rejection of activities in which a child with the patient's assigned gender might typically engage, dislike of one's sexual anatomy, and a desire to acquire the primary of secondary sex characteristics of the opposite gender (APA, 2022). As with adults, the child presenting with symptoms of gender dysphoria must be experiencing clinically significant distress and/or impairment to qualify for the diagnosis.

DOI: 10.4324/9781003586531-13

Clinical Vignette #1

Demographic Information and History

Name: Zack Nolan.

Demographic Information: 11-year-old White male.

Medical Diagnoses: None reported.

Reason for Referral: Zack was referred to the clinic by his school counselor, citing incidents of bullying and fights between his classmates. School counselor reports that some of his male classmates have bullied Zack for choosing to play with his female classmates throughout the school year. However, incidents have escalated to the point where Zack has now started fighting with these classmates for bullying him.

Clinical Interview Data

Interpreter Used: No.

Current Psychosocial Stressors: Zack will begin middle school next year and has expressed concerns about this new transition, specifically beginning a physical education class and having to change in the locker rooms with other students. Zack has also been getting into more fights with his older sister. Zack's mother reports Zack and his sister used to be close, as they used to play with the sister's dolls together and the sister would practice using makeup on her brother. Mother reports that their fighting has escalated because Zack will go into the sister's room to play with her makeup and wear her dresses and skirts without the sister's approval, which leads to his sister yelling at Zack for going through her belongings. Zack reports that he misses hanging out with his sister the way they used to. He also reports he wishes he was a girl because "everything would be easier," as he would not be bullied or yelled at by his sister for playing with makeup and wearing the clothes he wants to wear.

Protective Factors: Zack's mother reports that Zack is loving, friendly, and caring for others. She reports that Zack has never gotten into "big trouble" in school or at home until the recent fighting incident, to which the mother reports that Zack "finally lost his patience" with his classmates. The family has a strong bond, reporting that they have family game nights where they play video games together.

Developmental History: Zack's mother reports Zack is meeting all developmental milestones on time.

Academic History: Zack is currently in the 5th grade and is doing well academically. No IEP/504 plan has been established.

Social History: Zack reports that he enjoys being with the girls that he hangs out with at school and considers them great friends. His mother reports that Zack has never had any male friends, so she enrolled him in Little League in the hope that he could make more friends there. However, Zack does not enjoy Little League and wishes that his parents enrolled him in gymnastics because his friends in school are on the local gymnastics team. Zack reports that his classmates have bullied him ever since the first grade due to him always hanging out with the girls and enjoying "girl activities" such as arts and crafts, dancing, and dolls. Zack reports that when he plays "make-believe" games or character games with friends and family, he likes to choose the "pretty characters" who wear long dresses, wear lots of makeup, and have bright colors.

Household: Zack currently lives with his mother, father, and 14-year-old sister.

Previous Psychiatric History: Zack has no previous psychiatric diagnosis.

Family Psychiatric History: Zack's mother reports no familial psychiatric history.

History of Self-Harm: Zack's mother reports that when he was in the 1st grade, she saw him play with scissors in a manner that looked as though he was trying to cut his penis off. However, when mother confronted Zack, he reported that he was "kidding" and was just exploring how to use scissors.

Wellness Profile

Sleep: Zack's mother reports that Zack used to share a room with his sister and when their parents decided to allow the children their own rooms at the beginning of the school year, Zack had a sleep regression and would come into the parents' room or sister's room in the middle of the night. This only lasted a couple of weeks. Zack sleeps 8–9 hours at night.

Diet: Zack typically eats three times a day and will get a snack during recess on school days and one or two snacks in between meals on weekends. Zack's mother reports Zack has no issues with eating and eats fruits and vegetables without his mother having to ask him.

Elimination: No concerns in this area.

Technology: Zack's mother reports that she allows 1 to 2 hours of screentime for Zack on weekdays but does not restrict screentime on weekends. On weekends, Zack's mother reports he gets around 4–5 hours of screentime each day.

Physical Activity: Zack participates in Little League practices three times a week, with one to two games on weekends.

Substance Use/Abuse: Zack has never utilized alcohol or other substances.

Pain: 0.

Current Psychiatric Symptoms

Depression: Zack's mother reports that when he is at Little League, Zack withdraws and becomes a "shell of himself." He will not talk to his teammates in the dugout, and when he is on the field, he is not paying attention to the game but sits and looks for ladybugs or flowers in the outfield.

Anxiety: No symptoms reported.

Panic: No symptoms reported.

Mania: No symptoms reported.

Psychosis: No symptoms reported.

Trauma: No symptoms reported.

Eating Disorder: No symptoms reported.

Risky Behaviors/Sexual Activity: Zack and mother reported no risky behaviors.

Mental Status Exam

Appearance: *Dress*: appropriate. *Hygiene*: adequate. Appeared stated age.

Behavior: Appropriate, cooperative.

Speech: *Rate*: within normal limits. *Articulation*: within normal limits. *Volume*: quiet. *Coherence*: within normal limits.

Mood: Zack reported that he is "excited" to begin therapy because of all the new toys he can play with in the playroom. He noted that dolls, teddy bears, and arts and crafts are his favorite and asked if he could take some of them home.

Affect: Full, congruent to mood, appropriate to content of interview.

Thought Process: Logical, linear, goal directed.

Thought Content: Denied suicidal ideation, homicidal ideation, delusions, or hallucinations.

Orientation: Oriented to person, place, time, and situation.

Recent Memory: Intact.

Remote Memory: Intact.

Attention/Concentration: Sufficient.

General Knowledge: Within normal limits.

Language: Within normal limits.

Insight: Fair.

Judgment: Good.

Answer Key #1

Diversity Considerations

Zack is currently presenting with gender-non-conforming behaviors that may suggest gender dysphoria, but it is important to honor his self-expression and be slow to pathologize or label his presentation. The clinician must be sensitive to Zack's age, recognizing the important stage of identity development in which Zack has found himself. Specifically, the clinician must keep in mind that exploring gender roles and gender expression is not uncommon at Zack's age and may or may not ultimately evolve into transgender identity. Finally, there may be explicit and implicit gender expectations in all social areas for Zack. The clinician should explore how these social systems impact the Zack and his family's understanding of gender roles. Specifically, the clinician should consider how religious, regional, and familial beliefs, practices, and preferences may be impacting Zack.

Ethical and Legal Considerations

Because Zack is a minor, the clinician must consider both informed consent and assent at the outset of therapy, including explaining to all involved parties how privacy and confidentiality for a minor patient might be balanced with parent rights.

Depending on how therapy progresses and how Zack's identity evolves, the clinician may or may not need to consider additional aspects related to potential disagreements between Zack and his parents regarding Zack's gender identity. For example, if Zack ultimately identifies as transgender and his parents feel strongly that they cannot affirm such an identity, they may request that the clinician implement conversion therapy or reparative therapy. It is strongly encouraged that the clinician reviews relevant local laws, guidance from local licensing boards, and guidance from well-established professional organizations before considering such a request, as conversion therapy and reparative therapy are illegal in several states and discouraged by licensing boards and professional organizations. Similarly, if Zack ultimately identifies as transgender and his parents are supportive, the clinician might still need to review local laws as well as guidance from licensing boards and well-established professional organizations as providing gender-affirming care may be illegal in the area where Zack and the clinician live, study, and work. Legal consultation may be warranted if conflict is found to exist between local laws and guidance from licensing boards and well-established professional organizations.

Diagnostic Impressions and Justification

F64.2 Gender Dysphoria in Children.

Zack meets Criterion A because he reports wanting to be a girl so he can enjoy wearing cross-gender clothing and prefers playing cross-gender roles when playing make-believe. He prefers to interact with his female classmates and engage in the activities that are typically associated with females. This preference for cross-gender clothing and activities has caused clinically significant distress at school and home, meeting Criterion B.

Psychodynamic Case Conceptualization

Client gender expression and identity development are typically shaped by early attachment dynamics, unconscious desires, and familial relationships. Zack's closeness with his sister and shared play with traditionally feminine items may represent early objects of identification. The sister's growing distance may be triggering feelings of loss and abandonment in Zack, and his recent regressive behaviors may reflect attempts to reconnect with a comforting and affirming past. The bullying and pressure to conform to masculine norms may be intensifying internal conflict between authentic self-expression and the need for acceptance, leading to anxiety, frustration, and reactive aggression. Because the internalization of early caregivers can play a role in informing gender identity, the clinician may wish to explore Zack's relationship with his parents when formulating a thorough conceptualization. Additionally, from a psychodynamic perspective, gender can take on symbolic meaning as can forms of gender expression.

Psychodynamic goals can include creating a safe space for Zack to explore identity, integrate the self-states that might be contributing to internal conflicts, and tolerate emerging identity. It may also be appropriate to support Zack in bringing unconscious conflicts into conscious awareness, perhaps especially if these conflicts involve early caregivers. Because many children who experience gender dysphoria also report experiencing shame (Lemma, 2018), it may also be appropriate for the clinician to support Zack in developing compassion for the self while differentiating the self from internalized bias and prejudice taken in from society (Mollon, 2002).

Because Zack demonstrates interest in and excitement about the toys available, the clinician may wish to implement play therapy, art therapy, and/or sand tray therapy, all of which are treatment modalities with roots in psychodynamic theory. As with any other client, identification and exploration of transference may become relevant. Mentalization-based therapy may also be helpful to Zack as it could encourage curiosity regarding internal states instead of rigid identification or early foreclosure (Fonagy & Target, 2002).

Cognitive Behavioral Conceptualization

Zack may be experiencing negative core beliefs about himself as well as cognitive distortions related to how he is being perceived by others. The social invalidation experienced at the hands of others (such as the bullying at school and the increased arguing with his sister) may be maintaining both the cognitive distortions and overall feelings of distress.

Cognitive behavioral goals might include reducing the amount of distress Zack is experiencing associated with his symptoms of gender dysphoria.

Interventions could include restructuring maladaptive thoughts and teaching adaptive coping skills. This might include challenging maladaptive cognitions associated with internalized shame. Behavioral activation in the form of engagement with affirming communities may become relevant should Zack ultimately identify as transgender.

Biopsychosocial Conceptualization

Over the past decade, research has emerged indicating that gender dysphoria may have genetic or neuroanatomical underpinnings (Heylens et al., 2012; Guillamon et al., 2016). Additionally, some theorists have suggested that androgen exposure during the prenatal period may affect brain differentiation in a manner that ultimately contributes to gender dysphoria (Bao & Swaab, 2011). Additionally, Zack demonstrates emotional withdrawal with gender-congruent activities, such as Little League, which could suggest psychological distress linked to gender-conforming activities. Socially, Zack experiences bullying, loss of sibling connection, and limited acceptance of his gender-non-conforming behaviors. While he has a strong family bond and academic success, he lacks affirmation in peer and extracurricular settings, reinforcing his psychosocial vulnerability.

Appropriate treatment goals grounded in the biopsychosocial perspective include increasing Zack's knowledge about the human body while reducing anxiety regarding his own body as well as the physiological and psychological changes he is experiencing. Additionally, the clinician may wish to work toward improving overall emotional and behavioral regulation.

From a biopsychosocial perspective, providing psychoeducation regarding the human body, changes experienced during puberty, and the emotional and behavioral sequalae related to such changes, would be considered an appropriate intervention. CBT-based interventions could be utilized to challenge maladaptive thoughts while mindfulness-based interventions could be utilized to improve emotional and behavioral regulation. It may also be beneficial to provide the parents and sister with psychoeducation and, potentially, to collaborate with the school to reduce bullying. An additional recommendation would be for Zack to be enrolled in an extracurricular activity of his choosing, rather than having to endure an extracurricular activity that is causing him distress.

Clinical Case Vignette #2

Demographic Information and History

Name: Jacqueline Mendoza.

Demographic Information: 22-year-old Hispanic female.

Medical Diagnoses: No relevant medical diagnoses were reported.

Reason for Referral: Jacqueline referred herself to therapy due to confusion around her gender identity. Jacqueline describes herself as queer and has known that she is attracted to females since high school. However, in the past couple of years, Jacqueline has become increasingly more uncomfortable with the feminine aspects of her body and how she is treated as a woman. Jacqueline reports "never being inherently feminine" and is seeking therapy to gain a deeper understanding of this "confusion." Jacqueline believes she would be more comfortable if she were to begin identifying as a male in all aspects of her life and has been curious about exploring gender-affirming procedures and treatments but is worried about familial ramifications. Jacqueline reports that she recently began using male pronouns in her day-to-day life with close friends but is concerned that this news would get back to her family, causing more difficulties in her life.

Clinical Interview Data

Interpreter Used: No.

Current Psychosocial Stressors: Jacqueline was hesitant to seek therapy due to fear of her family not accepting her if she were to decide to identify as a male. She reports that when she came out as queer, she lost contact with distant family members and is still working to repair strained relationships with immediate family members.

Protective Factors: Jacqueline's girlfriend is supportive of Jacqueline exploring her gender identity and is committed to continuing the relationship if she were to decide to fully transition. Jacqueline also has friends who are members of the LGBTQ community or are allies of the community and she feels supported by them to explore this part of herself.

Developmental History: Jacqueline reports meeting all developmental milestones on time.

Academic History: Jacqueline maintained average grades throughout school but reports not being motivated in her education. Jacqueline completed an associate's degree and works as a bartender and part-time dog sitter. Jacqueline reports having "uncomfortable" interactions with patrons of her bar who hypersexualize her and believes that if she were a "real man" she would not be treated in the same manner.

Social History: Jacqueline reports that, while in school, she did not have many friends but preferred to play with the boys during recess. She reports being teased by other classmates for her masculine preferences, which led her to prefer isolation rather than continuing to play with the boys. However, once she began college, she began dressing a more masculine way and felt "more comfortable interacting with others." Jacqueline reports having had a girlfriend for one year and has recently moved to a new town with her. In this new town, Jacqueline has been able to make new friends at her bartending job and reports spending days off going to the movies and shopping with her friends and girlfriend. Jacqueline reports that she will sometimes be called a man by strangers, as she often wears men's clothes and has a short haircut. However, she reports feeling uncomfortable when strangers talk to her and treat her as a female.

Household: Jacqueline recently moved in with her girlfriend. Before this, Jacqueline was living with her mother, father, and two little sisters in her childhood home. Since coming out as queer, Jacqueline's relationship with her parents has been strained, which she anticipated due to her family's conservative values, but did not anticipate being kicked out of the home. Jacqueline reports she has a "decent" relationship with her sisters but is still trying to rebuild her relationship with her parents.

Previous Psychiatric History Jacqueline received counseling services at her college counseling center due to school-related stress. Jacqueline reported that she discussed previous trauma with this therapist and does not believe there are unresolved issues with previous trauma.

Family Psychiatric History: Jacqueline reports no familial psychiatric history.

History of Self-Harm: Jacqueline reports no history of self-harm but has disclosed that she has wanted to cut herself recently, specifically on her breasts. Jacqueline reports that she "hates them" and wishes to have them removed because they feel "wrong." Jacqueline has begun binding her breasts but reports that it does not make her feel better about having breasts, though she notes she is more likely to be identified as a male when she does.

Wellness Profile

Sleep: Jacqueline reports having difficulty falling asleep, but reports taking THC gummies to help her fall asleep.

Diet: Jacqueline reports usually eating three meals a day with an afternoon snack. Jacqueline also reports having protein shakes after lifting weights daily. No concerns with eating were reported.

Elimination: No concerns in this area.

Technology: Jacqueline reports spending approximately 5 hours a day on her phone and watches 3–4 hours of television daily.

Physical Activity: Jacqueline reports taking the dogs she watches on walks twice a day and that this occurs 4–5 days a week. Jacqueline also goes to the gym daily, as she is trying to "bulk up" her upper body to appear more masculine.

Substance Use/Abuse: Jacqueline reports utilizing THC in a gummy form to help with sleeping issues. No other substances reported.

Pain: 0/10.

Current Psychiatric Symptoms

Depression: Jacqueline reports that she always has felt that she has dealt with depression but feels that it has increased since being kicked out of her home. Jacqueline reports that she felt relieved from her depressive symptoms when she was living on her college campus and able to "be more authentic" by dressing in a masculine way and being able to date females without fear of criticism.

Anxiety: Jacqueline reports feelings of restlessness, irritability, muscle tension, sleep disturbance, and difficulty controlling worry most days.

Panic: No symptoms reported.

Mania: No symptoms reported.

Psychosis: No symptoms reported.

Trauma: Jacqueline reports having been sexually abused by her male cousin when she was 10 years old. When she told her parents, they did not believe her at first and refused to make a police report. After some "awkward" interactions with that side of the family, Jacqueline reports that her parents eventually began to believe her and reduced the amount of time spent with that side of the family.

Eating Disorder: No symptoms reported.

Risky Behaviors/Sexual Activity: No symptoms reported.

Mental Status Exam

Appearance: *Dress*: appropriate. *Hygiene*: adequate. Appeared stated age.

Behavior: Appropriate, cooperative.

Speech: *Rate*: within normal limits. *Articulation*: within normal limits. *Volume*: within normal limits. *Coherence*: within normal limits.

Mood: Jacqueline reports feeling excited to explore how she can live more authentically but is "terrified" about the ramifications that could occur if she were to inform her family she may wish to identify as male.

Affect: Full, congruent to mood, appropriate to content of interview.

Thought Process: Logical, linear, goal directed.

Thought Content: Denied suicidal ideation, homicidal ideation, delusions, and hallucinations.

Orientation: Oriented to person, place, situation, and time.

Recent Memory: Intact.

Remote Memory: Intact.

Attention/Concentration: Sufficient.

General Knowledge: Within normal limits.

Language: Within normal limits.

Insight: Fair.

Judgment: Good.

Answer Key #2

Diversity Considerations

Jacqueline presents with multiple intersecting, marginalized identities that need to be incorporated into the clinician's overall case conceptualization. Because Jacqueline reported being from a conservative, Hispanic background, family influences and culture should be considered in treatment. Specifically, the clinician may want to consider the role *familismo* may contribute to Jacqueline's distress, (*familismo* being the expectation in many Hispanic cultures that family needs and cultural expectations be honored above individual preferences and desires) (Campos et al., 2008). While religion may not necessarily play a role in the response of Jacqueline's family to her being queer, many conservative Hispanic families do value and participate in religious traditions that stigmatize non-heteronormative identities (Morales, 2010).

When working with this client, it is important to distinguish between sexual orientation and gender identity. At the same time, however, the intersection of sexual orientation and gender identity may warrant exploration if Jacqueline begins to report distress. Specifically, because Jacqueline currently identifies as a gay woman, but is considering and exploring identity as a man, she may experience anxiety about how to make meaning regarding these intersecting identities (Lev, 2004). Of note, because Jacqueline is only just beginning to explore the use of male pronouns and only with close friends, it may not be appropriate for the clinician to assume Jacqueline wishes the clinician to use male pronouns. This should be explored during intake, with the clinician ultimately using preferred pronouns and other forms of address indicated by Jacqueline.

Jacqueline's history of childhood sexual abuse and how it may be impacting her overall relationship with and experience of her body must also be taken into account. Specifically, research indicates that survivors of childhood sexual abuse often report higher levels of dissatisfaction with their bodies in general, and this may impact Jacqueline's overall symptoms of gender dysphoria and gender identity (Briere & Elliott, 2003; Steensma et al., 2013).

Finally, although the occupation of Jacqueline's girlfriend is not known, Jacqueline's report of working as a bartender and dog-sitter may indicate economic instability in the household, depending on how many hours Jacqueline is working. Because socioeconomic status is not clear, though it seems likely Jacqueline may have limited financial resources, issues around accessibility to care must be considered.

Ethical and Legal Considerations

As trauma was disclosed, trauma-informed care should be utilized, as well as ensuring there is ongoing risk assessment to gauge Jacqueline's self-harm ideation or behavior. While it is inappropriate to conceptualize gender identity solely as a response to trauma, the clinician should remain aware of the bidirectional nature of the relationship between trauma and identity. The clinician should follow gender-affirming guidelines as appropriate and ensure preferred pronouns are used once established, as well as provide informed resources on transitioning when requested. Due to the changing landscape related to gender-affirming care, clinician may also wish to review local laws as well as guidance by local licensing boards and well-established professional organizations.

Diagnostic Impressions and Justification

F64.0 Gender Dysphoria in Adolescents and Adults.
Jacqueline meets Criterion A because she reports persistent and clinically significant distress related to her assigned gender, including a strong desire to be recognized as male, discomfort with secondary sex characteristics, and a desire to transition socially and possibly medically.

Psychodynamic Case Conceptualization

Jacqueline's distress could be conceptualized as stemming from unresolved internal conflicts, specifically surrounding the conditional nature of their family system, early relational trauma, and identity formation challenges. Gender identity confusion could be related to unconscious conflicts regarding early attachment and early representations of gender roles, which may have been overly rigid given Jacqueline's description of her family as well as unresolved relational rupture with family. It is important to note that, from a psychodynamic perspective, gender dysphoria is not considered pathological but is instead understood as a sign of unresolved internal conflicts, etc. That being said, a process called defensive gendering can sometimes emerge to help a client disidentify with a vulnerable body (Mollon, 2002), which might feel protective to Jacqueline.

Ultimately, any treatment goals formulated for Jacqueline must be framed in a manner supportive of gender identity exploration and expression. Appropriate goals might include increasing Jacqueline's insight into how early caregiver relationships, relationships with members of her extended family, and her history of trauma may be informing her understanding of herself as well as her perspective regarding gender roles. It may be important to gently explore how disidentification with the female body could have emerged as a defense mechanism (Davies, 2004) without fostering a trauma narrative that could invalidate Jacqueline's current exploration of gender identity and expression.

For any client receiving psychodynamic care, establishing a secure holding environment is key to treatment; for this client, such an environment may be especially important given the amount of rejection she has experienced from her family. Interpreting transference response may also be appropriate, especially if Jacqueline internalizes the clinician as another "authority" figure set to judge her instead of care for her. The clinician may also wish to identify and challenge defense mechanisms protecting Jacqueline from guilt, shame, or gender-related anxiety. These interventions may all be implemented within the context of free association. Above all, the clinician must remember to provide competent care without pressuring Jacqueline to achieve identity resolution prematurely.

Cognitive Behavioral Conceptualization

Jacqueline's emotional distress and behavioral patterns could be influenced by maladaptive thought patterns shaped by past experiences of trauma, identity struggles, and negative social reinforcement, specifically from her family of origin. Increasing awareness of these patterns and promoting adaptive thinking and behavioral patterns could lessen Jacqueline's distress surrounding gender identity. It is important to note that behavioral avoidance may be maintaining Jacqueline's distress surrounding both intensifying gender dysphoria as well as anxiety associated with familial responses. Per Resick et al. (2008), some clients with trauma histories struggle to differentiate between trauma-related avoidance and identity-related distress.

Treatment goals grounded in cognitive behavioral therapy could include improving Jacqueline's ability to name and regulate affective states as well as her ability to identify cognitive distortions when they occur. It may also be appropriate to support her in replacing maladaptive cognitions and their underlying schemas with more adaptive/identity-affirming cognitions. Although Jacqueline indicated no unresolved issues associated with historical trauma, the clinician may wish to remain open to discussing events if Jacqueline chooses to do so.

Appropriate interventions may include utilizing worksheets or other tools to increase Jacqueline's emotional vocabulary, teaching adaptive coping skills, and using thought records. Behavioral experiments and graded exposure may also be appropriate interventions but only if considered to be safe in Jacqueline's community and/or with her co-workers, friends, and/or family. Should Jacqueline determine that there is a need to address historical trauma, integration of either trauma-focused CBT (TF-CBT) or cognitive processing therapy (CPT) may be appropriate.

Biopsychosocial Conceptualization

Jacqueline presents with sleep disturbances managed with THC, body dysphoria with urges toward self-harm, and a history of sexual trauma that may impact emotional regulation. There is likely a bidirectional relationship between reported sleep difficulties and emotional dysregulation and each is likely to exacerbate the other. Jacqueline's use of THC is concerning as it may cause her to avoid emotional processing (Turna et al., 2019) and therefore undermine the therapeutic process. Jacqueline struggles with depression, anxiety, and internalized shame rooted in past trauma and familial invalidation, compounded by gender dysphoria and identity-related stress. Overall distress is likely being maintained by dysfunctional core beliefs as well as negative automatic thoughts. Jacqueline benefits from a supportive partner and peer group, but past experiences of family rejection, gender-based objectification, and early non-conformity have contributed to ongoing relational and self-concept challenges as well as high vigilance in social settings. Jacqueline reports working two jobs but also appears to spend several hours each day on her phone which may indicated she has limited time to process through the distress she is experiencing and/or may have difficulty accessing needed care.

Treatment goals grounded in a biopsychosocial perspective include establishing a healthy and consistent sleep routine, including reducing dependency on THC, as well as increasing somatic awareness and integration, if it feels safe and comfortable for Jacqueline to do so.

Treatment interventions consistent with the biopsychosocial model include psychoeducation regarding sleep hygiene, sleep tracking, and relaxation training. Mindfulness-based approaches, such as progressive muscle relaxation, would likely also be helpful in promoting better sleep as well as managing overall distress. Yoga and massage may be helpful to Jacqueline, but, again, Jacqueline should only engage in such practices if the bodily awareness promoted by such practices are helpful to her. Psychoeducation regarding available community resources as well as gender-affirming medical resources may also be beneficial. If Jacqueline determines that gender-affirming surgery would be supportive of her emerging identity, couples counseling might be indicated to support Jacqueline and girlfriend in navigating the change.

Conclusion

Gender dysphoria, as categorized by the DSM-5-TR, refers to the often distressing incongruence a person might experience between the gender assigned at birth and their experienced or expressed gender identity. Gender dysphoria can present in children, adolescents, and adults. While gender dysphoria does present somewhat differently across the lifespan, overarching symptoms include clinically significant distress and/or impairment caused by the discrepancy between a person's gender identity and the primary and secondary sex characteristics present on their body. The clinical case vignettes included in this chapter serve to highlight the way in which gender dysphoria presents in childhood versus adulthood but clinicians are cautioned to remember that the experience of gender dysphoria is deeply personal and so it is crucial for clinicians to approach treatment compassionately and with humility. Because society's understanding of gender diversity continues to evolve, clinicians must also ensure that they are providing evidence-based care that also takes into account best practices so that mental health care services for patients experiencing gender dysphoria remain compassionate and inclusive.

References

APA (American Psychiatric Association). (2022). *Diagnostic and statistical manual of mental disorders* (5th ed., text rev.). American Psychiatric Association.

Bao, A. M., & Swaab, D. F. (2011). Sexual differentiation of the human brain: Relation to gender identity, sexual orientation and neuropsychiatric disorders. *Frontiers in Neuroendocrinology*, *32*(2), 214–226. https://doi.org/10.1016/j.yfrne.2011.02.007.

Briere, J., & Elliott, D. M. (2003). Prevalence and psychological sequelae of self-reported childhood physical and sexual abuse in a general population sample of men and women. *Child Abuse & Neglect*, *27*(10), 1205–1222. https://doi.org/10.1016/j.chiabu.2003.09.008.

Campos, B., Schetter, C. D., Abdou, C. M., Hobel, C. J., Glynn, L. M., & Sandman, C. A. (2008). Familism, social support, and stress: Positive implications for pregnant Latinas. *Cultural Diversity and Ethnic Minority Psychology*, *14*(2), 155–162. https://doi.org/10.1037/10999809.14.2.155.

Davies, J. M. (2004). Whose bad objects are we anyway? Repetition and our elusive love affair with evil. *Psychoanalytic Dialogues*, *14*(6), 711–732. https://doi.org/10.1080/10481881409348800.

Fonagy, P., & Target, M. (2002). Early intervention and the development of self-regulation. *Psychoanalytic Inquiry*, *22*(3), 307–335. https://doi.org/10.1080/07351692209348996.

Guillamon, A., Junque, C., & Gómez-Gil, E. (2016). A review of the status of brain structure research in transsexualism. *Archives of Sexual Behavior*, *45*(7), 1615–1648. https://doi.org/10.1007/s10508-016-0768-5.

Heylens, G., De Cuypere, G., Zucker, K. J., Schelfaut, C., Elaut, E., Vanden Bossche, H., De Baere, E., & T'Sjoen, G. (2012). Gender identity disorder in twins: A review of the case report literature. *The Journal of Sexual Medicine*, *9*(3), 751–757. https://doi.org/10.1111/j.1743-6109.2011.02567.x.

Lemma, A. (2018). *Transgender identities: A contemporary introduction*. Routledge.

Lev, A. I. (2004). *Transgender emergence: Therapeutic guidelines for working with gender variant people and their families*. Routledge.

Mollon, P. (2002). *Shame and jealousy: The hidden turmoil*. Karnac Books.

Morales, E. S. (2010). Contextual factors affecting the coming-out process for Latino gay men. *Cultural Diversity and Ethnic Minority Psychology*, *6*(3), 274–286. https://doi.org/10.1037/1099-9809.6.3.274.

Resick, P. A., Monson, C. M., & Chard, K. M. (2008). *Cognitive processing therapy: Veteran/military version*. US Department of Veterans Affairs. https://www.ptsd.va.gov/professional/treat/type/cpt_veteran_manual.asp.

Steensma, T. D., Kreukels, B. P. C., de Vries, A. L. C., & Cohen-Kettenis, P. T. (2013). Gender identity development in adolescence. *Hormones and Behavior*, *64*(2), 288–297. https://doi.org/10.1016/j.yhbeh.2013.02.020.

Turna, J., Patterson, B., & Van Ameringen, M. (2019). Is cannabis treatment for anxiety, mood, and related disorders ready for prime time? *Depression and Anxiety*, *36*(11), 1002–1017. https://doi.org/10.1002/da.22942.

Chapter 13

Disruptive, Impulse-Control, and Conduct Disorders

Veronica Regueiro

Disruptive, impulse-control, and conduct disorders, as characterized by the DSM-5-TR, are categorized as a group of disorders that generally present with emotional and behavioral dysregulation and, sometimes, violation of the rights of others (APA, 2022). These disorders can also sometimes cause patients to experience conflict with authority figures as a result of their symptoms (APA, 2022). Patients with disruptive, impulse-control, and conduct disorders often present as angry, irritable, argumentative, defiant, and/or aggressive (APA, 2022). Generally diagnosed in childhood or adolescence, this group of disorders can cause significant impairment in social, academic, and/or occupational domains (APA, 2022). Overall, prevalence rates for the disorders included in this chapter of the DSM are quite low, in the single digits for each diagnosis.

Oppositional defiant disorder, most commonly referred to as ODD, is characterized by a pattern of angry and/or irritable mood, argumentative and/or defiant behavior, and/or vindictiveness that lasts for at least 6 months and represents deviations from what is considered to be normative for the patient's age and gender, within the context of the patient's culture (APA, 2022). ODD presents in between 3 and 4 percent of the population (APA, 2022). Intermittent explosive disorder, most often referred to as IED, is characterized by recurrent behavioral outbursts and can take the form of either verbal or physical aggression, including harm to others and destruction of property (APA, 2022). IED presents in between 2 and 3 percent of the population (APA, 2022), and is therefore less often diagnosed and treated in clinical settings. Conduct disorder is generally characterized by repetitive and persistent patterns of violating society norms and/or the rights of others, which can include aggression toward other people or animals, destruction of property, deceitfulness, theft, and/or serious rule violations (APA, 2022). Interestingly, the prevalence of conduct disorder in male patients is approximately 4 percent whereas the prevalence rate in female patients is between 1 and 2 percent (APA, 2022), indicating the conduct disorders present in male patients approximately twice as often as in female patients. Additional diagnoses include pyromania and kleptomania. Patients who meet

DOI: 10.4324/9781003586531-14

diagnostic criteria for pyromania generally deliberately set fires, while patients who meet diagnostic criteria for kleptomania are generally unable to resist the urge to steal unneeded objects, generally because of the tension that builds within them before a theft occurs as well as the gratification experienced after (APA, 2022). Pyromania and kleptomania are relatively rare, occurring in less than 1 percent of the population.

Clinical Case Vignette #1

Demographic Information and History

Name: Alameda Chavez.

Demographic Information: 16-year-old Mexican American female.

Medical Diagnoses: None reported.

Reason for Referral: Alameda was referred due to a longstanding history of behavioral issues with which her foster mother, Mrs. Ramirez, would like support. Mrs. Ramirez was present for the intake and reported that Alameda has become progressively more argumentative, often overtly ignoring rules at both home and school. She reported that Alameda's irritability, defiance, and other behavioral issues began when Alameda was approximately 10–11 years old but have worsened significantly over the past several years. Mrs. Ramirez reported that Alameda often deliberately provokes or irritates others, which Alameda was able to acknowledge, stating that she sometimes like to "get a rise out of" her foster parents and teachers "just to see what they will do." Mrs. Ramirez reported frustration with the overall situation, stating that she "just can't deal with the weekly battles." She also reported having fostered multiple adolescents and described Alameda as "having the worst attitude" she has ever seen.

Clinical Interview Data

Interpreter Used: None needed.

Current Psychosocial Stressors: None reported besides the household conflict associated with the reason for referral.

Protective Factors: Alameda reported loving animals and volunteering at her local animal shelter on Saturdays. Mrs. Ramirez described Alameda as intelligent and reported caring deeply about her well-being. She reported being interested in adopting Alameda and her brother but stated that the biological parents have actively fought the adoption process.

Developmental History: Mrs. Ramirez reported having been told that Alameda met her developmental milestones generally within normal limits. Of note, she also reported being told that Alameda presented with frequent tantrums as a toddler and during preschool, sometimes having as many as 6–7 tantrums a week.

Academic History: Alameda reported having been suspended from school twice during the current semester. Of note, she reported that her teachers often treat her unfairly and that her school's rules "are stupid" and should not be imposed on someone who is almost an adult.

Social History: Alameda reported having several friends at school and stated that she enjoys going to the beach for nightly bonfires.

Household: Alameda lives with Mrs. Ramirez, a Hispanic woman who is an experienced foster mother. Alameda's biological brother also lives in the home. Alameda's biological parents have attempted to comply with family reunification requirements multiple times but have been unable to do so.

Previous Psychiatric History: No previous psychiatric history was reported.

Family Psychiatric History: Alameda reported her biological parents struggle with substance abuse and mental health issues.

History of Self-Harm: No history of self-harm was reported.

Wellness Profile

Sleep: Alameda reported that she generally goes to sleep at around midnight and wakes up at around 7 o'clock in the morning.

Diet: Alameda reported eating "whatever Mrs. Ramirez makes" but stated that she prefers to eat Takis, other spicy chips, hot wings, and gummy candies.

Elimination: No issues reported.

Technology: Alameda reported spending between 3 and 5 hours on social media and/or texting each day and also reported spending time watching television and movies on the weekends.

Physical Activity: Alameda denied engaging in any physical activity.

Substance Use/Abuse: Alameda denied past or current substance use.

Pain: None reported.

Current Psychiatric Symptoms

Depression: Alameda reported sometimes feeling sad and tired but denied any episodes of tearfulness and further stated only feeling sad once every 1–2 months. She did acknowledge feeling irritable and resentful approximately 1–2 days each week. Alameda reported sometimes experiencing suicidal ideation but denied ever having any intention to actually end her life.

Anxiety: Alameda reported experiencing some symptoms of anxiety including racing thoughts and muscle tension as well as general worry about her future.

Panic: Alameda denied symptoms of panic.

Mania: Alameda denied symptoms of mania or hypomania.

Psychosis: Alameda denied symptoms of psychosis.

Trauma: Alameda reported her biological parents were generally neglectful but denied any history of physical or sexual abuse.

Eating Disorder: Alameda denied symptoms of an eating disorder.

Risky Behaviors/Sexual Activity: Mrs. Ramirez reported that Alameda sometimes sneaks out in the middle of the night to spend time with friends from school. Alameda acknowledged engaging in such behavior and stated that at her age, she should be allowed to stay out later than what Mrs. Ramirez believes is appropriate. Alameda denied engaging in other risky behaviors.

Mental Status Exam

Appearance: Alameda was dressed casually. She has dark eyes and straight dark hair.

Behavior: Alameda was cooperative.

Speech: Alameda's speech was within normal limits.

Mood: Alameda described her mood as good.

Affect: Alameda's affect was congruent and appropriate.

Thought Process: Alameda's thought process was logical and linear.

Thought Content: Alameda denied suicidal ideation, homicidal ideation, delusions, or hallucinations.

Orientation: Alameda was oriented to person, place, time, and situation.

Recent Memory: Alameda's recent memory was intact.

Remote Memory: Alameda's remote memory was intact.

Attention/Concentration: Alameda's attention and concentration were within normal limits.

General Knowledge: Alameda's general knowledge was within normal limits.

Language: Alameda's language was within normal limits.

Insight: Alameda demonstrated fair insight.

Judgment: Alameda demonstrated fair judgment.

Answer Key #1

Diversity Considerations

While Alameda and Mrs. Ramirez are both Hispanic, it would be a mistake to assume that their cultural backgrounds and worldviews are identical. As an adolescent living in a foster home, Alameda may struggle with issues related to identity development and consolidation, specifically because she is away from her biological and extended family members during such a critical phase of development (Rivas-Drake et al., 2014). Although thoughtful consideration must be given to the information provided during the clinical interview, it is also important to remember that girls of color are not only often overpathologized in school settings but are also disproportionately diagnosed with behavioral disorders (Dettlaff & Boyd, 2020; Alegría et al., 2010). Girls presenting with behaviors deemed oppositional might also be more harshly judged and/or more punitively treated due to the incongruence between their behavioral presentations and social expectations related to stereotypically feminine presentations.

Ethical Considerations

Because Alameda is a foster child living in a foster home, there may be legal implications surrounding questions of consent relating to who may potentially have records released to them in the future. Specifically, clinicians should confirm that Mrs. Ramirez is legally able to consent to mental health treatment for Alameda, as the right to consent to mental health treatment may be with the court. Regardless of who is determined to be able to consent to treatment, Alameda should be given the opportunity to assent. Clear, explicit communication is recommended regarding privacy and confidentiality in the treatment of minors so that both Alameda and Mrs. Ramirez understand the balance between privacy and confidentiality and caregiver rights.

Legal Considerations

Although Alameda presented with a history of neglect, no child abuse report is required given ongoing involvement from the Department of Children and Family Services (DCFS). Still, the clinician must remain attuned to potential additional disclosure regarding abuse or neglect and clearly specify to Alameda status as a mandated reporter.

Diagnostic Impressions and Justification

F91.3 Oppositional Defiant Disorder, Moderate.
Alameda meets diagnostic criteria for a diagnosis of oppositional defiant disorder (ODD), moderate. Specifically, she was reported to be generally argumentative and defiant, often disregarding rules both at home and at school. She endorsed often feeling irritable and resentful and was able to acknowledge sometimes intentionally irritating others. Additionally, during the course of the clinical interview, she did not take responsibility for her own actions, blaming her difficulties at home and school on the unreasonableness of the adults responsible for her. Mrs. Ramirez reported ongoing and even worsening issues for the past 5–6 years and indicated that conflict in the home is occurring on at least a weekly basis. Based on the information gathered, Alameda's symptoms are negatively impacting her both at home and at school. While Alameda did not report a significant amount of distress associated with her symptoms, she did endorse some symptoms of anxiety and depression, which do often co-occur in children and adolescents diagnosed with ODD (APA, 2022). Because there is no evidence of a psychotic disorder, depressive disorder, or bipolar disorder, these diagnoses do not better account for her symptom presentation. Additionally, there is no evidence that her symptoms can be better accounted for by either a substance abuse disorder or disruptive mood dysregulation disorder.

Psychodynamic Case Conceptualization

Psychodynamic theory posits that early experiences with abuse and neglect can contribute to disrupted attachment, largely due to the deficits in attunement that can occur in such environments (Fonagy & Target, 2002). Alameda's oppositional and argumentative behaviors might serve as a sort of primitive defense (McWilliams, 2011) that protects her against affective experiences she might otherwise experience as overwhelming.

Because of Alameda's history, initial goals might include establishing a strong working relationship to facilitate the provision of corrective emotional experiences over the course of the therapeutic relationship. The clinician may also wish to work towards deepening Alameda's affective experience as well as improving her ability to tolerate difficult affects which may feel overwhelming to her. Over time, the clinician may wish to improve Alameda's insight into her overall internal experiences including unconscious motivations for her behaviors. Strengthening Alameda's ego functioning would also be an appropriate goal, so as to ultimately support her in depending less on the primitive defense mechanisms on which she currently relies. Similarly, over the course of treatment, it would be appropriate for the clinician to support Alameda in improving her overall interpersonal functioning.

As is the case when providing psychodynamic psychotherapy to an adult, the first intervention would be to establish a consistent and safe holding environment in which boundaries and empathic attunement could be employed. As Alameda begins to feel more comfortable in treatment, the clinician could facilitate exploration of the unconscious material through verbal narratives. Even when working with adolescents, clinicians are encouraged to interpret both transference and countertransference, to support adolescents such as Alameda into developing insight into their relational patterns. The clinician could also interpret the defense mechanisms with which Alameda presents and/or utilize clarification and confrontation to improve overall self-awareness. Because of Alameda's age and history, she may benefit from a course of art therapy, a treatment modality grounded in psychodynamic theory. Art therapy should, however, only be implemented by a trained art therapist.

Cognitive Behavioral Conceptualization

Alameda reported experiencing racing thoughts and while she did not disclose the content of these thoughts, it is possible that she is experiencing cognitive distortions such as overgeneralizing, all-or-nothing thinking, or jumping to conclusions, and that these thoughts are contributing to her overall behavioral presentation. It is also possible that Mrs. Ramirez is inadvertently reinforcing Alameda's behavioral issues. For example, if Alameda acts out and Mrs. Ramirez gives up on maintaining a boundary because she is tired of the conflict in the home, her avoidance may serve as a form of negative reinforcement.

Appropriate CBT goals would include reducing oppositional and defiant behaviors both at home and at school as well as improving Alameda's emotional regulation and interpersonal effectiveness. Alameda would also benefit from improving her problem-solving skills as well as her relationship with her foster mother.

The clinician may wish to begin with ABC analysis (antecedent-behavior-consequence analysis) to help Alameda identify patterns in her behavior as well as associated consequences. Alameda would benefit from cognitive restructuring, specifically to help her identify, challenge, and restructure the cognitive distortions contributing to her overall behavior. Cognitive reframing could support Alameda in managing any irritability arising from her thoughts. Mood logs and thought logs could support Alameda in improving her insight into her thoughts and feelings as well as their connection to her behaviors. Other worksheets could be used specifically to support Alameda in moving through the activities related to cognitive restructuring and reframing. Relaxation training as well as other mindfulness-based stress reduction techniques could help Alameda improve her overall emotional and behavioral regulation. Behavioral activation paired with contingency management could support Alameda in increasing her compliance with the expectations of her foster mother and teachers, specifically through the use of activity scheduling and token economies implemented both at home and at school. Additionally, role-playing activities may support Alameda in learning how to think through the potential outcomes related to her decisions especially with regard to her interpersonal relationships.

Biopsychosocial Conceptualization

There is some evidence that abnormalities in the prefrontal cortex and amygdala are associated with the development of ODD (APA, 2022). Because Alameda's biological parents reportedly struggle with mental health issues, Alameda may also present with a genetic predisposition that underlies her emotional and behavioral presentation. Underlying attachment issues resulting from the neglect to which Alameda was exposed as well as potentially learned behaviors may also be contributing to her presentation. There may also be aspects of the situation at home or school exacerbating her symptoms.

From a biopsychosocial perspective, it would be appropriate to formulate treatment goals that address multiple domains of functioning. Potential treatment goals include supporting Alameda in developing and maintaining habits to support a lifestyle that promotes emotional and behavioral regulation as well as cognitive flexibility. Improving overall self-concept would also be an appropriate goal. Additional treatment goals could include improving Alameda's relationship with both her foster mother and teachers.

When considering interventions that might support a lifestyle that promotes emotional and behavioral regulation, factors such as sleep, nutrition, and physical activity must be taken into consideration. The clinician may wish to begin by providing Alameda with psychoeducation regarding the bidirectional nature of the mind-body connection and then providing additional information regarding lifestyle interventions within that context. Specifically, Alameda would benefit from psychoeducation regarding the physiological and psychological benefit of sufficient high-quality sleep including how sleep hygiene could support such sleep. Psychoeducation regarding the impact of nutrition on mental health would also be beneficial, specifically within the context of additional information on the gut-brain relationship. Alameda would also benefit from psychoeducation regarding the role regular physical activity could play in improving her mood and reducing irritability. It would be appropriate to implement interventions curated from CBT to help Alameda learn how to identify and articulate her affective experience. Thought logs, mood logs, and journaling might all be helpful. The clinician may also with to encourage Alameda to engage in activities to promote identity development, self-efficacy, and self-concept such as volunteering or perhaps working with animals in another capacity. Additionally, because of the conflict reported between Alameda and the adults in her life, including those adults in treatment would be appropriate. Specifically, it would be appropriate to involve Alameda and Mrs. Ramirez in joint sessions designed to improve their interpersonal communication and conflict resolution skills as well as the overall quality of their relationship. With a signed ROI, the clinician could also collaborate with Alameda's school to ensure she is receiving appropriate behavioral support. A behavioral intervention plan (BIP) may be available to Alameda through her school. Token economies could also be implemented both at school and at home to improve her overall functioning in those settings. Of note, any collaboration with caregivers should have advocacy for Alameda at the forefront to ensure that her needs are being met and that the expectations set are developmentally appropriate. Because Alameda is a ward of the court, the clinician may wish to also collaborate with her social worker to ensure placement stability.

Clinical Case Vignette #2

Demographic Information and History

Name: Conrad Ford.

Demographic Information: 10-year-old Caucasian male.

Medical Diagnoses: None reported.

Reason for Referral: Conrad's parents, Mr. and Mrs. Ford, presented to the clinic with Conrad to request assistance with managing his emotional and behavioral dysregulation. Per their report, Conrad recently became so angry that he threw a chair at his mother after she asked him to put away his video game and prepare for bed. Mr. and Mrs. Ford also reported that during "his fits of rage," Conrad will frequently yell and scream at his parents and will curse at them. They also reported that approximately 3 months ago he became so angry he broke a window at the family's home. When asked for more details about Conrad's presentation, Mr. and Mrs. Ford reported that Conrad "really loses his temper" at least twice a week but seemed at a loss regarding why Conrad becomes so angry. Mr. and Mrs. Ford reported that the events immediately preceding Conrad's episodes of emotional and behavioral dysregulation include what they feel are generally benign, developmentally appropriate requests such as asking him to set the table for dinner, put away his toys, complete his homework, etc. They stated that while Conrad's "temper tantrums" generally last less than 30 minutes, they are difficult to manage. They reported feeling overwhelmed and confused by their son's behavior, describing him as a generally happy little boy who is funny, sweet, and caring.

Clinical Interview Data

Interpreter Used: No.

Current Psychosocial Stressors: Mr. and Mrs. Ford denied the presence of any psychosocial stressors potentially contributing to Conrad's presentation. Conrad also denied the presence of psychosocial stressors, reporting that he enjoys school and likes his friends even if they "fight sometimes."

Protective Factors: Mr. and Mrs. Ford described Conrad as funny, sweet, and caring, and stated that he excels in school as well as on his baseball team. Conrad reported that he enjoys watching superhero movies, with Captain America being his favorite superhero. He also reported loving his family's new puppy.

Developmental History: Mrs. Ford denied experiencing any prenatal or perinatal complications and stated that Conrad reached all of his developmental milestones within normal limits.

Academic History: Conrad reported receiving straight As in school and stated that art and history are his favorite subjects. He reported disliking math but said "math is easy but so boring." Mr. and Mrs. Ford denied Conrad ever undergoing a psychoeducational evaluation or having an IEP in place. Of note, Conrad and his parents both reported that Conrad's classroom has a card-pulling system whereby all children begin the day with green cards, move to yellow cards after their first infraction, and them move to orange and red cards if issues continue to arise. Conrad and his parents all reported that Conrad generally ends the day with green cards but will sometimes end the day with yellow cards as a result of arguing with a teacher or peer.

Social History: Conrad reported having several friends, especially on his baseball team. While his parents confirmed Conrad is generally well liked, they also stated that Conrad will sometimes "fall out" with a friend after being too argumentative and "not knowing how to just let some things go." They reiterated, however, that Conrad is generally well liked, has several friends, and generally gets along well with children he has known for long periods of time as well as new potential friends.

Household: Conrad reportedly lives with his biological parents, Mr. and Mrs. Ford. Per Mr. and Mrs. Ford, Conrad is an only child. Mr. and Mrs. Ford reported that Conrad has several cousins who often sleep over on the weekends and that Conrad gets along well with his cousins.

Previous Psychiatric History: Mr. and Mrs. Ford denied any previous psychiatric history for Conrad and/or themselves although Mr. Ford reported "having a really bad temper" when he was younger. He also reported that his own father, Conrad's grandfather, had also "had such a bad temper – he would just yell and scream sometimes for no big deal."

Family Psychiatric History: No additional family psychiatric history was reported.

History of Self-Harm: Conrad denied any history of non-suicidal self-injurious (NSSI) behaviors but his parents report that Conrad will sometimes become so upset that he hits himself on the head. Mr. and Mrs. Ford reported that when these instances occur, they intervene immediately and that Conrad has never been able to hit himself more than twice. Mr. and Mrs. Ford stated that Conrad has never needed to seek medical attention after these episodes, nor has he ever hit himself hard enough to leave a mark. They also stated that when hitting himself in the head, Conrad generally uses the flat of his hand or a fist, never an object. They also denied that Conrad engages in any head-banging.

Wellness Profile

Sleep: Mr. and Mrs. Ford reported that they try to have Conrad sleep 9–10 hours a night but that this time is cut short a couple of times each week because of Conrad's "temper tantrums."

Diet: Mr. and Mrs. Ford reported that Conrad consistently eats three full meals a day as well as 2–3 snacks and attributed his appetite to the amount of physical activity in which he engages as well as being "a growing boy." Mrs. Ford reported that she usually makes Conrad scrambled eggs, fruit, and toast for breakfast but that he will usually just eat cereal on the weekends, especially if he has an early baseball game scheduled. Mrs. Ford stated that she packs Conrad's lunch for school and that it typically includes a sandwich or Hot Pocket, baby carrots or celery with peanut butter, a piece of fruit, a bag of chips, and cookies or a brownie. Mrs. Ford reported that the family nearly always eats out for dinner as well as on the weekends, especially during baseball season, due to how baseball practices and games are scheduled.

Elimination: Conrad denied any concerns related to elimination.

Technology: Mr. and Mrs. Ford reported that Conrad "has more screen-time than what is probably good for him," acknowledging that he uses computers at school and also uses an iPad or phone at home and in the car. Mr. and Mrs. Ford reported knowing that "too much screentime isn't good" but also stated that the "battle to get Conrad to put away his iPad or whatever is just not worth it."

Physical Activity: Conrad reported playing tag and kickball at school during lunch and recess. He also reported attending baseball practice and games multiple times a week. Additionally, Conrad reported that his parents take him to ride his bike around a local college track on weekends if no baseball games are scheduled.

Substance Use/Abuse: Conrad and his parents all denied any possibility of Conrad engaging in substance use or abuse. Specifically, when asked about substance use or abuse, Conrad laughed and said, "Don't you know I'm only 10?"

Pain: 0/10.

Current Psychiatric Symptoms

Depression: Conrad denied any symptoms of depression and his parents confirmed his report, describing him as generally happy and sweet.

Anxiety: Conrad denied any symptoms of anxiety. Mr. and Mrs. Ford reported noticing some mild symptoms of anxiety but generally only "before a really important game, like if the team is getting close to making it to the championship."

Panic: Conrad denied any panic symptoms.

Mania: Conrad denied any symptoms of mania or hypomania.

Psychosis: Conrad denied any symptoms of psychosis.

Trauma: Conrad denied any history of trauma and his parents corroborated his report.

Eating Disorder: Conrad denied any symptoms of an eating disorder. Mrs. Ford reported that Conrad sometimes "gets picky" about his food but when asked to elaborate, specified that Conrad will often refuse to try vegetables with which he is not familiar and will only eat broccoli with cheese melted on it. Otherwise, she reported that Conrad regularly consumes items from all major food groups.

Risky Behaviors/Sexual Activity: Conrad denied engaging in any risky behaviors with the exception of breaking the window in his home and throwing the chair at his mother.

Mental Status Exam

Appearance: Conrad presented to the intake session wearing his baseball uniform as he was scheduled for baseball practice right after the session. His hygiene was appropriate for his age, and his height and weight also appeared appropriate for his age.

Behavior: Conrad was cooperative throughout the intake.

Speech: Conrad's speech was within normal limits.

Mood: "Fine!"

Affect: Conrad presented as generally euthymic.

Thought Process: Conrad's thought process was logical, linear, and goal directed.

Thought Content: Conrad denied any suicidal ideation, homicidal ideation, delusions, or hallucinations.

Orientation: Conrad was oriented to person, place, time, and situation.

Recent Memory: Conrad's recent memory was intact.

Remote Memory: Conrad's remote memory was intact.

Attention/Concentration: Conrad demonstrated sufficient attention and concentration.

General Knowledge: Conrad's general knowledge was within normal limits.

Language: Conrad's receptive and expressive language skills were within normal limits.

Insight: Conrad's insight appeared to be developmentally appropriate.

Judgment: Conrad's judgment appeared fair.

Answer Key #2

Diversity Considerations

Because Conrad is a Caucasian male from a two-parent household, his overall demographic profile matches with the majority population evaluated and treated in many clinical settings. It is important, however, to avoid making assumptions about Conrad and/or his family based on the perception of cultural homogeneity. Norms associated with subcultures can influence behavior, parenting practices, and other facets of human behavior and functioning (Sue et al., 2019). For example, in some cultures, boys are socialized to engage in more externalizing behaviors such as impulsivity and aggression, and these behaviors are normalized. In Western societies, boys have historically been socialized to suppress vulnerable emotions and instead express distress through displays of anger and/or aggression (Chaplin & Aldao, 2013). Internalized gender norms can also influence the way parents respond to children's behaviors, which can, in some situations, lead to responses that reinforce dysregulation.

Conrad's age also needs to be taken into account as a diversity variable, particularly as his age indicates that he is entering into a developmental period characterized by (hopefully) emerging capacities related to executive functioning and emotional regulation. Most 10-year-olds are expected to demonstrate some ability to self-regulate but may struggle with doing so successfully when their affective experiences exceed their still-developing capacities (Steinberg, 2014). There may be an aspect of Conrad's presentation influenced by his age as there may be developmental limitations associated with emotional vocabulary or impulse control (Morris et al., 2007).

Broader societal influences also need to be taken into account when considering the diversity variables impacting any patient's presentation. In modern societies, with easy access to technology and where technology is frequently overused, lifestyle disruptions and emotional and behavioral dysregulation have become more common. These factors influence both childhood routines and parenting practices and must be approached with the same cultural humility as other societal influences that impact behavior across the lifespan.

Ethical Considerations

Because Conrad is 10 years old, the informed consent process should be completed with his parents, as they are the individuals legally able to consent to treatment. The question of assent should not be ignored, however, and care must be taken to include Conrad in the informed consent process so as to obtain his assent to treatment. When engaging in this conversation, the clinician must be sure to use language appropriate for both Conrad and his parents to ensure that all three of them are able to understand the information provided regarding the nature, purpose, risks, and benefits of psychotherapy as well as the limitations of privacy and confidentiality. Clear conversations regarding privacy and confidentiality are especially important when working with minors, as some parents may assume clinicians are required to provide daily detailed updates pertaining to treatment when some level of privacy should actually be maintained for the child to ensure he feels safe and respected throughout the therapeutic process. At the same time, it is imperative for any child entering treatment, including Conrad, to understand that there are limits to privacy and confidentiality and that his parents may be informed of statements he may make regarding harm to himself or others.

Because Conrad is 10 years old, it is reasonable to assume that effective treatment would necessarily include his parents. In this situation, a clinician may be tempted to serve both as Conrad's individual therapist as well as the family's therapist but dual relationships can at times impair objectivity and so clinicians finding themselves in this situation are encouraged to maintain clear, consistent professional boundaries so that focus can remain on the identified patient. Of note, clinicians working with minor patients must also remain vigilant to the possibility of being triangulated by members of the family and therefore be careful to maintain neutrality in order to ensure the ethical and effective delivery of interventions.

Legal Considerations

No additional legal considerations noted at this time.

Diagnostic Impressions and Justification

F63.81 Intermittent Explosive Disorder.

The DSM-5-TR that best explains Conrad's overall presentation is intermittent explosive disorder. Specifically, he is presenting with repeated occurrences of verbal aggression, including temper tantrums, which his parents reported as occurring at least twice a week. They also reported two episodes of physical aggression, one during which property was destroyed but one that did not result in the destruction of property. Based on his parents' report, Conrad has been symptomatic for at least 3 months. Given that Conrad and his parents all denied any current psychosocial stressors, and that Mr. and Mrs. Ford reported that Conrad's behavioral outbursts generally occur in response to normal day-to-day parent/child interactions, it seems fair to say that the magnitude of the expressed anger and aggression is out of proportion to the immediately preceding events. There was no mention of primary or secondary gain; that is, it does not seem as though Conrad is intentionally acting out as a means of achieving a tangible end. Additionally, Conrad's symptoms are causing interpersonal conflict with his parents. Because Conrad is over 6 years of age, he falls into the age range where IED may be considered as a possible diagnosis. Finally, no other medical or mental health issues can be implicated with regard to Conrad's presentation. His medical history was reported to be unremarkable, and no evidence was presented to support the possibility of a neurodevelopmental disorder. Additionally, no mood symptoms indicative of a depressive disorder, disruptive mood dysregulation, or bipolar disorder were reported. Because of his age, it would likely be inappropriate to consider seriously the presence of psychosis or problematic personality features, but even if he were old enough for such possibilities to be considered, there is no evidence to suggest the presence of either. As such, IED is the diagnosis that best explains Conrad's presentation.

Psychodynamic Case Conceptualization

IED can be best understood as the external manifestation of unresolved internal conflicts and deficits in ego functioning. Historically, psychodynamic theory has understood the ability to tolerate frustration, modulate affect, and inhibit impulses as a sign of a mature ego. Because Conrad is emotionally and behaviorally dysregulated, it seems likely that his ego is somehow deficient or impaired which is why he struggles to tolerate frustration. His aggression is evidence that he is likely employing primitive defenses such as projection and splitting and it may also serve as a cathartic release of psychic tension. It is important to note that while Conrad appears to have loving and securely attached parents, they did report a history of intergenerational emotional and behavioral dysregulation specifically associated with expressions of anger.

Treatment goals grounded in psychodynamic theory could include improving affective regulation, improving impulse control, and improving insight into interpersonal process and internalized object relations. The clinician could also support Conrad in strengthening his ego functioning while promoting the integration of conflicted ego states. Additionally, the clinician could support Conrad in reducing his reliance on primitive defense mechanisms while helping him develop more adaptive strategies for having his needs met. Finally, it is important for clinicians to remember that the therapeutic relationship itself can serve as a corrective emotional experience.

As is consistent in psychodynamic psychotherapy, treatment should begin with the establishment of a consistent and safe holding environment to help contain Conrad's dysregulated emotions and behavior. Within that context, the clinician should provide Conrad with empathic attunement. Because of his age, Conrad could benefit from either traditional talk therapy, art therapy, or play therapy. Regardless of the treatment modality utilized, the clinician should support Conrad in learning how to identify and articulate his affective states. Developmentally appropriate language and metaphors could be utilized to support symbolization of affect. Talk therapy, play, or art could help Conrad explore relational themes and internalized dynamics with his parents. While Conrad is very young, interpretations can still be utilized but should be implemented gently and in a developmentally appropriate manner. Interpretations could include interpretation of transference specifically with regard to how Conrad might re-enact family relationships within the context of the therapeutic relationship. It would also be important throughout the course of treatment to model appropriate integrated responses to any emotional or behavioral dysregulation Conrad might display. A clinician using play therapy should specifically help Conrad channel his aggressive impulses into creative or constructive outlets as that could potentially support ego development.

Cognitive Behavioral Conceptualization

There are several factors that need to be considered when applying CBT to Conrad's case. First and foremost, because he is only 10 years old, he is likely still developing metacognitive abilities, which may make it difficult for him to reflect on and reframe internal states. This does not indicate any sort of a deficit but rather reflects normative psychological functioning for most 10-year-olds. Second, given Mr. Ford's report that he himself used to have a "bad temper" as did his own father, one must consider whether or not Conrad has been exposed to adults using verbal or physical aggression when angry, as such situations would allow for those adults to model potentially maladaptive methods of communicating distress. That being said, Conrad's presentation is also likely being impacted by cognitive distortions. Specifically, he may be engaging in catastrophizing when even minor demands are placed upon him or engaging in dichotomous thinking, both of which would likely contribute to emotional and behavioral dysregulation. Conrad also appears to lack developmentally appropriate adaptive coping skills to help him manage his affective states especially when distressed. Based on the information reported, Conrad's caregivers and environment are currently reinforcing his emotional and behavioral dysregulation. Clear examples of negative reinforcement were shared by Conrad's parents, and they may be reinforcing his behaviors in other ways, contributing to an overall pattern of learned behavior whereby explosive episodes are utilized to exert control.

Appropriate treatment goals stemming from CBT include increasing Conrad's ability to self-monitor as well as his overall emotional awareness. Once Conrad's ability to self-monitor has improved, he would benefit from learning how to restructure maladaptive cognitions as well as from gaining adaptive coping skills so as to improve his overall emotional and behavioral regulations. Last, improving Conrad's problem-solving skills, communication skills, and conflict resolution skills would serve as worthwhile goals grounded in CBT.

Emotion wheels, feelings thermometers, emotion cards, and charades are all developmentally appropriate interventions that can be used to help Conrad learn how to identify and label his own affective states. Therapeutic art activities, such as a feelings self-portrait or body mapping, can also be utilized to help Conrad learn the physiological cues associated with anger. Additionally, developmentally appropriate films, such as *Inside Out* can help teach Conrad emotional literacy skills in engaging ways. Once Conrad has learned how to recognize and label his own affective states, he can begin to learn about the thoughts he has that contribute to those states. Thought bubble exercises or comic strip activities can be used to help him learn how to connect thoughts with feelings and then subsequent behaviors. Thought bubble exercises and comic strip activities can also be used to teach Conrad how to replace maladaptive thoughts with adaptive thoughts. Additionally, Conrad can be taught adaptive coping strategies to help him learn how to regulate both his emotional and physiological responses when becoming upset. For example, the clinician can teach him deep breathing, progressive muscle relaxation, etc., in a developmentally appropriate manner. Role-playing can be utilized to support Conrad in rehearsing the skills being taught as well as in learning when to deploy his new skills. Because Conrad appears to enjoy physical activity, he can also be taught how to use short bursts of intensive exercises to manage potentially overwhelming affective states. Of note, because Conrad is only 10 years old, his parents' involvement in treatment will be crucial in helping Conrad improve his overall emotional and behavioral regulation. Specifically, it would be important to provide Conrad's parents with training regarding effective behavioral reinforcement strategies. The clinician can, for example, work with Conrad's parents to implement a home behavior chart as well as a token economy.

Biopsychosocial Conceptualization

Research indicates that IED may have an underlying neurobiological component related to increased reactivity in the amygdala as well as dysregulated serotonergic functioning (APA, 2022). That being said, because Conrad is only 10 years old, it is important to note that his brain is not yet fully developed and that some of his presentation can therefore be explained by general neurodevelopmental immaturity. Given the paternal history of difficulty managing emotions and behaviors, there may be a genetic component but there could also be aspects of learned behavior influencing Conrad's presentation. His behaviors could have been learned as the result of a parent modeling such behaviors but could also have been learned by his parents inadvertently reinforcing his behaviors. Cognitive distortions are likely playing a role in Conrad's presentation as are potential attachment issues. For example, while Conrad's parents present as concerned and engaged, they reported feeling helpless and overwhelmed in the face of his dysregulation, which may suggest that they have responded inconsistently to Conrad's distress. Inconsistent patterns of responding on the part of caregivers can contribute to the development of insecure attachment patterns, which can then in turn result in aggressive protest behaviors. It is also important to consider the broader social context and how socialization involving concepts related to masculinity and emotional suppression may be playing a role in exacerbating Conrad's emotional and behavioral dysregulation.

Treatment goals grounded in the biopsychosocial model could include improving Conrad's ability to manage his impulses by improving his emotional insight and overall emotional and behavioral regulation. It would also be appropriate to help Conrad learn how to reframe cognitive distortions so that they become more adaptive. Finally, the clinician could help Conrad improve his overall functioning within his family system as well as his parents' skills in managing the moments of distress he experiences.

While Conrad is quite young and physicians from different specialties differ with regard to the appropriateness of administering psychotropic medication to young children, recommending that Conrad's parents consult with a child psychiatrist may be helpful in providing them with support and information regarding available treatment options especially if they find that psychological interventions are not effective in improving Conrad's presentation. Clinicians could teach Conrad mindfulness-based adaptive coping strategies such as deep breathing, progressive muscle relaxation, guided imagery, etc., in a developmentally appropriate manner. Interventions curated from various evidence-based treatment modalities such as CBT, DBT, etc., could also support Conrad in learning how to identify and articulate his affective experiences. Therapeutic play and/or therapeutic art could be helpful in addressing the affective experiences Conrad may find difficult to articulate, especially at the beginning of treatment. Once Conrad has developed some insight into his cognitions and affective experiences, cognitive restructuring could be utilized to help hm reframe cognitive distortions. Because Conrad is a young child, the involvement of his parents will be crucial to achieving optimal treatment outcomes. Specifically, they would benefit from parent training to help them provide Conrad with more consistent and containing responses as well as developmentally appropriate boundaries supported by both positive reinforcement and natural consequences. If needed, the family system can be referred to family therapy as well. Finally, introducing some changes to Conrad's lifestyle may further support increased emotional and behavioral regulation. While he is already a physically active child, he may benefit from physical activities that could support his awareness of his body while teaching concepts related to self-mastery. Martial arts may be particularly effective in supporting these goals while also providing opportunities for catharsis in the form of sparring.

Clinical Case Vignette #3

Demographic Information and History

Name: Mei Ling Wong.

Demographic Information: 18-year-old Chinese American female.

Medical Diagnoses: None reported.

Reason for Referral: Mei Ling was ordered to mandated therapy services after multiple psychiatric hospitalizations as well as repeated encounters with local law enforcement. She was ordered to attend psychotherapy after her third arrest for initiating a physical altercation at a local nightclub during which she obtained a broken beer bottle and attempted to use it to injure another female patron. Previous involvement with law enforcement resulted from prior physical altercations and also because Mei Ling was caught shoplifting from various local stores on different occasions, including Sephora, Ulta, Target, and Pottery Barn. Of note, during the clinical interview, Mei Ling reported concern regarding how her behavioral and legal history might influence her future plans.

Clinical Interview Data

Interpreter Used: No.

Current Psychosocial Stressors: Mei Ling reported that "money is always tight" and that she frequently has to work multiple jobs to be able to afford rent as well as other basic necessities. She also reported some conflict with her roommates and stated that she "has never had a good relationship" with her parents.

Protective Factors: Mei Ling presented as intelligent and articulate during the clinical interview. She reported enjoying makeup and skincare and stated that she has "a ton of followers on Tik Tok" who watch the tutorials she posts. Mei Ling reported wanting to become "a real influencer" indicating long-term goals aligned with her interests.

Developmental History: Mei Ling reported believing that she met her developmental milestones within normal limits.

Academic History: Mei Ling reported having received average grades while in high school and stated she could have performed better academically but found school "so stupid and so boring." She reported "ditching class all of the time" beginning in the fifth or sixth grade. She denied ever having undergone a psychoeducational evaluation while enrolled in school and reported that she was "always in the normal classes." Mei Ling reported graduating from high school within the past year, and that she has been working in the food industry since prior to graduation. She reported having been previously employed by Panda Express, Chipotle, Mod Pizza, and Papa John's but stated she only worked at each restaurant for approximately 6–9 months because she "was always in trouble for such stupid things" like regularly being late for her shift and not following restaurant procedures for opening and closing. Mei Ling reported currently working as a contractor for GrubHub and stated that she is considering applying for a seasonal position at her local Amazon warehouse when the holiday season commences. Mei Ling reported generally doing well in her work at GrubHub and that she benefits from the flexibility offered by contract work.

Social History: Mei Ling reported that she was often reprimanded during junior high and high school for bullying other students. She reported feeling somewhat guilty when considering her behavior as a young adolescent, but then stated, "It was a tough school, eat or be eaten. I figured it was better to eat." She reported having one close friend throughout her childhood and having dated multiple male classmates. Mei Ling denied currently dating anyone and said she spends most of her time with her roommates or with her co-workers.

Household: Mei Ling reported living in a two-bedroom apartment with three other young women. When asked about her parents, Mei Ling reported that she only communicates with them once or twice each month because "they are crazy strict and hate everything." Mei Ling reported that she "couldn't wait to not live with them anymore" while she was growing up and that she attempted to run away from home multiple times as an adolescent. Mei Ling reported that she immigrated to the United States with her parents when she was just 6 months old and that while she is sure her early childhood was "fine," she does not remember ever getting along with her parents. Per Mei Ling, her parents "were always working at their restaurant and had no idea what was going on in [her] life but still thought they could tell [her] what to do all of the time." Mei Ling indicated her parents should not be considered a source of support and did not agree to sign an ROI so they could be included in her care.

Previous Psychiatric History: Mei Ling reported a longstanding history of depression and anxiety as well as a history of NSSI behaviors that resulted in a string of psychiatric hospitalizations throughout high school whenever teachers noticed the cuts along her arms and thighs. Mei Ling reported her parents consistently complied with "whatever recommendations the school or shrinks would make" but did not believe in the benefit of psychotherapy and so would not permit her to engage in more treatment than that deemed necessary by school officials or medical professionals.

Family Psychiatric History: Mei Ling reported that her father "is probably an alcoholic" because of the copious amounts of alcohol he consumes after work each day. She also reported that both of her parents "are probably depressed but who knows? Feelings don't matter."

History of Self-Harm: Mei Ling denied any current NSSI behaviors and reported she last cut 2 months ago. When asked about her motivation to remain safe, Mei Ling reported having recently met "a really cute guy" and being concerned that he might find her scars unattractive.

Wellness Profile

Sleep: Mei Ling reported that she generally sleeps 5–6 hours each night.

Diet: Mei Ling reported that she usually eats one meal consisting of fast food each day but will "sometimes sneak something out of a GrubHub order" she is delivering if the package is easy to open and she thinks no one will notice the missing food. Of note, Mei Ling reported feeling guilty about sometimes eating some of the food she is meant to deliver but became defensive when questioned further by the clinician, stating that she has no one on whom she can depend, and that she has to take care of herself the best she can.

Elimination: Mei Ling denied experiencing any gastrointestinal distress or elimination issues.

Technology: Mei Ling reported that she spends most of the day on her phone, scrolling through Tik Tok and Instagram as well as creating and editing content.

Physical Activity: Mei Ling reported disliking exercise but stated she will often walk, if possible, in an effort to save gas.

Substance Use/Abuse: Mei Ling reported occasionally using cannabis but stated her usage has decreased significantly since leaving the food industry. She reported currently "smoking out" once a month, when her roommates are willing to share their cannabis with her.

Pain: 3/10. Mei Ling reported overall body aches related to both the physical altercation in which she engaged at the bar as well as her arrest and was noted to have some bruising along one arm as well as on the right side of her face.

Current Psychiatric Symptoms

Depression: Mei Ling reported feeling down and fatigued.

Anxiety: Mei Ling reported anxious thoughts related to her financial situation as well as muscle tension and heart palpitations.

Panic: Mei Ling denied any symptoms related to panic.

Mania: Mei Ling denied any symptoms of mania or hypomania.

Psychosis: Mei Ling denied any symptoms of psychosis.

Trauma: Mei Ling reported that her parents "just yelled" at her "all of the time" and frequently used corporal punishment as their primary form of discipline.

Eating Disorder: Mei Ling denied any symptoms of an eating disorder.

Risky Behaviors/Sexual Activity: Mei Ling initially denied engaging in any risky behaviors but then asked, "Does hooking up count?" She ultimately reported having had approximately one new sexual partner each month for the past year and then indicated that her "hook-ups" would sometimes purchase items she might need such as groceries or give her "money for rent and stuff."

Mental Status Exam

Appearance: Mei Ling presented to the clinical interview wearing torn jeans, platform heels, and a bralette with an oversized cardigan.

Behavior: Mei Ling initially presented as resistant and resentful but became more cooperative as the session progressed.

Speech: Mei Ling's speech was generally within normal limits.

Mood: Mei Ling reported her mood as "whatever." When asked for clarification she shrugged and again said, "It's whatever. How would you feel if you had to come talk to some stranger for no reason?"

Affect: Mei Ling's affect was generally blunted.

Thought Process: Mei Ling's thought process was generally logical, linear, and goal directed.

Thought Content: Mei Ling denied suicidal ideation, homicidal ideation, delusions, and hallucinations.

Orientation: Mei Ling was oriented to person, place, situation, and time.

Recent Memory: Mei Ling's recent memory was intact.

Remote Memory: Mei Ling's remote memory was intact.

Attention/Concentration: Mei Ling's attention and concentration were sufficient.

General Knowledge: Mei Ling's general knowledge was within normal limits.

Language: Mei Ling's receptive and expressive language skills were within normal limits.

Insight: Mei Ling presented with fair insight.

Judgment: Mei Ling presented with poor judgment.

Answer Key #3

Diversity Considerations

Because Mei Ling identifies as a Chinese American who immigrated to the United States during infancy and also reported a significant amount of conflict with her parents, it is important to consider the role acculturative stress might play in her presentation. Specifically, she may be experiencing some form of internal conflict related to having to navigate the values and norms of more traditional Chinese culture, as embodied by her parents, with the values and norms of majority culture in the United States (Schwartz et al., 2010). Her comments regarding her parents indicate a significant amount of intergenerational conflict which is not uncommon in immigrant families (Yasui & Dishion, 2007). Because young immigrants, especially those who arrive in the United States as infants, often acculturate faster than their parents, the clinician should consider how a potential acculturation gap could have contributed to Mei Ling's oppositional behaviors as well as her estrangement from her family. In the United States, individuals of Asian descent are often referred to as the "model minority" and Mei Ling may have been exposed to stereotypes related to that construct as well as other stereotypes associated with Asian women, leading her to ultimately act out in a maladaptive fashion as a reaction to or rejection of these stereotypes.

The information Mei Ling shared during the clinical interview appears to indicate that she is struggling with challenges associated with low socioeconomic status (SES), including food scarcity and potential housing instability. These factors, in combination with her racial and immigrant identities, may intersect in ways that increase her vulnerability to psychosocial stress (Williams & Mohammed, 2009). Taken together, these factors suggest that Mei Ling is struggling to survive, and her associated behaviors could be easily overpathologized.

This context becomes especially relevant when considering Mei Ling's admission of sometimes receiving access to basic needs from a sexual partner after engaging in sexual activity. While Mei Ling did not self-identify as a sex worker, her report does raise concerns regarding survival sex which must be properly considered within the context of gender-based power differentials, economic marginalization, and sexual exploitation (Lazarus et al., 2012).

Ethical Considerations

First and foremost, clinical attention must be given to Mei Ling's history of NSSI behavior. While she denied any current suicidal ideation, she reported what appears to be a long history of NSSI with the most recent occurrence being just 2 months prior to the clinical interview. As such, a much more comprehensive safety assessment is warranted with commensurate safety planning as indicated based on the results of the assessment.

Because Mei Ling has achieved the age of majority, she is legally able to provide consent for her own treatment. That being said, she has been mandated to attend psychotherapy and so the clinician must take care to explain the nuances involved with informed consent versus assent as well as the unique nature of mandated treatment related to limits of confidentiality and the consequences of non-compliance (Knapp et al., 2013). Of note, because Mei Ling identities as a content creator, additional unique boundary issues are also salient in this case. Clinicians should avoid reviewing any content Mei Ling is posting on social media as doing so could potentially compromise their ability to remain objective within the context of the therapeutic relationship. If Mei Ling happens to mention somehow incorporating the clinician into the online content she is posting, the clinician should reinforce appropriate professional boundaries (Zur, 2015).

There are aspects of Mei Ling's presentation that could potentially result in significant countertransference on the part of a clinician that may negatively impact the clinician's ability to be compassionate and effective. Clinicians are strongly encouraged to remember ethical principles related to respect for patient autonomy and dignity – this case, so as to avoid pathologizing Mei Ling and some of the survival strategies in which she has reportedly engaged. Clinicians working with Mei Ling should also consider the impact of low socioeconomic status on patient access to healthcare, including mental health care, and how difficulty accessing services can comprise a system barrier to care.

Legal Considerations

Because Mei Ling is being mandated to attend treatment, it is important for the treating clinician to understand whatever duty to the court must be taken into account for the local jurisdiction. Legal obligations owed by the clinician can often include providing regular updates regarding progress being made in treatment including information regarding a patient's overall compliance and level of risk (Melton et al., 2017). It is incumbent upon the clinician to discuss this aspect of mandated treatment with Mei Ling as part of the informed consent process so that Mei Ling does not feel betrayed or blindsided when the clinician sends certain information to the court. Because Mei Ling has a history of initiating physical altercations with others, the clinician must clearly inform her of the mandated reporting required by clinicians associated with the 1976 Tarasoff ruling.

While it is outside the scope of this volume to serve as a resource for the specialty practice of forensic psychology, it is important to note that Mei Ling may be eligible for a mental health diversion or restorative justice program, depending on the jurisdiction in which she resides. Such programs allow young adults with mental health disorders to seek alternatives to incarceration but do require treatment compliance as well as regular check-ins with the court (Lurigio & Snowden, 2009). Of note, Mei Ling may wish her clinician to communicate with her attorney, especially if a mental health diversion or restorative justice program is being considered, and if this is the case, the clinician will need to ensure that any and all appropriate ROIs are signed.

Diagnostic Impressions and Justification

F91.2 Conduct Disorder, Adolescent-Onset Type, Moderate.

While there is certainly nuance to consider in Mei Ling's situation, she does meet diagnostic criteria for conduct disorder given the reported repetitive and persistent pattern of behavior in which she has violated the basic rights of others, violated major age-appropriate societal norms, or both. It is clear from her report that this pattern of behavior extends much further back than the 12 months required by the DSM-5-TR. At the same time, she was very recently arrested and ordered into treatment, meeting the DSM-5-TR requirement that at least one symptom be presented within the immediately preceding 6 months. By her own report, Mei Ling meets at least 6 of the 15 criteria listed in the DSM-5-TR, exceeding the required 3 needed to qualify for the diagnosis. Specifically, Mei Ling reported a history of having bullied others throughout junior high and high school and has been arrested multiple time for initiating physical altercations, most recently having been arrested for using a weapon during an altercation. She has reportedly also been in trouble with local law enforcement several times due to shoplifting, often from more expensive stores such as Sephora and Ulta. She reported having run away from home at least twice prior to turning age 18, and also reported frequently being truant from school beginning about the fifth or sixth grade. Given Mei Ling's reported conflict with her parents, roommates, and others (including local law enforcement) as well as her difficulties in maintaining employment, it seems reasonable to suggest that she is experiencing impairment in multiple domains of functioning.

Because Mei Ling is 18 years old, she can only be diagnosed with conduct disorder if diagnostic criteria for antisocial personality disorder are not met. While there is significant overlap between the two diagnoses, there is some evidence to suggest that Mei Ling is engaging in some behaviors out of a sense of desperation so that she can have her basic needs met and engage in the work she wants to do as a content creator. There is also some evidence to suggest that she feels at least some remorse regarding both her past and current behaviors. Additionally, even given all the problematic aspects of Mei Ling's presentation, she does appear to be future focused and actively working toward the career she would ultimately like to have. While clinicians may differ in their overall conceptualization of Mei Ling's case, it seems possible that, with the appropriate support and community resources, Mei Ling symptoms could fully remit, especially given the environmental contributors, including a lack of financial resources. Her overall presentation actually seems to have improved in some ways since moving out of her parents' home. For example, while she bullied peers in junior high and high school, she did not give any indication that she was fired from her jobs due to treating co-workers poorly and, in fact, indicated that most of her socialization recently has been with her roommates and co-workers. Additionally, while she frequently chose to miss school, she does not appear to have chosen to miss work; rather, she was often late to her shift. Her concern for her future, now having been ordered into treatment, may also serve as motivation for change. Within this context, it is important to note that she did comply with the order to present for treatment and that. while initially resistant, she became more cooperative as the clinical interview progressed. These distinct aspects of Mei Ling's overall presentation seem to indicate that her emotional and behavioral difficulties are not rooted in a pervasive and inflexible characterological etiology but rather serve as maladaptive responses to the difficult situations she has been experiencing since childhood. As such, a diagnosis of conduct disorder seems more appropriate than a diagnosis of antisocial personality disorder at this point. As noted in the DSM-5-TR, all patients ultimately diagnosed with antisocial personality disorder must have first received a diagnosis of conduct disorder but not all patients with conduct disorder progress to the point of being diagnosed with antisocial personality disorder.

The DSM-5-TR allows for several specifiers associated with the conduct disorder diagnosis. Because it seems as though Mei Ling's symptoms manifested when she was between 11 and 13 years old, the adolescent-onset specifier is more appropriate than the childhood-onset specifier. Additional specifiers can be utilized to identify the presence of limited prosocial emotions, lack of remorse or guilt, callousness, lack of concern regarding performance, and shallow affect. There is no evidence currently indicating that any of those specifiers could be appropriately applied to Mei Ling at this point. Finally, there are specifiers that can allow for the delineation of mild, moderate, and severe symptoms, depending on the level of impairment being experienced by the patient.

Psychodynamic Case Conceptualization

Psychodynamic theory posits that early caregiver relationships inform internalized relational templates and other aspects of each individual's internal world. Mei Ling's description of her parents as well as her current relationship with them suggests that she experienced some disrupted attachment, which likely undermined her ability to develop secure attachment, the foundation for trusting adult relationships as well as the ability to self-regulate and become successfully autonomous in adulthood. Mei Ling also appears to be experiencing significant unconscious conflicts associated with internalized aggression and unresolved relational trauma. Mei Ling's difficulties in inhibiting her impulses and regulating her emotions and behaviors overall seem indicative of compromised ego functioning as well as dependence on primitive defenses such as acting out, splitting, and minimizing. Mei Ling's desire to work as a content creator on social media is particularly interesting from a psychodynamic perspective. It is possible that her desire to work as a content creator and influencer serves as a projection of a false self whose purpose is to garner external validation while masking internalized feelings of inadequacy. Specifically, Mei Ling's focus on beauty and skincare may represent an overinvestment in narcissistic defenses.

Treatment goals informed by psychodynamic theory could include increasing Mei Ling's insight into unconscious conflicts, of which she may not be aware, and strengthening ego functions, so that she can engage in improved affect tolerance and impulse control. She would also benefit from exploring internalized objects. Additionally, Mei Ling would benefit from developing a more coherent sense of self. Overall, treatment should be aimed at improving her emotional and behavioral regulation.

As is generally the case in psychodynamic psychotherapy, treatment should begin with the clinician establishing a safe and consistent holding environment in which the therapeutic relationship can ultimately develop. As treatment progresses, it will be important for the clinician to interpret both defense mechanisms in which Mei Ling may engage during treatment as well as transference that might become evident. Clarification and confrontation can also be utilized to help Mei Ling develop insight into the unconscious motivations driving behavior, including those that appear to be aimed at meeting previously unmet developmental needs. Mentalization can be incorporated into treatment to support Mei Ling's ability to reflect on her own internal states as well as the internal states of others. Once the working-through stage of treatment has been reached, Mei Ling and her clinician can work through the unconscious internal conflicts affecting Mei Ling's presentation.

Cognitive Behavioral Conceptualization

Mei Ling is currently being impacted by several situational factors contributing to her presentation, including financial stress and interpersonal conflict with multiple individuals, while her behavioral patterns are being maintained by the negative reinforcement that comes with avoidance, the positive reinforcement available on social media platforms, and a lack of adaptive coping strategies that can be deployed in moments of distress. Mei Ling's presentation is also likely being influenced by negativistic core beliefs regarding her own unworthiness as well as the general untrustworthiness of others. Intermediate beliefs in the form of assumptions and attitudes as well as negative automatic thoughts are, in all likelihood, also contributing to Mei Ling's presentation.

Because Mei Ling initially presented as resistant to treatment, the first goal of CBT would ideally be to increase her motivation to participate in psychotherapy even though treatment is, in her particular case, court ordered. Once Mei Ling is more amenable to treatment services, the clinician can help her improve insight into the relationship between her cognitions, emotions, and behaviors and also help her restructure maladaptive cognitions. Mei Ling would also benefit from improving her ability to utilize adaptive coping strategies when overwhelmed by emotions.

Motivational interviewing can be implemented at the outset of treatment to explore any ambivalence Mei Ling may continue to experience after the clinical interview as well as to explore more about the goals she identified. Psychoeducation can then be provided regarding the collaborative nature of CBT, the CBT triangle, and the distinct functions of both primary and secondary emotions, after which Mei Ling can begin keeping a mood log and a thought log. Socratic questioning can be utilized to help Mei Ling examine evidence both for and against maladaptive thoughts. The clinician can teach Mei Ling mindfulness-based adaptive coping strategies to help her learn how to better manage her episodes of emotional and behavioral dysregulation. Additionally, the clinician can utilize behavioral activation as a proactive approach to managing Mei Ling's symptoms. Finally, because of how dysregulated Mei Ling can become as well as her history of NSSI behaviors, a full course of dialectical behavior therapy should not be ruled out as DBT has been proven to be effective in improving patients' distress tolerance skills and maintain safety.

Biopsychosocial Conceptualization

Given that Mei Ling reported that her parents are probably depressed and that her father may struggle with substance abuse, genetic factors contributing to Mei Ling's presentation cannot be ruled out, although difficulties related to acculturation as well as other currently unknown factors may also contribute to her parents' presentations. Mei Ling also reported a history of chronic sleep deprivation as well as chronically poor nutrition and a generally sedentary lifestyle, all of which can negatively impact mood. Additionally, Mei Ling reported some cannabis use, although apparently less now than when she was working in the food industry. While her use of cannabis does not appear chronic and seems to be occasional, it may still contribute to emotional blunting and/or avoidance, which, in the long run, can negatively influence her overall ability to cope with overwhelming affective states. Psychological factors contributing to Mei Ling's presentation include likely disrupted attachment stemming from both early caregiver experiences as well as the somewhat disengaged parenting she reported experiencing as an older child and adolescent. Additionally, it is likely that maladaptive core beliefs play a role in Mei Ling's emotional and behavioral dysregulation. It is also important to consider the aspects of Mei Ling's history that seem indicative of trauma as well as the fact that trauma is dysregulating and disorganizing to the human person, often in ways that result in later emotional and behavioral dysregulation. It is equally important to consider the continued state of chronic deprivation in which Mei Ling lives as well as the stressors and risks associated with her SES and their implication as social determinants of health.

Because Mei Ling initially presented as resistant to treatment, the clinician's first goal can be to improve her level of intrinsic motivation as well as change talk. Treatment goals informed by the biopsychosocial model could include supporting Mei Ling in improving sleep, nutrition, and overall physical health while pursuing referrals to address any underlying neurobiological issues contributing to her dysregulated mood and behavior. Additional goals could include reducing dependence on maladaptive defense mechanisms while increasing the use of adaptive defense mechanisms. Finally, treatment goals can include improving social and financial stability as well as access to community-based resources.

Motivational interviewing can be utilized to support Mei Ling in exploring any resistance to treatment while helping her clarify her values and goals. Mei Ling would benefit from psychoeducation regarding the mind/body connection, especially with regard to the roles sleep, nutrition, and physical activity can play in supporting optimal mental and physical health outcomes. Referrals to a psychiatrist as well as a registered dietitian should be considered while the clinician can provide psychoeducation regarding sleep hygiene and the harmful effect cannabis can have, especially on a still-developing brain. Interventions curated from CBT and DBT could support Mei Ling in improving her ability to tolerate distress and restructure the cognitions likely contributing to her distress. The clinician could also provide Mei Ling with information regarding low-income housing if needed, and should definitely provide her with resources to related to food acquisition and healthcare as well as information related to resources for vocational training.

Clinical Case Vignette #4

Demographic Information and History

Name: Wayne Hollenbeck.

Demographic Information: 32-year-old Caucasian male.

Medical Diagnoses: None reported.

Reason for Referral: Wayne presented to the clinic at the recommendation of his attorney after he was arrested on suspicion of intentionally starting two fires, one in northern California and one in southern California. During the clinical interview, he acknowledged having intentionally set the fires, stating, "My lawyer told me not to tell you this, but I don't get the point of being here if I'm not supposed to tell you anything. Aren't you supposed to keep things secret?"

Clinical Interview Data

Interpreter Used: No.

Current Psychosocial Stressors: Wayne reported he was recently arrested and initially held without bail, but that a judge recently agreed to allow bail (which was provided by his parents). He reported disliking the detention facility where he was held after being arrested and stated that there are ongoing legal proceedings related to his case.

Protective Factors: Wayne presented as calm and amenable throughout the clinical interview. He also reported having a close and supportive relationship with his mother. Wayne reported enjoying physical activity and stated that he exercises regularly.

Developmental History: Wayne reported believing that he met his developmental milestones within normal limits.

Academic History: Wayne reported having received average grades in junior high and high school. He reported having enjoyed his physics and chemistry classes but otherwise did not generally enjoy school. He denied any history of having undergone a psychoeducational evaluation as well as any history of special education. Wayne denied ever having attended college and reported that he began working immediately after high school as a delivery driver for a large national chain. Wayne reported "still technically" being employed by the company although currently on leave and also informed the clinician that he has been serving as a volunteer firefighter for several years.

Social History: Wayne reported getting along well with neighbors and said that he usually socializes with co-workers as well as friends from the local fire station. He denied currently dating anyone, stating, “It’s hard to date when I live with my folks.”

Household: Wayne reported living with his parents and siblings (two sisters and two brothers) in his childhood home.

Previous Psychiatric History: Wayne denied any history of having received mental health services but did report often feeling sad and lonely as an adolescent.

Family Psychiatric History: Wayne denied any family history of mental illness but also acknowledged that mental health is not generally discussed in his family as the men are supposed to be “tough, you know, and keep everything inside.”

History of Self-Harm: Wayne denied any history of NSSI behaviors.

Wellness Profile

Sleep: Wayne reported that he generally sleeps 6–8 hours each night and also occasionally naps during the day.

Diet: Wayne reported that his diet primarily consists of whatever his mother prepares. He stated that she cooks simple meals daily, usually consisting of beef or chicken with potatoes or other vegetables.

Elimination: Wayne denied experiencing any gastrointestinal distress or elimination issues.

Technology: Wayne reported that he has been spending much of the day on his phone or computer, playing games or participating in various online forums such as Reddit, but that prior to his arrest he was too busy working “and doing other things” to spend much time online.

Physical Activity: Wayne reported that he occasionally goes to the gym to lift weights and also enjoys hiking and camping. Of note: Wayne also reported that he enjoys rock climbing.

Substance Use/Abuse: Wayne reported regularly using cannabis. He reported smoking three to four times a week and occasionally making edibles at home with his siblings. Of note: Wayne reported that he began collecting lighters when he began using cannabis at around 14 years of age and further reported owning over 100 lighters. Wayne also reported that he will usually consume three to four beers when at home in the evenings.

Pain: 0/10.

Current Psychiatric Symptoms

Depression: Wayne reported sometimes feeling sad and fatigued, but that his symptoms are transitory. He attributed feeling down to still living with his parents and "not being where [he] wants to be in life."

Anxiety: Wayne reported occasionally experiencing racing thoughts and muscle tension, specifically when anticipating a conflict with his father or his union boss at his place of employment. Of note: Wayne reported "almost overwhelming relief" when watching flames, stating, "It's almost like a meditation, you know? I could be totally stressed out, just getting more and more tense every day, but then I watch the flames and everything just feels better."

Panic: Wayne denied any symptoms related to panic.

Mania: Wayne denied any symptoms of mania or hypomania.

Psychosis: Wayne denied any symptoms of psychosis.

Trauma: Wayne denied any history of trauma but did say that his father "was pretty rough" on him as a child and adolescent. When Wayne was again asked about any history of abuse he said, "No, no, no – nothing like that. But you know how men from that generation are. Nothing is ever good enough but they want you to be perfect. He was a bully. He still is a bully. But he never hit any of us for anything."

Eating Disorder: Wayne denied any symptoms of an eating disorder.

Risky Behaviors/Sexual Activity: Wayne denied engaging in any risky behaviors.

Mental Status Exam

Appearance: Wayne presented to the clinical interview wearing jeans and a polo shirt.

Behavior: Wayne presented as calm and cooperative during the interview, sitting very still on the couch and watching the clinician carefully throughout the session.

Speech: Wayne's speech was generally within normal limits.

Mood: Wayne briefly shrugged when asked about his mood then said, "About what you would expect." When asked to clarify, he stated, "I'm worried that there's something seriously wrong with me. What do you want me to say?"

Affect: Wayne's affect was generally restricted.

Thought Process: Wayne's thought process was generally logical, linear, and goal directed.

Thought Content: Wayne denied suicidal ideation, homicidal ideation, delusions, and hallucinations.

Orientation: Wayne was oriented to person, place, situation, and time.

Recent Memory: Wayne's recent memory was intact.

Remote Memory: Wayne's remote memory was intact.

Attention/Concentration: Wayne's attention and concentration were sufficient.

General Knowledge: Wayne's general knowledge was within normal limits.

Language: Wayne's receptive and expressive language skills were within normal limits.

Insight: Wayne presented with fair insight.

Judgment: Wayne presented with poor judgment.

Answer Key #4

Diversity Considerations

One of the most salient aspects of Wayne's presentation seems to be his internalization of traditional masculine gender norms consistent with hegemonic masculinity, which promotes toughness and emotional suppression and negatively impact psychological openness as well as help-seeking behaviors (Mahalik et al., 2003). It is possible that, if these traits were valued in his family while he was growing up and/or modeled by his father, the overall family dynamic may have prevented him from receiving needed mental health services as an adolescent, thereby contributing to the development of maladaptive coping mechanisms. Additionally, these values could have been further reinforced by his work as a delivery driver and volunteer firefighter, as the professional identities associated with both roles can emphasize resilience and stoicism. Overall, Wayne appears to belong to a White working-class patriarchal community where psychological vulnerability was equated with weakness, a common phenomenon in such demographic groups (Courtenay, 2000).

Ethical Considerations

A primary ethical consideration associated with Wayne's case involves the question of patient-clinician confidentiality as, during the clinical interview, Wayne spontaneously disclosed that he did indeed commit the crimes of which he has been accused and for which he has been arrested. The ethical codes for most helping professions, including psychology, counseling, social work, and medicine, allow for privacy and confidentiality in the vast majority of situations a patient may report, except for when the clinician has a legal responsibility to disclose information, such as in the case of mandated reports. It can be argued that the primary responsibility of the clinician is to honor privacy and confidentiality but the legal exceptions mandate clinicians to break privacy and confidentiality in very specific, and only very specific, situations. While it is outside the scope of this volume to fully explore the ethical considerations and nuances associated with each case, Wayne's situation is unique because he confessed to a crime during the course of the clinical interview. It can be argued that crimes that have already occurred, especially when they are already known to local law enforcement agencies, fall outside the scope of mandated reporting laws and requirements, although this might differ from jurisdiction to jurisdiction. Most mandated reporting laws require that authorities be contacted when minors and dependent adults are being abused and/or neglected or when a patient poses an imminent risk of harm to others, as in the case of Tarasoff reporting or dangerous patient scenarios. While any clinician working with Wayne must remain vigilant to the possibility that he may pose a threat to others in the future, his one disclosure pertaining to the fires he set seems protected due to ethical codes, legal statutes, and best practice guidelines pertaining to maintaining privacy and confidentiality for patients. That being said, it is also important to note that Wayne reported presenting for treatment at the suggestion of his attorney. While the language used indicates that Wayne is presenting for psychotherapy services voluntarily, it is recommended that the clinician confirm there is not actually a court order or diversion plan of some sort in place as the information included during the provision of informed consent is necessarily different when a patient has been ordered into treatment versus when the patient is presenting voluntarily. Specifically, guidelines and practices pertaining to privacy and confidentiality change when psychotherapy treatment has been ordered and so clarity regarding whether Wayne truly is presenting voluntarily is crucial. Additionally, again because it appears to have been the attorney who generated the referral, it would be important for the clinician to clarify whether Wayne is to be receiving psychotherapy services or if the attorney perhaps intended that some sort of evaluation be conducted. Because the answer to that question could again change the information shared during the informed consent process, clarity regarding the attorney's intention in generating the referral is needed. Additionally, if it is revealed that the attorney is interested in some sort of an evaluation, the clinician would need to consider seriously whether conducting such an evaluation is part of his/her/their scope of practice. As is always the case when a third party is involved in treatment, the clinician would need an ROI to speak with the attorney, but given the nuanced and complex nature of Wayne's presentation, including the context in which he is presenting for treatment, obtaining such an ROI and speaking with the attorney is recommended.

While Wayne denied the presence of any homicidal ideation during the clinical interview, his report of intentionally setting fires is very concerning, especially given that he is located in California, a state where "fire season" is an openly acknowledged unofficial season in some parts of the state and where fires have historically been devastating to local communities. As such, it would be incumbent upon any clinician working with Wayne to regularly assess for safety as needed so as to monitor any evolving risk factors. Because legal statutes related to what is often referred to as a duty to protect or a duty to warn differs from jurisdiction to jurisdiction, it is strongly recommended that clinicians clearly understand the laws where they practice. In some states, for example, a clearly identified victim is needed before the clinician can break privacy and confidentiality. In other states, the general threat of violence being committed in a public space is sufficient.

Legal Considerations

As noted in the preceding section, Wayne's case is complex, requiring careful consideration of ethical and legal precepts. The need to determine the nature of the referral has already been noted (i.e., determining if the attorney referred Wayne for psychotherapy or an evaluation). From a legal perspective, if the clinician determines that the attorney made the referral for evaluative purposes and if such work falls within the clinician's scope of practice and competency, Wayne must be informed that the clinician's duty is not just to him but also potentially to the referring party or the court itself and that patient-clinician privilege might then be waived especially in the case of the evaluation results being subpoenaed.

If the clinician moves forward with the evaluation and either Wayne's attorney or the court asks the clinician to evaluate Wayne's mental state at the time he set one or both fires, the clinician would need to ensure familiarity with the M'Naghten Rule, the legal standard used in many jurisdictions to determine whether or not a patient understood the nature of his/her/their own actions at the time an offense was committed. Less relevant may be the question of whether or not Wayne is competent to stand trial, given that he presented as fully oriented and articulate, and had already consulted with his attorney and followed the attorney's advice. That being said, the clinician should still remain vigilant regarding Wayne's ability to participate in a trial if needed.

Diagnostic Impressions and Justification

F63.1 Pyromania.

Based on the information gathered during the clinical interview, the diagnosis that seems to best fit the most concerning aspects of Wayne's presentation is pyromania. Wayne spontaneously disclosed having set the two fires for which he was arrested. He also reported that watching flames is almost meditative for him, releasing built-up tension and helping him find a sense of relief. The DSM-5-TR includes a criterion for pyromania related to a patient's sense of pleasure, gratification, and/or relief when exposed to or experiencing a fire and specifies participating in their aftermath. Within this context, it is important to note that Wayne reported serving as a volunteer firefighter. While he did not disclose what motivated him to become a volunteer firefighter, it would be interesting to explore whether or not serving as a volunteer firefighter might provide him with the opportunity to engage with fire or the aftermath of a fire and thus serve as a vehicle for pleasure, gratification, or relief. Wayne also reported some interest in fire paraphernalia, noting that he collects lighters and has over 100.

No other factors or diagnoses appear to account for Wayne's presentation. It does not appear, based on his report, that there was any primary or secondary gain associated with setting the fire. It also does not appear as though he set the fire because he was angry or acting out in a vengeful manner. There is no reported history of neurodevelopmental disorder to account for his behavior, nor did he report any psychiatric symptoms associated with a psychotic process. There is also no other evidence to suggest a history of conduct disorder or antisocial personality disorder.

Psychodynamic Case Conceptualization

Based on Wayne's report, it seems as though he experienced his father as critical and emotionally withholding when he was growing up, and also as though that is still his experience of his father, even as an adult. Wayne's relationship with his father could have led him to develop a harsh superego characterized by internalized shame, causing him to develop unconscious feelings of inadequacy. While Wayne's relationship with his father could have contributed to some form of intrapsychic ambiguity, his relationship with his mother seems to reflect some sort of maternal enmeshment, which may in turn be representative of a developmental arrest in the separation/individual process. Because Wayne reported that watching fire brings him a sense of overwhelming relief, it can be posited that his fire-setting behaviors serve as a form of maladaptive affect regulation and may actually be representative of suppressed rage. Additionally, setting fires may somehow provide Wayne with a sense of power and control in a situation where he might otherwise feel helpless and inadequate. Based on his report and on his presentation in clinic, Wayne appears to engage in intellectualization, projection, and displacement as defense mechanisms. Wayne's work as a volunteer firefighter is especially interesting as may serve as a form of reaction formation against his own aggressive impulses by allowing him to undo his destructive tendencies in a socially sanctioned manner. Other aspects of Wayne's presentation seem to indicate that he has struggled and/or is currently struggling to develop a coherent adult identity, specifically because of his continued dependence on his family, especially his mother. Finally, fire itself is a deeply symbolic medium in a variety of cultures, and it may therefore be interesting to consider what fire means specifically for Wayne. For some individuals, fire represents rage and destruction while for others fire serves as a symbol of purification and transformation. In Wayne's case, setting fires may serve as a symbol of taking back power and control from whatever figures he feels have stolen his power. Given his likely underlying feelings of inadequacy and shame, fire may also represent as attempt to somehow cleanse himself from whatever deficiencies he feels he possesses.

Treatment goals grounded in psychodynamic theory could include helping Wayne develop insight into the unconscious internal conflicts likely contributing to his fire-setting behaviors as well as the symbolic meaning fire might hold for him. The clinician could also support Wayne in identifying and articulating his affective states while strengthening his ego functioning. Additionally, the clinician could support Wayne in modifying any internalized maladaptive object relations while helping him resolve the developmental arrest that appears to be present.

As is always the case in psychodynamic psychotherapy, the clinician should begin by establishing a safe and consistent holding environment, which can then serve as the context for all other interventions. The clinician can support Wayne in engaging in free association and, when Wayne is ready, provide interpretations of the defense mechanisms and transference manifesting within the therapeutic alliance. Ultimately, the therapeutic relationship established between Wayne and his clinician could provide the opportunity for Wayne to experience a corrective emotional experience, which could then lead to a reparative relationship, ultimately providing Wayne with a reorganized internal working model less dependent on maladaptive affect regulation strategies.

Cognitive Behavioral Conceptualization

Wayne's overall presentation is likely being influenced by maladaptive core beliefs that are influencing the way in which he is interpreting the world around him as well as impacting his interactions with others. It is also likely that Wayne is experiencing negative automatic thoughts related to his own worthiness (or lack thereof) and that these automatic thoughts reflect more deeply rooted cognitive distortions, such as dichotomous thinking, catastrophizing, and minimization.

Overall, Wayne's behavioral pattern seems indicative of avoidance-based coping, which is being reinforced by the relief he feels after engaging in a maladaptive coping strategy such as substance use and fire-setting.

Given Wayne's history and the current presenting problem, an initial goal of treatment should be to establish a collaborative therapeutic relationship that invites trust and provides structure. While Wayne is apparently presenting for treatment voluntarily, he is involved in a challenging legal situation and did choose to begin treatment at the recommendation of his attorney. As such, another important initial goal might be to formally assess his readiness for change and address any ambivalence that might arise from such a conversation. Once a collaborative therapeutic relationship has been established, the clinician could support Wayne in improving his insight into his affective experiences and also improving his repertoire of adaptive coping strategies. It would also be helpful if the clinician could help Wayne identify and restructure both cognitive distortions and maladaptive core beliefs.

Wayne would benefit from psychoeducation regarding the CBT model to help him develop insight into the relationship between his cognitions, affective experiences, and behaviors. Motivational interviewing could be utilized to address any reported ambivalence and support Wayne in committing to change. An emotion wheel can be utilized to support Wayne in developing the emotional vocabulary needed to effectively articulate his emotional experiences. Additionally, thought logs and mood logs can be used to help him learn how to identify cognitions and feelings. Wayne would also benefit from learning adaptive coping strategies to replace the maladaptive coping strategies in which he currently engages. Specifically, interventions curated from mindfulness-based stress reduction and dialectal behavior therapy may be helpful as they could teach him to be more aware of his affective experience without judgment or reactivity and also tolerate any emotional reactivity he may experience. Socratic questioning, the downward arrow technique, and behavioral experiments could all be implemented to evaluate and reframe cognitive distortions while challenging maladaptive core beliefs.

Biopsychosocial Conceptualization

Wayne did not report having been diagnosed with any neurodevelopmental disorders or medical issues but did report fairly significant substance use, specifically, cannabis and alcohol, nearly every day of the week. It is very likely that his substance use is impacting his executive functioning skills, including his ability to inhibit his impulses, as well as impacting his mood. Chronic cannabis use specifically, especially when begun during adolescence, is associated with long-term affect regulation difficulties (Volkow et al., 2014). From a psychological perspective, Wayne's presentation appears to be impacted by significantly maladaptive coping strategies, likely rooted in cognitive distortions along with issues related to developmental arrest. Unfortunately, the almost cathartic experience he reported when watching fire is likely reinforcing the use of fire-setting as a way of managing overwhelming affective experiences. Based on his report, he seems to have struggled with mental health issues for a significant period but, due to the culture in his family around mental health and potentially the socialization of men with regard to their expression (or lack thereof) of emotion, was not able to receive the support he needed as an adolescent. The underlying etiology of Wayne's difficulty articulating his emotional experiences is likely multifactorial and includes the modeling provided by his father, but alexithymia should not be ruled out. While Wayne denied any history of abuse, it seems reasonable to suspect that he experienced some form of disrupted attachment given the information he shared regarding his father. Finally, it is important to consider the role Wayne's environment plays in shaping both his past and current emotional and behavioral presentation. Based on Wayne's report, his family appears to adhere to a traditional patriarchal structure where male emotional expression is discouraged and stoicism is modeled. Wayne reported having what appears to be generally adequate social connections but also seems to want more intimate and gratifying relationships, which he feels prevented from recognizing because he continues to live in his family home. Additionally, it seems likely that the legal proceedings associated with his fire-setting and subsequent arrest are causing some sort of distress, both because of the direct impact of the proceedings on his life but also because of the ways in which his employer, co-workers, and family members may be responding.

From a biopsychosocial perspective, an appropriate treatment goal would be to support Wayne in reducing his substance use, especially given the role substance use is playing in maintaining his symptoms. It would be appropriate to support Wayne in developing insight into his affective experiences while also improving his repertoire of adaptive coping strategies. Additionally, it is recommended that the clinician help Wayne learn how to both identify and address maladaptive thought patterns and core beliefs. If Wayne expresses a desire to move out of his family's home or otherwise indicates that living with his family is not congruent with his culture, the clinician could then support him in progressing some autonomy from his family of origin in a developmentally appropriate manner. Wayne would also benefit from increased meaningful social support.

Motivational interviewing could be used at the outset of treatment to assess Wayne's readiness to change and also to help him develop insight into the role substance abuse may be playing in his life. The clinician may also wish to provide Wayne with psychoeducation regarding the long-term effects of both cannabis and alcohol use on both his body and his mind. There is a variety of interventions that could support Wayne in developing insight into his cognitions and affective states, including emotion wheels, journaling, etc. Because of how dysregulated Wayne can become, implementing interventions from DBT to improve his overall distress tolerance would likely be helpful. Additionally, interventions commonly utilized in CBT could support Wayne in identifying and challenging maladaptive cognitions and beliefs. Assertiveness training may support Wayne in beginning to navigate relational boundaries with his family while encouraging him to explore additional vocational opportunities that may allow for greater autonomy as well as a career that perhaps better aligns with his values. While Wayne currently engages with various online communities, he would benefit from in-person social interactions. Given that he enjoys a wide variety of activities such as hiking and rock climbing, he may benefit from joining social groups with similar interests.

Clinical Case Vignette #5

Demographic Information and History

Name: Tala Pole.

Demographic Information: 28-year-old Native American woman.

Medical Diagnoses: Cerebral palsy (CP; wheelchair dependent); epilepsy (seizures well controlled with medication)

Reason for Referral: Tala presented to the clinic at the insistence of her mother and grandmother after she was caught shoplifting for the third time. Tala reported that she had been attempting to steal a small stuffed animal when she was caught, and she also stated that she has previously stolen a variety of small items such as lip gloss, gum, and mints. Per Tala, she had not been aware that the store's security guard was standing at the end of the aisle when she attempted to place the small stuffed animal in her backpack, but he had apparently been watching her because he had recognized her from a previous encounter. Tala reported having shoplifted several times as an adolescent without ever having been caught and that she only recently began to shoplift again after feeling "the urge just build up and up and up." Tala endorsed significant regret regarding her shoplifting but also reported that "it just feels so good" whenever she is able to shoplift without getting caught.

Clinical Interview Data

Interpreter Used: No.

Current Psychosocial Stressors: Tala denied any psychosocial stressors outside the potential legal consequences of her shoplifting behaviors.

Protective Factors: Tala reported having a close and supportive relationship with her mother and grandmother. She reported feeling connected to her extended family members as well as other members of her tribe. Tala reported regularly engaging in cultural activities with members of her tribe, and she also reported having kept in touch with several friends from the small private college she attended.

Developmental History: Tala reported that she was born prematurely, at 30 weeks gestation, via emergency Cesarean section, but was unable to provide additional information. She did report having been held in the neonatal intensive care unit (NICU) for an unspecified period and that she was somewhat delayed in meeting developmental milestones related to gross motor movements such as crawling and walking. She also stated, however, that she met all other developmental milestones within normal timeframes.

Academic History: Tala denied any history of psychoeducational testing or having received special education services. She reported having attended private school throughout her academic career, including when she attended college, and she reported having had a 504 plan in place during certain aspects of her educational trajectory, to allow for accommodations associated with her reliance on her wheelchair. Tala reported having majored in sociology and that she has recently been considering attending graduate school. Tala reported being currently employed in the human resources department of her local hospital but said she may want to pursue a master's degree in social work to facilitate a career change.

Social History: Tala reported having an active and busy social life, including regularly meeting friends for brunch or dinner. She also reported that she has been "talking to" a man she met on a dating app and that she is considering meeting him in person.

Household: Tala reported living at her family home with her mother and grandmother. She reported having a younger brother who lives out of state and is currently pursuing a doctoral degree in anthropology. She also reported having a younger sister who recently married and moved to a different part of the state. Of note: Tala reported that her father passed away several years ago due to cirrhosis of the liver.

Previous Psychiatric History: Tala denied any history of mental health concerns or ever having receiving psychotherapy services.

Family Psychiatric History: Tala reported that her father drank heavily for most of her life. She denied any other family psychiatric history.

History of Self-Harm: Tala denied any history of NSSI behaviors.

Wellness Profile

Sleep: Tala reported that she generally sleeps 8–9 hours each night. She denied any concerns regarding sleep onset or maintenance.

Diet: Tala reported that she usually skips breakfast as she "is not a morning person" and that she usually eats lunch out with colleagues. Tala also reported that she frequently eats dinner out on the weekends but that, during the week, she eats dinner at home with her mother and grandmother. Tala reported that she prefers to "eat clean" although she will make exceptions when eating out.

Elimination: Tala denied experiencing any gastrointestinal distress or elimination issues.

Technology: Tala reported that she will sometimes scroll through Instagram or check her dating app but otherwise does not engage in much technology use outside of her work.

Physical Activity: Tala reported having previously played adaptive sports but that she "stopped sometime during college." She reported now attending an adaptive yoga class once a week and using resistance bands and free weights at home to exercise her upper body.

Substance Use/Abuse: Tala denied any history of substance use or abuse.

Pain: 0/10.

Current Psychiatric Symptoms

Depression: Tala reported sometimes feeling sad and down but that these feelings are transitory.

Anxiety: Tala denied any symptoms of anxiety apart from her concern regarding what would happen to her if she continues to steal.

Panic: Tala denied any symptoms related to panic.

Mania: Tala denied any symptoms of mania or hypomania.

Psychosis: Tala denied any symptoms of psychosis.

Trauma: Tala denied any history of trauma.

Eating Disorder: Tala denied any symptoms of an eating disorder.

Risky Behaviors/Sexual Activity: Tala denied engaging in any risky behaviors.

Mental Status Exam

Appearance: Tala presented as petite and slight.

Behavior: Tala was cooperative and forthcoming.

Speech: Tala's speech was generally within normal limits.

Mood: Tala reported feeling anxious and upset, stating repeatedly, "What's wrong with me? I don't want to steal. I want to stop! I just can't do it."

Affect: Tala's affect was constricted and tearful, so congruent with reported mood.

Thought Process: Tala's thought process was generally logical, linear, and goal directed.

Thought Content: Tala denied suicidal ideation, homicidal ideation, delusions, and hallucinations.

Orientation: Tala was oriented to person, place, situation, and time.

Recent Memory: Tala's recent memory was intact.

Remote Memory: Tala's remote memory was intact.

Attention/Concentration: Tala's attention and concentration were sufficient.

General Knowledge: Tala's general knowledge was within normal limits.

Language: Tala's receptive and expressive language skills were within normal limits.

Insight: Tala presented with fair insight.

Judgment: Tala presented with poor judgment.

Answer Key #5

Diversity Considerations

Because Tala identifies as Native American and also reported being active within her tribal community, it is recommended that the clinician explore Tala's specific tribal affiliation and any variables associated with her specific tribe that should be taken in account during the course of psychotherapy. In general, indigenous communities tend to approach health and wellness through holistic approaches and so Tala should be asked if there are any particular culturally congruent practices in which she would want to engage as a part of treatment. Clinicians working with indigenous patients should, as much as possible, honor the traditional knowledge systems to which their patients have access. It is also recommended that clinicians remember that many marginalized communities, including the members of indigenous communities, may not trust healthcare providers or the legal system and so more time and care should be invested in the development of the therapeutic alliance. Because Tala must navigate both her traditional culture and mainstream American culture, she may receive conflicting messages about most, if not all, domains of life, including healthcare and mental health. These messages may impact her manner in which she chooses to approach treatment as well as her overall presentation.

While Tala appears to be fairly independent, she is wheelchair dependent, a diversity variable that can cause her to encounter structural barriers as well as the possible internalization of ableist narratives.

Ethical Considerations

While Tala appears to have initiated psychotherapy services voluntarily, her presenting problem does include both historical and ongoing issues related to shoplifting, which, if the shoplifting continues, could have significant legal consequences. Because nothing Tala has reported up to this point consists of information that would require a clinician to file a mandated report, the clinician must maintain Tala's confidentiality.

Legal Considerations

While a significant aspect of Tala's presenting problem is the shoplifting in which she has engaged, she did not report any ongoing legal proceedings. During the informed consent process, it is recommended that the clinician clearly explain to Tala what might happen should any legal action be taken against her, up to and including that courts will sometimes subpoena records. As such, the clinician should ensure that all documentation is completed in a timely manner that adheres to the highest of professional standards.

Diagnostic Impressions and Justification

F63.3 Kleptomania.

Tala meets the DSM-5-TR diagnostic criteria for kleptomania as she struggles against impulses to steal items she does not need. The items she steals are also of no significant value. Tala's confusion regarding her own behavior seems to indicate that she does, indeed, steal impulsively and, also, is unable to stop herself although she experiences distress related to this behavior. Of note: she did report feeling gratified immediately after each theft. Based on the information Tala reported, it does not seem as though she has been shoplifting out of anger or a desire to extract revenge. It also does not seem as though there is another psychological issue such as psychosis or mania contributing to her symptoms.

Psychodynamic Case Conceptualization

From a psychodynamic perspective, it is likely that Tala's repeated shoplifting is an outward manifestation of unresolved internal conflict stemming from early childhood experiences. It is important to note that, while Tala did not report any significant trauma such as sexual abuse of physical abuse, her history is significant for medical trauma. Specifically, she was born prematurely and placed in the NICU, after which she was diagnosed with CP and epilepsy. Early childhood experiences that result in such significant medical diagnoses and require ongoing medical intervention and support can disrupt the development of body autonomy and mastery while also interrupting the child's ability to develop a sense of personal agency. Tala also reported that her father abused alcohol, ultimately passing away from related complications, which may have disrupted the development of an internalized paternal object. It is interesting to note that the items Tala steals are small and potentially comforting and childlike (e.g., the small stuffed animal). This may indicate a sort of regression into earlier developmental stages as well as a desire to exert control over her environment or maybe even over her past. Tala's reported confusion about her own behavior may indicate conflict between ego ideals and impulsive drives with the actual shoplifting behavior representing underlying desire for autonomy and self-soothing. In this way, Tala's shoplifting behavior could be a manifesting of these underlying conflicts and drives, serving as a maladaptive way of expressing distress while also having previously unmet developmental needs met. Because Tala is able to reflect on her own behavior, there is evidence that suggests an observing ego allowing her to be introspective – at the same time, however, her overall behavioral presentation is indicative of defense mechanisms such as repression and denial, which are likely impeding her ability to access the more salient symbolic meanings associated with her behavior.

Appropriate treatment goals would be to increase Tala's insight into her unresolved internal conflicts and motivations as well as early object relations. The clinician could also support Tala in strengthening her overall ego functions, which would in turn support her developing more adaptive coping strategies while improving her judgment. It may also be important to identify and work through any points of developmental fixation or regression that might be impacting Tala's presentation, so as to address the potential developmental arrest. Finally, because Tala identifies as Native American and is an active participant in her own cultural traditions, and is also wheelchair dependent due to her medical diagnosis of CP, it may be important for the clinician to support Tala in developing a cohesive narrative regarding her lived experience as a

Native American woman with a disability that affirms both her vulnerabilities and agency.

Within the context of psychodynamic psychotherapy, appropriate interventions include establishing a safe and consistent holding environment wherein any affect, including shame, ambivalence, and grief, can be articulated, thereby moving the patient from having to externalize her behaviors toward improved insight and emotional integration. Such a holding environment can create the opportunity to corrective emotional experiences that can ultimately result in a reparative relationship. It would also be appropriate to interpret any transference that emerges within the therapeutic alliance as well as the potential symbolic meanings associated with Tala's shoplifting. Because of how grounded Tala is in her culture, it may be interesting and helpful to explore any relevant cultural metaphors or tribal narratives that resonate with Tala as she explores and works through both her history and current behavioral presentation. This intervention may support Tala in developing a cohesive self-narrative that fully incorporates all aspects of her identity. Finally, it may be appropriate to support Tala in processing through any unresolved grief related to the passing of her father as well as any grief associated with her own disrupted developmental trajectory due to her medical diagnoses of CP and epilepsy.

Cognitive Behavioral Conceptualization

From the perspective of CBT, Tala's repeated engagement in shoplifting can be understood as a maladaptive behavior being maintained by cognitive distortions as well as reinforcement contingencies. Specifically, Tala's behavior may be driven by negative core beliefs associated with her feelings of self-worth or agency, with the short-term emotional relief she experiences after shoplifting serving as the reinforcer. It is, of course, also possible that certain cognitions are allowing her to rationalize her behavior, so as to reduce guilt in the moment she is shoplifting, thereby serving as negative reinforcement. That being said, because Tala reported experiencing guilt and recrimination in the long run, her behaviors are also likely contributing to her underlying negative core beliefs. Tala's likely negative core beliefs and cognitive distortions may have developed in response to her physical disability as well as the early loss of her father, with social messages associated with dependence, inadequacy, or otherness further compounding her symptoms. Overall, Tala appears trapped in a self-perpetuating cycle of emotional and behavioral dysregulation resulting in maladaptive coping strategies that run the risk of negatively impacting multiple domains of living.

CBT treatment goals could include supporting Tala in learning how to identify and restructure the cognitive distortions related to her shoplifting behaviors while also developing insight into the deeper underlying core beliefs in which these cognitive distortions are likely rooted. It would also be important to teach

Tala how to recognize behavioral triggers so she can ultimately improve her overall ability to regulate her affect and behavior without having to resort to maladaptive coping strategies such as shoplifting. This does, of course, mean that improving Tala's repertoire of adaptive coping strategies as well as her problem-solving skills would also serve as important treatment goals.

The clinician could utilize a variety of CBT interventions to support Tala in reaching her treatment goals, such as Socratic questioning and guided discovery, to help her consider the evidence both for and against the automatic thoughts contributing to her behaviors. The downward arrow technique could also be utilized to explore underlying core beliefs potentially driving her behavior and associated distress. Tala would benefit significantly from learning adaptive coping strategies that can be based in a variety of evidence-based manualized treatment grounded in CBT, such as DBT, MBSR, and/or ACT. Behavioral activation can also be utilized to support participation in reinforcing prosocial activities, which can then reduce vulnerability to impulsive behavior. Thought records, mood logs, and other homework assignments can be provided to Tala to support her overall engagement in the therapeutic process, so as to more effectively facilitate change.

Biopsychosocial Conceptualization

Tala reported a medical history significant for CP and epilepsy, both of which are neurodevelopmental in nature and, in all likelihood, related to her premature birth and subsequent admission to the NICU. Tala reported that her CP requires her to utilize a wheelchair, which she does successfully, and that her epilepsy is well controlled. That being said, the presence of neurological conditions as well as Tala's premature birth and NICU stay may have contributed to atypical developmental experiences, specifically, difficulties associated with sensorimotor integration and executive functioning skills. Tala denied any additional neurodevelopmental diagnoses and also denied having required any special education services while in school, but it is possible that her medical diagnoses and her associated disability may have impacted her opportunities for autonomy, self-efficacy, and mastery. It is also important to note that chronic medical conditions can contribute to psychological distress, especially when associated with social stigma, environmental barriers, or both. It should also be noted that Tala's NICU stay may also have disrupted early attachment processes. Tala's overall presentation is interesting because she does, in general, present as very high functioning, with decent insight into her behavior as well as motivation to change, but she is also clearly impaired with regard to impulse control, as she is unable to inhibit her impulse to shoplift. Tala's presentation does seem to indicate the presence of internal conflict as well as overreliance on maladaptive coping strategies to regulate her mood. While Tala denied any history of trauma, she also reported that her father utilized alcohol in a manner that ultimately ended his life, which may have contributed to disrupted attachment, unresolved grief, and/or feelings abandonment. Tala reported having several significant protective factors in place, including a supportive relationship with her mother and grandmother, long-lasting friendships, and engagement with her cultural community as well as consistent employment and future goals. However, her experiences as a disabled Native American woman may also at times expose her to both explicit and implicit forms of discrimination, which could over time potentially contribute to internalized ableism, chronic stress, and feelings of frustration and marginalization.

When formulating treatment goals grounded in the biopsychosocial perspective, it is appropriate to consider the ways in which psychological treatment can support physiological functioning. In Tala's case, it would be appropriate to consider goals that could support optimal neurological and physiological functioning while increasing her participation in health maintenance behaviors that support emotional and behavioral regulation. Tala would also benefit from improving insight into her affective states and behaviors, especially as they relate to her shoplifting. The clinician could also support Tala in developing additional adaptive coping strategies. It may also be beneficial for the clinician to support Tala in identifying specific goals she would like to achieve both during the course of therapy and after.

With the appropriate ROI in place, the clinician could coordinate care with Tala's neurologist. If the clinician is trained as a health psychologist or neuropsychologist, the clinician could also provide psychoeducation regarding epilepsy and seizure thresholds as well as interventions to support Tala's seizure threshold. Given that little to no information is known regarding Tala's history of medical interventions, the clinician may wish to consider referrals to clinic-based occupational therapy (OT) as well as clinic-based physical therapy (PT), so that the requisite professionals can assess Tala and determine what, if any, OT and PT interventions may be appropriate. The PT might, for example, be able to recommend modified/adaptive versions of physical exercise that could enhance mood and help Tala regulate her emotions and behaviors. Interventions taken from CBT and DBT could help Tala identify and challenge distorted cognitions while improving her distress tolerance skills. Additionally, interventions taken from ACT might support Tala in clarifying her values and long-term goals and then support her in determining how aligned her choices and behaviors are with those values and long-term goals. Of note, because Tala identifies as Native American and is very much involved in her culture, it may be appropriate to consider collaborating with tribal health, elders, and/or spiritual leaders, if Tala wishes their involvement in treatment and is willing to sign the requisite ROIs.

Conclusion

In conclusion, the disruptive, impulse-control, and conduct disorders outlined in this chapter represent a complex and clinically significant category of psychiatric conditions that emerge primarily in childhood and adolescence but can certainly contribute to enduring problematic patterns of behavior, impairment, and distress across the lifespan, both for the identified patient as well as for relatives and other loved ones. Whether a patient presents with ODD, IED, conduct disorder, pyromania, or kleptomania, accurate case conceptualization and diagnosis as well as evidence-based treatment is needed to mitigate the impairment and distress associated with these disorders. The five clinical case vignettes included in this chapter are meant to serve as an introduction to the various diagnoses included in the associated chapter of the DSM-5-TR, reflecting the potential nuances associated with each disorder while also capturing the contextual factors possibly associated with each diagnosis. Hopefully the clinical case vignettes included in this chapter also facilitated critical thinking regarding diversity-related factors, ethical considerations, and legal considerations.

Readers familiar with the DSM-5-TR might note that a clinical case vignette was not provided for antisocial personality disorder, which does appear in the associated DSM-5-TR chapter. Antisocial personality disorder is categorized as a Cluster B personality disorder in the DSM-5-TR, which means it is characterized by dramatic, emotional, and/or erratic behavior (APA, 2022). In addition, antisocial personality disorder is specifically characterized by a pervasive disregard for the rights of others as well as frequent violation of those rights. Diagnostic criteria for antisocial personality disorder includes failure to conform to social norms, deceitfulness, impulsivity, irritability, reckless disregard for the safety of self and/or others, consistent irresponsibility, and a lack of remorse with regard to how one's comments, choices, and behaviors may injure others (APA, 2022). A patient must be at least 18 years old to qualify for a diagnosis of antisocial personality disorder but must also have been diagnosed with conduct disorder before turning 15 years. When evaluating a patient for antisocial personality disorder, the clinician must also consider whether another personality disorder better accounts for the patient's presentation as well as whether another psychiatric disorder, such as schizophrenia, might be present. While some members of the general public or pop psychology sources might refer to the symptom cluster present in antisocial personality disorder as psychopathy, psychopathy is not an official diagnosis in the DSM-5-TR. Patients with antisocial personality disorder are often stigmatized, especially by media sources, but antisocial personality disorder represents a severe characterological disturbance that can significantly negatively impact the life of the patient. Additional information regarding antisocial personality disorder as well as a representative clinical case vignette can be found in Chapter 14: Personality Disorders.

Ultimately, the purpose of this chapter has been to lay the foundation for understanding disruptive, impulse-control, and conduct disorders and encourage clinicians to think critically about diversity-related variables, ethics, and laws while working with patients who meet the diagnostic criteria for the disorders outlined in this chapter. Readers are encouraged to continue considering how patient presentations are shaped by biological, psychological, and social factors as well as how creating compassionate, relational environments can both facilitate and sustain behavioral transformation.

References

Alegría, M., Green, J. G., McLaughlin, K. A., & Loder, S. (2010). *Disparities in child and adolescent mental health and mental health services in the US.* William T. Grant Foundation. https://wtgrantfoundation.org/library/uploads/2015/10/Alegria-Disparities-in-Child-and-Adolescent-Mental-Health.pdf.

APA (American Psychiatric Association). (2022). *Diagnostic and statistical manual of mental disorders* (5th ed., text rev.). American Psychiatric Publishing.

Chaplin, T. M., & Aldao, A. (2013). Gender differences in emotion expression in children: A meta-analytic review. *Psychological Bulletin, 139*(4), 735–765. https://doi.org/10.1037/a0030737.

Courtenay, W. H. (2000). Constructions of masculinity and their influence on men's well-being: A theory of gender and health. *Social Science & Medicine, 50*(10), 1385–1401. https://doi.org/10.1016/S0277-9536(99)00390-1.

Dettlaff, A. J., & Boyd, R. (2020). Racial disproportionality and disparities in the child welfare system: Why do they exist, and what can be done to address them? *The Annals of the American Academy of Political and Social Science, 692*(1), 253–274. https://doi.org/10.1177/0002716220980329.

Fonagy, P., & Target, M. (2002). Early intervention and the development of self-regulation. *Psychoanalytic Inquiry, 22*(3), 307–335. https://doi.org/10.1080/07351692209348990.

Knapp, S., Younggren, J. N., VandeCreek, L., Harris, E., & Martin, J. N. (2013). *Assessing and managing risk in psychological practice: An individualized approach* (2nd ed.). American Psychological Association.

Lazarus, L., Chettiar, J., Deering, K., Nabess, R., Shannon, K. (2012). Risky health environments: Women sex workers' struggles to find safe, secure and non-exploitative housing in Canada's poorest postal code. *Social Science & Medicine, 73*(11), 1600–1607.

Lurigio, A. J., & Snowden, J. (2009). Putting therapeutic jurisprudence into practice: The growth, operations, and effectiveness of mental health court. *Justice System Journal, 30*(2), 196–218.

Addis, M. E., & Mahalik, J. R. (2003). Men, masculinity, and the contexts of help seeking. *American Psychologist, 58*(1), 5–14. https://doi.org/10.1037/0003-066X.58.1.5.

Mahalik, J. R., Burns, S. M., & Syzdek, M. (2007). Masculinity and perceived normative health behaviors as predictors of men's health behaviors. *Social Science & Medicine, 64*(11), 2201–2209. https://doi.org/10.1016/j.socscimed.2007.02.035.

McWilliams, N. (2011). *Psychoanalytic diagnosis: Understanding personality structure in the clinical process* (2nd ed.). Guilford Press.

Melton, G. B., Petrila, J., Poythress, N. G., & Slobogin, C. (2017). *Psychological evaluations for the courts: A handbook for mental health professionals and lawyers* (4th ed.). Guilford Press.

Morris, A. S., Silk, J. S., Steinberg, L., Myers, S. S., & Robinson, L. R. (2007). The role of the family context in the development of emotion regulation. *Social Development*, *16*(2), 361–388. https://doi.org/10.1111/j.1467-9507.2007.00389.x.

Rivas-Drake, D., Syed, M., Umaña-Taylor, A., Markstrom, C., French, S., Schwartz, S. J., Lee, R., & Ethnic and Racial Identity in the 21st Century Study Group. (2014). Feeling good, happy, and proud: A meta-analysis of positive ethnic-racial affect and adjustment. *Child Development*, *85*(1), 77–102. https://doi.org/10.1111/cdev.12175.

Schwartz, S. J., Unger, J. B., Zamboanga, B. L., & Szapocznik, J. (2010). Rethinking the concept of acculturation: Implications for theory and research. *American Psychologist*, *65*(4), 237–251.

Steinberg, L. (2014). *Age of opportunity: Lessons from the new science of adolescence*. Houghton Mifflin Harcourt.

Sue, D. W., Sue, D., Neville, H. A., & Smith, L. (2019). *Counseling the culturally diverse: Theory and practice* (8th ed.). Wiley.

Volkow, N. D., Baler, R. D., Compton, W. M., & Weiss, S. R. B. (2014). Adverse health effects of marijuana use. *New England Journal of Medicine*, *370*(23), 2219–2227. https://doi.org/10.1056/NEJMra1402309.

Williams, D. R., & Mohammed, S. A. (2009). Discrimination and racial disparities in health: Evidence and needed research. *Journal of Behavioral Medicine*, *32*(1), 20–47.

Yasui, M., & Dishion, T. J. (2007). The ethnic context of child and adolescent problem behavior: Implications for child and family interventions. *Clinical Child and Family Psychology Review*, *10*(2), 137–179. https://doi.org/10.1007/s10567-007-0016-9.

Zur, O. (2015). *Boundaries in psychotherapy: Ethical and clinical explorations*. American Psychological Association.

Chapter 14

Personality Disorders

Emily Longfellow

The DSM-5-TR defines personality disorders as enduring patterns of inner experience and behavior that significantly differ from cultural expectations (APA, 2022). Symptoms associated with personality disorders, regardless of the specific personality disorder, generally emerge during adolescence or early adulthood and are pervasive, inflexible, and stable over time (APA, 2022). Like many other disorders included in the DSM-5-TR, personality disorders generally cause impairment in important areas of functioning and include cognitive changes and affective changes (APA, 2022). While personality disorders are rare, they are not as rare as thought by the general public, given that they are estimated to affect between 9 and15 percent of the general population (APA, 2022). Diagnosing personality disorders requires careful consideration and assessment, as well as thorough understanding of a patient's cultural context (as behavioral presentations considered normative in one culture may be perceived as pathological in another). Additionally, while personality disorders tend to emerge in adolescence and early adulthood, clinicians are encouraged to remember that personality traits in adolescence might fluctuate and so the diagnosis of a personality disorder should only be considered on personality traits that have become stable over time and across contexts.

The categorical model of understanding personality disorders groups all 10 personality disorders into 3 clusters with other similar personality disorders. Cluster A includes personality disorders considered to result in odd or eccentric behavior, including paranoid personality disorder, schizoid personality disorder, and schizotypal personality disorder (APA, 2022). Paranoid personality disorder is generally characterized by a pervasive mistrust of others with significant suspicions regarding the motives and intentions of others (APA, 2022). Schizoid personality disorder is characterized by marked detachment from social relationships while schizotypal personality disorder is characterized by extreme discomfort in close relationships accompanied by cognitive and/or perceptual disturbances (APA, 2022). Cluster B includes personality disorders understood to result in erratic behaviors often experienced as overly dramatic or overly

DOI: 10.4324/9781003586531-15

emotional by others, including antisocial personality disorder, borderline personality disorder, histrionic personality disorder, and narcissistic personality disorder (APA, 2022). Generally speaking, antisocial personality disorder is subsequently characterized by a pattern of disregard for the rights of others as well as regular violation of the rights of others (APA, 2022). Borderline personality disorder is characterized by significant impulsivity that occurs within the context of unstable interpersonal relationships as well as disturbances in self-image, cognition, and affect (APA, 2022). Histrionic personality disorder is characterized by extreme emotionality and attention-seeking behavior, and narcissistic personality disorder is characterized by a need for grandiosity and admiration as well as a lack of empathy for the experiences of others (APA, 2022). Finally, Cluster C, which includes avoidant personality disorder, dependent personality disorder, and obsessive-compulsive personality disorder, can be generally understood as the cluster representing personality disorders that result in excessively anxious or fearful behaviors (APA, 2022). Avoidant personality disorder is subsequently characterized by extreme social inhibition and feelings of inadequacy while dependent personality disorder is characterized by submissive and clinging behaviors born out of an intense fear of separation (APA, 2022). Obsessive-compulsive personality disorder is characterized by intense preoccupation with perfectionism and control (APA, 2022).

The DSM-5-TR also includes an alternative model for understanding personality disorders that considers dimensional traits as well as functional impairments as core components of each personality disorder. This alternative model assesses personality disorders using just two criteria: level of personality functioning and pathological personality traits (APA, 2022). Level of personality functioning takes into account both impairments in self-concept and impairments in interpersonal functioning (APA, 2022). Pathological personality traits consist of five domains: negative affectivity, detachment, antagonism, disinhibition, and psychoticism, measured across 25 facets (APA, 2022). While the alternative model does not yet include all 10 personality disorders included in the categorical model, it does include antisocial personality disorder, avoidant personality disorder, borderline personality disorder, narcissistic personality disorder, obsessive-compulsive personality disorder, and schizotypal personality disorder.

Clinical Case Vignette #1

Demographic Information and History

Name: CeCe Hart.

Demographic Information: 37 years old, White female.

Medical Diagnoses: No relevant medical diagnoses were reported.

Reason for Referral: CeCe was referred to the clinic by her employee assistance program (EAP) after finalizing her divorce from her husband. CeCe utilized her employer's EAP to assist in the divorce, stating she wanted him "out of her life as quickly as possible." She believed he was cheating on her with multiple women. However, her husband insisted he had never had an affair. Her contact person for the EAP recommended CeCe receive counseling. CeCe was hesitant, as she reported not having had a good experience in the past. CeCe presented for treatment at the request of her EAP, but she was unsure if she could trust anyone to discuss the hardships of her divorce.

Clinical Interview Data

Interpreter Used: No.

Current Psychosocial Stressors: CeCe recently got a divorce from her partner and was worried about paying rent without his financial support. CeCe reported not having a support system on which she can rely.

Protective Factors: CeCe has a steady remote job and has two dogs she loves and cares for.

Developmental History: CeCe reported meeting all developmental milestones on time.

Academic History: CeCe completed high school and some college courses, but she dropped out of college in her sophomore year.

Social History: Throughout her life, CeCe has never had close friends; as she reported that once she gets close to others, they will either begin using what she has said against her or lie to her to "spite" her. She believes everyone is "out to get her" and has "given up" wanting to have close relationships. CeCe was once married but recently got divorced due to believing her partner was unfaithful to her. CeCe does not have any siblings and has a strained relationship with her parents.

Household: CeCe lives in an apartment alone with her two dogs. Her ex-husband moved out within the past year during the divorce.

Previous Psychiatric History: CeCe received psychotherapy in her first year of college for symptoms of stress and worry but terminated treatment prematurely because she did not believe her therapist had her best interests at heart.

Family Psychiatric History: CeCe reported no family psychiatric history.

History of Self-Harm: CeCe reported no history of self-harm.

Wellness Profile

Sleep: CeCe reported having difficulty falling asleep, as she will get out of bed multiple times to ensure she has locked all the windows and doors. She consistently fears someone may break into her apartment. CeCe frequently wakes up if she hears noises in her apartment and worries it could be an intruder. This fear then prevents her from falling back asleep quickly. She reported getting approximately 6–7 hours of sleep each night.

Diet: CeCe reported eating three meals a day with an occasional afternoon snack. She reported taking multivitamins and supplements regularly. No concerns with eating were reported.

Elimination: No symptoms reported.

Technology: CeCe reported she spends about 6–7 hours on her computer each weekday. She reported watching television about 2–3 hours a day. CeCe reported minimal time on her phone and has deactivated all social media accounts, as she does not want people to know where she is or what she is doing.

Physical Activity: CeCe will take her dogs on a walk once a day 5–6 times a week for about 30 minutes. CeCe will choose a different time and walking route each walk because of concerns that someone could be stalking her at any given time.

Substance Use/Abuse: CeCe reported having a glass of wine with dinner once a week.

Pain: 0/10.

Current Psychiatric Symptoms

Depression: No symptoms reported.

Anxiety: CeCe reported constant concern about people around her exploiting or harming her. Specifically, she worries her co-workers are conspiring to get her fired, though she does not interact with them much, other than through quick emails or messages. She believes the messages she receives from co-workers are “passive-aggressive” and thinks they talk poorly about her to their boss. She reported not wanting to get into another romantic relationship, as she believes “all men cheat.”

Panic: CeCe reported no panic symptoms but is always hyperaware of her surroundings.

Mania: No symptoms reported.

Psychosis: No symptoms reported.

Trauma: CeCe was a witness to domestic violence as a child, but no reports or criminal investigations were completed. CeCe also reported emotional and physical abuse from her father and that her mother was neglectful in not protecting her from her father.

Eating Disorder: No symptoms reported.

Risky Behaviors/Sexual Activity: No concerning behaviors reported.

Mental Status Exam

Appearance: *Dress*: appropriate. *Hygiene*: adequate. Appeared stated age.

Behavior: Appropriate but guarded.

Speech: *Rate*: fast. *Articulation*: within normal limits. *Volume*: within normal limits. *Coherence*: within normal limits.

Mood: CeCe reported feeling "scared" of the interviewer because she is unsure what the interviewer will do with the gathered information.

Affect: Constricted, congruent to mood, appropriate to content of interview.

Thought Process: Circumstantial, loosening of associations.

Thought Content: Denied suicidal ideation, homicidal ideation, delusions, and hallucinations.

Orientation: Oriented to person, place, and time.

Recent Memory: Intact.

Remote Memory: Intact.

Attention/Concentration: Sufficient.

General Knowledge: Average.

Language: Within normal limits.

Insight: Poor.

Judgment: Fair.

Answer Key #1

Diversity Considerations

CeCe's background as a White American woman may influence her emphasis on independence, mistrust of others, and reluctance to seek mental health care due to potential stigma. Cultural and gender-related factors may shape her experiences of trauma, social isolation, and perceived safety concerns. Specifically, given that CeCe reported emotional abuse, physical abuse, and neglect during her childhood as well as domestic violence within her home, she may strongly distrust any dynamics she perceives to be patriarchal in nature.

Ethical Considerations

None at this time.

Legal Considerations

As an EAP referral, CeCe will have a limited number of sessions available to her. Treatment must adhere to the short time allotted to CeCe. The clinician must also act in accordance with both client privacy laws and requirements set forth by the EAP, and any nuances associated with employer reporting must be included in the initial informed consent.

Diagnostic Impressions and Justification

F60.0 Paranoid Personality Disorder.
CeCe meets Criterion A because she has a pervasive pattern of distrust, as seen by her relationships with people throughout her life. She believes friends are "out to get her" without any evidence to back this assumption. CeCe requested a divorce from her husband due to suspicions of infidelity without evidence confirming he had an affair. She perceives messages from her co-workers as attacks and reads hidden meanings behind remarks that could be interpreted as benign. CeCe meets Criterion B because these behaviors are not better explained by psychotic features.

Psychodynamic Case Conceptualization

CeCe's history of emotional and physical abuse from her father, combined with neglect from her mother, likely contributed to an insecure attachment style, leading to deep-seated mistrust and hypervigilance in relationships. Her mistrust, difficulty in forming close relationships, and belief that her husband was unfaithful, even in the absence of evidence, suggest a projection of unresolved fears from her past onto current relationships. Additionally, her hypervigilance indicates unconscious anxiety stemming from her early experiences. This conceptualization is rooted in the theory that CeCe's early childhood experiences contributed to a problematic internal working model as well as internalized objects characterized by hostility and betrayal. Because CeCe did not have a consistent nurturing caregiver, ego development was also likely impacted. CeCe appears to have a poorly integrated sense of self and engages in primitive defenses such as projection and splitting. CeCe is also likely being impacted by unconscious internal conflicts related to dependence versus autonomy and trust versus self-protection.

Appropriate psychodynamic treatment goals might include establishing a stable and reliable therapeutic alliance and increasing CeCe's insight into both unconscious internal conflicts and difficult interpersonal patterns. CeCe would also benefit from an increased capacity to tolerate difficult affective states as well as improved ego functioning, which may ultimately support her in decreasing her dependence on primitive defenses.

In psychodynamic treatment, the first intervention is always the use of a consistent and predictable therapeutic frame, with the second being empathic attunement to facilitate affective containment. CeCe would benefit from an exploration of early childhood dynamics as well as gentle interpretations, as needed, to address transference dynamics. Clarification and confrontation can also be used as needed to help CeCe improve both reality testing and general insight

Cognitive Behavioral Conceptualization

CeCe's difficulties can be conceptualized through the five-part CBT model, which posits that situations give rise to thoughts, which in turn influence emotions, behaviors, and physical sensations. Ultimately, CeCe presents with several cognitive distortions that contribute to a negative cycle in which her interpretations of events confirm and reinforce her maladaptive beliefs, increasing her emotional distress and behavioral avoidance. Cognitive distortions cause intense anxiety and fear, which then prompt avoidance behaviors like minimizing communication with colleagues and disengaging from collaborative tasks. Similarly, during daily walks with her dogs, CeCe fears that someone may be stalking her. As a result, she changes her route and times each day in an effort to stay undetected, reinforcing her belief that the world is unsafe and that constant vigilance is necessary for self-preservation. At the core of CeCe's presentation are deeply held negative beliefs about the trustworthiness of others and the reliability of safety in interpersonal and environmental contexts. These beliefs likely stem from her early experiences of interpersonal trauma, including witnessing domestic violence and enduring emotional and physical abuse from her father, compounded by the perceived neglect from her mother. These assumptions function as rigid rules that guide CeCe's daily behavior and decision making, ultimately serving as safety behaviors that maintain her distress.

Appropriate CBT treatment goals include helping CeCe identify and challenge maladaptive beliefs while improving emotional regulation. CeCe would also benefit by learning adaptive coping strategies, especially in activating situations such as at work with colleagues and when walking her dogs. Another appropriate CBT would be to reduce avoidance behaviors. Lastly, CBT could focus on strengthening CeCe's insight into how her automatic thoughts influence her emotions and behaviors, with the long-term goals of improving interpersonal relationships.

Several CBT interventions may be helpful to CeCe over the course of treatment. Psychoeducation could be incorporated at the beginning of treatment to help CeCe understand how anxiety and past trauma contribute to her distorted perceptions of threat and interpersonal danger. CeCe would also benefit from psychoeducation regarding common cognitive biases. The downward arrow could be used to uncover deeper beliefs, which would then be reframed through Socratic questioning and schema dialogue. Cognitive restructuring techniques could be used to address automatic negative thoughts while behavioral experiments could allow CeCe to test the validity of her beliefs in structured, real-life scenarios. CeCe would also benefit from learning adaptive coping skills such as diaphragmatic breathing, progressive muscle relaxation, and grounding techniques. Finally, behavioral activation strategies could be implemented.

Biopsychosocial Conceptualization

CeCe did not report any significant medical history but her persistent hyperarousal suggests possible dysregulation within the autonomic nervous system, likely exacerbated by chronic stress. Her sleep disturbances and elevated physiological arousal may reinforce cognitive distortions and contribute to emotional dysregulation. CeCe presents with cognitive distortions that seem rooted in rigid, maladaptive beliefs as well as dichotomous thinking. Her history of witnessing abuse and experiencing inconsistent caregiving has likely contributed to core beliefs around betrayal, danger, and abandonment, which can help make sense of her social isolation. Finally, CeCe's presentation may be somewhat impacted by societal narratives around gender-based betrayal and mistrust.

Treatment goals grounded in the biopsychosocial approach can include reducing the CeCe's chronic hyperarousal and improving the quality of her sleep as well as helping her identify, examine, and reframe cognitive distortions. The biopsychosocial model can also address her social isolation by increasing her engagement with others. Addressing the impact of past relational trauma on current social functioning will be essential.

Interventions may include psychoeducation regarding the mind-body connection as well as techniques such as diaphragmatic breathing, progressive muscle relaxation, and guided imagery. Sleep hygiene strategies might also be helpful as well as CBT interventions to help CeCe identify and challenge distorted cognitions related to mistrust, betrayal, and perceived persecution. Behavioral experiments could be used as well as schema therapy. Assertiveness training and communication skills training can support CeCe in re-engaging socially while maintaining a sense of control.

Clinical Case Vignette #2

Demographic Information and History

Name: Cory Whitlock.

Demographic Information: 45 years old, African American male.

Medical Diagnoses: No relevant medical diagnoses were reported.

Reason for Referral: Cory was referred to clinic per his sister's request after his sister requested a wellness check on Cory. Cory's sister reported to police she had not heard from Cory in weeks and was worried when he did not pick up his phone when she called. When police arrived, Cory answered the door and reported he did not answer the phone because he did not want to talk to his sister. Cory's sister encouraged him to go to therapy because she is worried he may be experiencing depression. Cory reported he has always been a "recluse" and does not enjoy social interactions.

Clinical Interview Data

Interpreter Used: No.

Current Psychosocial Stressors: Cory reported being "not excited" about the responsibilities that come from his promotion. Cory has a remote job where he works independently most of the time. However, his promotion will require him to do weekly check-ins with his subordinates. Cory reported this new responsibility does not cause him stress, but he states he is "not looking forward to it."

Protective Factors: Cory reported being "content" with how he lives his life, including his employment, relationship status, and familial connections.

Developmental History: Cory reported he had a speech delay as a child and meeting all other developmental milestones on time.

Academic History: Cory received an associate's degree. He reported maintaining "average" grades throughout his time in school.

Social History: Cory reported not having many friends throughout his life and only interacts with co-workers on an "as-needed" basis. Cory maintains regular contact with his sister, but he reported she is the one who always reaches out first and encourages him to visit their parents in their home.

Household: Cory lives in an apartment by himself. He has a mother and father who live in a nursing home in a nearby city and a sister who lives with her husband and daughter.

Previous Psychiatric History: Cory reported no previous psychiatric history.

Family Psychiatric History: Cory reported his sister receives therapy for anxiety-related symptoms.

History of Self-Harm: Cory denied a history of self-harm behaviors.

Wellness Profile

Sleep: Cory reported he sleeps 8–9 hours nightly. He reported no difficulties with sleep.

Diet: Cory reported eating three meals a day with a late-night snack some nights. He reported no concerns in this area.

Elimination: No symptoms reported.

Technology: Cory reported spending 8 hours a day on his computer for work. Cory reported his TV is on "all day" while he is working, eating, and while he goes to sleep. Cory reported not spending much time on his phone and does not utilize social media.

Physical Activity: Cory reported he will go on a walk around his neighborhood once a week.

Substance Use/Abuse: Cory reported drinking a beer with dinner nightly.

Pain: 0/10.

Current Psychiatric Symptoms

Depression: Cory reported symptoms of anhedonia. Cory reported feeling "indifferent" about the activities he chooses to do but said he does not enjoy completing activities with others.

Anxiety: No symptoms reported.

Panic: No symptoms reported.

Mania: No symptoms reported.

Psychosis: No symptoms reported.

Trauma: No symptoms reported.

Eating Disorder: No symptoms reported.

Risky Behaviors/Sexual Activity: No concerning behaviors reported.

Mental Status Exam

Appearance: *Dress*: appropriate. *Hygiene*: adequate. Appeared stated age.

Behavior: Appropriate, cooperative.

Speech: *Rate*: within normal limits. *Articulation*: within normal limits. *Volume*: within normal limits. *Coherence*: within normal limits.

Mood: Cory reported he felt "indifferent" but "irritated" that he had to present to therapy because his sister was concerned for him.

Affect: Flat, congruent to mood, appropriate to content of interview.

Thought Process: Logical, linear, goal directed.

Thought Content: Denied suicidal ideation, homicidal ideation, delusions, and hallucinations.

Orientation: Oriented to person, place, and time.

Recent Memory: Intact.

Remote Memory: Intact.

Attention/Concentration: Sufficient.

General Knowledge: Average.

Language: Within normal limits.

Insight: Fair.

Judgment: Fair.

Answer Key #2

Diversity Considerations

Cory is an African American man. This carries significant implications for understanding his psychological presentation and treatment experience particularly because African American men in the United States may face chronic exposure to systemic racism, discrimination, and cultural stereotypes, which can contribute to a mistrust of institutions, including law enforcement and mental health systems (Hammond, 2010). Cory's reluctance to engage with others, including his sister and the therapist, may reflect not only personality style but also culturally mediated coping mechanisms shaped by historical and/or generational trauma. Additionally, African American men are less likely to seek mental health services voluntarily and may underreport emotional distress (Neighbors et al., 2007). Cory's flat affect and "indifference" may therefore partially reflect socialized emotional suppression as well as his reluctance to engage with a system he does not trust. Additionally, because the client is a man, he may be influenced by traditional gender role expectations, especially those that discourage emotional vulnerability, dependency, or expressions of sadness. That being said, Cory's guardedness and expressed irritation at being referred to therapy may reflect internalized stigma toward mental health treatment, which is prevalent in many African American communities.

Ethical Considerations

This case illustrates the importance of informed consent and respecting a client's autonomy. It highlights the importance of understanding a client's perspective of their symptoms and differentiating between distress and the client's lifestyle choices.

Legal Considerations

Cory presented to therapy at the suggestion of his sister, following a police-initiated wellness check but presented as cognitively intact and oriented, suggesting no legal barriers to consent. That being said, the clinician may wish to confirm that Cory's agreement to engage in treatment is free from coercion, even if initiated by a concerned family member. Coerced treatment without legal mandate may be ethically and legally invalid and, at this point, there is no evidence to suggest that Cory either is conserved or needs to be conserved. Additionally, although Cory's sister initiated the referral, no information may be disclosed to her without Cory's explicit, written consent, which will be an important boundary to maintain if the sister attempts to follow up with the clinician regarding her brother's care.

Diagnostic Impressions and Justification

F60.1 Schizoid Personality Disorder.

Cory meets Criterion A because he does not desire close relationships and chooses activities that are done individually. He only interacts with close relatives when they initiate contact and does not appear to have an interest in many activities, including sexual experiences. Cory also demonstrated flat affect throughout the intake interview and appeared emotionally detached when interacting with others. Cory meets Criterion B because he is not experiencing mania or psychosis. Therefore, his symptoms are not better explained by other disorders, such as schizophrenia or bipolar disorder.

Psychodynamic Case Conceptualization

Cory's overall presentation seems grounded in maladaptive defensive mechanisms and possible early relational disruptions. His emotional indifference, flat affect, and preference for solitude suggest the use of distancing defenses to protect against affective experiences that might otherwise feel too overwhelming. His irritability at the initiation of therapy and resistance to external concern may reflect unconscious conflicts around autonomy, shame, or perceived intrusions, which could possibly become re-enacted in the therapeutic relationship, should Cory choose to remain in treatment.

From a psychodynamic perspective, an initial goal might include improving Cory's capacity for affect recognition and tolerance while increasing his insight into unconscious relational patterns, especially those associated with his avoidance of closeness, irritation with the concern of others, and generalized emotional flatness. Long-term psychodynamic services may help Cory develop a more cohesive and integrated sense of self. This process may allow Cory to eventually consider alternative ways of relating to others with more emotional authenticity and less guardedness.

Interventions stemming from psychodynamic theory could begin with supportive techniques to help build a safe therapeutic alliance, followed by interpretations when appropriate to gently point out patterns in Cory's thoughts, behaviors, and emotional responses. Interpretations could focus on transference dynamics or other interpersonal relationships. Additionally, Cory may benefit from interventions that encourage mentalization.

Cognitive Behavioral Conceptualization

Cory's presentation appears influenced by core beliefs and automatic thoughts that discourage social engagement, while his flat affect and disinterest in relationships may reflect underlying schemas related to self-sufficiency, mistrust, or a diminished sense of reward from interpersonal connection. Cory's reaction to his sister's concern may be understood as a behavioral expression of his core beliefs about autonomy, control, or the perceived intrusiveness of others. Additionally, the solitary activities in which he engages further reinforce his isolation and restrict opportunities for corrective social experiences, thereby maintaining the cycle of disengagement. Overall, his resistance to initiating contact with others or participating in more activating behaviors may stem from maladaptive assumptions that remain unchallenged in the absence of external feedback. These cognitions may also explain his diminished anticipatory pleasure in response to upcoming responsibilities at work, such as leading meetings, which require social presence and engagement with others. While he does not report subjective anxiety, his avoidance may reflect a covert form of social discomfort that has become entrenched and normalized within his worldview.

Appropriate CBT goals would include helping Cory identify his automatic thoughts and test the validity of his beliefs about others and social interaction. It may be important to increase Cory's engagement in valued activities.

Behavioral activation would be of paramount importance. Structured interventions would aim to support a gradual increase in rewarding behaviors and corrective interpersonal experiences, which may in turn foster improved emotional responsiveness, motivation, and quality of life. It is important to note that because Cory does not necessarily report distress related to his lifestyle, primary focus should be on behavioral activation and other interventions that ensure no occupational impairment arises, as he appears to be at risk of developing some difficulties at work.

Biopsychosocial Conceptualization

Cory did not report any relevant medical conditions or issues with sleep or nutrition but his lifelong pattern of social disengagement and early speech delay may suggest an underlying Cory's hesitation to engage in social interactions, including with family members and those with whom he works, may reflect entrenched maladaptive beliefs about autonomy, mistrust, or emotional vulnerability, which may be reinforced by cultural factors as well as gender-based expectations of men. Because of his lifestyle, Cory has minimal social support outside of his sister and, while he may be content with this, it appears as though he may be at risk of developing issues at work given recent changes to his position.

Interventions grounded in the biopsychosocial model could include improving Cory's insight, increasing his meaningful social engagement, and supporting his overall well-being, although any goals set should be consistent with Cory's own goals for his life and not superimposed onto him by the clinician. An additional goal could be to improve Cory's awareness of maladaptive cognitive schemas contributing to emotional flattening and interpersonal detachment.

Treatment interventions grounded in the biopsychosocial model could begin with psychoeducation about the impact of social isolation on neurobiological and emotional functioning as well as support in identifying and challenging core beliefs that reinforce social isolation. Behavioral activation can be introduced to increase engagement in meaningful activities, even if solitary at first, to reinforce routine and improve mood regulation. Once ready to engage more frequently with others, Cory can begin to increase contact with his sister or initiate brief, structured interactions with colleagues. Assertiveness training as well as social skills training may be helpful in setting him up for success.

Clinical Case Vignette #3

Demographic Information and History

Name: Travis Johnson.

Demographic Information: 25 years old, Native American male.

Medical Diagnoses: No relevant medical diagnoses were reported.

Reason for Referral: Travis was referred for therapy after pleading guilty to charges of assaulting a peace officer. Law enforcement was called when Travis was at a shopping mall complex, hiding behind planters, stating he was being followed by someone who looked just like him. Witnesses reported he was yelling "he follows" repeatedly. When police contacted Travis to encourage him to leave the shopping mall, Travis picked up a planter and threw it at an officer. Travis was taken into custody by officers after using physical force to detain Travis.

Clinical Interview Data

Interpreter Used: No.

Current Psychosocial Stressors: Travis is currently experiencing homelessness and has been homeless since he dropped out of college when he was 20 years old.

Protective Factors: Travis reported he has strong ties to his indigenous religion and believes his ancestors are still connected to him; he reported that he communicates with them regularly.

Developmental History: Travis reported meeting all developmental milestones on time.

Academic History: Travis completed high school and received average grades until college. Travis dropped out of college. He began displaying "odd" behaviors in class, such as ducking under desks because he felt the FBI was watching him, and skipping class because he got a "message from the ancestors" that there would be a natural disaster if he went to class.

Social History: While growing up, Travis had difficulty maintaining close friends. Once he moved out of state for college, he had even more difficulty establishing close relationships with his roommates and classmates. Since he became homeless, Travis has connected with other individuals experiencing homelessness. He will join homeless encampments on some nights and sleep by himself on others when he fears the others "are out to get him."

Household: Travis is currently living a transient lifestyle. He grew up with his mother, father, and younger brother, but lost contact with them when he moved out of his home state 7 years ago for college.

Previous Psychiatric History: Travis reported he was previously held on a 5150 hold 3 years ago because the police were called on him due to his erratic behavior while high on methamphetamine near a school.

Family Psychiatric History: Travis reported no previous family psychiatric history.

History of Self-Harm: Travis reported no history of self-harm.

Wellness Profile

Sleep: Travis reported he used to sleep well at night but, over the past 3 years, he has needed less and less sleep. Travis reported experiencing 3–4 hours a day, but in the form of shorter naps.

Diet: Travis averages one meal a day, stating his methamphetamine usage makes him less hungry.

Elimination: No symptoms reported.

Technology: Travis reported no use of technology, as he does not have access to a television, smartphone, or computer.

Physical Activity: Travis reported walking "all day."

Substance Use/Abuse: Travis reported smoking methamphetamine 3–4 times a week for the past 3 years. Travis reported that, after smoking a "point," he will be high for many hours. Travis reported he has made no attempts to stop using but his intake of methamphetamine has decreased in recent weeks due to not being able to afford it.

Pain: 0/10.

Current Psychiatric Symptoms

Depression: No symptoms reported.

Anxiety: Travis reported having anxiety symptoms when he is high on methamphetamine.

Panic: No symptoms reported.

Mania: No symptoms reported.

Psychosis: Travis presented with symptoms of delusions, but these specific delusions do not last longer than a couple of hours before shifting to a new delusion. Travis reported bodily delusions, such as out-of-body experiences.

Trauma: No symptoms reported.

Eating Disorder: No symptoms reported.

Risky Behaviors/Sexual Activity: Travis reported that he starting smoking methamphetamine 3 years ago.

Mental Status Exam

Appearance: *Dress*: inappropriate, wore a woman's skirt as a shirt and made a necktie into a headband. *Hygiene*: inadequate. Travis could not report the last time he took a shower or brushed his teeth. Appeared stated age.

Behavior: Lack of eye contact with assessor, detached.

Speech: *Rate*: inconsistent throughout interview. *Articulation*: within normal limits. *Volume*: quiet, soft. *Coherence*: inconsistent throughout interview.

Mood: Travis reported that he feels "weird" and he "does not trust" the interviewer.

Affect: Flat, incongruent to mood, inappropriate to content of interview.

Thought Process: Flight of ideas.

Thought Content: Denied suicidal ideation, homicidal ideation, and hallucinations. Denied delusions but presented with active delusions.

Orientation: Oriented to person. Not oriented to place, situation, or time.

Recent Memory: Impaired.

Remote Memory: Impaired.

Attention/Concentration: Distractible.

General Knowledge: Average.

Language: Within normal limits.

Insight: Poor.

Judgment: Poor.

Answer Key #3

Diversity Considerations

Travis identifies as Native American and reported strong ties to his traditional indigenous religion and spiritual beliefs, particularly in relation to communication with ancestors. These beliefs must be understood and interpreted within the context of Travis's culture and spirituality rather than pathologized as symptoms of psychosis without nuanced clinical interpretation. For many Native American individuals, spirituality includes ongoing relationships with ancestors, visions, and spiritual messages (Gone, 2013). For this client, then, it will be important to carefully evaluate the symptoms with which he is presenting and differentiate culturally normative spiritual experiences from psychotic symptoms. Further complicating his presentation is the methamphetamine use. In some communities, clinicians may be able to consult with cultural liaisons, Native healers, or tribal elders when evaluating belief systems and behaviors as well as potentially helpful treatments. Some communities may have access to culturally congruent healing practices such as sweat lodge ceremonies or talking circles. Because Travis is Native American, he may also carry the psychological burden of historical trauma, including colonization, forced assimilation, displacement, and systemic racism (Brave Heart, 2003). His disconnection from family, homelessness, and substance use may reflect indirect expressions of unresolved or unrecognized generational trauma. It may be appropriate to consider referral to a clinic that is able to provide culturally congruent care specifically for members from Travis's tribe.

Ethical Considerations

Given Travis's fluctuating mental status, delusions, and poor insight, his capacity to provide informed consent may be impaired and so clinicians must carefully consider his presentation and potentially consult with other professionals to determine whether he can consent to care. If legally mandated to participate in treatment, informed assent should still be sought, emphasizing respect for his agency, and with clear explanations regarding the limits of confidentiality in mandated settings. As noted above, there are diversity issues to consider, which must be navigated ethically by not forcing Eurocentric models of health onto

Table 14.1 Assessment data

*MCMI-IV**	*Base Rate Scores*
Clinical Personality Patterns	
Schizoid	73
Avoidant	55
Melancholic	46
Dependent	23
Histrionic	30
Turbulent	32
Narcissistic	45
Antisocial	30
Sadistic	25
Compulsive	35
Negativistic	40
Masochistic	25
Severe Personality Pathology	
Schizotypal	87
Borderline	45
Paranoid	43
Clinical Syndromes	
Generalized anxiety	60
Somatic symptom	75
Bipolar spectrum	44
Persistent depression	58
Alcohol use	50
Drug use	86
Post-traumatic stress	30
Severe Clinical Syndromes	
Schizophrenic spectrum	73
Major depression	58
Delusional	73

Note: *MCMI-IV: Millon Clinical Multiaxial Directory (4th ed.).

him but by carefully considering his overall presentation prior to providing a diagnosis. Additionally, MCMI (Millon Clinical Multiaxial Directory) results must be interpreted with caution, as standardized norms may not be validated across indigenous populations. Additional ethical concerns may become relevant as treatment reaches an end as Travis's homelessness poses ethical challenges around continuity of care and equity of access.

Legal Considerations

Travis has a history of being held on a 5150, which in California is an involuntary psychiatric hold. It indicates prior contact with civil commitment procedures due to psychiatric instability and substance use. Travis may still meet criteria for a 50 as active delusions, homelessness, and poor judgment, may meet the gravely disabled criteria. If civil commitment is pursued, which in California would be an LPS conservatorship, Travis would be entitled to legal representation, a probable cause hearing, and judicial review. Travis's methamphetamine use may complicate the legal question of eligibility for involuntary psychiatric treatment, as substance-induced psychosis alone is not sufficient for LPS conservatorship unless accompanied by a primary psychiatric condition. Additionally, Travis was arrested for assault on a peace officer and referred for mental health treatment through the court system, indicating that he is a defendant in criminal proceedings with possible diversion to treatment. If diversion to treatment is not permitted by the court and legal proceedings are begun, the clinician involved in the case may need to respond to court orders or subpoenas and should therefore follow requisite guidelines pertaining to case documentation. Of note: if a client is enrolled in a federally recognized tribe and committed his offense on tribal land or has existing legal ties to a tribal jurisdiction, tribal courts may have concurrent or exclusive jurisdiction, depending on the setting and charges.

In the United States, there is a longstanding legal obligation rooted in treaties and federal Indian law that federal and state systems coordinate culturally appropriate services for Native individuals. Clinicians must therefore determine whether Travis is eligible for services through Indian Health Services or tribally operated programs.

Diagnostic Impressions and Justification

F21 Schizotypal Personality Disorder.
Travis meets Criterion A due to his ideas of reference and persistent pattern of lacking close relationships. He began displaying "odd" behaviors in early adulthood, and his odd/paranoid thinking directs his "eccentric" behaviors. Travis meets Criterion B of symptoms not occurring during other psychiatric diagnoses because, of the psychotic features of other diagnoses, only delusions are present and there have been no depressive or manic episodes.

Psychodynamic Case Conceptualization

Travis's presentation likely stems from early relational disturbances, identity fragmentation, and defensive operations shaped by trauma and cultural dislocation. He engages in primitive defenses such as splitting, projection, and denial, which serve to externalize intolerable internal conflicts and maintain psychic cohesion in the face of overwhelming anxiety. The emergence of bizarre and shifting delusional content may reflect ego regression to an early developmental stage wherein the boundaries between self and other are insufficiently differentiated. His spiritual communication with ancestors and distrust of others may represent attempts at self-cohesion and meaning-making in the absence of secure relational anchors. The intensity of his delusional system may also be understood as a symbolic expression of unmet dependency needs and persecutory anxieties, reflecting unresolved early object loss or failed maternal attunement.

The overarching goal of psychodynamic treatment with this client would be the gradual strengthening of ego functions to support reality testing, affect regulation, and relational capacity. Specific goals might include the development of insight into unconscious processes underlying his delusional experiences, the integration of fragmented self-states, and the establishment of a more coherent and adaptive identity. Therapy should aim to foster a therapeutic alliance in which Travis could potentially begin to experience the clinician as a trustworthy and containing other, thereby allowing for the exploration of deeply rooted fears of abandonment, annihilation, and betrayal. Another important goal might be to explore the transference and countertransference dynamics that emerge in the therapeutic relationship, using these as a window into Travis's internalized object relations and defensive strategies.

Given the fragility of Travis's ego structure and his active psychosis, psychodynamic interventions must begin at a supportive-expressive level, emphasizing containment, empathic attunement, and the consistent provision of a nonjudgmental therapeutic frame. Interventions may include reflective listening, clarification of affective states, and validation of subjective experience, which aim to promote emotional articulation and reduce psychic fragmentation. As the therapeutic alliance strengthens, the clinician may gently interpret defensive operations and explore the symbolic meaning of delusional content, especially as these relate to internalized fears, dependency conflicts, and object representations. Attention to transference phenomena such as idealization, devaluation, or projection of persecutory figures can be used to bring unconscious relational patterns into awareness, while maintaining a stabilizing stance.

Cognitive Behavioral Conceptualization

Travis's presentation reflects the interaction of distorted cognitions, maladaptive core beliefs, and dysfunctional behavioral patterns that have developed and solidified over time, likely as a result of cumulative psychosocial adversity, substance use, and untreated psychotic symptoms. His persecutory and somatic delusions may represent extreme cognitive distortions rooted in maladaptive schemas related to mistrust, vulnerability, and identity confusion. These beliefs appear to be reinforced by chronic social isolation, substance-induced perceptual changes, and the lack of corrective experiences within supportive environments. His homelessness and disconnection from his family have likely exacerbated negative automatic thoughts involving perceived threat and danger, contributing to a hypervigilant cognitive style. Additionally, methamphetamine use functions as both a maladaptive coping strategy to manage distress and a physiological amplifier of psychotic symptomatology. His spiritual beliefs, while potentially protective, may also interact with delusional content in a manner that blurs reality testing and reinforces magical thinking.

The primary treatment goals within a CBT framework are to enhance the client's testing, reduce the intensity and frequency of distressing psychotic experiences, and build adaptive coping skills for managing psychosocial stressors. A critical goal might be the identification and restructuring of maladaptive beliefs and cognitive distortions, particularly those associated with threat perception, mistrust of others, and self-referential ideation. Equally important would be increasing the client's awareness of the relationship between substance use and symptom exacerbation, thereby promoting motivation for harm reduction or abstinence. The treatment should also aim to build behavioral activation strategies to improve daily functioning, sleep hygiene, and social engagement. Finally, enhancing Travis's problem-solving abilities and self-efficacy may be crucial to addressing his homelessness and supporting his long-term stabilization.

CBT interventions with Travis should likely begin with the establishment of a structured, collaborative therapeutic relationship that provides safety, predictability, and transparency, all of which are key conditions for working with patients experiencing psychosis. Psychoeducation regarding the nature of psychotic symptoms, the effects of methamphetamine, and the stress-vulnerability model could be foundational for increasing insight and promoting engagement. Specific cognitive strategies may include the use of thought records to identify and examine delusional beliefs, guided discovery to explore alternative explanations, and cognitive restructuring to reduce conviction in maladaptive interpretations. Behavioral strategies such as activity scheduling, sleep hygiene interventions, and coping skills training might support Travis's functional recovery and reduce reliance on substance use. Additionally, the use of graded exposure and behavioral experiments may help reduce avoidance behaviors and challenge hypervigilant threat perceptions.

Biopsychosocial Conceptualization

Travis's symptoms are likely being compounded by the neurotoxic effects of chronic methamphetamine use. The presence of persecutory delusions, disorganized thought processes, and impaired insight suggests significant neurocognitive dysfunction, potentially exacerbated by stimulant-induced neurochemical dysregulation. Travis evidences cognitive distortions and poor reality testing, which may be related to both substance use and longstanding personality vulnerabilities, as evidenced by elevated scores on schizotypal and schizoid personality scales. His detachment, mistrust, and emotional constriction suggest impaired social-cognitive development and deficits in affective attunement. Travis has experienced profound social disconnection from family, peers, and his broader support systems, which, when combined with homelessness and cultural marginalization, has likely intensified his psychological distress and reduced his access to stabilizing resources. While his indigenous spiritual beliefs may serve as a culturally meaningful coping mechanism, they may also be conflated with delusional content in the absence of grounding influences or culturally responsive care.

Interventions grounded in a biopsychosocial approach include stabilization of psychiatric symptoms, reduction of substance use, and improvement in Travis's functional capacity and quality of life. Travis likely needs to be evaluated for antipsychotic medication and managing the physiological effects of stimulant use. Additional goals could include fostering adaptive coping strategies and addressing trauma-related vulnerabilities and cognitive distortions. Social goals might involve securing safe housing, reconnecting Travis with community supports, and facilitating access to culturally responsive services, including those informed by indigenous healing practices.

Interventions grounded in a biopsychosocial perspective could include the implementation of a harm-reduction model to address Travis's methamphetamine use, incorporating motivational interviewing and, when feasible, referral to dual-diagnosis treatment. Supportive therapy, cognitive-behavioral strategies for psychosis (CBTp), and psychoeducation might improve Travis's adaptive coping skills, reduce symptom distress, and improve reality testing. Case management would be essential to securing stable housing, accessing public assistance, and coordinating care with culturally competent providers. It may also be important to support cultural reintegration, perhaps through linkage to tribal health programs, spiritual leaders, or indigenous community organizations.

Clinical Case Vignette #4

Demographic Information and History

Name: Brandon Brown.

Demographic Information: 35 years old, White male.

Medical Diagnoses: No relevant medical diagnoses were reported.

Reason for Referral: Brandon was referred to the clinic as a part of his probationary terms following a recent arrest at a local shopping mall. Brandon has an extensive criminal history and recently pleaded guilty to grand theft and assault of a peace officer.

Clinical Interview Data

Interpreter Used: No.

Current Psychosocial Stressors: Brandon is currently unemployed and has had difficulty maintaining employment, as he has gotten fired from previous jobs.

Protective Factors: Brandon reported to the session on time and stated he would complete all sessions to complete the terms of his probation.

Developmental History: Brandon reported meeting all developmental milestones on time.

Academic History: Brandon reported poor academic performance while in school and got expelled in his sophomore year of high school for multiple fights and bringing drugs onto campus. Brandon reported he did not return to school to complete his GED.

Social History: Brandon reported he has had few friends throughout his life, but explained he and these people get into physical and verbal fights occasionally. Brandon reported having several romantic partners in the past, but stated the relationships were never "serious."

Household: Brandon reported he "couch hops" with friends, family members, or romantic partners. Brandon reported he has not stayed in one place for more than a couple of weeks at a time.

Previous Psychiatric History: Brandon has received psychotherapy in the past to complete the terms of probation for previous charges. He reported it was "a waste of time" and reported no previous diagnoses.

Family Psychiatric History: Brandon reported he is unaware of any family psychiatric history.

History of Self-Harm: Brandon reported no history of self-harm or suicidal ideation.

Wellness Profile

Sleep: Brandon reported usually falling asleep at 1 or 2 am and will sleep until noon. He reported infrequent wakings throughout the night and does not nap during the day.

Diet: Brandon reported eating three meals a day, usually consisting of fast food or food made by the person he is staying with. He states he will snack on chips and popcorn throughout the day 3–4 days a week.

Elimination: No symptoms reported.

Technology: Brandon reported utilizing a smartphone for multiple hours at a time and reported watching approximately 4–5 hours of TV daily. He states he will usually use social media on his phone and watch TV simultaneously.

Physical Activity: Brandon reported limited physical activity, stating he will go on walks around the neighborhood occasionally and ride a bike to the store when needed.

Substance Use/Abuse: Brandon reported drinking "a couple" beers daily and denies any substance use. However, in his criminal record, he has had arrests for DUI (driving under the influence) alcohol and DUI drugs and has been arrested with heroin and cocaine on his person on different occasions.

Pain: 0/10.

Current Psychiatric Symptoms

Depression: No symptoms reported.

Anxiety: No symptoms reported.

Panic: No symptoms reported.

Mania: No symptoms reported.

Psychosis: No symptoms reported.

Trauma: Brandon reported no instances of trauma in his past. However, it is known that Brandon was the one who found his father after his father's suicide when Brandon was 12 years old.

Eating Disorder: No symptoms reported.

Risky Behaviors/Sexual Activity: Brandon reported he began drinking alcohol during his freshman year of high school. He also reported having unprotected sex with multiple sexual partners since the age of 15.

Mental Status Exam

Appearance: *Dress*: appropriate. *Hygiene*: inadequate. Appeared stated age.

Behavior: uncooperative, guarded.

Table 14.2 Assessment data

*MMPI-3**	*T Scores*
Over-reporting	75
Somatic Cognitive Functioning	
RC1	51
MLS	45
NUC	62
EAT	47
COG	63
Emotional Dysfunction	
EID	75
RCd	45
SUI	44
HLP	51
SFD	59
NFC	40
RC2	75
RC7	50
STR	59
WRY	44
CMP	42
ARX	51
ANP	53
BRF	56
NEGE	57
INTR	65
Thought Dysfunction	
THD	55
RC6	56
RC8	51
PSYC	60
Behavioral Dysfunction	
BXD	80
RC4	82
FML	65
JCP	74
SUB	74
RC9	46
IMP	49
ACT	50
AGG	78
CYN	43
DISC	76
Interpersonal Functioning	
SFI	42
DOM	42
AGGR	78
DSF	52
SAV	60
SHY	49

Note: *MMPI-3: Minnesota Multiphasic Personality Inventory (3rd ed.).

Speech: *Rate*: within normal limits. *Articulation*: within normal limits. *Volume*: within normal limits. *Coherence*: within normal limits.

Mood: Brandon reported being "annoyed" for having to complete therapy.

Affect: Constricted, congruent to mood, appropriate to content of interview.

Thought Process: Logical, linear, goal directed.

Thought Content: Denied suicidal ideation, homicidal ideation, delusions, and hallucinations.

Orientation: Oriented to person, place, and time.

Recent Memory: Intact.

Remote Memory: Intact.

Attention/Concentration: Sufficient.

General Knowledge: Within normal limits.

Language: Within normal limits.

Insight: Fair.

Judgment: Poor.

Answer Key #4

Diversity Considerations

It is important to consider Brandon's identity within the larger sociocultural context which may include broader patterns of racial and socioeconomic disadvantage, particularly given his criminal history, homelessness, and limited social support. The impact of cultural stigmatization may play a significant role in his interactions with the criminal justice system and his resistance to therapy. Specifically, his consistent unemployment, transient housing situation, and history of criminal activity all may reflect broader social inequalities that can contribute to feelings of hopelessness, marginalization, and instability. Additionally, his continued reliance on "couch hopping" and dependence on others for basic needs may perpetuate feelings of inadequacy and undermine his sense of self-worth. These socioeconomic stressors may exacerbate any underlying psychological conditions, such as aggression, poor impulse control, and interpersonal difficulties, that Brandon displays. Socioeconomic challenges can also influence Brandon's treatment engagement, as he may feel disconnected from institutional structures that he perceives as punitive or unsupportive, potentially fostering mistrust of authority figures, including therapists.

Ethical Considerations

Brandon's autonomy may be compromised by his probationary status, which could raise concerns about coercion or involuntary treatment. Although Brandon has been referred for therapy as part of his probation terms, it is important to maintain a focus on informed consent, ensuring that he understands the purpose of therapy beyond legal obligations and has the ability to make decisions about his participation. The ethical principle of justice mandates that Brandon's treatment be delivered equitably, ensuring he receives appropriate care regardless of his criminal history, socioeconomic status, or substance use. Given his legal and social marginalization, Brandon may be at risk of receiving substandard care if providers are influenced by bias or stereotypes. It is important to ensure that Brandon has access to the same level of care as any other client, including treatment for substance abuse, anger management, and emotional regulation.

Because Brandon's therapy is part of his probation requirements, there may be concerns about whether his participation or progress in therapy will be disclosed to legal authorities. Ethical guidelines stipulate that confidentiality should be maintained unless there is a clear risk of harm to the client or others, or when mandated by law. In Brandon's case, it will be necessary to discuss the limits of confidentiality upfront and ensure that he understands the potential legal implications of his treatment. For instance, if Brandon were to disclose any intentions to harm others or engage in illegal activities, the therapist would be ethically and legally required to breach confidentiality.

Legal Considerations

Because Brandon's referral to therapy is a condition of his probation, his treatment must be framed within the context of court-mandated mental health services. This status carries significant legal implications, as participation in the therapeutic process is no longer entirely voluntary but partially compelled by the state. Clinicians must be acutely aware of the statutory requirements of court-ordered treatment, including documentation protocols, attendance reporting, and progress updates that may be required by probation officers or judges. It is essential that the therapist clearly delineates the purpose and scope of the intervention, ensuring that Brandon is informed of the ways in which his participation – or lack thereof – may affect his legal standing. Failure to engage in treatment or non-compliance with court conditions could result in legal consequences, such as probation revocation or incarceration, thus placing the clinician in a position of dual accountability to both the client and the court. Records must be kept in accordance with Health Insurance Portability and Accountability Act (HIPAA) regulations and applicable state laws governing the confidentiality of mental health information. Additionally, given the possibility of court subpoenas, clinicians should create documentation with the expectation that records may be reviewed by judges, attorneys, or probation officers. Accurate, concise, and professionally worded records could not only protect the clinician legally but also support the integrity of the therapeutic process.

Diagnostic Impressions and Justification

F60.2 Antisocial Personality Disorder.
Brandon meets Criterion A because, since his high school years, he has failed to conform to lawful behaviors and is consistently irresponsible, as evidenced by his failure to maintain a job and his lengthy and consistent criminal history, indicating a lack of respect for the rights of others. Brandon demonstrates impulsivity, as well as aggressive behaviors. He meets Criteria B and C because he is over the age of 18 and has shown signs of conduct disorders since before the age of 15. Criterion D is met due to Brandon not displaying symptoms of psychosis, mania, or depressive episodes.

Psychodynamic Case Conceptualization

Brandon presents with a personality structure marked by significant impairments in ego functioning as well as difficulty in forming stable object relations. His early expulsion from school, chronic legal problems, poor employment history, and unstable interpersonal relationships suggest disruptions in early developmental stages, potentially related to attachment insecurity and unresolved trauma. The discovery of his father's suicide at age 12, an event that, surprisingly, Brandon did not acknowledge as traumatic, may represent a repressed psychic wound that has contributed to a disorganized internal world and the use of primitive defense mechanisms such as denial, projection, and acting out. His aggressive behavior, transient living arrangements, and substance use history may serve as maladaptive efforts to assert control, manage internal chaos, and suppress intolerable affect states linked to unresolved grief and rage rooted in unacknowledged trauma.

Treatment goals grounded in psychodynamic theory include fostering insight into unconscious internal conflicts, enhancing ego strength, and developing more adaptive defense mechanisms. Given his oppositional stance and guarded affect, initial therapeutic aims would include establishing a reliable and nonjudgmental therapeutic alliance that can tolerate his resistance and ambivalence about treatment. Eventually, focus would shift toward helping Brandon identify the symbolic meanings of his antisocial behavior and emotional disengagement. Particular attention should be paid to unresolved grief surrounding his father's suicide, as this unacknowledged trauma may underscore his affective constriction, hostility, and compulsive need to reject authority figures. Additional goals would include helping Brandon recognize patterns of relational disruption and to begin developing internal capacities for emotional regulation, reality testing, and reflective functioning.

Psychodynamic interventions would begin with the consistent and empathic application of the therapeutic frame to create a holding environment in which Brandon can begin to experience emotional safety and containment. Interpretation of resistance and transference phenomena would likely be important, particularly as Brandon may project his internalized aggression or mistrust onto the therapist in the form of defiance or disengagement. Clarification and confrontation may be used initially to explore the meanings behind his resistance, while deeper interpretive work would aim to uncover unconscious fantasies, conflicts, and affective state, especially those related to loss, abandonment, and authority. Attention to countertransference is essential, as Brandon's interpersonal style may evoke frustration, helplessness, or rejection in the therapist, mirroring the dynamics of his early relational environments. Over time, as Brandon becomes more capable of self-reflection, interventions would aim to help him integrate previously dissociated affect and develop a more cohesive and adaptive sense of self.

Cognitive Behavioral Conceptualization

Brandon's longstanding behavioral dysregulation, oppositional behavior, and antisocial conduct can likely be explained as learned patterns of maladaptive cognition and behavior, reinforced over time through environmental contingencies and cognitive distortions. Brandon's early expulsion from school, substance use, and repeated legal involvement likely contributed to core beliefs characterized by mistrust of authority, low self-efficacy, and a diminished sense of personal responsibility. These core beliefs may have evolved into intermediate assumptions as well as an entrenched schema of skepticism toward institutional systems and interpersonal vulnerability. Additionally, maladaptive behavioral patterns such as substance use, aggression, and impulsive decision making likely serve as both maladaptive avoidance mechanisms and maladaptive emotion regulation strategies. Brandon's inability to maintain stable relationships or employment reinforces these negative beliefs, perpetuating a self-fulfilling cycle of perceived failure and oppositional behavior.

CBT treatment goals appropriate for Brandon might include increasing insight into the relationship between his thoughts, emotions, and behaviors while supporting the development of prosocial cognitive and behavioral alternatives. Early treatment objectives might include enhancing motivation for change and fostering engagement by using motivational interviewing strategies. Subsequent goals could involve identifying and challenging cognitive distortions while also targeting skill development in anger management, impulse control, problem solving, and interpersonal communication. Additionally, the treatment should work toward restructuring Brandon's maladaptive schemas, especially those related to trust, control, and self-worth, while developing a capacity for realistic goal setting, accountability, and behavioral self-monitoring.

Appropriate CBT interventions could begin with psychoeducation about the CBT model to help Brandon understand how his thinking patterns influence his behavior and emotional reactions. Given his reluctance toward treatment, motivational interviewing techniques should be employed to foster change talk. Cognitive restructuring would be central to the intervention process, particularly in identifying and modifying maladaptive core beliefs and automatic thoughts that fuel aggression, entitlement, or antisocial behavior. Behavioral strategies such as contingency management, behavioral activation, and social skills training may be useful in reinforcing adaptive behaviors and reducing avoidance patterns. Role playing and behavioral rehearsal can be employed to improve interpersonal functioning and reduce impulsivity during emotionally charged situations. As Brandon demonstrates increased insight and engagement, self-monitoring tools such as thought records and behavior logs might be introduced to strengthen the skills being taught in therapy as well as generalization to real-world contexts.

Biopsychosocial Conceptualization

Brandon did not report and significant medical conditions, but his longstanding alcohol use, likely underreported substance abuse history, and poor hygiene suggest compromised physical well-being and potential neurocognitive impairment secondary to substance misuse. Brandon also presents with behavioral dysregulation, including impulsivity, aggression, and antisocial tendencies, as evidenced by elevated MMPI-3 scores. He also demonstrates elements of emotional disengagement and diminished interpersonal dysfunction, further supported by poor academic history, unstable housing, and a dismissive attitude toward treatment. Additionally, Brandon's transient living arrangements, unstable employment, limited social support, and extensive legal history reflect chronic environmental instability. Despite his denial of trauma, the known fact that he discovered his father's suicide at age 12 years introduces the likelihood of unresolved childhood trauma, which may be contributing to maladaptive behavioral patterns and affective detachment. It is also important to recognize the chronic stress impacting him.

From a biopsychosocial perspective, reducing substance use, enhancing behavioral regulation, and improving Brandon's interpersonal and occupational functioning are all appropriate goals. A routine medical evaluation may be warranted to assess any underlying health impacts currently affecting Brandon. An initial goal may be to increase motivation for treatment with subsequent goals aimed at improving emotional awareness and developing skills for impulse control and affect regulation. Additional goals might include stabilizing housing, strengthening prosocial supports, and facilitating access to vocational or educational services. Given Brandon's limited insight and resistance to treatment, early goals must also focus on engagement, alliance building, and leveraging his probation requirement as a pathway to sustained participation in care.

Interventions grounded in the biopsychosocial model should involve coordinated, multidisciplinary care, with possible referral to a substance use specialist or integrated dual diagnosis treatment program to address alcohol misuse and assess for stimulant or opioid dependence. Motivational interviewing may help address Brandon's ambivalence toward treatment, while cognitive-behavioral strategies can be implemented to target aggression, risk-taking, and poor judgment. Social skills training and emotion regulation work grounded in mindfulness-based stress reduction may also be beneficial. Case management will likely be essential for facilitating access to stable housing, vocational rehabilitation, and legal advocacy. Community-based programs tailored to individuals with criminal justice involvement may offer structure, accountability, and culturally competent support.

Clinical Case Vignette #5

Demographic Information and History

Name: Nicole Wang.

Demographic Information: 31 years old, Asian American female.

Medical Diagnoses: No relevant medical diagnoses were reported.

Reason for Referral: Nicole was referred to the hospital after police were called to her apartment when neighbors heard screaming and things being thrown in the home. When police entered the home, they found Nicole holding a large kitchen knife and threatening to harm herself after getting into an argument with her boyfriend. The law enforcement officers were able to take Nicole into custody without incident but deemed her to be a threat to herself and others and placed her on a 5150 hold.

Clinical Interview Data

Interpreter Used: Yes.

Current Psychosocial Stressors: Nicole is currently going through a breakup with her boyfriend of 5 months. Nicole reported she believed this man was "the one," and they would have been engaged within the coming weeks. However, Nicole also reported their relationship was "off and on" for years, and he "does not deserve her." This breakup led to the incident that led to this hospitalization.

Protective Factors: Nicole has a job as a hairdresser and makes a steady enough income to afford her rent and other bills. Nicole's parents live in the same city and meet with Nicole for dinner or coffee on a biweekly basis.

Developmental History: Nicole reported meeting all developmental milestones on time.

Academic History: Nicole completed high school with honors and completed some college credits before dropping out to attend cosmetology school. Nicole completed cosmetology school after taking a break to earn money to pay for tuition (after gambling her tuition money away). Nicole is providing cosmetology services in her apartment while looking for a salon to offer her a role.

Social History: Nicole reported growing up with her parents and younger brother in the same home since immigrating to the United States from China when Nicole was entering high school. Nicole reported having many friends throughout her life, but states these friends have "come and gone." When asked why she feels these friends have "come and gone," Nicole began to cry and stated some friends were "selfish" while other friends left the friendship because Nicole was a "horrible friend" and she "does not deserve friends because [she] is the worst person alive."

Household: Nicole lives with two roommates she met online while looking for a room to rent. Nicole reported tension between her roommates, stating they are "teaming up against her" and "constantly complaining" about Nicole's messy habits and how Nicole will bring over men without consulting with her roommates beforehand. Nicole lives in the same city where she attended high school and still sees her parents regularly. Nicole has a younger brother who lives out of state while attending graduate school.

Previous Psychiatric History: Nicole went to her college's counseling center while enrolled for a couple of months as she was referred by her Resident Advisor for difficulties with her roommates. Nicole also has had a previous 5150 hold 5 years prior for another suicide attempt that was triggered by her parents "kicking her out" of their home. Nicole reported her parents kicked her out due to "being a terrible daughter," but her parents reported that she refused to get a job, and they believed she would be motivated to get a job if she had to pay rent somewhere. In this incident, Nicole threatened to drive her car off a freeway overpass and got into a physical struggle with her father while trying to take her car keys and leave the home. Her mother called 911 and Nicole was placed on a 5150 hold at this time.

Family Psychiatric History: Nicole's mother currently attends individual therapy for anxiety-related symptoms.

History of Self-Harm: Nicole has had one other suicide attempt before the reason for referral. Nicole self-harmed in the form of overdosing on ibuprofen 3 years ago and has threatened to cut herself but has never completed this act. When Nicole overdosed on ibuprofen, a roommate found her in the bathroom and made her throw up to get the medication out of her system. No medical treatment occurred after this incident.

Wellness Profile

Sleep: Nicole reported inconsistent sleep patterns. Nicole states there will be some nights where she can sleep for 8–10 hours without issues, but then there will be other nights where she has difficulty falling and staying asleep, where she will only get 3–4 hours of sleep in total.

Diet: Nicole reported eating three meals a day with an occasional snack in the afternoon on some days. She reported there are times when she "feels fat" and has binged and purged. Nicole reported this has occurred once or twice a year since she was 18 years old.

Elimination: No symptoms reported.

Technology: Nicole reported an average of 6 hours on social media daily. Nicole also reported watching TV daily but could not specify the amount of time she spends watching TV as she will complete other tasks while watching TV, such as folding laundry or washing dishes.

Physical Activity: Nicole reported she attends pilates classes three times a week at her local gym.

Substance Use/Abuse: Nicole reported drinking alcohol "socially" and states this occurs about once a month. Nicole reported drinking in excess to the point of a "blackout" on most occasions.

Pain: 0/10.

Current Psychiatric Symptoms

Depression: Nicole reported experiencing a depressed mood some days for as long as she can remember. Nicole also reported irritability and feelings of worthlessness and "emptiness." Nicole expressed previous suicidal thoughts but reported no current suicidal ideation during the intake interview.

Table 14.3 Assessment data

*MCMI-IV**	*Base Rate Scores*
Clinical Personality Patterns	
Schizoid	43
Avoidant	30
Melancholic	60
Dependent	55
Histrionic	75
Turbulent	75
Narcissistic	43
Antisocial	45
Sadistic	20
Compulsive	65
Negativistic	34
Masochistic	32
Severe Personality Pathology	
Schizotypal	35
Borderline	90
Paranoid	55
Clinical Syndromes	
Generalized anxiety	56
Somatic symptom	45
Bipolar spectrum	40
Persistent depression	55
Alcohol use	60
Drug use	25
Post-traumatic stress	44
Severe Clinical Syndromes	
Schizophrenic spectrum	32
Major depression	45
Delusional	32

Note: *MCMI-IV: Millon Clinical Multiaxial Directory (4th ed.).

Anxiety: Nicole reported difficulty controlling worry about her relationships. She reported when she enters a relationship with a romantic partner, she believes he is "the one," even if she has only known him for a couple of days or weeks. However, when conflict occurs in the relationship, she is quick to believe the relationship is going to end.

Panic: No symptoms reported.

Mania: No symptoms reported.

Psychosis: No symptoms reported.

Trauma: Nicole reported being a victim of sexual assault while in high school from a boy she knew from school. Nicole did not report this incident, and no investigation took place.

Eating Disorder: Nicole reported she has binged and purged once or twice a year since she was 18 years old.

Risky Behaviors/Sexual Activity: Nicole reported drinking in excess to the point of "blackout" about once a month for the past couple of years. Nicole reported having had multiple sexual partners in the previous 10 years and never used any form of birth control during this time. Nicole reported having to get multiple tests completed for sexually transmitted infections (STIs) in previous years.

Mental Status Exam

Appearance: *Dress*: appropriate. *Hygiene*: adequate. Appeared stated age.

Behavior: Appropriate, cooperative.

Speech: *Rate*: within normal limits. *Articulation*: within normal limits. *Volume*: within normal limits. *Coherence*: within normal limits.

Mood: Nicole reported feeling a wide range of emotions throughout the interview, stating "a lot of emotions" were brought up while talking about certain topics.

Affect: Full, labile, hyperthymic, congruent to mood, appropriate to content of interview.

Thought Process: Circumstantial.

Thought Content: Endorsed suicidal ideation, denied homicidal ideation, denied delusions and hallucinations.

Orientation: Oriented to person, place, and situation.

Recent Memory: Intact.

Remote Memory: Intact.

Attention/Concentration: Sufficient.

General Knowledge: Within normal limits.

Language: Within normal limits.

Insight: Fair.

Judgment: Poor.

Answer Key #5

Diversity Considerations

Cultural background and immigration experience likely play a pivotal role in Nicole's psychological functioning and worldview. The transition from China to the United States during her high school years likely disrupted her social identity development and may have been accompanied by experiences of cultural dissonance, marginalization, or acculturative stress (Berry, 2005). Nicole's expressions of self-blame, intense emotional lability, and relational volatility may partly reflect internalized cultural expectations about success, filial piety, and interpersonal harmony common in many East Asian cultures (Kim, 2007). Her report of being "a terrible daughter" and the distress related to her parents' disapproval may signify shame-based coping influenced by collectivist values (Choi & Chentsova-Dutton, 2012). The fact that an interpreter was used during the interview suggests potential language-related barriers, which could contribute to feelings of isolation or difficulty articulating emotional distress in a clinical setting. Of note: mental health stigma within Asian American communities may impact Nicole's willingness to engage fully in mental health services. Cultural stigma surrounding psychiatric illness and suicide can lead to concealment of symptoms, somatization, or ambivalence toward therapeutic processes (Leong & Lau, 2001). Nicole's ambivalence toward past psychotherapy and minimal family involvement during crises may reflect such cultural influences. This highlights the importance of culturally adapted psychoeducation and collaborative treatment planning that honors Nicole's values and reduces internalized stigma (Sue et al., 2009).

Nicole's gender identity and experiences as a woman are also salient. Her emotional distress appears closely linked to romantic relationships, with intense idealization and devaluation of partners – a pattern possibly rooted in attachment insecurity but also influenced by societal gender norms that reinforce relational dependency and self-worth based on romantic validation (Gilligan, 1982). Furthermore, Nicole disclosed a history of sexual trauma during high school, which, while unreported, may contribute to persistent feelings of worthlessness and relational dysregulation. This history underscores the importance of trauma-informed care that recognizes the intersection of gender-based violence and mental health (Herman, 1992).

Additionally, Nicole appears to experience economic instability. Although she is employed as a hairdresser and earns enough to meet basic financial obligations, her informal work setting and transient housing arrangements with individuals she meets online suggest marginal economic security. These conditions may exacerbate her emotional vulnerabilities and limit access to stable healthcare, community resources, or a support system – factors particularly important for individuals with prior psychiatric hospitalizations.

Ethical Considerations

Because Nicole was admitted to the hospital under a 5150 hold following a suicide threat and possession of a knife during a domestic argument, the clinician must be vigilant in balancing Nicole's right to self-determination with the imperative to ensure her safety and the safety of others Although emergency circumstances justify temporary suspension of certain rights, the clinician should endeavor to restore Nicole's autonomy as soon as clinically appropriate, including providing clear explanations of her legal status, treatment options, and the role of consent in ongoing care. Because of Nicole's history of prior suicide attempts, threats of self-harm, and labile affective states, the clinician is also ethically required to conduct a thorough suicide risk assessment and implement appropriate interventions, which may include safety planning.

Because of Nicole's history of police involvement, family conflict, and the use of an interpreter, confidentiality concerns are magnified by the need for third-party involvement, increasing the importance of clear documentation and informed consent processes regarding what information will be shared and with whom. Consideration must also be given to whether an interpreter is available in the facility where Nicole is being held and, if not, how clinicians will be able to ensure clear, effective communication with Nicole.

Legal Considerations

Because Nicole is being held under a 5150, the clinician must ensure that all legal criteria are met and that documentation supports the necessity of the hold, including behavioral observations, suicide risk, and estimated threat level. Furthermore, Nicole's previous 5150 hold history adds complexity, as clinicians must evaluate whether she meets criteria for a more extended involuntary treatment (e.g., 5250 or LPS conservatorship) if risk persists. Involuntary hospitalization always complicates the traditional informed consent process, yet Nicole retains the right to be informed about the nature of her treatment, potential risks and benefits, and the extent of her rights within the facility.

Diagnostic Impressions and Justification

F60.3 Borderline Personality Disorder.

Nicole meets the criteria because she demonstrates a persistent pattern of unstable relationships, as evidenced by her relationships with her boyfriend and roommates as well as reported past relationships. Nicole demonstrates alternating between the extremes of idealization and devaluation in her views about others and herself. She also displays impulsive behaviors, including binge drinking, risky sexual behaviors, binge eating and purging, and self-harm behaviors.

Psychodynamic Case Conceptualization

Nicole's presentation can likely be attributed to relational disturbances rooted in early developmental experiences and internalized object relations. Her emotional lability, interpersonal instability, and self-destructive behaviors suggest features consistent with borderline personality disorder. Nicole's intense fear of abandonment, alternating idealization and devaluation of relationships, and chronic feelings of emptiness reflect unresolved early attachment disruptions and failure to integrate self and object representations into cohesive wholes (Fonagy & Bateman, 2008). Her impulsivity, self-harming behaviors, and affective instability may represent attempts to manage overwhelming internal states and ward off feared annihilation or rejection. Nicole's relationship with her parents appears ambivalent, marked by a longing for approval and proximity yet complicated by feelings of rejection and unworthiness, suggesting the presence of both dependency and aggression within her internalized parental objects. Her traumatic experience of sexual assault in adolescence, which went unreported and unprocessed, likely exacerbated internal conflict, guilt, and shame, contributing to self-punitive fantasies and reinforcing a fragmented sense of self (Davies & Frawley, 1994).

The overarching psychodynamic treatment goal may be to foster the development of a more stable and coherent sense of self and to facilitate the integration of fragmented affective experiences. Specific goals include improving affect tolerance, reducing maladaptive defenses, enhancing reflective functioning, and fostering secure therapeutic attachment (Fonagy et al., 2002). Additionally, treatment should aim to bring unconscious conflicts into conscious awareness, particularly those related to abandonment, self-worth, and dependency. Establishing insight into the cyclical re-enactments of early relational patterns in current relationships, especially with romantic partners and friends, will support Nicole in developing healthier object relations. The therapeutic process also aims to reduce self-harming behaviors by identifying their symbolic meaning and addressing the underlying emotional states they express or defend against.

Therapeutic intervention will emphasize the establishment of a consistent and empathic therapeutic relationship to serve as a holding environment. The therapist should attend to transference dynamics, particularly idealization and devaluation, and interpret these within the context of Nicole's internalized relational templates. Clarification, confrontation, and interpretation of defense mechanisms, especially projective identification and splitting could be employed to deepen insight and enhance ego strength. The clinician should gently explore Nicole's early object relations and traumatic experiences, especially those related to abandonment and betrayal, in order to facilitate the mourning of unattainable ideals and the acceptance of relational ambivalence. Emphasis on mentalization-based techniques may be particularly useful given the high borderline features identified on the MCMI-IV, fostering Nicole's capacity to reflect on her own and others' mental states and reduce interpersonal misattunement (Bateman & Fonagy, 2004). Throughout treatment, interventions should be paced in accordance with Nicole's tolerance for affect and insight, with attention on maintaining the therapeutic alliance amid potential ruptures.

Cognitive Behavioral Conceptualization

Nicole's presentation is likely the result of maladaptive core beliefs, dysfunctional thought patterns, and ineffective coping behaviors that perpetuate emotional dysregulation and self-harming tendencies. Her core beliefs may have originated from early adverse experiences, including her unprocessed sexual trauma, perceived rejection from caregivers, and prior relational instability. Nicole's intermediate beliefs and cognitive distortions (e.g., catastrophizing, mind-reading, and dichotomous thinking) are frequently activated in interpersonal contexts, particularly when she perceives signs of rejection or invalidation. For instance, when her romantic relationship ended, she interpreted the event through an absolutist lens, which contributed to suicidal ideation and impulsive behavior. Her behaviors function as maladaptive strategies to manage overwhelming affect and to elicit emotional responses from others, thus maintaining a maladaptive cycle of negative reinforcement.

Appropriate CBT treatment goals include the identification and modification of core beliefs as well as helping Nicole recognize and restructure automatic thoughts and cognitive distortions, particularly those triggered by interpersonal stress. The clinician may also wish to support Nicole in developing improved emotional regulation skills as well as improved interpersonal effectiveness. Finally, the clinician should ensure that treatment supports a reduction in self-harming behaviors.

Interventions grounded in CBT could begin with psychoeducation about the CBT model and the role of thoughts, emotions, and behaviors in maintaining psychological distress. Cognitive restructuring could help Nicole identify and challenge distorted cognitions and replace them with more balanced alternatives. Emotion regulation skills, including relaxation training, mindfulness, and distress tolerance techniques, may be integrated from dialectical behavior therapy (DBT) to support affective stability (Linehan, 1993). Additionally, assertiveness training, communication skills rehearsal, and role play may be beneficial.

Biopsychosocial Conceptualization

Nicole's MCMI-IV results reveal clinically significant elevations in the borderline, histrionic, and turbulent personality domains, suggesting a biologically mediated predisposition to affective instability and impulsivity. Sleep dysregulation and disordered eating also point to possible disruptions in neurobiological systems involved in emotion regulation and reward processing. While there is no reported family history of major psychiatric disorders aside from her mother's anxiety, Nicole's presentation may reflect heritable temperamental traits, such as emotional sensitivity, which interact with environmental stressors to heighten her vulnerability to mood and behavioral instability (Crowell et al., 2009). Additionally, her pattern of excessive alcohol consumption to the point of blackout suggests impaired inhibitory control, which may compound her emotional dysregulation and impulsivity. She presents with longstanding difficulties in identity formation, low self-worth, and unstable interpersonal attachments; and her distorted cognitive appraisals reflect deeply entrenched maladaptive core beliefs and negative self-schema. Nicole's fear of abandonment, unstable relationships, and identity diffusion are prototypical of borderline personality features, as reflected in her MCMI-IV profile and clinical history. Moreover, her history of interpersonal loss, coupled with perceived rejection, can often precipitate suicidal crises and dysregulated behaviors. Her transient but intense relationships – idealizing romantic partners quickly and devaluing them just as swiftly – demonstrate insecure attachment patterns and an underdeveloped sense of self. Her coping repertoire appears limited to avoidance, substance use, and affective outbursts, which further impair her functioning and social relationships. Nicole's inconsistent romantic and social history – characterized by unstable attachments and impulsive sexual behavior – may reflect both a need for external validation and a maladaptive attempt to regulate internal distress. Her reliance on social media and difficulty in maintaining close relationships further complicate her ability to build a sustainable social support network. Finally, Nicole's identity as a Chinese immigrant who entered the United States during adolescence is likely salient to her clinical presentation. Cultural expectations related to filial piety, emotional suppression, and achievement may contribute to Nicole's internalized guilt, feelings of inadequacy, and shame (Sue et al., 2019). Her estrangement from stable peer relationships, and her tenuous living arrangements with roommates who are reportedly critical of her, further exacerbate her sense of isolation and perceived rejection. Although she maintains regular contact with her parents and has financial independence through her work as a hairdresser, her support system may be emotionally limited or she may experience it as conditional, given past conflicts with her family and her tendency to self-blame for these ruptures.

Treatment goals should include stabilizing sleep patterns and reducing high-risk behaviors such as binge drinking, which may exacerbate mood instability and impulsivity. Additional goals could center on improving Nicole's affect regulation, enhancing her distress tolerance, and fostering a more coherent and stable sense of self. Specific aims should include reducing suicidal ideation, mitigating symptoms of depression and emotional lability, and addressing maladaptive interpersonal patterns, particularly within romantic relationships. Nicole would also benefit from stronger social support, improved communication and boundaries within peer and roommate relationships, and an increase in her sense of safety and stability within her living situation.

Appropriate biopsychosocial interventions for Nicole might include a referral to a psychiatrist for a comprehensive medication evaluation, especially as selective serotonin reuptake inhibitors or mood stabilizers may offer benefit if mood symptoms persist. Interventions borrowed from dialectical behavior therapy (DBT) or mentalization-based therapy (MBT) may be helpful in targeting emotional dysregulation and impulsivity. It may also be helpful to refer to a case manager to facilitate conflict resolution with roommates and assess safer housing options. Additionally, involving Nicole's family, if appropriate and desired, through culturally responsive family psychoeducation may improve relational dynamics and promote a more supportive post-discharge environment.

Clinical Case Vignette #6

Demographic Information and History

Name: Brittney Martinez.

Demographic Information: 25 years old, gay Hispanic female.

Medical Diagnoses: No relevant medical diagnoses were reported.

Reason for Referral: Brittney was referred to treatment by her girlfriend because her girlfriend felt Brittney's behaviors were negatively impacting their relationship. Brittney reported in the last fight she and her girlfriend had, her girlfriend became upset with Brittney's flirtatious behavior with several people at a work party. According to Brittney, she has had fights like this in the past with her current girlfriend and other people she has been romantically involved with. Brittney stated her girlfriend threatened to break up with her if she did not attend therapy.

Clinical Interview Data

Interpreter Used: Yes.

Current Psychosocial Stressors: Brittney reported difficulties at work, stating there has been "drama" between her and her co-workers because of her flirtatious behavior at her work party. Brittney noted, due to her behavior at this party, human resources (HR) is now investigating sexual harassment accusations against Brittney. Brittney disclosed this is not the first time HR has contacted her about her presentation in work settings, stating she has been written up for dressing "provocatively."

Protective Factors: Brittney's religious faith is important to her. Brittney reported she feels close to her girlfriend and family "as long as they are not in a fight." Brittney also reported not being worried about her job status because she has been making enough money on social media to "maintain her lifestyle."

Developmental History: Brittney reported meeting all developmental milestones on time.

Academic History: Brittney completed high school and received a bachelor's degree in communications.

Social History: Brittney reported she has many friends and loved ones whom she can rely on for support.

Household: Brittney has lived with her girlfriend for 8 months. She is the only child of divorced parents, who divorced while she was in high school. Brittney reported having a closer relationship with her mother than her father.

Previous Psychiatric History: Brittney reported no previous psychiatric history.

Family Psychiatric History: Brittney reported her father received treatment for alcohol abuse while he was going through his divorce.

History of Self-Harm: Brittney reported she has threatened to kill herself previously during a fight with her current girlfriend. However, Brittney did not receive therapeutic services after this incident.

Wellness Profile

Sleep: Brittney reported no issues with sleep or sleep disturbances.

Diet: Brittney reported starting the day with oatmeal and a cup of coffee. Brittney reported she will typically order food to be delivered to her workplace for lunches and will make dinner with her girlfriend. Brittney reported having snacks of trail mix or fruit on some occasions.

Elimination: No symptoms reported.

Technology: Brittney reported spending approximately 7 hours on social media daily to create content for her personal account and a secondary account where Brittney creates sexual content for a profit.

Physical Activity: Brittney reported using a walking treadmill while at work and will hike on the weekends one to two times a month.

Substance Use/Abuse: Brittney reported drinking alcohol 3–4 days a week. She reported she does not feel as though her drinking is a problem, but after the events of her work party, many people have told her she had "too much to drink."

Pain: 0/10.

Current Psychiatric Symptoms

Depression: Brittney reported feelings of sadness and loneliness occasionally. She specified her mood typically fluctuates when she is having interpersonal conflicts with friends, family, or loved ones.

Anxiety: No symptoms reported.

Panic: No symptoms reported.

Mania: No symptoms reported.

Psychosis: No symptoms reported.

Trauma: Brittney reported there have been several occasions in her life where she has been "traumatized." When asked about these occasions, Brittney summarized that people had "hurt her" because she felt they would avoid her, or she would feel uncared for if the person did not pay attention to her in group scenarios.

Eating Disorder: No symptoms reported.

Risky Behaviors/Sexual Activity: Brittney reported she has had multiple sexual partners within the past 10 years. Brittney stated this caused tension in her current relationship but stated she "can't help if people want to be with [her]."

Mental Status Exam

Appearance: *Dress*: inappropriate, client presented to the intake interview wearing only a bralette and a pair of shorts. When asked to "cover up" by the receptionist, Brittney went into her car and found a zip-up jacket but left the jacket unzipped, with her breasts exposed throughout the interview. *Hygiene*: adequate. Appeared stated age.

Behavior: Seductive, charming, entitled.

Speech: *Rate*: within normal limits. *Articulation*: exaggerated. *Volume*: within normal limits. *Coherence*: within normal limits.

Mood: Brittney reported feeling "distressed" at the beginning of the interview and displayed a sorrowful affect. However, at the end of the interview, Brittney expressed "deep gratitude" for speaking with her and displayed a neutral to happy affect.

Affect: Hyperthymic and labile, congruent to mood, inappropriate to content of interview.

Thought Process: Logical, linear, goal directed.

Thought Content: Endorsed suicidal ideation; denied homicidal ideation, delusions, and hallucinations.

Orientation: Oriented to person, place, and time.

Recent Memory: Intact.

Remote Memory: Intact.

Attention/Concentration: Distractible.

General Knowledge: Within normal limits.

Language: Within normal limits.

Insight: Fair.

Judgment: Poor.

Answer Key #6

Diversity Considerations

Because Brittney is a 25-year-old gay Hispanic woman, she exists at the intersection of multiple marginalized groups, each of which may inform her experience of distress, identity formation, and relational functioning. Minority stress, which is defined as the chronic experience of discrimination, microaggression, or social invalidation, may contribute to or exacerbate her symptoms, particularly within interpersonal domains. Her reported difficulties with intimacy, fear of abandonment, and heightened sensitivity to perceived rejection may partially reflect internalized stigma or attachment disruptions potentially shaped by her cultural or familial background. Ethnic identity must also be understood within a broader cultural framework. Brittney identifies as Hispanic, and cultural values such as *familismo*, *marianismo*, and collectivism may influence her relational style, gender role expectations, and emotional expression. While Brittney's faith may provide comfort and a sense of meaning, it may also conflict with aspects of her sexual orientation or lifestyle, potentially contributing to internal conflict or shame. This, however, depends on the religious tradition in which she participates and whether or not the church to which she belongs supports her lifestyle.

Ethical Considerations

Brittney's flirtatious and seductive behavior, with which she presented during the intake session, may present potential boundary issues during treatment if she continues to present in a manner deemed inappropriate by clinic staff and/or if her attire becomes problematic in the clinic for other patients, including minor patients. This may require a firm yet compassionate maintenance of professional boundaries to prevent boundary violations or countertransference issues. Additionally, Brittney's endorsement of past suicidal ideation during interpersonal conflict mandates a thorough risk assessment and ongoing monitoring to ensure her safety, consistent with the ethical principle of beneficence and the legal obligation to intervene when a client is at risk of harm to self.

Legal Considerations

This case may include some legal considerations given the workplace misconduct allegations. Per her report, Brittney is currently under investigation by her employer's HR department for alleged sexual harassment, and there exists the possibility that legal proceedings such as employment litigation or even a civil suit by the alleged victims could involve subpoenas for clinical records or clinician testimony. Clinicians must inform Brittney of the limits of confidentiality, especially regarding court-ordered disclosures.

Diagnostic Impressions and Justification

F60.4 Histrionic Personality Disorder.
Brittney meets the criteria because of her pervasive patterns of attention-seeking behavior. Brittney displayed theatrical but shallow expression of affect that rapidly shifted throughout the intake interview. In discussing her past, Brittney used dramatized vocabulary about events but was unable to provide details or context for these events. Also, Brittney displays herself in an overtly provocative manner that is inappropriate in the context of the interaction with the

interviewer. Her flirtatious behavior, reliance on social media, and history of suicidal threats in conflicts may indicate difficulties with emotional regulation and validation-seeking.

Psychodynamic Case Conceptualization

Brittney's presentation seems to reflect a deep-seated need for validation and affection, likely rooted in early attachment disruptions. Brittney's description of her childhood, notably her parents' divorce and her father's struggles with alcohol abuse, suggests the possibility of insecure attachment patterns. Her sexualized behavior may indicate that she utilizes reaction formation as a defense mechanism, wherein she compensates for feelings of emotional neglect and low self-esteem by engaging in behaviors that provide her with external validation (Freud, 1936). Her use of alcohol seems to serve as both a coping mechanism and a form of self-soothing in the face of distressing emotional experiences, potentially exacerbating her impulsivity and poor judgment (Baker et al., 2008).

Treatment goals grounded in psychodynamic theory may include the integration of fragmented aspects of her sense of self as well as the exploration and resolution of unconscious internal conflicts related to attachment and self-worth. A key treatment objective may be to explore early childhood relationships with her parents, particularly the impact of parental divorce and her father's substance abuse on her attachment style and sense of security (Fonagy et al., 2002). Additionally, it might be essential to help Brittney gain insight into her unconscious defensive mechanisms, particularly her use of sexuality and flirtation as means of self-soothing or avoiding feelings of inadequacy. A secondary goal would be to help Brittney develop more effective interpersonal strategies by increasing insight into relational patterns, with a focus on addressing issues of boundary formation and impulsivity.

Transference-focused therapy (TFP) may be a useful intervention, allowing Brittney to explore her unconscious patterns in the therapeutic relationship and gain insight into how these patterns manifest in her personal and professional life (Clarkin et al., 2007). In particular, the transference may provide insight into her relationship with authority figures and her expectations in romantic relationships. Techniques such as interpretation and confrontation may be employed to explore the root causes of her behavior, helping Brittney link her flirtatiousness to her unmet emotional needs and deep-seated fears of abandonment.

Cognitive Behavioral Conceptualization

Brittney's presentation appears to be impacted by cognitive distortions and negative core beliefs. Her behaviors also seem to be reinforced by cognitive distortions such as catastrophizing and overgeneralization, particularly in the context of her interactions with romantic partners.

CBT would focus on challenging these core beliefs, modifying the cognitive distortions that fuel her impulsive behaviors, and teaching Brittney more adaptive coping mechanisms for handling distress in her relationships and work environments. Specifically, CBT could aim to address her negative core beliefs about self-worth, including the belief that attention from others is necessary for her to feel valued or loved. CBT could also focus on helping Brittney develop more adaptive coping skills to manage distressing emotions, especially in romantic relationships and work environments.

Cognitive restructuring techniques may be the most helpful in identifying and challenging Brittney's cognitive distortions. Behavioral interventions, including exposure therapy, would also be used to help Brittney confront situations where she might typically engage in flirtation or provocative behavior, without resorting to these behaviors as a way of gaining validation. By gradually confronting these situations, Brittney can learn that her fears of abandonment or rejection are often exaggerated and that her worth does not depend on external validation. Additionally, emotion regulation training would be introduced to help Brittney manage the distress that arises in her relationships and work settings. Techniques such as mindfulness and distress tolerance would be taught to help Brittney cope with feelings of rejection and loneliness without resorting to self-destructive behaviors. Specifically, she may benefit from enrollment in dialectical behavior therapy (DBT).

Biopsychosocial Conceptualization

Brittney did not report a significant medical history but she may have been underreporting due to her high volume of sexual partners and the lack of clarity regarding whether she has consistently practiced safer sex since becoming sexually active. There may be genetic factors influencing her presentation, however, as her father had a history of alcohol abuse, which may indicate a family history of substance use disorders or emotional dysregulation, both of which can increase vulnerability to similar patterns in Brittney. Overall, Brittney's behaviors appear to be driven by cognitive distortions and are likely being exacerbated by issues both at work and at home.

One appropriate treatment goal grounded in the biopsychosocial model would be to reduce Brittney's alcohol consumption by addressing its role as a maladaptive coping mechanism for emotional regulation, while exploring alternative adaptive coping strategies. Treatment could also focus would be on addressing cognitive distortions and helping Brittney develop more adaptive beliefs about herself and her relationships. Specifically, the goal would be to reduce her need for external validation and improve her self-esteem by challenging underlying beliefs that she is unworthy of love or attention unless she seeks it from others. Additionally, emotion regulation skills would be a priority, helping Brittney to manage distressing emotions without resorting to impulsive behaviors.

Improving her relationship with her girlfriend and reducing the negative impact of workplace stressors may also serve as valuable goals.

Motivational interviewing and harm reduction strategies could be employed to help Brittney manage her drinking patterns in a way that minimizes harm and supports her overall emotional regulation, while also helping her increase her engagement in change talk as well as possible sobriety. CBT interventions could be utilized to challenge Brittney's cognitive distortions and negative core beliefs, particularly those related to self-worth and interpersonal relationships. For example, cognitive restructuring would focus on helping Brittney recognize that her worth is not contingent on others' attention and that her behavior does not need to be flirtatious or provocative to maintain connections. Given the conflict Brittney has had with her girlfriend, they may benefit from a referral to couples counseling. Brittney may also wish to enroll in Alcoholics Anonymous. While not much is known about Brittney's engagement with her religious tradition, she did report it as a protective factor and therefore increased engagement with her religious community could be encouraged as an additional method for increasing social support.

Clinical Case Vignette #7

Demographic Information and History

Name: Jay Williams.

Demographic Information: 37 years old, White male.

Medical Diagnoses: No relevant medical diagnoses were reported.

Reason for Referral: Jay was referred to the clinic by his workplace's HR department after an incident with Jay's boss following an annual performance review. Jay was displeased with the feedback he had received from his boss, as he was expecting a promotion. However, Jay's boss had given Jay poor ratings for inadequate sales and completing tasks with "a lack of urgency." Jay responded to his boss by screaming and using profanities, stating he was "more deserving" of his boss's job and would be "better respected" by his subordinates if he were to have authority. Jay was written up for this incident and is required to attend therapy to maintain his employment.

Clinical Interview Data

Interpreter Used: No.

Current Psychosocial Stressors: Jay recently went through a divorce with his wife of 5 years. Jay's ex-wife received full custody of the children, while Jay gets to see his son and daughter every other weekend. Jay reported tension has grown between him and his ex-wife because he believes she is mad she "could not take him for his money" when she asked for child support. Jay reported he was pleased he was able to hire a good lawyer to ensure he would not have to pay child support at all.

Protective Factors: Jay has friends he sees weekly. Jay has expressed feeling excited to have the "freedom" to date again.

Developmental History: Jay reported meeting all developmental milestones on time.

Academic History: Jay completed high school.

Social History: Jay has been friends with a member of a country club and has golfed with friends from the country club every weekend for the past 4 years. Jay admits that, though he could afford to become a member himself, he would rather use his friend's membership because his friend "owes him" for dog-sitting previously. Jay reported he is his mother's "favorite child." Jay's mother comes to visit him biweekly and makes him dinner. Jay only contacts his ex-wife when he needs to discuss discuss dropping off or picking up his children for their regular visits.

Household: Jay lives by himself in an apartment he moved into after his divorce. Jay's mother and father are also divorced. Jay's mother lives in a nearby city and his father lives in a different state. Jay has a closer relationship with his mother than his father.

Previous Psychiatric History: Jay reported no previous psychiatric history.

Family Psychiatric History: Jay reported no familial psychiatric history.

History of Self-Harm: Jay has no history of self-harm and denies suicidal ideation.

Wellness Profile

Sleep: Jay reported sleeping 7–8 hours a night and reported no issues with sleep disturbances.

Diet: Jay reported eating three meals a day and will have a protein shake after his morning workouts. No concerns with eating were reported.

Elimination: No symptoms reported.

Technology: Jay reported spending 3–4 hours a day watching television after work and will spend approximately 1–2 hours on his phone daily.

Physical Activity: Jay reported going to the gym every morning before work to lift weights for approximately 2 hours.

Substance Use/Abuse: Jay reported averaging 10 alcoholic beverages weekly. He reported having beer after work and beer and hard liquor on the weekends while golfing or going to a bar.

Pain: 0/10.

Current Psychiatric Symptoms

Depression: No symptoms reported.

Anxiety: No symptoms reported.

Panic: No symptoms reported.

Mania: No symptoms reported.

Psychosis: No symptoms reported.

Trauma: No symptoms reported.

Eating Disorder: No symptoms reported.

Risky Behaviors/Sexual Activity: Per reason for referral, Jay demonstrates impulsivity when confronted with a lack of admiration.

Mental Status Exam

Appearance: *Dress*: appropriate. *Hygiene*: adequate. Appeared stated age.

Behavior: Appropriate, cooperative.

Speech: *Rate*: within normal limits. *Articulation*: within normal limits. *Volume*: within normal limits. *Coherence*: within normal limits.

Mood: Jay reported feeling "annoyed" that he must participate in therapeutic services. Jay stated he "should not have to come to therapy" because he believes his boss is the one in the wrong.

Affect: Full, stable, congruent to mood, appropriate to content of interview.

Thought Process: Logical, linear, goal directed.

Thought Content: Denied suicidal ideation, homicidal ideation, delusions, and hallucinations.

Orientation: Oriented to person, place, and time.

Recent Memory: Intact.

Remote Memory: Intact.

Attention/Concentration: Sufficient.

General Knowledge: Within normal limits.

Language: Within normal limits.

Insight: Poor.

Judgment: Poor.

Answer Key #7

Diversity Considerations

Jay may be influenced by dominant cultural narratives around masculinity, authority, and emotional expression; and his resistance to therapy and attribution of fault to his supervisor and ex-wife may reflect socialized expectations that discourage help seeking and externalize blame when personal efficacy is challenged.

Ethical Considerations

Because Jay is required to attend therapy by his place of employment, he may have limited sessions available to him and his employer may be expecting some sort of report regarding treatment adherence. The clinician must remain aware of these dynamics and ensure conversations pertaining to them are included in the informed consent process as needed. Whenever third parties are involved in mental health care, clinicians also need to ensure they are sharing the absolute minimum amount of information necessary to complete their assigned tasks.

Legal Considerations

No additional legal considerations.

Diagnostic Impressions and Justification

F60.81 Narcissistic Personality Disorder.
Jay meets the criteria for narcissistic personality disorder because he has a pervasive need for admiration and a lack of empathy. Jay demonstrates through his behaviors at work and his relationship with his mother and ex-wife that he believes he is "special" and feels he is entitled to special treatment, which

is demonstrated in his arrogant attitudes and behaviors. Jay appears to lack empathy for his ex-wife and his boss regarding his, Jay's, behaviors and he lacks insight into his exploitative behaviors.

Psychodynamic Case Conceptualization

Jay's overall personality features seem suggestive of narcissistic defenses, including grandiosity, entitlement, and difficulty tolerating criticism or perceived slights. As is often the case with narcissistic patients, Jay's intense reaction to negative feedback at work may be indicative of a fragile self-esteem that is defended against through externalizing blame and asserting dominance. Jay's relational history, including a contentious divorce, limited paternal connection, and possible enmeshment with his mother, may reflect unresolved oedipal dynamics and arrested identity development rooted in early caregiving relationships. His overidentification with external markers of success and inability to tolerate perceived humiliation or dependency likely serve as defenses against unconscious feelings of inadequacy, rejection, or shame.

The primary treatment goals in psychodynamic therapy for Jay may involve increasing his insight into the unconscious internal conflicts driving his interpersonal dysfunction, particularly his intense reactions to perceived slights and his reliance on defensive grandiosity. Enhancing affect tolerance, especially around feelings of shame, inadequacy, or abandonment, is essential for fostering emotional growth and so should also be included as a goal. Additional goals may include facilitating more adaptive relational patterns by exploring transference dynamics as they emerge in the therapeutic relationship, as well as encouraging the gradual relinquishment of rigid self-ideals in favor of a more integrated and authentic sense of self. Treatment should also address Jay's difficulty with authority figures, likely rooted in past experiences with his father and reinforced through adult relational schemas, thereby supporting the development of greater psychological flexibility and emotional regulation in hierarchical or evaluative environments.

Appropriate interventions grounded in psychodynamic theory may include interpretations formulated to bring unconscious material into conscious awareness, particularly focusing on defense mechanisms such as projection, idealization, and devaluation. Clarification and confrontation may be used to help Jay examine discrepancies between his self-perception and the impact of his behavior on others, while interpretation can illuminate the unconscious meanings behind his aggressive or entitled reactions. Working with transference may become central, as Jay may project both idealized and devalued authority figures onto the therapist, recreating relational dynamics that mirror his internal conflicts.

Cognitive Behavioral Conceptualization

Jay presents with maladaptive core beliefs related to entitlement, self-importance, and mistrust of others, which appear to contribute to persistent interpersonal difficulties and emotional dysregulation, particularly in response to criticism or perceived slights. His behavioral responses likely serve to reduce cognitive dissonance and preserve self-esteem but ultimately reinforce interpersonal conflict and occupational instability.

CBT-based treatment goals for Jay will likely involve identifying, evaluating, and restructuring maladaptive core beliefs and automatic thoughts that contribute to his interpersonal and occupational difficulties. Specifically, treatment should aim to increase Jay's awareness of the connection between his cognitions, emotional reactions, and behaviors in situations involving authority, criticism, or social evaluation. Treatment should also target skills in emotional regulation, assertiveness, and distress tolerance to improve his ability to navigate workplace and interpersonal stressors.

CBT interventions for Jay should begin with psychoeducation about the cognitive model, including the role of core beliefs and automatic thoughts in shaping behavior and emotion. Thought records might help Jay identify patterns of distorted thinking, particularly in high-conflict situations. Cognitive restructuring techniques could be used to challenge and reframe dysfunctional beliefs while behavioral experiments may be introduced to test these cognitions and promote experiential learning. Role-playing and social skills training might support the development of assertive communication and empathy, while problem-solving strategies can aid in managing interpersonal disputes. Additionally, incorporating anger management techniques and stress-reduction practices such as mindfulness-based techniques may be essential in addressing Jay's impulsive reactions and promoting behavioral regulation.

Biopsychosocial Conceptualization

Jay did not report a significant medical history and actually endorsed living a fairly healthy and active life. That being said, his average intake of 10 alcoholic beverages weekly might represent a maladaptive coping mechanism, particularly given his recent psychosocial stressors. Jay presents with poor judgment, low frustration tolerance, and rigid belief systems that likely stem from longstanding cognitive and emotional schemas centered on self-aggrandizement and externalization of blame. Jay's divorce and loss of primary custody of his children as well as having to move out of the family home may have threatened his self-concept, intensifying compensatory behaviors such as exaggerated self-presentation and oppositionality toward authority. Jay's overall social environment seems characterized by strained family dynamics, limited paternal involvement, and recent marital dissolution.

Treatment goals grounded in the biopsychosocial model should be formulated to enhance Jay's self-awareness, interpersonal functioning, and emotional regulation. It will be important to monitor Jay's alcohol use to reduce the risk of substance-related harm and ensure that his physical health behaviors are not masking psychological distress. Jay would also benefit from improving conflict resolution skills, fostering mutuality in relationships, and encouraging responsible co-parenting practices.

Interventions could include cognitive restructuring to challenge core beliefs around superiority and entitlement along with psychoeducation regarding the impact of narcissistic traits on relationships and workplace dynamics which may facilitate greater insight and motivation for change. Because Jay presents with poor insight, he may not be particularly open to change at this time, in which case motivational interviewing could be implemented. Family or co-parenting therapy may also be beneficial in restructuring dynamics with his ex-wife and fostering more adaptive involvement with his children.

Clinical Case Vignette #8

Demographic Information and History

Name: Cindy Hunt.

Demographic Information: 65 years old, White female.

Medical Diagnoses: No relevant medical diagnoses were reported.

Reason for Referral: Cindy is presenting to the clinic after her sister referred her for therapy to work on her "self-esteem." Cindy reported to her sister she left her third book club in 2 months because she did not think the other women in the group liked her. Cindy's sister convinced Cindy to come to therapy because this has been a pattern of behavior in Cindy's life. Cindy reported she believes she is "unlovable" and "not good enough" to be in certain circumstances, such as water aerobics classes or book clubs.

Clinical Interview Data

Interpreter Used: No.

Current Psychosocial Stressors: Cindy's brother recently passed away and she reported feeling guilty about not being close to him throughout their lives.

Protective Factors: Cindy is strong in her Christian faith and is not experiencing financial stressors.

Developmental History: Cindy reported meeting all developmental milestones on time.

Academic History: Cindy maintained average grades throughout middle and high school. Cindy spent most of her adult life working as an overnight front desk host at a local hotel.

Social History: Cindy reported she has had multiple friendships and romantic relationships throughout her life, very few lasting longer than a couple of years. Cindy reported she is always worried her friends and boyfriends secretly hate her. She explained that over the years friendships would take a long time to form and would slowly diminish because Cindy would back out of plans last minute or stop reaching out to her friends. Cindy reported she even declined a proposal from her most serious boyfriend because she was concerned he "could not love her."

Household: Cindy reported she lived with her parents, brother, and sister throughout her childhood. Throughout her young adult life, Cindy lived with multiple friends but eventually moved out because she feared she was being an "annoying roommate." Cindy also lived with her most serious boyfriend but moved out after she declined his proposal. Since this event, Cindy has lived on her own.

Previous Psychiatric History: Cindy reported no history of prior psychiatric treatment.

Family Psychiatric History: Cindy reported no familial psychiatric history.

History of Self-Harm: Cindy reported no history of self-harm behaviors.

Wellness Profile

Sleep: Cindy reported difficulties sleeping before events where she must socialize with other people because she fears she will be criticized or rejected when she gets to the event. On nights when she sleeps well, Cindy reported an average of 7–8 hours of sleep.

Diet: Cindy reported having oatmeal in the mornings for breakfast, a salad or sandwich for lunch, and a smaller dinner. Cindy reported she will snack on vegetables or nuts in between lunch and dinner some days.

Elimination: No symptoms reported.

Technology: Cindy reported watching television an average of 3–4 hours a day.

Physical Activity: Cindy reported going on walks around her neighborhood three to four times a week. Cindy reported she enjoys the activities that are found in group fitness classes at her gym but fears she will "make a fool" of herself if she joins the classes.

Substance Use/Abuse: Cindy reported having two to three alcoholic drinks per week, usually wine. Cindy reported no other substance usage.

Pain: 0/10.

Current Psychiatric Symptoms

Depression: Cindy reported she has lost interest in joining clubs, such as book clubs, stating she has been discouraged because she does not believe the other members will want her to join the club. She reported she is "not as well read" as the other members and worries she will embarrass herself if she were to stay in the club.

Anxiety: Cindy reported experiencing muscle tension, panic attacks, and difficulty controlling worry, specifically when having to interact with other people. Cindy explains she specifically works the overnight shifts at the hotel because fewer people check in during those hours, and therefore, she would be less likely to have a panic attack. In other areas of her life, Cindy worries her friends do not want to be with her, even when they initiate the gathering.

Panic: Cindy reported experiencing heart palpitations, sweating, shaking, and chest pain.

Mania: No symptoms reported.

Psychosis: No symptoms reported.

Trauma: Cindy reported her mother and father utilized corporal punishment throughout her childhood. Cindy explained that this included hitting her, kicking her, and being locked in her small closet for long periods.

Eating Disorder: No symptoms reported.

Risky Behaviors/Sexual Activity: No symptoms reported.

Mental Status Exam

Appearance: *Dress*: appropriate. *Hygiene*: adequate. Appeared stated age.

Behavior: Appropriate, cooperative, guarded.

Speech: *Rate*: within normal limits. *Articulation*: within normal limits. *Volume*: within normal limits. *Coherence*: within normal limits.

Mood: Cindy reported she felt "stressed" and "scared" that the interviewer was going to think she was "crazy."

Affect: Full, congruent to mood, appropriate to content of interview.

Thought Process: Logical, linear, goal directed.

Thought Content: Denied suicidal ideation, homicidal ideation, delusions, and hallucinations.

Orientation: Oriented to person, place, and time.

Recent Memory: Intact.

Remote Memory: Intact.

Attention/Concentration: Sufficient.

General Knowledge: Within normal limits.

Language: Within normal limits.

Insight: Fair.

Judgment: Fair.

Answer Key #8

Diversity Considerations

One key cultural considerations is Cindy's age, and also, therefore, potentially the generation to which she belongs, which may influence her perspectives on self-esteem, relationships, and gender roles. Additionally, while religion often provides a sense of community, structure, and emotional support, if Cindy's particular religious tradition also places significant emphasis on perfectionism or moral standards, it could compound her feelings of unworthiness and fear of judgment, especially in social contexts where she perceives others as more capable or deserving.

Ethical Considerations

No ethical considerations at this time.

Legal Considerations

No legal considerations at this time.

Diagnostic Impressions and Justification

F60.6 Avoidant Personality Disorder.
Cindy meets the diagnostic criteria because she displays consistent patterns of social inhibition, feelings of inadequacy, and hypersensitivity to negative evaluations that impact many aspects of her life. She maintains a work schedule specifically to avoid interactions with others and consistently ruminates and worries about receiving disapproval or rejection from others. Cindy is reluctant to join new activities or make new connections with others because of feelings of inferiority, as seen in her avoidance of going to the gym and joining a book club.

Psychodynamic Case Conceptualization

Cindy appears to present with defense mechanisms stemming from her childhood developed to protect her against feelings of rejection as well as an unconscious desire to avoid further humiliation or emotional pain. Her fear of being "unlovable" and "not good enough" could be rooted in unresolved internal conflicts based in the early attachment experiences reported. Her adult relationships reflect patterns of seeking connection but simultaneously sabotaging them through withdrawal or self-sabotage, which could be a manifestation of her internal conflict between the desire for closeness and the fear of being hurt or rejected.

In psychodynamic psychotherapy, the primary treatment goals for Cindy may be to increase self-awareness, reduce defensive patterns of avoidance and withdrawal, and foster a more cohesive and integrated sense of self. One possible goal could be to help Cindy identify and confront her unconscious fears of rejection and criticism, working to replace these fears with healthier, more adaptive ways of relating to others. Additionally, Cindy would benefit from understanding the impact of her unresolved grief and guilt regarding her brother's death, as these emotions likely exacerbate her anxiety and avoidance behaviors. Ultimately, the treatment will aim to help Cindy develop more fulfilling and stable relationships, free from the internalized fear of rejection that has hindered her social functioning.

Treatment interventions grounded in psychodynamic theory could focus on enhancing insight and self-awareness, with an emphasis on exploring unconscious internal conflicts, especially those related to early attachment experiences and punitive parenting. Interventions such as free association could be utilized to help Cindy access repressed memories and emotional material that may be contributing to her current difficulties. It may also be important for the clinician to provide interpretations of transference as it arises, observing Cindy's reactions to the therapeutic relationship, and using this as a tool to examine how Cindy's relational patterns may be re-enacted in the therapy space. As in all psychodynamic psychotherapy the clinician's role will be to provide a consistent and empathic presence, providing Cindy with a corrective emotional experience.

Cognitive Behavioral Conceptualization

Cindy's presentation is likely being caused by negative automatic thoughts as well as problematic core beliefs that contribute to maladaptive behaviors and emotional distress. She presents with clear cognitive distortions, such as overgeneralization and catastrophizing, where she interprets social interactions through a lens of fear and inadequacy. This leads to anticipatory anxiety before social events and a tendency to withdraw from potentially rewarding social opportunities, reinforcing her belief that others will reject or criticize her. Cindy's avoidance of social situations is a safety behavior designed to protect her from the anticipated negative evaluation of others, but it also prevents her from gaining evidence to disconfirm her negative beliefs about herself. Additionally, Cindy's reported panic attacks, including physical symptoms such as heart palpitations and sweating, are likely triggered by her cognitive distortions, which amplify her fear of rejection and social failure. These panic attacks reinforce Cindy's avoidance patterns, maintaining the cycle of anxiety and isolation.

As is generally the case with CBT, treatment goals should challenge and modify her maladaptive thoughts, beliefs, and behaviors, with a focus on reducing anxiety and increasing participation in social activities. By learning how to recognize negative thought patterns, Cindy can develop more balanced, realistic beliefs about herself and her social interactions. Another key goal should be to reduce Cindy's avoidance behaviors and increase her engagement in social situations. This would involve gradual exposure to feared social situations, such as attending group fitness classes or joining book clubs, while actively confronting her anxiety and challenging her automatic negative thoughts during these experiences. Additionally, addressing Cindy's panic attacks is an important goal, as reducing the frequency and intensity of these attacks will help her feel more confident in her ability to manage anxiety.

CBT interventions should focus on a combination of cognitive restructuring, behavioral activation, and exposure techniques as Cindy would benefit from all three forms of intervention. The clinician can guide Cindy in examining the evidence for and against her negative thoughts, using worksheets as valuable visual aids and helping her develop more realistic and adaptive beliefs about herself and her social interactions. Cognitive restructuring may also be able to target Cindy's deeply held beliefs about her worth and lovability, aiming to replace these with more positive and accurate self-conceptions. Behavioral interventions could involve gradually increasing Cindy's participation in social situations through exposure exercises. Relaxation training may also be helpful in supporting Cindy to manage her physical symptoms of anxiety during these exposures, as well as thought-stopping techniques to interrupt negative self-talk.

Biopsychosocial Conceptualization

While Cindy denied any significant medical history, her panic attacks, characterized by heart palpitations, sweating, and chest pain, may be a result of heightened physiological arousal in response to anxiety-provoking social situations. Her autonomic nervous system likely overreacts to perceived threats, triggering these physical symptoms. Additionally, her underlying cognitive distortions contribute to her social anxiety and avoidance. Unfortunately, Cindy's isolation and withdrawal from social activities serves to reinforce her belief that she is unworthy of connection, creating a cycle of avoidance that perpetuates her emotional distress. The recent loss of her brother has also triggered feelings of guilt and sadness, adding another layer of psychosocial stress to her already complex emotional landscape.

Treatment goals grounded in the biopsychosocial approach could begin by reducing the frequency and intensity of Cindy's panic attacks by teaching her relaxation techniques, breathing exercises, and grounding techniques to help regulate her physiological response to anxiety. Cindy would also benefit from learning how to identify and reframe her negative cognitions about herself. Treatment interventions can also be formulated to increase Cindy's engagement in social activities and improve her interpersonal relationships.

Interventions can focus on teaching Cindy relaxation techniques such as diaphragmatic breathing, progressive muscle relaxation, and mindfulness meditation to help regulate her autonomic nervous system and reduce the intensity of her panic attacks when they strike. Psychoeducation regarding the physiological aspects of anxiety could also serve to increase Cindy's understanding of her symptoms and empower her to manage them more effectively. Additionally, cognitive restructuring and other CBT interventions such as keeping thought records could help Cindy identify, evaluate, and replace distorted thoughts with more balanced and realistic beliefs. Behavioral interventions could include gradual exposure to social situations that Cindy avoids in order to allow her to gain evidence that her fears of rejection or criticism are often unfounded and to build self-efficacy in social settings. Cindy should also be encouraged to engage in activities that foster a sense of accomplishment and enjoyment.

Clinical Case Vignette #9

Demographic Information and History

Name: Kylie Garcia.

Demographic Information: 42 years old, Black Hispanic female.

Medical Diagnoses: No relevant medical diagnoses were reported.

Reason for Referral: Kylie was referred to the clinic by her adult son, who recommended she seek mental health services after her divorce. Kylie and her husband separated 2 years ago, and their divorce was finalized 4 months ago. Since the separation, Kylie moved in with her son and his family until she got "on her feet." Kylie reported her husband wanted a divorce because, after their son moved out and began his own family, he felt Kylie was "too emotional" when left home alone (while he went to work or was out-of-town for work-related events) and he felt "smothered" by Kylie.

Clinical Interview Data

Interpreter Used: Yes.

Current Psychosocial Stressors: Kylie has recently gone through a divorce after being married for 20 years. Kylie reported this divorce has "confirmed her worst fears" of being left alone to take care of herself. Kylie reported the distress of the divorce has "disrupted her entire life" and she feels as though she will "never recover."

Protective Factors: Kylie reported holding a strong faith in Catholicism and attends mass weekly with her son and his family.

Developmental History: Kylie reported meeting all developmental milestones on time.

Academic History: Kylie maintained average grades throughout her education. Kylie attended college for a couple of years with the hope of becoming a nurse. However, Kylie dropped out to work full-time to financially support her future husband through his education. After her husband obtained his "dream job," Kylie quit her job to stay at home to raise her child so her husband could focus on his career.

Social History: During her marriage, Kylie was a stay-at-home mother and was focused solely on raising her son. Kylie did not have many friends at this time and relied on her husband as her sole social support. However, once their son moved out of the house to go to college, Kylie's ex-husband recommended she join a club or get a part-time job so she could make friends and have something to do. However, Kylie reported she felt uncomfortable starting something new without her husband helping her choose what to do or having him there. Since the divorce, Kylie has also stopped attending weekly Bible study because she had been going to a couples Bible study with her husband. Kylie reported she has considered joining a women's group at her church but has not because she fears the other women will judge her because of her divorce and that she will "look stupid" when she speaks up in front of a group.

Household: Kylie currently lives with her son, daughter-in-law, and one-year-old grandchild. Before Kylie's divorce, Kylie had only lived with her parents and then moved in with her husband when they got married.

Previous Psychiatric History: Kylie reported no previous psychiatric history.

Family Psychiatric History: Kylie reported no familial psychiatric history.

History of Self-Harm: Kylie reported no history of self-harm behaviors.

Wellness Profile

Sleep: Kylie reported consistent patterns of sleep nightly. Kylie reported getting 6–7 hours of sleep nightly but will occasionally be woken up by the cries of her grandchild if she cries during the night. Kylie reported no concerns about her sleep routine.

Diet: Kylie reported no concerns surrounding her diet and eating patterns. Kylie reported eating three "balanced" meals daily and will have dessert once or twice a week.

Elimination: No symptoms reported.

Technology: Kylie reported watching the morning news daily for 2–3 hours and watching other television programs for 2–3 hours in the evening. Kylie uses her smartphone for communicating through text messages and phone calls, as well as using social media for an hour or two daily.

Physical Activity: Kylie reported she used to go to group fitness classes at her gym twice a week with her ex-sister-in-law. However, since the separation from her ex-husband, Kylie has not wanted to go to the gym because she does not want to go alone and is fearful of reaching out to her ex-sister-in-law to see if she would still want to go to the gym with her.

Substance Use/Abuse: Kylie reported drinking wine and cocktails once or twice monthly when she goes out to dinner with her family. Kylie reported never having used other substances previously.

Pain: 0/10.

Current Psychiatric Symptoms

Depression: Kylie reported having a depressed mood and a sense of worthlessness since her divorce. Kylie reported she is only able to get out of these "funks" when she receives reassurance from friends or family.

Anxiety: Kylie reported having difficulty concentrating, panic attacks, and difficulty controlling worry since her separation. However, Kylie reported having these symptoms whenever she and her ex-husband got into fights, and she worried he would leave her.

Panic: Kylie reported feeling symptoms of panic including trembling, sobbing, feelings of choking, chest pain and discomfort, and fear of losing control when confronted with the idea of losing someone important to her. Kylie reported these symptoms occurring when talking with her ex-husband about their separation and divorce and, most recently, when her son referred her to therapy.

Mania: No symptoms reported.

Psychosis: No symptoms reported.

Trauma: Kylie reported having been a victim of domestic violence throughout her marriage. Kylie reported her husband would hit her with his hands during fights, but her son had never witnessed the abuse while he was growing up. Kylie reported no reports were made to law enforcement and no criminal investigations occurred regarding domestic abuse allegations against her ex-husband.

Eating Disorder: No symptoms reported.

Risky Behaviors/Sexual Activity: No symptoms reported.

Mental Status Exam

Appearance: *Dress*: appropriate. *Hygiene*: adequate. Appeared stated age.

Behavior: Appropriate, cooperative

Speech: *Rate*: within normal limits. *Articulation*: within normal limits. *Volume*: within normal limits. *Coherence*: within normal limits.

Mood: Kylie reported feeling "frustrated" that her son referred her to therapy. She stated she believed he wanted her to go to therapy so she "could get out of his house." However, Kylie reported she has not relayed her frustration to her son because she fears she will "lose his support."

Affect: Full, labile, congruent to mood, appropriate to content of interview.

Thought Process: Logical, linear, goal directed.

Thought Content: Denied suicidal ideation, homicidal ideation, delusions, and hallucinations.

Orientation: Oriented to person, place, and time.

Recent Memory: Intact.

Remote Memory: Intact.

Attention/Concentration: Sufficient.

General Knowledge: Average.

Language: Within normal limits.

Insight: Fair.

Judgment: Fair.

Answer Key #9

Diversity Considerations

Kylie identifies as both Hispanic and Black, which positions her within two culturally rich, but distinct, ethnic groups. The intersection of these identities may result in unique cultural experiences that influence her coping mechanisms, communication styles, and views on mental health especially as, within many Hispanic and Black cultures, there may be stigma associated with seeking mental health support. This stigma can be rooted in values of family loyalty, religious beliefs, and communal support, where issues are often handled privately or within the family unit. Kylie's initial reluctance to attend therapy due to her son's referral reflects potential cultural reservations about seeking external help and the challenge of navigating a more individualized approach to mental health care. Additionally, Kylie may be facing gender-related societal pressures, such as ageism and the perceived role of women in traditional familial structures. As a mother who devoted much of her adult life to supporting her husband's career and raising their child, Kylie might also be experiencing identity challenges now that her son has grown, and her marriage has ended.

Kylie's strong Christian faith, particularly her regular attendance at mass with her son and his family, provides her with a protective factor that could support her during this difficult transition. Religion and spirituality can offer significant emotional comfort, but they may also present challenges in therapy if religious beliefs about relationships, marriage, or family are inconsistent with therapeutic goals. For example, Kylie's adherence to Catholic teachings about divorce and marriage may be a source of guilt or self-judgment, particularly as she navigates the aftermath of her divorce. As such, it is essential to integrate her religious beliefs respectfully into treatment and explore how they influence her current distress, self-worth, and coping mechanisms.

Ethical Considerations

None at this time.

Legal Considerations

None at this time.

Diagnostic Impressions and Justification

F60.7 Dependent Personality Disorder.
Kyle meets the criteria because she demonstrates an excessive need to be taken care of by others, which leads to submissiveness and clingy behavior. This can be seen in part in her decision to stop her educational and career trajectory to support her husband, but such a decision should not be overpathologized as it may simply represent a culturally normative adherence to traditional values. After her separation, Kyle immediately sought another relationship to replace her husband's relationship with her son and his family. She has difficulty completing tasks on her own, like going to the gym without her sister-in-law. This hesitancy seems to stem from feelings of helplessness and insecurity in her ability to make good decisions.

Psychodynamic Case Conceptualization

Kylie's overall presentation suggests the presence of unresolved unconscious internal conflicts rooted in early attachment issues and developmental challenges. Her current distress, which includes feelings of worthlessness and fear of abandonment, may be understood as a reflection of unconscious anxieties related to separations and attachments. The fear of being alone and the pervasive sense of inadequacy are likely tied to early experiences in which Kylie's emotional needs may not have been fully met, possibly due to her limited social support and the emotionally constricted environment in her marriage. Her difficulty in establishing independent social connections after her son moved out and her hesitations to engage in activities like joining a women's group can be understood as an extension of this unresolved dependency. Additionally, Kylie's internalization of her husband's criticisms during the marriage, particularly her perception of herself as "too emotional," suggests a history of negative self-judgments and the development of a fragile sense of self-worth.

Appropriate treatment goals stemming from psychodynamic theory includes resolving underlying unconscious internal conflicts related to attachment, emotional dependency, and self-worth. Additionally, treatment can aim to help Kylie develop a more secure sense of self and increase her emotional autonomy, allowing her to form healthier, more balanced relationships in the future. Building on her faith and existing protective factors, the treatment will also work on enhancing her emotional resilience and self-esteem, particularly in situations where she feels vulnerable to rejection or isolation.

Psychodynamic interventions for Kylie should be founded on the creation of a safe and supportive therapeutic relationship where unconscious material can be explored through free association and examination of transference. The clinician may also utilize interpretation to address how Kylie's feelings of inadequacy and anxiety may stem from early relational conflicts that were not fully resolved.

Cognitive Behavioral Conceptualization

Kylie's overall presentation is clearly being impacted by maladaptive cognitions and behaviors that have been reinforced by her recent divorce, the emotional distance in her marriage, and the resulting fears of isolation. These core beliefs likely contribute to her heightened anxiety, as she anticipates rejection or judgment from others. Her avoidance behaviors, such as withdrawing from social activities, reflect maladaptive coping strategies that temporarily alleviate anxiety but ultimately reinforce her negative beliefs about herself and her relationships. Kylie's difficulty in managing her emotions is compounded by her rumination on past negative experiences, which further reinforces her sense of worthlessness and unlovability. Cognitive distortions such as catastrophizing and overgeneralizing exacerbate her symptoms and contribute to a cycle of depression and anxiety.

The primary treatment goals using CBT would focus on identifying and modifying her maladaptive thought patterns and behaviors. Specifically, therapy would aim to challenge her negative core beliefs related to abandonment and self-worth and such beliefs would be examined through the identification of cognitive distortions, particularly the tendency to overgeneralize and catastrophize negative events. In addition to addressing cognitive distortions, treatment would aim to reduce Kylie's anxiety and depressive symptoms by encouraging her to gradually confront feared social situations, such as re-engaging in social activities like the women's group at her church or participating in fitness classes. Furthermore, the therapy would focus on improving Kylie's emotional regulation by teaching her practical adaptive coping strategies.

CBT interventions for Kylie could begin with psychoeducation regarding the relationship between thoughts, feelings, and behaviors, helping her understand how her negative thought patterns contribute to her emotional distress. Cognitive restructuring could help Kylie identify and challenge cognitive distortions, particularly her tendency to overgeneralize negative experiences and assume that others will judge her harshly. This could involve examining the evidence for and against her automatic thoughts and developing more balanced and realistic perspectives. Additionally, the clinician could introduce behavioral interventions, such as exposure therapy, to help Kylie gradually face situations that trigger her anxiety, such as attending social events or re-engaging in group activities, in a safe and controlled manner. These exposures would aim to reduce her avoidance behaviors and reinforce the idea that she can tolerate discomfort without catastrophic consequences. The therapist would also teach Kylie practical skills to manage her anxiety and emotional responses, such as deep breathing, progressive muscle relaxation, and mindfulness exercises. As Kylie works through these interventions, she would be encouraged to monitor her progress and use journaling or thought records to track shifts in her thinking and emotional responses. These interventions would help Kylie develop a more balanced view of herself, increase her confidence in social interactions, and ultimately break the cycle of anxiety and depression.

Through this CBT approach, Kylie would be better equipped to challenge and change the unhelpful cognitive and behavioral patterns that have contributed to her emotional distress, promoting long-term emotional well-being and a healthier, more positive view of herself and her relationships.

Biopsychosocial Conceptualization

Kylie's overall presentation appears to be exacerbated by her negative cognitions and beliefs, particularly her fear of abandonment and feelings of worthlessness, which have been intensified by the emotional trauma of her divorce. These psychological patterns seem to stem from her experiences of emotional dependence on her husband and her lack of independent social engagement, particularly after becoming a stay-at-home mother. Kylie's avoidance suggests maladaptive coping strategies in response to anxiety. Importantly, Kylie is navigating a significant life transition following her divorce, which has impacted her social support network. Her lack of social connection outside of her immediate family is contributing to her emotional distress, further reinforcing her sense of loneliness and fear of being judged.

Appropriate biopsychosocial treatment goals could involve helping Kylie manage her physical symptoms of anxiety, such as panic attacks and chest pain. Another goal could include challenging and reframing Kylie's negative core beliefs about herself, particularly her fears of abandonment and worthlessness. Kylie would also benefit from increased social engagement and rebuilding her social support network.

One intervention grounded in the biopsychosocial model could include teaching relaxation techniques to help Kylie manage the physiological symptoms of anxiety, such as heart palpitations, shaking, and chest pain. Additionally, CBT strategies would be incorporated to address Kylie's psychological symptoms. Specifically, cognitive restructuring could be used to challenge her negative core beliefs and behavioral interventions, such as exposure therapy, could be used to gradually reduce Kylie's avoidance behaviors and increase her engagement with social situations (such as attending church events or seeking social support from friends). One form of social support from which Kylie might benefit would be a divorce recovery group hosted by her local Catholic church.

Clinical Case Vignette #10

Demographic Information and History

Name: Jameson Jones.

Demographic Information: 37-year-old White male.

Medical Diagnoses: No relevant medical diagnoses reported.

Reason for Referral: Jameson was referred to therapy by his couples therapist whom he sees with his wife due to continuing arguments about how the "house should operate," including parenting their 7-year-old son, and Jameson "not following through" on tasks he commits to because he prioritizes his career. Recently, Jameson reported he missed his son's baseball game because he went to work on a Saturday to complete a report his boss wanted finished the day prior. Jameson reported that, though it may take him longer to complete work tasks, his boss appreciates his attention to detail, and he cannot understand why his wife does not appreciate this trait of his. Jameson's wife first brought them to couples therapy because of their recurring arguments and feeling constantly criticized by Jameson. Jameson was referred to individual therapy because he was told it could help his marriage to gain insight as to why he prioritizes some things, such as work, over others, such as spending time with his family.

Clinical Interview Data

Interpreter Used: No.

Current Psychosocial Stressors: Jameson has been receiving pressure from his boss about the amount of work he has been doing. Jameson reported his boss recently had a meeting with him regarding the amount of work he gets done compared to his peers. Jameson does not believe this will result in him getting fired but reported being "frustrated" with his boss as his work is "perfect" while his co-workers "sloppily and carelessly" turn in reports.

Protective Factors: Jameson is strong in his Jewish faith and is rule oriented. Jameson reported caring for his family and having "great" problem-solving skills.

Developmental History: Jameson reported meeting all developmental milestones on time.

Academic History: Jameson had average grades throughout school but was marked down points in his assignments for turning them in late. Jameson finds himself in similar patterns at his job, explaining he turns in reports to his boss lately consistently because of editing and re-editing the reports. Jameson reported his boss "learned better than to give him hard deadlines." However, recently Jameson reported his boss has been less accepting of him turning in reports late, though the reports have great attention to detail.

Social History: Jameson reported having "decent" relationships with co-workers, though he does not go to work-related functions because he does not view them as "friends." Other than his family, Jameson does not report having friends or socializing with other people.

Household: Jameson currently lives with his wife and 7-year-old son. Before marrying his wife, Jameson lived by himself in his adult years because he preferred having his apartment "his way."

Previous Psychiatric History: Jameson has been receiving couples therapy for the past 4 months. Jameson has never received individual psychiatric services previously.

Family Psychiatric History: Jameson reported his sister went to therapy when she got to college. Jameson reported he believes she began therapy to process childhood trauma from their father.

History of Self-Harm: No concerning symptoms reported.

Wellness Profile

Sleep: Jameson reported missing a couple of hours of sleep on nights when he stays late at work to finish reports. On nights he gets home on time, Jameson reported getting 7–8 hours of sleep nightly. On the nights he stays late at work, Jameson reported he could get less than 3 hours of sleep and has even stayed at the office to sleep there instead of commuting back home for an hour or two of sleep.

Diet: Jameson reported no concerns surrounding his diet and eating patterns. Jameson reported eating three "balanced" meals daily and will have a "protein-filled" snack. Jameson reported caring a lot about his physical health and believes having a healthy diet is "crucial."

Elimination: No symptoms reported.

Technology: Jameson limits his screentime to 3 hours of television and an hour of social media daily. Jameson spends most of his workday in front of a computer going over statistics and typing reports.

Physical Activity: Jameson reported running 3 miles every morning before going to work and will lift weights four times a week during his lunch break.

Substance Use/Abuse: Jameson reported having "a couple" of beers after work most days of the week.

Pain: 0/10.

Current Psychiatric Symptoms

Depression: No symptoms reported.

Anxiety: Jameson reported difficulty concentrating on tasks that require multiple steps, primarily focusing on one step of the task until it is completed "correctly." Jameson reported irritability and muscle tension when things are left askew by others, both at home and at work, which causes him distress.

Panic: No symptoms reported.

Mania: Jameson reported distractibility when completing some tasks, specifically when he hyperfocuses on specific aspects of tasks.

Psychosis: No symptoms reported.

Trauma: Jameson and his sister were victims of physical and verbal abuse from their father and witnessed domestic violence in their home. Jameson reported his father would get drunk after work and abuse him, his sister, or his mother if the house was not clean or if they made simple mistakes.

Eating Disorder: No symptoms reported.

Risky Behaviors/Sexual Activity: Jameson reported no risky behaviors. Jameson reported he "would never" break any laws or policies at work and has "zero empathy" for those breaking any rule.

Mental Status Exam

Appearance: *Dress*: appropriate. *Hygiene*: adequate. Appeared stated age.

Behavior: Cooperative, guarded.

Speech: *Rate*: within normal limits. *Articulation*: within normal limits. *Volume*: within normal limits. *Coherence*: within normal limits.

Mood: Jameson reported feeling "frustrated" with being referred to individual therapy, as he felt couples therapy "was enough." He stated he does not understand why people get "upset" when he "just does things that make sense and are right."

Affect: Full, labile, congruent to mood, appropriate to content of interview.

Thought Process: Logical, linear, goal directed.

Thought Content: Denied suicidal ideation, homicidal ideation, delusions, and hallucinations.

Orientation: Oriented to person, place, and time.

Recent Memory: Intact.

Remote Memory: Intact.

Attention/Concentration: Sufficient.

General Knowledge: Within normal limits.

Language: Within normal limits.

Insight: Poor.

Judgment: Fair.

Answer Key #10

Diversity Considerations

Jameson's upbringing within a Jewish faith tradition likely shapes his views regarding family dynamics, work ethic, and social responsibilities. His identification with Jewish values, including his rule-oriented nature and his emphasis on discipline and responsibility, could influence both his stress reactions and his interpersonal relationships. It is crucial to understand how these cultural beliefs and values might shape Jameson's interpersonal expectations, especially in his marriage and with his colleagues, although knowledge of which branch of Judaism he belongs to would be helpful (i.e., orthodox, conservative, etc.). The impact of intergenerational trauma in Jameson's case is also significant. The verbal and physical abuse he experienced from his father, along with witnessing domestic violence, likely continues to affect his current relationships. Additionally, generational trauma related to the history of the Jews may be impacting him. Conversely, as a White man in the workplace, his experiences of power and authority may differ significantly from others who may experience institutional barriers or discrimination, which is worth considering when discussing his professional expectations and the way he internalizes feedback from his boss. Granted, the manner in which Jameson expresses his Jewish identity may influence this variable. Again, because Jameson is a man, he may have internalized traditional masculine ideals that shape his emotional responses and interpersonal behaviors. These norms could influence his difficulty in expressing vulnerability or seeking emotional support outside of the family unit. His discomfort with individual therapy may reflect a broader cultural norm in which men are expected to be self-sufficient and control their emotions, particularly in the context of work and family life.

Jameson's adherence to his Jewish faith and involvement in religious practices may be an important protective factor for his emotional well-being. His strong faith could offer him a source of comfort, meaning, and moral guidance, especially in times of personal distress. His faith might also play a role in his sense of duty and responsibility toward his family. Understanding how his religious practices influence his views on family, work, and responsibility is essential to formulating a culturally sensitive approach to therapy. For example, his frustration with the notion of "doing things that make sense and are right" may reflect his internalization of religious or cultural teachings about personal and family duties.

Ethical Considerations

Given that Jameson is concurrently involved in couples therapy, coordination between the individual and couples clinicians is essential to avoid role confusion or conflicting treatment goals. With Jameson's consent, clear communication between the providers could be established to maintain ethical boundaries and provide continuity of care across settings.

Legal Considerations

None at this time.

Diagnostic Impressions and Justification

F60.5 Obsessive-Compulsive Personality Disorder.
Jameson meets the criteria because he displays a pervasive pattern of perfectionism and a need for control. This perfectionism interferes with task completion while also giving more time and energy towards work rather than leisurely activities. He demonstrates rigidity and stubbornness and does not delegate tasks to others due to worry about the task not being done correctly.

Psychodynamic Case Conceptualization

Jameson's overall presentation, including his symptomology, appears rooted in unresolved early developmental trauma. It seems like that Jameson developed a harsh superego and defense mechanisms such as reaction formation, displacement, and intellectualization to cope with early experiences of helplessness and danger. His compulsive work behaviors, prioritization of productivity over relationships, and intolerance for disorder or deviation from rules suggest the internalization of an idealized image of control and order as a defense against the chaos of his early family environment. His limited social relationships, emotional distance from peers, and lack of insight into the emotional needs of others further reflect deficits in early object relations and impaired capacity for affect regulation.

The primary goals of psychodynamic treatment with Jameson likely should center on enhancing insight into the unconscious internal conflicts underlying his perfectionism, control-seeking behaviors, and emotional rigidity. It would be helpful to increase Jameson's awareness of how early relational dynamics, particularly with his abusive father, continue to shape his internal object world and current interpersonal relationships. Additionally, goals can include facilitating integration of previously disavowed or conflicted emotional experiences, supporting ego development, and helping Jameson rework internalized critical object representations.

Psychodynamic psychotherapy generally emphasizes the therapeutic alliance as a vehicle for insight and transformation, and such should also be the case for Jameson. Interpretations should focus on unconscious internal conflicts, transference patterns, and the activation of Jameson's internalized relational schemas within the therapeutic dyad. Interventions could also include gentle exploration of the symbolic meaning of his compulsive work habits, late report submissions, and rigidity, linking these behaviors to early experiences of unpredictability and punishment.

Cognitive Behavioral Conceptualization

Jameson's symptoms and distress are likely being maintained by dysfunctional automatic thoughts as well as behavioral patterns that reinforce those beliefs and perpetuate a negative cycle of emotional distress, particularly irritability and anxiety. His attentional bias toward rules, order, and structure may serve as a compensatory strategy to manage underlying cognitive distortions around safety, control, and self-worth, all of which contribute to impaired functioning in his interpersonal relationships and increasing distress in both work and family domains.

Treatment should focus on identifying, challenging, and restructuring Jameson's maladaptive core beliefs and cognitive distortions related to perfectionism, control, and interpersonal expectations. A major goal will be to increase Jameson's cognitive flexibility as well as developing more adaptive problem-solving strategies, improving emotional regulation skills, and fostering more constructive communication patterns within his marriage. Treatment will also target behavioral activation in the social domain by increasing Jameson's engagement in meaningful interpersonal activities and reducing avoidant behaviors that reinforce his social isolation. Importantly, goals will include helping Jameson realign his value system so that familial relationships are integrated more fully into his sense of purpose and well-being, thereby decreasing conflict and improving relational satisfaction.

Treatment should begin with psychoeducation regarding the CBT model, especially the multidirectional relationship between thoughts, feelings, and behaviors. Cognitive restructuring techniques could be used to help Jameson identify and modify core beliefs and automatic thoughts that underlie his perfectionistic and control-driven behaviors. This could include the use of cognitive logs, thought records, and Socratic questioning to facilitate insight and challenge distortions such as all-or-nothing thinking, catastrophizing, and mind reading. Behavioral interventions could focus on exposure tasks related to tolerating imperfection and implementing graded practice in social situations. Finally, values clarification exercises and mindfulness techniques may be incorporated to promote present-focused awareness, reduce cognitive fusion with rigid rules, and support meaningful life choices in alignment with both work and family priorities.

Biopsychosocial Conceptualization

While Jameson did not report any significant health concerns, disrupted sleep occasionally results from overworking. He uses alcohol moderately and reported no history of psychiatric illness or medical conditions, indicating a relatively stable biological foundation. He likely presents with deeply internalized schemas around safety, control, perfectionism, and a rule-governed sense of morality. His psychological rigidity and difficulty tolerating ambiguity or disorder appear to function as maladaptive coping strategies aimed at managing residual anxiety and internalized fear. Unfortunately, Jameson's world is markedly constrained. Outside of work and family, he reported limited social contact and no significant friendships. His marriage is currently strained due to criticism, lack of follow-through on familial obligations, and emotional distance. Jameson's cultural identity, particularly his strong Jewish faith and value placed on rules and structure, plays a central role in his worldview and may further inform his cognitive style and interpersonal expectations.

Treatment goals could focus on promoting emotional flexibility, improving relational functioning, and integrating past trauma into a cohesive narrative that allows for healing and behavioral change. It would also help Jameson develop greater insight into how early trauma shapes his current schemas, emotional responses, and interpersonal behavior. Facilitating the development of self-compassion, emotional awareness, and distress tolerance will be essential. Additional goals could include increasing Jameson's engagement with meaningful social interactions beyond work and family, rebuilding emotional intimacy with his spouse, and learning to adapt expectations in relationships where his rigid standards may be causing conflict. Finally, the treatment plan should support Jameson in reconciling the protective aspects of his cultural and spiritual identity with a more flexible and empathetic approach to interpersonal relationships.

Biopsychosocial interventions could include cognitive restructuring, mindfulness-based strategies, and emotional skills training in empathy, validation, and conflict resolution may also be necessary. Encouraging Jameson to cultivate meaningful social engagement outside of his nuclear family will further support emotional growth and reduce reliance on rigid coping strategies. Attention to his cultural and religious values can serve as a strength-based component in therapy, fostering adaptive meaning-making and moral reasoning without reinforcing perfectionism or judgmental attitudes.

Conclusion

Personality disorders represent enduring, inflexible, and pervasive patterns of behavior and inner experience that significantly deviate from cultural expectations and contribute to functional impairments across cognitive, affective, interpersonal, and behavioral domains. Despite their relative rarity, personality disorders affect a notable portion of the general population, underscoring the importance of accurate diagnosis that is both culturally informed and developmentally contextualized. The DSM-5-TR offers two frameworks for understanding these disorders: the traditional categorical model, which organizes 10 personality disorders into 3 behaviorally distinct clusters, and the alternative model, which conceptualizes personality pathology through impairments in functioning and pathological traits. Both models reflect ongoing efforts within the field to balance clinical utility with empirical precision, and they emphasize the complexity inherent in assessing and treating personality pathology. Future clinical and research efforts should continue to explore integrative approaches that accommodate individual variability while promoting culturally responsive and evidence-based diagnostic and treatment practices.

References

APA (American Psychiatric Association). (2022). *Diagnostic and statistical manual of mental disorders* (5th ed., text rev.). American Psychiatric Association.

Baker, J. N., von Hoebel, S., & Cash, T. F. (2008). Narcissism and self-esteem in young adult women: A comparison of self-report and behavioral measures. *Personality and Individual Differences*, *45*(6), 588–594

Bateman, A. W., & Fonagy, P. (2004). Mentalization-based treatment of BPD. *Journal of Personality Disorders*, *18*(1), 36–51. https://doi.org/10.1521/pedi.18.1.36.32772.

Berry, J. W. (2005). Acculturation: Living successfully in two cultures. *International Journal of Intercultural Relations*, *29*(6), 697–712. https://doi.org/10.1016/j.ijintrel.2005.07.013.

Brave Heart, M. Y. H. (2003). The historical trauma response among Natives and its relationship with substance abuse: A Lakota illustration. *Journal of Psychoactive Drugs*, *35*(1), 7–13.

Choi, Y., & Chentsova-Dutton, Y. E. (2012). Parental socialization of emotion expression: Cultural and emotional specificity. *Emotion Review*, *4*(3), 271–280. https://doi.org/10.1177/1754073912439764.

Clarkin, J. F., Yeomans, F. E., & Kernberg, O. F. (2007). *Psychodynamic psychotherapy for personality disorders: A clinical handbook*. Guilford Press.

Crowell, S. E., Beauchaine, T. P., & Linehan, M. M. (2009). A biosocial developmental model of borderline personality: Elaborating and extending Linehan's theory. *Psychological Bulletin*, *135*(3), 495–510. https://doi.org/10.1037/a0015616.

Davies, J. M., & Frawley, M. G. (1994). *Treating the adult survivor of childhood sexual abuse: A psychoanalytic perspective*. Basic Books.

Fonagy, P., & Bateman, A. W. (2008). The development of borderline personality disorder – A mentalizing model. *Journal of Personality Disorders*, *22*(1), 4–21. https://doi.org/10.1521/pedi.2008.22.1.4.

Fonagy, P., Target, M., Steele, M., Steele, H., & Hagen, R. (2002). Attachment and reflective function: Their role in self-organization. *Development and Psychopathology*, *14*(4), 799–815.

Freud, S. (1936). *The ego and the mechanisms of defense*. Hogarth Press.

Gilligan, C. (1982). *In a different voice: Psychological theory and women's development*. Harvard University Press.

Gone, J. P. (2013). Redressing First Nations historical trauma: Theorizing mechanisms for indigenous culture as mental health treatment. *Transcultural Psychiatry*, *50*(5), 683–706.

Hammond, W. P. (2010). Psychosocial correlates of medical mistrust among African American men. *American Journal of Community Psychology*, *45*(1–2), 87–106.

Herman, J. L. (1992). *Trauma and recovery: The aftermath of violence – from domestic abuse to political terror*. Basic Books.

Kim, B. S. K. (2007). Adherence to Asian and European American cultural values and attitudes toward seeking professional psychological help among Asian American college students. *Journal of Counseling Psychology*, *54*(4), 474–480. https://doi.org/10.1037/0022-0167.54.4.474.

Leong, F. T. L., & Lau, A. S. L. (2001). Barriers to providing effective mental health services to Asian Americans. *Mental Health Services Research*, *3*(4), 201–214. https://doi.org/10.1023/A:1013177014788.

Linehan, M. M. (1993). *Cognitive-behavioral treatment of borderline personality disorder*. Guilford Press.

Neighbors, H. W., Musick, M. A., & Williams, D. R. (2007). The African American minister as a source of help for serious personal crises: Bridge or barrier to mental health care? *Health Education & Behavior*, *25*(6), 759–777.

Sue, S., Zane, N., Nagayama Hall, G. C., & Berger, L. K. (2009). The case for cultural competency in psychotherapeutic interventions. *Annual Review of Psychology*, *60*, 525–548. https://doi.org/10.1146/annurev.psych.60.110707.163651.

Sue, D. W., Sue, D., Neville, H. A., & Smith, L. (2019). *Counseling the culturally diverse: Theory and practice* (8th ed.). Wiley.

Conclusion

Veronica Regueiro

This volume, the product of the combined clinical education, training, and experience of multiple licensed clinical psychologists and doctoral students, explores a broad range of clinical case vignettes, each reflecting a distinct disorder curated from the DSM-5-TR. Hopefully, the clinical case vignettes included in this volume have highlighted the multifaceted nature of mental health disorders as well as the importance of compassionate person-centered care. Each chapter has attempted to capture the nuanced nature of patient identities as well as the centrality of ethical and legal practice grounded in both cultural competence and cultural humility. Intentional consideration of diversity, equity, inclusion, and cultural humility is crucial to the provision of compassionate patient-centered care that reflects the dignity of the person and allows for human flourishing, rather than symptom management. It is our hope that this book has served as a valuable tool for faculty members, clinical supervisors, and training directors, as well as their students, and that the foundational knowledge included in each chapter supports excellence in clinical practice.

What began as a response to a practical need has evolved into a far more meaningful endeavor for all the authors involved in this project. The completion of this volume, representative of the efforts of many diverse professionals at various institutions across the United States, represents one small but very important contribution toward supporting the faculty, clinical supervisors, and training directors responsible for shaping the future of mental health. This collection is ultimately intended to support the development of critical thinking and diagnostic skills in graduate and doctoral students and hopefully we have accomplished that. Graduate and doctoral training lays the foundation for understanding psychopathology as well as alleviating suffering and some of the most effective training tools in the pursuit of these goals are clinical case vignettes. Clinical case vignettes bridge theory and practice, allowing for critical thinking as well as exposure to diverse situations with minimal risk.

DOI: 10.4324/9781003586531-16

Theoretical Orientation in Clinical Practice

A clearly defined theoretical orientation is essential to both the ethical and effective practice of clinical psychology as well as the other professions that contribute to the field of mental health. Theoretical orientations provide clinicians with structured frameworks for understanding psychopathology as they help clinicians organize patient information into meaningful patterns. Theoretical orientations also provide shared language for training and interdisciplinary collaboration purposes. The lack of a clearly defined theoretical orientation can sometimes result in reactive clinical decision making based on subjective experience instead of objective, evidence-based practice, which can ultimately compromise patient outcomes.

Psychodynamic theory, rooted in classical psychoanalysis but modernized by several clinicians since Freud, represents just one of the three theoretical orientations utilized to conceptualize the clinical case vignettes presented in this volume. Psychodynamic theory emphasizes the role of unconscious processes, internal conflicts, and relational dynamics in the formation of psychopathology. Often underrepresented in training programs and also often viewed as less accessible due to its difficulty in being manualized, psychodynamic psychotherapy has nevertheless demonstrated empirical evidence and remains relevant specifically because of its adaptability and integrative capacity. CBT, the second theoretical orientation utilized to conceptualize clinical case vignettes in this volume is widely recognized specifically for its structured, evidence-based, manualized approach. Based on both cognitive psychology and behaviorism, CBT emphasizes the role of thoughts and behaviors in the development and maintenance of psychopathology. CBT is highly adaptable, and multiple third-wave treatments have been born from it, including ACT, DBT, and MBCT. CBT does have some critics but is ultimately considered to be the standard of care for many disorders found in the DSM-5-TR. Differing significantly from both psychodynamic theory and CBT is the biopsychosocial model, the third theoretical orientation utilized in the volume to conceptualize clinical case vignettes. Developed in response to both biological and psychological models of psychopathology, the biopsychosocial model instead proposes that psychopathology is born out of complex interactions between biology, psychology, and the social environment. As such, the biopsychosocial model promotes a somewhat more holistic approach to patient care and is endorsed by many professional practice organizations. One significant concern pertaining to the biopsychosocial model, however, is that while it offers a helpful framework for conceptualizing psychopathology, it lacks clear guidelines pertaining to appropriate treatment goals and interventions.

Ultimately, clearly defined and operationalized theoretical orientations are foundational to ethical and effective clinical practice, not only because they provide clinicians with structured frameworks within which they can understand and address psychopathology, but also because they provide consistency and a shared language across settings. That being said, there is no one theoretical orientation that can offer a truly comprehensive understanding of the person. Each theoretical orientation offers just one lens, one perspective, through which the person, suffering, and flourishing can be understood. Together, however, these theoretical orientations capture the complexity of the human experience and highlight the utility of theory-driven care.

Legal and Ethical Obligations

Just as a well-defined theoretical orientation can serve as the foundation for competent compassionate care, so too can adherence to legal statutes and ethical principles. Because legislation and ethical codes evolve in response to new research findings, practice issues, etc., mental health clinicians must bear the responsibility of keeping themselves up-to-date regarding changes implemented by the federal government, state law, licensing boards, and professional practice organizations. Compliance with both federal and state law as well as adherence to a professional ethics code not only ensures that patients are provided with high quality care but also mitigates liability and maintains public trust in the professionals serving the field of mental health.

Licensed clinical psychologists follow the ethics code published by the American Psychological Association but all major professional organizations representing mental health clinicians have developed ethics codes to help guide the practice of their constituencies. Precepts common to most ethics codes include beneficence and non-maleficence, fidelity and responsibility, integrity, justice, and respect for the rights and dignity of others. Most mental health clinicians are also adjured to practice only within the scope of their respective competencies and to adopt a position of lifelong learning for the duration of their careers.

Diversity, Equity, Inclusion, and Cultural Humility

Conceptualizing and diagnosing patients in any mental health setting is a foundational skill that creates the opportunity for appropriate treatment. The process of conceptualization and diagnosing requires not just symptom identification but also exploration of symptom etiology, duration, and severity, all within the context of a patient's history and context. An accurate diagnosis can open the door to effective treatment within the context of a compassionate person-centered approach to care. The DSM-5-TR, the most recent iteration of the DSM, incorporates developmental and cultural considerations into each diagnostic classification to support clinicians in providing culturally congruent care while allowing for context-specific diagnoses. Diversity considerations are integral to the diagnostic process as they allow clinicians to understand the role of various diversity factors in the development, manifestation, and maintenance of symptoms. As science and society have both progressed, seismic shifts have been reflected in the DSM, with factors now considered diversity variables slowly de-pathologized over time, allowing the DSM to reflect at least some of the aspects considered normative in the society in which it was produced. Some of the most significant changes to the DSM over time have included the ways in which homosexuality and the distress related to transgenderism have been qualified. Additional updates to the DSM have included acknowledgment of how one's sociocultural context can influence diagnosis, with some marginalized groups being disproportionately diagnosed with certain severe persistent mental illness while other groups have been disregarded. Whether one's particular demographic group is being overpathologized or disregarded, the stage is set for the proliferation of disparities in the mental health care system, which can negatively impact treatment and access to care for marginalized groups. Clinicians are encouraged to consider carefully the influence of diversity variables on symptom presentation and diagnosis as well as clinical care and, perhaps more importantly, to consider the intersectionality of identity when appropriate. Models such as Hay's ADDRESSING framework or Sue's Tripartite Framework can support clinicians in thinking comprehensively through the various diverse identities with which patients often present. The gradual evolution of cultural considerations and diversity variables in diagnostic systems like the DSM underscores the importance of incorporating diversity, equity, and inclusion (DEI) into clinical practice. As diagnostic criteria have changed over time to reflect advances in the psychological and medical sciences, it can only be assumed that diagnostic criteria will continue to evolve to keep pace with research. By prioritizing DEI and cultural humility, clinicians can provide patient care that honors patient dignity, promotes justice, and fosters healing. Not only is this approach considered best practice – it is an ethical imperative in providing equitable care.

Mental health clinicians are increasingly expected to provide compassionate, competent care to diverse patients, but it is unrealistic to expect that any one clinician be able to master every diversity variable with which a patient might present. As such, cultural humility, characterized by lifelong learning, self-reflection and critique, and acknowledging the limitations of education and training, can encourage clinicians to remain non-defensive and open to learning. Cultural humility also stresses the importance of acknowledging the power differential between clinicians and patients, creating the space for patients to serve as the experts in their own lives. Cultural humility requires a profound understanding of humility itself, which involves acknowledging that there are as many ways of knowing and experiencing the world as there are people. Clinicians are encouraged to consider their own multifaceted identities in order to understand how their intersecting identities have shaped their worldviews and therefore, of course, their interactions with patients. For clinicians wanting to utilize object measures in their clinical practice, the MCHS, based in part on a concept analysis of cultural humility, could be valuable. The CHS may also be helpful and can be administered to patients to elicit feedback. Use of these measures can support clinicians in identifying their areas of strength related to cultural humility as well as their areas for growth. The CFI, included in the DSM-5-TR, offers clinicians a structured set of questions designed to facilitate conversations regarding how cultural factors shape patients' identities, interpretations of symptoms, and expectations of care. While not explicitly grounded in cultural humility, the CFI does offer guidance regarding how to initiate discussions pertaining to the role culture plays in patient expressions of distress. Ultimately, the practice of cultural humility must extend beyond good intentions and invite both individual and institutional commitment. Psychological safety may serve as a foundational aspect of the practice of cultural humility in healthcare settings and can potentially lead clinicians and their students to co-create clinical culture grounded in both individual introspection and system change.

Ultimately, the process of diagnostic formulation and conceptualization are deeply interconnected with cultural humility, each reinforcing the ethical imperative to provide compassionate person-centered care. While many tools exist to provide clinicians with guidance and support, it is ultimately the responsibility of each individual clinician to intentionally apply the concept of cultural humility in healing spaces. Cultural humility is the necessary and ideal complement to diagnostic rigor, encouraging the use of validated tools while also acknowledging that patients must serve as the experts regarding their own lived experiences. In the end, no tool can replace a clinician's authentic commitment to equity and accountability.

Psychopathology and Human Flourishing

This volume has, as far as it is possible to do so with such a limited number of words, attempted to provide a general exploration of the DSM-5-TR, specifically for the purpose of supporting mental health clinicians as they work to heal patients and train students and supervisees. Through an integrated structure that allows for the conceptualization of demographic information and symptom report through multiple perspectives, this volume offers a multidimensional understanding of psychopathology as it manifests in diverse populations. Each chapter includes clinical case vignettes exemplifying diagnoses curated from specific chapters of the DSM-5-TR to reflect both the psychopathology symptomatic of a particular disorder but also the context of the patient. Diversity variables were highlighted throughout, as were variables associated with ethical and legal practice. The theoretical orientations utilized emphasize the diversity of explanatory models as well as how conceptualization of a patient through a particular lens ultimately informs treatment planning. Overall, this book has sought to offer a multifaceted, practice-oriented exploration of psychopathology enriched by theoretical diversity as well as attention to legal and ethical obligations. It is through the practice of both diagnostic rigor and cultural humility that mental health clinicians can cultivate competency and compassion.

Mental health clinicians occupy a uniquely impactful position within the broader health and social service systems in which they work, frequently bearing witness to the ways in which individual suffering, cultural context, and systemic inequity interact with one another. It is because mental health clinicians serve in such spaces that they are called upon to not simply manage symptoms of mental illness or improve functioning but to actively promote human flourishing. Within a context of ethical and legal fidelity, cultural humility, and competent evidence-based practice grounded in robust understanding of theoretical orientations, human flourishing is possible. When mental health clinicians consistently present themselves as competent, fair, and trustworthy, they cultivate the safety, trust, and respect essential for healing and growth. Mental health clinicians who are willing to demonstrate cultural humility and actively work to incorporate culturally informed interventions into care not only mitigate the risk of harm to their patients but also empower their patients to affirm their identities and reclaim agency. It is within the context of theory, culture, and law and ethics that human flourishing becomes a realistic goal of mental health clinicians. It is by honoring the dignity of the person, affirming the rich diversity of the human experience, and implementing effective interventions that mental health clinicians can create conditions in which patients might be able to grow beyond the constraints of mental illness into having fuller and more meaningful lives. Ultimately, the work of any mental health clinician is not simply clinical – it is deeply humanistic and profoundly transformative.

Continuing the Journey

In no academic volume is the conclusion meant to signify the end of learning but rather a gateway into more nuanced inquiry and deeper understanding. In that spirit, below is a curated selection of recommended readings developed to extend the learning process beyond the pages of this one textbook. In this conclusion, we hope you find both an invitation and a bridge into a collection of readings that will inspire you to think deeply and practice compassionately so that you can more meaningfully engage with the lived experiences of your patients. Stay curious, always asking *why* instead of only *what*. Challenge yourself personally and professionally. Commit yourself to the ideals of excellence, integrity, and justice that represent the best of what mental health care has to offer. Most importantly, in the ever-evolving field of mental health, eschew certainty and move forward with the disciplined openness that can transform a mental health clinician into a catalyst for individual and collective transformation.

Recommendations for Future Reading

Anxiety Disorders

American Psychiatric Association. (2022). *Diagnostic and statistical manual of mental disorders* (5th ed., text rev.; DSM-5-TR). American Psychiatric Publishing.

Barlow, D. H. (2021). *Anxiety and its disorders: The nature and treatment of anxiety and panic* (2nd ed.). Guilford Press.

Craske, M. G., & Stein, M. B. (2022). *Anxiety disorders*. In G. F. Koob, M. Le Moal, & R. F. Thompson (Eds.), *Encyclopedia of behavioral neuroscience* (2nd ed., pp. 164–169). Elsevier. https://doi.org/10.1016/B978-0-12-819641-0.00039-6.

Hofmann, S. G., Asnaani, A., Vonk, I. J., Sawyer, A. T., & Fang, A. (2012). The efficacy of cognitive behavioral therapy: A review of meta-analyses. *Cognitive Therapy and Research*, *36*(5), 427–440. https://doi.org/10.1007/s10608-012-9476-1.

Kaczkurkin, A. N., & Foa, E. B. (2015). Cognitive-behavioral therapy for anxiety disorders: An update on the empirical evidence. *Dialogues in Clinical Neuroscience*, *17*(3), 337–346. https://doi.org/10.31887/DCNS.2015.17.3/akaczkurkin.

LeDoux, J. (2015). *Anxious: Using the brain to understand and treat fear and anxiety*. Viking.

Roy-Byrne, P. P. (2015). Treatment-refractory anxiety; definition, risk factors, and treatment challenges. *Dialogues in Clinical Neuroscience*, *17*(3), 191–206. https://doi.org/10.31887/DCNS.2015.17.3/proybyrne.

Stein, D. J., Scott, K. M., de Jonge, P., & Kessler, R. C. (2017). Epidemiology of anxiety disorders: From surveys to nosology and back. *Dialogues in Clinical Neuroscience*, *19*(2), 127–136. https://doi.org/10.31887/DCNS.2017.19.2/dstein.

Watson, D., & O'Hara, M. W. (2017). Anxiety disorders, comorbidity, and risk for depression: Clinical and theoretical implications. In L. B. Alloy & J. H. Riskind (Eds.), *Cognitive vulnerability to emotional disorders* (pp. 115–138). Routledge.

Biopsychosocial Model

Borrell-Carrio, F., Suchman, A. L., & Epstein, R. M. (2004). The biopsychosocial model 25 years later: Principles, practice, and scientific inquiry. *Annals of Family Medicine*, *2*(6), 576–582. https://doi.org/10.1370/afm.245.

Engel, G. L. (1977). The need for a new medical model: A challenge for biomedicine. *Science*, *196*(4286), 129–136. https://doi.org/10.1126/science.847460.

Engel, G. L. (1980). The clinical application of the biopsychosocial model. *The American Journal of Psychiatry*, *137*(5), 535–544. https://doi.org/10.1176/ajp.137.5.535.

Frankel, R. M., Quill, T. E., & McDaniel, S. H. (Eds.). (2003). *The biopsychosocial approach: Past, present, future*. University of Rochester Press.

Lehman, B. J., David, D. M., & Gruber, J. A. (2017). Rethinking the biopsychosocial model of health: Understanding health as a dynamic system. *Social and Personality Psychology Compass*, *11*(8), e12328. https://doi.org/10.1111/spc3.12328.

Suls, J., & Rothman, A. (2004). Evolution of the biopsychosocial model: Prospects and challenges for health psychology. *Health Psychology*, *23*(2), 119–125. https://doi.org/10.1037/02786133.23.2.119.

Wade, D. T., & Halligan, P. W. (2017). The biopsychosocial model of illness: A model whose time has come. *Clinical Rehabilitation*, *31*(8), 995–1004. https://doi.org/10.1177/0269215517709890.

White, K. P. (2005). The biopsychosocial model and its limitations. In G. Fink (Ed.), *Encyclopedia of stress* (2nd ed., Vol. 1, pp. 307–312). Academic Press.

Zachariae, R. (2009). Psychoneuroimmunology: A bio-psycho-social approach to health and disease. *Scandinavian Journal of Psychology*, *50*(6), 645–651. https://doi.org/10.1111/j.1467-9450.2009.00779.x.

Biosocial Theory

Beauchaine, T. P., & Zalewski, M. (2016). Biosocial influences on the development of borderline personality disorder. *Development and Psychopathology*, *28*(4pt1), 1211–1231. https://doi.org/10.1017/S0954579416000797.

Crowell, S. E., Beauchaine, T. P., & Linehan, M. M. (2009). A biosocial developmental model of borderline personality: Elaborating and extending Linehan's theory. *Psychological Bulletin*, *135*(3), 495–510. https://doi.org/10.1037/a0015616.

Bipolar and Related Disorders

American Psychiatric Association. (2022). *Diagnostic and statistical manual of mental disorders* (5th ed., text rev.; DSM-5-TR). https://doi.org/10.1176/appi.books.9780890425787.

Basco, M. R., & Rush, A. J. (2005). *Cognitive-behavioral therapy for bipolar disorder* (2nd ed.). Guilford Press.

Goodwin, F. K., & Jamison, K. R. (2007). *Manic-depressive illness: Bipolar disorders and recurrent depression* (2nd ed.). Oxford University Press.

Miklowitz, D. J. (2019). *The bipolar disorder survival guide: What you and your family need to know* (3rd ed.). Guilford Press.

Miklowitz, D. J., & Johnson, S. L. (2021). *Bipolar disorder: A family-focused treatment approach* (2nd ed.). Guilford Press.

Phillips, M. L., Kupfer, D. J., & Frank, E. (2013). *Bipolar disorder: Diagnosis and assessment*. In B. J. Sadock, V. A. Sadock, & P. Ruiz (Eds.), *Kaplan & Sadock's comprehensive textbook of psychiatry* (10th ed., pp. 1710–1722). Wolters Kluwer.

Post, R. M., & Leverich, G. S. (2008). *Treatment of bipolar illness: A casebook for clinicians and patients*. W. W. Norton.

Soreff, S. M., & Xiong, G. L. (2020). Bipolar affective disorder. https://www.ncbi.nlm.nih.gov/books/NBK153185/.

Vieta, E., & Suppes, T. (2008). Maintenance therapy of bipolar disorder. *Psychopharmacology Bulletin*, *41*(2), 41–52.

Yatham, L. N., & Maj, M. (Eds.). (2011). *Bipolar disorder: Clinical and neurobiological foundations*. Wiley-Blackwell.

Cognitive Behavioral Therapy

Beck, A. T., Rush, A. J., Shaw, B. F., & Emery, G. (1979). *Cognitive therapy of depression*. Guilford Press.

Beck, J. S. (2011). *Cognitive behavior therapy: Basics and beyond* (2nd ed.). Guilford Press.

Clark, D. A., & Beck, A. T. (2012). *The anxiety and worry workbook: The cognitive behavioral solution*. Guilford Press.

Dobson, K. S., & Dozois, D. J. A. (Eds.). (2019). *Handbook of cognitive-behavioral therapies* (4th ed.). Guilford Press.

Ellis, A. (1962). *Reason and emotion in psychotherapy*. Lyle Stuart.

Ellis, A., & Dryden, W. (2007). *The practice of rational emotive behavior therapy* (2nd ed.). Springer Publishing.

Hofmann, S. G., Asnaani, A., Vonk, I. J., Sawyer, A. T., & Fang, A. (2012). The efficacy of cognitive behavioral therapy: A review of meta-analyses. *Cognitive Therapy and Research*, *36*(5), 427–440. https://doi.org/10.1007/s10608-012-9476-1.

Kuyken, W., Padesky, C. A., & Dudley, R. (2009). *Collaborative case conceptualization: Working effectively with clients in cognitive-behavioral therapy*. Guilford Press.

Leahy, R. L. (2017). *Cognitive therapy techniques: A practitioner's guide* (2nd ed.). Guilford Press.

Persons, J. B. (2008). *The case formulation approach to cognitive-behavior therapy*. Guilford Press.

Wright, J. H., Brown, G. K., Thase, M. E., Basco, M. R., & Beck, A. T. (2017). *Cognitive therapy for depression: A practical and comprehensive guide* (2nd ed.). American Psychiatric Publishing.

Cultural Humility

American Psychological Association. (2017). *Multicultural guidelines: An ecological approach to context, identity, and intersectionality*. https://www.apa.org/about/policy/multicultural guidelines.

Fisher-Borne, M., Cain, J. M., & Martin, S. L. (2015). From mastery to accountability: Cultural humility as an alternative to cultural competence. *Social Work Education*, *34*(2), 165–181. https://doi.org/10.1080/02615479.2014.977244.

Foronda, C., Baptiste, D. L., Reinholdt, M. M., & Ousman, K. (2016). Cultural humility: A concept analysis. *Journal of Transcultural Nursing*, *27*(3), 210–217. https://doi.org/10.1177/1043659615592677.

Gallardo, M. E. (Ed.). (2014). *Developing cultural humility: Embracing race, privilege, and power*. SAGE Publications.

Hook, J. N., Davis, D. E., Owen, J., Worthington, E. L., Jr., & Utsey, S. O. (2013). Cultural humility: Measuring openness to culturally diverse clients. *Journal of Counseling Psychology*, *60*(3), 353–366. https://doi.org/10.1037/a0032595.

Isaacson, M. (2014). Clarifying concepts: Cultural humility or competency. *Journal of Professional Nursing*, *30*(3), 251–258. https://doi.org/10.1016/j.profnurs.2013.09.011.

Mosher, D. K., Hook, J. N., Captari, L. E., Davis, D. E., DeBlaere, C., & Owen, J. (2017). Cultural humility: A therapeutic framework for engaging diverse clients. *Practice Innovations*, *2*(4), 221–233. https://doi.org/10.1037/pri0000055.

National Association of Social Workers. (2015). *Standards and indicators for cultural competence in social work practice*. https://www.socialworkers.org/Practice/Practice-Standards Guidelines.

Substance Abuse and Mental Health Services Administration. (2014). *Improving cultural competence* (TIP Series 59, HHS Publication No. SMA 15-4849). US Department of Health and Human Services. https://store.samhsa.gov/product/TIP-59-Improving Cultural-Competence/SMA15-4849.

Sue, S., Cheng, J. K. Y., Saad, C. S., & Chu, J. P. (2012). Asian American mental health: A call to action. *American Psychologist*, *67*(7), 532–544. https://doi.org/10.1037/a0028900.

Tervalon, M., & Murray-García, J. (1998). Cultural humility versus cultural competence: A critical distinction in defining physician training outcomes in multicultural education. *Journal of Health Care for the Poor and Underserved*, *9*(2), 117–125. https://doi.org/10.1353/hpu.2010.0233.

Yeager, K. A., & Bauer-Wu, S. (2013). Cultural humility: Essential foundation for clinical researchers. *Applied Nursing Research*, *26*(4), 251–256. https://doi.org/10.1016/j.apnr.2013.06.008.

Disruptive, Impulse-Control, and Conduct Disorders

American Psychiatric Association. (2022). *Diagnostic and statistical manual of mental disorders* (5th ed., text rev.; DSM-5-TR). https://doi.org/10.1176/appi.books.9780890425787.

Barkley, R. A. (2013). *Defiant children: A clinician's manual for assessment and parent training* (3rd ed.). Guilford Press.

Bloomquist, M. L. (2012). *Skills training for children with behavior disorders: A parent and practitioner guidebook* (2nd ed.). Guilford Press.

Frick, P. J., & Matlasz, T. M. (2020). *Conduct disorder: A biopsychosocial model*. Springer.

Kazdin, A. E. (2005). *Parent management training: Treatment for oppositional, aggressive, and antisocial behavior in children and adolescents*. Oxford University Press. https://doi.org/10.1093/med:psych/9780195386004.001.0001.

Kazdin, A. E. (2008). Evidence-based treatment and practice: New opportunities to bridge clinical research and practice, enhance the knowledge base, and improve patient care. *American Psychologist*, *63*(3), 146–159. https://doi.org/10.1037/0003-066X.63.3.146.

Kendall, P. C. (Ed.). (2011). *Child and adolescent therapy: Cognitive-behavioral procedures* (4th ed.). Guilford Press.

Mash, E. J., & Barkley, R. A. (Eds.). (2014). *Child psychopathology* (3rd ed.). Guilford Press.

Pelham, W. E., Fabiano, G. A., & Waxmonsky, J. G. (2021). Treatment of disruptive behavior disorders. In J. M. Rey (Ed.), *IACAPAP e-textbook of child and adolescent mental health* (Chapter D.1). International Association for Child and Adolescent Psychiatry and Allied Professions. https://iacapap.org.

Shaw, D. S. (2013). Future directions for research on the development and prevention of early conduct problems. *Journal of Clinical Child & Adolescent Psychology*, *42*(3), 418–428. https://doi.org/10.1080/15374416.2013.779662.

Depressive Disorders

American Psychiatric Association. (2022). *Diagnostic and statistical manual of mental disorders* (5th ed., text rev.; DSM-5-TR). American Psychiatric Publishing.

Beck, A. T., Rush, A. J., Shaw, B. F., & Emery, G. (1979). *Cognitive therapy of depression*. Guilford Press.

Cuijpers, P. (2020). *Depression: A global public health problem*. Springer.

Cuijpers, P., Karyotaki, E., Weitz, E., Andersson, G., Hollon, S. D., van Straten, A., & Ebert, D. D. (2016). The effects of psychotherapies for major depression in adults on remission, recovery and improvement: A meta-analysis. *Journal of Affective Disorders*, *202*, 511–517. https://doi.org/10.1016/j.jad.2016.05.036.

Gilbert, P. (2016). *Depression: The evolution of powerlessness* (2nd ed.). Routledge.

Gotlib, I. H., & Hammen, C. L. (Eds.). (2014). *Handbook of depression* (3rd ed.). Guilford Press.

Insel, T. R., & Charney, D. S. (2003). Research on major depression: Strategies and priorities. *JAMA*, *289*(23), 3167–3168. https://doi.org/10.1001/jama.289.23.3167.

Kendler, K. S. (2016). The phenomenology of major depression and the representativeness and nature of DSM criteria. *American Journal of Psychiatry*, *173*(8), 771–780. https://doi.org/10.1176/appi.ajp.2016.15121509.

Klein, D. N., & Santiago, N. J. (2003). Dysthymia and chronic depression: Introduction, classification, risk factors, and course. *Journal of Clinical Psychology*, *59*(8), 807–816. https://doi.org/10.1002/jclp.10161.

National Institute for Health and Care Excellence. (2022). *Depression in adults: Treatment and management* (NICE Guideline NG222). https://www.nice.org.uk/guidance/ng222.

Dissociative Disorders

American Psychiatric Association. (2022). *Diagnostic and statistical manual of mental disorders* (5th ed., text rev.; DSM-5-TR). American Psychiatric Publishing.

Brand, B. L., Loewenstein, R. J., & Lanius, R. A. (2014). Dissociative disorders: An overview of assessment, phenomenology, and treatment. *Psychiatric Clinics of North America*, *37*(2), 333–349. https://doi.org/10.1016/j.psc.2014.03.001.

Chu, J. A., & Bowman, E. S. (2016). *Treating dissociative disorders: The therapeutic relationship, phase-oriented treatment, and the search for authenticity*. American Psychiatric Publishing.

Howell, E. F. (2011). *Understanding and treating dissociative identity disorder: A relational approach*. Routledge.

International Society for the Study of Trauma and Dissociation. (2011). Guidelines for treating dissociative identity disorder in adults, third revision. *Journal of Trauma & Dissociation*, *12*(2), 115–187. https://doi.org/10.1080/15299732.2011.537247.

Lanius, R. A., Paulsen, S. L., & Corrigan, F. M. (Eds.). (2014). *Neurobiology and treatment of traumatic dissociation: Toward an embodied self.* Springer.

Lyssenko, L., Schmahl, C., Bockhacker, L., Vonderlin, R., Bohus, M., & Kleindienst, N. (2018). Dissociation in psychiatric disorders: A meta-analysis of studies using the Dissociative Experiences Scale. *American Journal of Psychiatry*, *175*(1), 37–46. https://doi.org/10.1176/appi.ajp.2017.17010025.

Reinders, A. A. T. S., Willemsen, A. T. M., Vos, H. P. J., den Boer, J. A., & Nijenhuis, E. R. S. (2012). Fact or factitious? A psychobiological study of authentic and simulated dissociative identity states. *PLoS One*, *7*(6), e39279. https://doi.org/10.1371/journal.pone.0039279.

Şar, V., Dorahy, M. J., & Krüger, C. (2017). Revisiting the etiological and nosological aspects of dissociative identity disorder: A biopsychosocial perspective. *Psychology Research and Behavior Management*, *10*, 137–146. https://doi.org/10.2147/PRBM.S113734.

Diversity, Equity, and Inclusion

American Psychological Association. (2017). *Multicultural guidelines: An ecological approach to context, identity, and intersectionality*. https://www.apa.org/about/policy/multicultural-guidelines.

American Psychiatric Association. (2023). *APA's framework for addressing health equity in psychiatry*. https://www.psychiatry.org/psychiatrists/structural-racism-task-force.

Comas-Díaz, L., & Jacobsen, F. M. (2020). Ethnocultural allodynia as psychological pain: A culturally based diagnostic formulation. *American Psychologist*, *75*(6), 823–834. https://doi.org/10.1037/amp0000651.

Gallardo, M. E. (Ed.). (2014). *Developing cultural humility: Embracing race, privilege and power*. SAGE Publications.

Hall, G. C. N., Yip, T., & Zárate, M. A. (2016). On becoming multicultural in a monocultural research world: A conceptual approach to studying ethnocultural diversity. *American Psychologist*, *71*(1), 40–51. https://doi.org/10.1037/a0039734.

National Association of Social Workers. (2015). *Standards and indicators for cultural competence in social work practice*. https://www.socialworkers.org/Practice/Practice-Standards Guidelines.

Substance Abuse and Mental Health Services Administration. (2014). *Improving cultural competence* (Treatment Improvement Protocol Series No. 59). U.S. Department of Health and Human Services. https://store.samhsa.gov/product/TIP-59-Improving-Cultural Competence/SMA15-4849

Sue, D. W., & Sue, D. (2022). *Counseling the culturally diverse: Theory and practice* (9th ed.). Wiley.

Truong, K. L., Paradies, Y., & Priest, N. (2014). Interventions to improve cultural competency in healthcare: A systematic review of the literature. *BMC Health Services Research*, *14*, Article 99. https://doi.org/10.1186/1472-6963-14-99.

US Department of Health and Human Services, Office of Minority Health. (2018). *National standards for culturally and linguistically appropriate services (CLAS) in health and health care*. https://thinkculturalhealth.hhs.gov/clas.

Walker, R., & Bigelow, D. A. (2011). Mental health and racial/ethnic disparities: A framework for culturally competent care. *Psychiatric Services*, *62*(2), 209–211. https://doi.org/10.1176/ps.62.2.pss6202_0209.

Williams, D. R., Lawrence, J. A., & Davis, B. A. (2019). Racism and health: Evidence and needed research. *Annual Review of Public Health*, *40*, 105–125. https://doi.org/10.1146/annurevpublhealth-040218-043750.

Feeding and Eating Disorders

American Psychiatric Association. (2022). Diagnostic and statistical manual of mental disorders (5th ed., text rev.; DSM-5-TR). https://doi.org/10.1176/appi.books.9780890425787.

Attia, E., & Walsh, B. T. (2009). Behavioral management for anorexia nervosa. *New England Journal of Medicine*, *360*(5), 500–506. https://doi.org/10.1056/NEJMct0804535.

Bailey, A. P., Parker, A. G., Colautti, L. A., Hart, L. M., Liu, P., & Hetrick, S. E. (2014). Mapping the evidence for the prevention and treatment of eating disorders in young people. *Journal of Eating Disorders*, *2*(1), 5. https://doi.org/10.1186/2050-2974-2-5.

Fairburn, C. G. (2008). *Cognitive behavior therapy and eating disorders*. Guilford Press.

Forman, S. F., & McKenzie, N. (2013). The psychobiology of eating disorders – A neural systems perspective. *Adolescent Medicine: State of the Art Reviews*, *24*(1), 21–32.

Garner, D. M. (2017). *Eating Disorder Inventory – 3: Professional manual*. Psychological Assessment Resources.

Hilbert, A. (Ed.). (2017). *Binge-eating disorder: Advances in research and clinical practice*. Guilford Press.

Kaye, W. H., Wierenga, C. E., Bailer, U. F., Simmons, A. N., & Bischoff-Grethe, A. (2013). Nothing tastes as good as skinny feels: The neurobiology of anorexia nervosa. *Trends in Neurosciences*, *36*(2), 110–120. https://doi.org/10.1016/j.tins.2013.01.003.

Keel, P. K., & Forney, K. J. (2013). Psychosocial risk factors for eating disorders. *International Journal of Eating Disorders*, *46(5),* 433–439. https://doi.org/10.1002/eat.22094.

Lock, J., & Le Grange, D. (2015). *Treatment manual for anorexia nervosa: A family-based approach* (2nd ed.). Guilford Press.

Murray, S. B., Nagata, J. M., Griffiths, S., Calzo, J. P., Brown, T. A., & Mitchison, D. (2022). The enigma of male eating disorders: A critical review and synthesis. *Clinical Psychology Review*, *93*, 102131. https://doi.org/10.1016/j.cpr.2022.102131.

National Eating Disorders Association (NEDA). (n.d.). *Feeding and eating disorders*. https://www.nationaleatingdisorders.org/.

Peebles, R., & Sieke, E. H. (2021). Avoidant/restrictive food intake disorder: A current clinical review. *Current Opinion in Pediatrics*, *33*(4), 346–352. https://doi.org/10.1097/MOP.0000000000001015.

Smolak, L., & Levine, M. P. (2015). *The Wiley handbook of eating disorders*. Wiley-Blackwell.

Strother, E., Lemberg, R., Stanford, S. C., & Turberville, D. (2012). Eating disorders in men: Underdiagnosed, undertreated, and misunderstood. *Eating Disorders*, *20*(5), 346–355. https://doi.org/10.1080/10640266.2012.715512.

Treasure, J., Duarte, T. A., & Schmidt, U. (2020). Eating disorders. *The Lancet*, *395*(10227), 899–911. https://doi.org/10.1016/S0140-6736(20)30059-3.

Watson, H. J., & Bulik, C. M. (2013). Update on the treatment of anorexia nervosa: Review of clinical trials, practice guidelines and emerging interventions. *Psychological Medicine*, *43*(12), 2477–2500. https://doi.org/10.1017/S0033291712002620.

Westmoreland, P., Krantz, M. J., & Mehler, P. S. (2016). Medical complications of anorexia nervosa and bulimia. *American Journal of Medicine*, *129*(1), 30–37. https://doi.org/10.1016/j.amjmed.2015.06.031.

Gender Dysphoria

American Psychiatric Association. (2022). *Diagnostic and statistical manual of mental disorders* (5th ed., text rev.; DSM-5-TR). https://doi.org/10.1176/appi.books.9780890425787.

Ashley, F. (2020). *Gender-affirming care and the limits of informed consent*. University of Toronto Press.

Budge, S. L., Orovecz, J. J., & Thai, J. L. (2015). Transgender emotional and coping processes: Facilitative and avoidant coping throughout gender transitioning. *The Counseling Psychologist*, *43*(7), 881–917. https://doi.org/10.1177/0011000015609045.

Drescher, J. (2014). Controversies in gender diagnoses. *The Psychiatric Clinics of North America*, *37*(4), 545–561. https://doi.org/10.1016/j.psc.2014.08.004.

Drescher, J., & Byne, W. (2012). *Treating transgender children and adolescents: An interdisciplinary discussion*. Routledge.

Hidalgo, M. A., Ehrensaft, D., Tishelman, A. C., Clark, L. F., Garofalo, R., Rosenthal, S. M., & Spack, N. P. (2013). The gender affirmative model: What we know and what we aim to learn. *Human Development*, *56*(5), 285–290. https://doi.org/10.1159/000355235.

Lev, A. I. (2004). *Transgender emergence: Therapeutic guidelines for working with gender variant people and their families*. Haworth Press.

Matsuno, E., & Budge, S. L. (2017). Non-binary/genderqueer identities: A critical review of the literature. *Current Sexual Health Reports, 9*(3), 116–120. https://doi.org/10.1007/s11930017-0111-8.

Meyer-Bahlburg, H. F. L. (2010). From mental disorder to iatrogenic hypogonadism: Dilemmas in conceptualizing gender identity variants as psychiatric conditions. *Archives of Sexual Behavior*, *39*(2), 461–476. https://doi.org/10.1007/s10508-009-9532-4.

Olson, K. R., Durwood, L., DeMeules, M., & McLaughlin, K. A. (2016). Mental health of transgender children who are supported in their identities. *Pediatrics*, *137*(3), e20153223. https://doi.org/10.1542/peds.2015-3223.

Puckett, J. A., Matsuno, E., Dyar, C., & Mustanski, B. (2019). Mental health and resilience in transgender individuals: What type of support makes a difference? *Journal of Family Psychology*, *33*(8), 954–964. https://doi.org/10.1037/fam0000561.

Safer, J. D., Coleman, E., Feldman, J., Garofalo, R., Hembree, W., Radix, A., & Sevelius, J. (2016). Barriers to healthcare for transgender individuals. *Current Opinion in*

Endocrinology, Diabetes and Obesity, *23*(2), 168–171. https://doi.org/10.1097/MED.0000000000000227.
Turban, J. L., King, D., Reisner, S. L., & Keuroghlian, A. S. (2020). Pubertal suppression for transgender youth and risk of suicidal ideation. *Pediatrics*, *145*(2), e20191725. https://doi.org/10.1542/peds.2019-1725.
WPATH. (2022). *Standards of care for the health of transgender and gender diverse people, Version 8*. World Professional Association for Transgender Health. https://www.wpath.org/publications/soc.

Obsessive Compulsive and Related Disorders

Abramowitz, J. S. (2018). *Getting over OCD: A 10-step workbook for taking back your life* (2nd ed.). Guilford Press.
Abramowitz, J. S., McKay, D., & Taylor, S. (Eds.). (2008). *Clinical handbook of obsessive compulsive disorder and related problems*. Johns Hopkins University Press.
American Psychiatric Association. (2022). *Diagnostic and statistical manual of mental disorders* (5th ed., text rev.; DSM-5-TR). American Psychiatric Publishing.
Foa, E. B., Yadin, E., & Lichner, T. K. (2012). *Exposure and response (ritual) prevention for OCD: Therapist guide* (2nd ed.). Oxford University Press.
Frost, R. O., & Steketee, G. (2014). *Stuff: Compulsive hoarding and the meaning of things*. Mariner Books.
Grant, J. E., Odlaug, B. L., & Kim, S. W. (2010). A clinical review of trichotillomania. *Current Psychiatry Reports*, *12*(4), 301–307. https://doi.org/10.1007/s11920-010-0120-8.
Insel, T. R., & Wang, P. S. (2010). Rethinking mental illness. *JAMA*, *303*(19), 1970–1971. https://doi.org/10.1001/jama.2010.555.
Mataix-Cols, D., Frost, R. O., Pertusa, A., Clark, L. A., Saxena, S., Leckman, J. F., & Stein, D. J. (2010). Hoarding disorder: A new diagnosis for DSM-5? *Depression and Anxiety*, *27*(6), 556–572. https://doi.org/10.1002/da.20693.
Pauls, D. L., Abramovitch, A., Rauch, S. L., & Geller, D. A. (2014). Obsessive-compulsive disorder: An integrative genetic and neurobiological perspective. *Nature Reviews Neuroscience*, *15*(6), 410–424. https://doi.org/10.1038/nrn3746.
Phillips, K. A. (2005). *The broken mirror: Understanding and treating body dysmorphic disorder* (rev. ed.). Oxford University Press.
Rachman, S. J. (2009). *Obsessions, compulsions, and religious behavior*. Oxford University Press.
Salkovskis, P. M. (Ed.). (1996). *Frontiers of cognitive therapy*. Guilford Press.
Snorrason, I., Belleau, E. L., & Woods, D. W. (2021). Body-focused repetitive behaviors: From phenomenology to treatment. *Harvard Review of Psychiatry*, *29*(2), 104–116. https://doi.org/10.1097/HRP.0000000000000280.
Steketee, G., & Frost, R. O. (2007). *Compulsive hoarding and acquiring: Therapist guide*. Oxford University Press.
Tolin, D. F., Frost, R. O., & Steketee, G. (2014). *Hoarding disorder: A comprehensive clinical guide*. Academic Press.
Twohig, M. P., Hayes, S. C., & Masuda, A. (2006). A preliminary investigation of acceptance and commitment therapy as a treatment for chronic skin picking.

Behaviour Research and Therapy, *44*(10), 1513–1522. https://doi.org/10.1016/j.brat.2005.10.002.

Veale, D., & Neziroglu, F. (2010). *Body dysmorphic disorder: A treatment manual*. Wiley-Blackwell.

Wilhelm, S., Phillips, K. A., & Steketee, G. (2013). *Cognitive-behavioral therapy for body dysmorphic disorder: A treatment manual*. Guilford Press.

Woods, D. W., & Twohig, M. P. (2008). *Trichotillomania: An ACT-enhanced behavior therapy approach*. New Harbinger Publications.

Personality Disorders

American Psychiatric Association. (2022). *Diagnostic and statistical manual of mental disorders* (5th ed., text rev.; DSM-5-TR). https://doi.org/10.1176/appi.books.9780890425787.

Bateman, A. W., & Fonagy, P. (2016). *Mentalization-based treatment for personality disorders: A practical guide*. Oxford University Press.

Beck, A. T., Freeman, A., & Davis, D. D. (2004). *Cognitive therapy of personality disorders* (2nd ed.). Guilford Press.

Clark, L. A. (2007). Assessment and diagnosis of personality disorder: Perennial issues and an emerging reconceptualization. *Annual Review of Psychology*, 58, 227–257. https://doi.org/10.1146/annurev.psych.57.102904.190200.

Clarkin, J. F., Yeomans, F. E., & Kernberg, O. F. (2006). *Psychotherapy for borderline personality: Focusing on object relations*. American Psychiatric Publishing.

Hopwood, C. J., Wright, A. G. C., Krueger, R. F., Schade, N., Markon, K. E., & Morey, L. C. (2013). DSM-5 pathological personality traits and the Five-Factor Model: A conceptual and empirical integration. *Journal of Abnormal Psychology*, *122*(3), 843–853. https://doi.org/10.1037/a0032800.

Kernberg, O. F. (1984). *Severe personality disorders: Psychotherapeutic strategies*. Yale University Press.

Krueger, R. F., & Markon, K. E. (2014). The role of the DSM-5 personality trait model in moving toward a quantitative and empirically based approach to classifying personality and psychopathology. *Annual Review of Clinical Psychology*, *10*, 477–501. https://doi.org/10.1146/annurev-clinpsy-032813-153732.

Linehan, M. M. (1993). *Cognitive-behavioral treatment of borderline personality disorder*. Guilford Press.

Livesley, W. J. (2003). *Practical management of personality disorder*. Guilford Press.

McWilliams, N. (2011). *Psychoanalytic diagnosis: Understanding personality structure in the clinical process* (2nd ed.). Guilford Press.

Millon, T., Grossman, S., Millon, C., Meagher, S., & Ramnath, R. (2004). *Personality disorders in modern life* (2nd ed.). Wiley.

Morey, L. C., & Hopwood, C. J. (2019). Stability and change in personality disorders. *Annual Review of Clinical Psychology*, *15*, 499–526. https://doi.org/10.1146/annurev-clinpsy050718-095525.

Pincus, A. L., & Lukowitsky, M. R. (2010). Pathological narcissism and narcissistic personality disorder. *Annual Review of Clinical Psychology*, 6, 421–446. https://doi.org/10.1146/annurev.clinpsy.121208.131215.

Widiger, T. A., & Mullins-Sweatt, S. N. (2009). Five-factor model of personality disorder: A proposal for DSM-V. *Annual Review of Clinical Psychology*, *5*, 197–220. https://doi.org/10.1146/annurev.clinpsy.032408.153542.

Widiger, T. A., & Oltmanns, J. R. (2017). The classification of personality disorders: A review of current and emerging models. *Annual Review of Clinical Psychology*, *13*, 291–315. https://doi.org/10.1146/annurev-clinpsy-032816-045057.

Psychodynamic Theory

Gabbard, G. O. (2017). *Psychodynamic psychiatry in clinical practice* (5th ed.). American Psychiatric Publishing.

Kohut, H. (1977). *The restoration of the self.* International Universities Press.

Luborsky, L., & Crits-Christoph, P. (1998). *Understanding transference: The core conflictual relationship theme method* (2nd ed.). American Psychological Association. https://doi.org/10.1037/10385-000.

McWilliams, N. (2004). *Psychoanalytic psychotherapy: A practitioner's guide.* Guilford Press.

McWilliams, N. (2011). *Psychoanalytic diagnosis: Understanding personality structure in the clinical process* (2nd ed.). Guilford Press.

Mitchell, S. A., & Black, M. J. (2016). *Freud and beyond: A history of modern psychoanalytic thought* (2nd ed.). Basic Books.

Shedler, J. (2010). The efficacy of psychodynamic psychotherapy. *American Psychologist*, *65*(2), 98–109. https://doi.org/10.1037/a0018378.

Westen, D. (1998). The scientific legacy of Sigmund Freud: Toward a psychodynamically informed psychological science. *Psychological Bulletin*, *124*(3), 333–371. https://doi.org/10.1037/0033-2909.124.3.333.

Relational Frame Theory

Barnes-Holmes, D., Barnes-Holmes, Y., & Cullinan, V. (2000). Relational frame theory and Skinner's verbal behavior: A possible synthesis. *The Behavior Analyst*, *23*(1), 69–84. https://doi.org/10.1007/BF03392011.

Barnes-Holmes, Y., Hussey, I., McEnteggart, C., Barnes-Holmes, D., & Foody, M. (2017). Relational frame theory: A functional approach to understanding and alleviating human suffering. *Current Opinion in Psychology*, *13*, 11–15. https://doi.org/10.1016/j.copsyc.2016.04.010.

Hayes, S. C., Barnes-Holmes, D., & Roche, B. (2001). *Relational frame theory: A post-Skinnerian account of human language and cognition.* Springer Science + Business Media. https://doi.org/10.1007/978-1-4615-0557-5.

Törneke, N. (2010). *Learning RFT: An introduction to relational frame theory and its clinical application.* New Harbinger Publications.

Villatte, M., Villatte, J. L., & Hayes, S. C. (2016). *Mastering the clinical conversation: Language as intervention.* Guilford Press.

Schizophrenia Spectrum and Other Psychotic Disorders

American Psychiatric Association. (2013). Schizophrenia spectrum and other psychotic disorders. In *Diagnostic and statistical manual of mental disorders* (5th ed., pp. 87–122). https://doi.org/10.1176/appi.books.9780890425596.dsm02.

American Psychiatric Association. (2020). The American Psychiatric Association practice guideline for the treatment of patients with schizophrenia. *American Journal of Psychiatry*, *177*(9), 868–872. https://doi.org/10.1176/appi.ajp.2020.177901.

Buckley, P. F., & Schulz, S. C. (Eds.). (2019). *The American Psychiatric Association Publishing textbook of schizophrenia* (2nd ed.). American Psychiatric Association Publishing. https://www.appi.org/American_Psychiatric_Association_Publishing_Textbook_of_Schiophrenia_Second_Edition.

Frith, C., & Johnstone, E. (2003). *Schizophrenia: A very short introduction*. Oxford University Press.

Gottesman, I. I. (1991). *Schizophrenia genesis: The origins of madness*. W. H. Freeman.

Kingdon, D. G., & Turkington, D. (2005). *Cognitive therapy of schizophrenia*. Guilford Press.

Mueser, K. T., & Jeste, D. V. (Eds.). (2008). *Clinical handbook of schizophrenia*. Guilford Press.

Saks, E. R. (2007). *The center cannot hold: My journey through madness*. Hyperion.

Torrey, E. F. (2019). *Surviving schizophrenia: A family manual* (7th ed.). Harper Perennial.

Wang, E. W. (2019). *The collected schizophrenias: Essays*. Graywolf Press.

Somatic Symptoms and Related Disorders

American Psychiatric Association. (2022). *Diagnostic and statistical manual of mental disorders* (5th ed., text rev.; DSM-5-TR). https://doi.org/10.1176/appi.books.9780890425787.

Barsky, A. J., & Borus, J. F. (1999). Functional somatic syndromes. *Annals of Internal Medicine*, *130*(11), 910–921. https://doi.org/10.7326/0003-4819-130-11-199906010-00016.

Dimsdale, J. E. (Ed.). (2007). *Somatization: A joint responsibility of medicine and psychiatry*. American Psychiatric Publishing.

Edwards, M. J., & Bhatia, K. P. (2012). Functional (psychogenic) movement disorders: Merging mind and brain. *The Lancet Neurology*, *11*(3), 250–260. https://doi.org/10.1016/S14744422(11)70310-6.

Henningsen, P., Zipfel, S., & Herzog, W. (2007). Management of functional somatic syndromes. *The Lancet*, *369*(9565), 946–955. https://doi.org/10.1016/S0140-6736(07)60159-7.

Kirmayer, L. J., & Sartorius, N. (2007). Cultural models and somatic syndromes. *Psychosomatic Medicine*, *69*(9), 832–840. https://doi.org/10.1097/PSY.0b013e31815b002c.

Kroenke, K. (2007). Efficacy of treatment for somatoform disorders: A review of randomized controlled trials. *Psychosomatic Medicine*, *69*(9), 881–888. https://doi.org/10.1097/PSY.0b013e31815b000d.

Lipowski, Z. J. (1988). Somatization: The concept and its clinical application. *American Journal of Psychiatry*, *145*(11), 1358–1368. https://doi.org/10.1176/ajp.145.11.1358.

Looper, K. J., & Kirmayer, L. J. (2002). Behavioral medicine approaches to somatoform disorders. *Journal of Consulting and Clinical Psychology*, *70*(3), 810–827. https://doi.org/10.1037/0022-006X.70.3.810.

Sharpe, M., & Carson, A. (2001). "Unexplained" somatic symptoms, functional syndromes, and somatization: Do we need a paradigm shift? *Annals of Internal Medicine*, *134*(9 Pt 2), 926–930. https://doi.org/10.7326/0003-4819-134-9_Part_2-200105011-00014.

Stone, J., Carson, A., & Sharpe, M. (2005). Functional symptoms and signs in neurology: Assessment and diagnosis. *Journal of Neurology, Neurosurgery & Psychiatry*, *76*(suppl_1), i2–i12. https://doi.org/10.1136/jnnp.2004.061655.

Van Dessel, N., Den Boeft, M., van der Wouden, J. C., Kleinstäuber, M., Leone, S. S., Terluin, B., Numans, M. E., & van Marwijk, H. W. J. (2014). Non-pharmacological interventions for somatoform disorders and medically unexplained physical symptoms (MUPS) in adults. *Cochrane Database of Systematic Reviews*, *2014*(11), CD011142. https://doi.org/10.1002/14651858.CD011142.pub2.

Wileman, L., May, C., & Chew-Graham, C. (2002). Medically unexplained symptoms and the problem of power in the primary care consultation: A qualitative study. *Family Practice*, *19*(2), 178–182. https://doi.org/10.1093/fampra/19.2.178.

Woolfolk, R. L., & Allen, L. A. (2016). *Treating somatization: A cognitive-behavioral approach*. Guilford Press.

Trauma and Stressor-Related Disorders

American Psychiatric Association. (2013). *Diagnostic and statistical manual of mental disorders* (5th ed.). American Psychiatric Association.

Briere, J., & Scott, C. (2014). *Principles of trauma therapy: A guide to symptoms, evaluation, and treatment* (2nd ed.). SAGE Publications.

Cloitre, M., Shevlin, M., Brewin, C. R., & Bisson, J. I. (2017). The International Trauma Questionnaire: Development of a self-report measure of ICD-11 PTSD and complex PTSD. *European Journal of Psychotraumatology*, *8*(1), 1–15. https://doi.org/10.1080/20008198.2017.1400963.

Foa, E. B., Keane, T. M., & Friedman, M. J. (2009). *Effective treatments for PTSD: Practice guidelines from the International Society for Traumatic Stress Studies* (2nd ed.). Guilford Press.

Friedman, M. J., Resick, P. A., & Keane, T. M. (2014). *Handbook of PTSD: Science and practice*. Guilford Press.

Herman, J. L. (1997). *Trauma and recovery: The aftermath of violence – from domestic abuse to political terror*. Basic Books.

Horowitz, M. J. (2001). *Stress response syndromes* (3rd ed.). Jason Aronson.

Kilpatrick, D. G., & Resick, P. A. (2009). The nature of trauma and PTSD. In T. M. Weisner, J. L. Garofalo, & P. A. Resick (Eds.), *Post-traumatic stress disorder: DSM-5 and beyond* (pp. 3–25). Routledge.

Maercker, A., & Brewin, C. R. (2015). A cognitive-behavioral approach to trauma-related disorders. In M. J. Friedman, T. M. Keane, & P. A. Resick (Eds.), *Handbook of PTSD: Science and practice* (pp. 251–267). Guilford Press.

McFarlane, A. C., & van Hooff, M. (2013). The impact of traumatic stress on the development of post-traumatic stress disorder (PTSD). *Psychiatry*, *76*(5), 337–343. https://doi.org/10.1016/j.psych.2013.04.004.

Nijenhuis, E. R. S., & van der Hart, O. (2011). Trauma-related dissociation: Conceptual clarity and the link with PTSD. *European Journal of Trauma & Dissociation*, *5*(3), 107–114. https://doi.org/10.1016/j.ejtd.2010.12.003.

Resick, P. A., Monson, C. M., & Chard, K. M. (2017). *Cognitive processing therapy for PTSD: A comprehensive manual*. Guilford Press.

Shapiro, F. (2001). *EMDR: Eye movement desensitization and reprocessing: Basic principles, protocols, and procedures* (2nd ed.). Guilford Press.

van der Kolk, B. A. (2006). *Trauma and memory: Brain and body in a search for the living past*. In B. A. van der Kolk, A. C. McFarlane, & L. Weisaeth (Eds.), *Trauma and its impact on the body and the brain* (pp. 3–29). Guilford Press.

van der Kolk, B. A. (2014). *The body keeps the score: Brain, mind, and body in the healing of trauma*. Viking.

Yehuda, R. (2002). Post-traumatic stress disorder. In J. L. Hellerstein, A. L. L. Hammen, & R. J. DeRubeis (Eds.), *The Oxford handbook of mood disorders* (pp. 663–681). Oxford University Press.

Zoellner, L. A., & Feeny, N. C. (2019). Posttraumatic stress disorder and related disorders. In D. H. Barlow (Ed.), *The Oxford handbook of clinical psychology* (pp. 292–320). Oxford University Press.

Index

Note: Locators in **bold** refer to tables. Alphabetization is word-by-word.

Made in the USA
Monee, IL
13 September 2026

62977123R00256